NEW YORK, NEW YORK

Also by Oliver E. Allen

NEW YORK,

A History of the World's Most

NEW YORK

Exhilarating and Challenging City

Oliver E. Allen

ATHENEUM • NEW YORK • 1990
COLLIER MACMILLAN CANADA • TORONTO
MAXWELL MACMILLAN INTERNATIONAL
NEW YORK • OXFORD • SINGAPORE • SYDNEY

Atheneum
Macmillan Publishing Company
866 Third Avenue
New York, NY 10022

Collier Macmillan Canada, Inc.
1200 Eglinton Avenue, Suite 200
Don Mills, Ontario M3C 3N1

Library of Congress Cataloging-in-Publication Data
Allen, Oliver E.
    New York, New York / Oliver E. Allen.
        p. cm.
    Includes bibliographical references.
    ISBN 0-689-11960-7
    1. New York (N.Y.)—History. I. Title.
  F128.3.A45 1990
  974.7'1—dc20   90-473

Macmillan books are available at special discounts for bulk purchases for sales promotions, premiums, fund-raising, or educational use. For details, contact:

Special Sales Director
Macmillan Publishing Company
866 Third Avenue
New York, NY 10022

10 9 8 7 6 5 4 3 2 1

Designed by Erich Hobbing

PRINTED IN THE UNITED STATES OF AMERICA

To the memory of F.L.A.
In his time, an enthusiast of New York

Contents

Contents

Illustrations

Illustrations

Sketch by Archibald Robertson of the rural outskirts of the city, 1798

The Five Points, 1827

Maritime New York: East River and lower Manhattan, 1836

South Street, late nineteenth century

West Side docks, Hudson River, 1869

(between pages 174 and 175)

St. John's Park, Varick Street, in the 1840s

Immigrants disembarking near the lower tip of Manhattan in the 1840s

The fire that destroyed the Merchants' Exchange, December 16, 1835

Lower Manhattan after it was rebuilt, in a sketch by J. W. Hill, 1848

Tradesmen and storekeepers on lower Hudson Street, 1865

Photograph by Mathew Brady, 1867, of Broadway between Spring and Prince streets

Astor Place Riot of 1849

Civil War Draft Act riots, July 1863

New York, looking south from the Latting Observatory on 42nd Street, 1853

Inventor Charles T. Harvey on his elevated railway, 1868

Mayor Fernando Wood in the Gem Saloon

Thomas Nast's famous cartoon attacking the Tweed Ring, *Harper's Weekly*, 1871

Tammany Hall

George Washington Plunkitt

Richard Croker

Jay Gould

Jim Fisk and Jay Gould shown fleeing to New Jersey in a rowboat, March 11, 1868

Panic on the New York Stock Exchange, April 13, 1872

Manhattan in 1876, photographed by John H. Beal

Harlem Lane (St. Nicholas Avenue) in a Currier & Ives print, 1870

Preface

No one is neutral about New York. This sprawling and incredible place, rich beyond measure both in material wealth and in its energetic people, and a cultural bonanza to boot, seems expressly designed to provoke strong feelings. Few cities in the world are so admired—or so envied, feared, or even cordially disliked. What is it that has brought about this oddly mixed reputation? Why is New York the city that so many people love to hate?

Having lived in or around it almost all my life, I have long been fascinated, as have other denizens of the city and a great many non-New Yorkers, by its special character, so full of contradictions and so provocative. So when I came to write a history of the city I decided it made sense to tell the story in terms of what made New York the way it is: what forces, events, and people shaped this powerhouse and made it so special over the almost four centuries during which it has prospered on the shores of its extraordinary harbor.

The key to the city's history, I felt, was that very harbor, for it brought two things that have always been dominant: money and people. New York's story is the endless intertwining of these two forces, the money that produced Wall Street and the people who have flooded in and are still coming; they have made the city unique.

Telling the story from this vantage point has necessarily caused me to leave out much that others might say is essential. Among other things, it has given the book a decided Manhattan slant. That is how I saw the story. To enthusiasts of other boroughs and to everyone else who complains that something has been slighted, I say yes, you may be right; but in covering nearly 400 years it was necessary to leave out quite a lot, and what has remained is what I felt was particularly germane to the specialness of New York.

I would like to express my thanks to Peter Goldmark, who got me going on the project; to Thomas A. Stewart, Lee Goerner, Cynthia Merman, and Donald Fehr, capable and supportive editors all; to Joel Honig for superlative copy editing; to my agent, Emilie Jacobson, for her good advice throughout; and to Deborah Allen, whose keen eye and good sense have been wonderful.

Special thanks go also to Milton M. Klein, John A. Kouwenhoven, and John Steele Gordon; to all the hardworking and helpful hands at the New York Public Library (but especially Barbara Hillman, Dom Pilla, and Patrick Bunyan) and at The New-York Historical Society (especially Diana Arecco); to Gretchen Viehmann at the Museum of the City of New York; and to Kenneth Cobb at New York's Municipal Archives, Ellen Wallenstein at the New York City Parks Photo Archive, and David Wright at the Pierpont Morgan Library.

O.E.A.

New York, July 1990

NEW YORK, NEW YORK

Prologue:
The Incomparable Setting

If you stand on the observation deck of the World Trade Center facing south and look out over the lower end of Manhattan and the harbor around and beyond it, you can grasp the two forces that have from the very beginning shaped New York City and determined its extraordinary character.

Immediately below, with its jumbled buildings and narrow canyons throbbing with the muffled roar of traffic, air conditioners, and other manifestations of urban crowding, is the downtown financial center, symbolized by Wall Street: the nation's money market, the focus of the implacable economic muscle that has made New York unquestionably the most powerful city in the world and has caused it to be idolized, feared, hated, and wondered at throughout the globe.

Yet out in the harbor beyond the end of Manhattan, alone and silent in the middle distance, stands a totally different symbol, the Statue of Liberty, representing New York's (even more than the nation's) centuries-old spirit of welcome, the city's role as a haven and refuge, a place of hope whose door is never closed. This is the other—and equally vital—side of New York.

And lying between and around these two seemingly contradictory images—indeed, permitting them to have coexisted harmoniously, and for the most part highly profitably, since New York's earliest days more than 350 years ago—is the body of water that caused the city to be founded here in the first place: the great harbor, one of the wonders of the earth.

That founding calls to mind another notion: the point of land right below in the near foreground can reasonably claim to be the birthplace of the nation. For the lower tip of Manhattan is where the first European inhabitants of what would become New York City established their tiny settlement—where Peter Minuit made his legendary purchase of Manhattan Island. And that settlement, more than any other from those early days, grew in time to become a microcosm of the America we know today. The history books, of course, do not see it that way. To them the nation's birthplace is Plymouth, Massachusetts, or Jamestown, Virginia. But both Plymouth and Jamestown symbolize a rural, Anglo-Saxon, almost utopian world that may be comforting to recall as the wellspring of our liberties but is not the United States we know in the twentieth century. New York has always been the kind of place the country has become. "The rest of the country and New York," says the historian Milton M. Klein, "have for three hundred years or more marched to the tune of the same drummer; New York was or was always becoming what the rest of the nation turned out to be."[1] New York, in other words, developed into a heterogeneous, basically tolerant and strongly materialistic community, and so did the country. And New York's residents are in fact composite Americans: energetic, cosmopolitan, materialistic, and brash—but also, Klein points out, convivial, humane, tolerant, and idealistic. Other Americans insist that New York is not America. But, like it or not, it is.

In the age of air travel and truck transport even New Yorkers themselves tend to forget how vital the harbor has always been, and how huge. A couple of generations ago, when travel between continents was by ship, passengers on ocean liners arriving in New York were made well aware of how stupendous it is. For as their ship came up through the Narrows and they got their first glimpse of the storied Manhattan skyline gleaming in the morning sun, they were bound to marvel at the busy maritime scene around them, with untold numbers of large and small craft—freighters, tankers, barges, flatboats laden with railroad cars, tugs, ferries, other liners—churning in all directions across the waters of the great Upper Bay. There seemed no end to the activity or to the expanse of water. Today, although the amount of waterborne traffic is vastly reduced, something of the port's physical size and complexity can at least be glimpsed from the Trade Center's observation deck. It extends in all directions, astonishingly widespread, actually comprising several interconnecting harbors. The saying goes that New York's harbor can hold all the world's navies at once, or all the merchantmen, and there is no reason to doubt it.

Spreading out in the center, to the south, is the Upper Bay, which ocean liners used to traverse, a broad and almost landlocked body some five miles long and three wide in which, if necessary, thousands of ships and other craft can anchor safely—as they did during the 1986 Statue of Liberty centennial. Brooklyn's ample docking facilities line the bay's eastern edge, to the left, and nearby is Governor's Island, a military base, which the Dutch called Nut Island after the trees growing there and which actually was the site of a temporary Dutch settlement before Manhattan was deemed a likelier place for a trading post. Extending northward from the Upper Bay on either side are the East River (to the left) and the Hudson River (to the right). Although each of these bodies is merely a part of the overall harbor, each would be large and well situated enough to make New York a thriving, world-class port all on its own.

But there's more. Off to the southwest (and dimly seen on a good day in the far right distance) is another, separate body of water connected to the Upper Bay by a strait known as Kill Van Kull (*kil* is Dutch for channel, while Newark Bay was once known as "the Cull," so this is the passage leading from the Cull, or Kull). Newark Bay is technically part of New Jersey but in actuality is an arm of New York's harbor, which since 1921 has been administered by the states of New York and New Jersey acting together through a port authority. This large affair is today much the busiest section of the port, as its geography enables it to handle with great efficiency the container traffic that dominates modern shipping.

Far off to the south, way out beyond the Statue of Liberty and past the Narrows (which separates Long Island on the left and Staten Island on the right and serves as the harbor's formal entrance) can be seen the Lower Bay. It is a mammoth 100-square-mile expanse that affords additional copious anchorage and also provides extra protection for the harbor by means of a series of shoals and sand bars. Its outer limit is marked by Sandy Hook, which is more than sixteen miles from the Trade Center and is barely visible even in clear weather, a dim line on the horizon. Far-reaching, the harbor is also a unifier. Its waters surround the city's seven million residents and reach out to unite the eighteen million who inhabit the Greater New York metropolitan region. This heaven-sent phenomenon is responsible for making New York City what it is.

The story of New York can be seen as an outgrowth of, and the

3

interplay between, the two forces that stem from the harbor: economic power and the spirit of openness. Everything flows from these two. Unlike the city's early archrivals Boston and Philadelphia, both of which were founded as religious colonies (one Puritan, the other Quaker), New York from the beginning was all business, a wideopen trading town. The Dutch put their stamp on it: New Amsterdam, as they called it, was to be purely and simply a mercantile center, a marketplace, and anyone could come and set up shop. The British, taking over in 1664, continued the tradition, and New York early on enjoyed a greater degree of political freedom and religious liberty than did other colonies. Even during the short period when it served as the new nation's first capital, its mercantile aura was a strong presence.

The business image has stuck: in 1807 a visitor noted that every "thought, word, look, and action of the multitude seemed to be absorbed by commerce,"[2] while as recently as 1948 another guest saw the city as a vast retail showcase in which "all the rich loot of civilization" was for sale.[3] But successful trading brought much else. Commerce necessitated the banking industry (many of the largest American banks are headquartered here), while the need to protect shipping fostered marine and other insurance enterprises. So, too, the desire to put spare cash to work and the need to finance shipping gave rise to the investment community, whose central ornament is the New York Stock Exchange, surely the world's most influential trading place. Money and power in turn led eventually to the city's primacy in the communications industry and in almost every kind of artistic and cultural endeavor.

With the profusion of money and power has come arrogance, and this has not endeared the city to the rest of the nation. New York's insolence has often seemed so overwhelming that it has masked the city's tradition of accepting—indeed, of caring for—people of every stripe. As the major port of entry to this continent it has always been a city of immigrants, and it is by far the most cosmopolitan city in the country, if not the world. And if only to keep the peace, New Yorkers perforce have had to become tolerant. If they had not, remarked the noted essayist E. B. White, they "would explode in a radio-active cloud of hate and rancor and bigotry."[4] They have indeed exploded at times in the past, but in the main they have gotten along with each other, if only because they must.

The city's dynamic energy and its continuing acceptance of new peoples have combined to keep it incessantly changing. If its hectic mood is predictable from one day to the next, its physical appearance is not. New York's celebrated skyline, that icon of our times, is constantly adding new towers of every conceivable shape, and the city's footprint has a way of changing too as the waterfront is periodically relocated outward. Most of the World Trade Center itself, completed in the 1970s, rises where once there was just water, having been constructed on made land that did not exist in Dutch times; and now there is new land out beyond that too (called Battery Park City), with streets and buildings set out almost as if they had been there forever.

Looking out from the Trade Center, contemplating the city's immensity, envisioning the unbelievable range of human activity taking place in its five boroughs and absorbing the full-throated hum that rises from its endless streets and buildings, an observer may find it hard to realize that although New York is much the country's oldest big city (predating both Boston and Philadelphia), as recently as four centuries ago this entire surrounding was silent. All was wilderness. The land was forested to the water's edge and peopled by Algonquin Indians, whose fires sent wispy columns of smoke up through the trees into the quiet air. The great Hudson River, flowing past the wooded islands, made hardly a sound.

But of all the geological flukes that produced what one observer has called the area's "peculiar topography,"[5] by far the most significant is the Hudson. Its width and great depth (50 to 60 feet deep as it passes the city, but below the silt on its bottom lies bedrock that is probably 200 to 300 feet down) suggest that what we are looking at is the terminus of a very lengthy river, something on the order of the Mississippi-Missouri (3,860 miles) or the Yangtze (3,430 miles). Yet the Hudson is barely 315 miles long. Some geologists think that in the distant past the Great Lakes may have emptied not into the St. Lawrence River as now but into an ancestor of the Mohawk and the Hudson, leading across what is now upper New York State and south to the sea. This would account for the river's deep cleft, as well as for the break in the Appalachian Mountains west of Albany that later made possible the epochal Erie Canal. In any event, millions of years ago the Hudson cut a fjordlike channel for itself south from the Albany area and, during a period when the world's oceans had receded, dug a further course some 130 miles long out to the southeast below the New York area, to what was then the edge of the sea. At one spot, today far under the surface of the Atlantic, it carved out a gorge wider and deeper than the Grand Canyon.

Meanwhile two other rivers had cut deep valleys that joined the Hudson in what is now the Upper Bay. One of them approached from the northeast—from Connecticut and Long Island Sound—by way of the cut known as Hell Gate (which appropriately is two hundred feet deep in some places); its course is now the misnamed East River, not a river at all but a strait. The other came in from the west, through the Kill Van Kull, and is represented today by New Jersey's Passaic and Hackensack rivers and by Newark Bay. The combined river then flowed out through the Narrows—which must have been a magnificent gorge back then—to the distant sea. When in time the ocean's waters rose again, they engulfed the meeting place and the lower courses of the old rivers to create New York's harbor. But so deep are the residual channels that the entire port, although made up of onetime rivers, is tidal and the Hudson for most of its course is technically an estuary, an arm of the sea that feels the influence of tides as far upriver as Troy, north of Albany.

A final fluke should be mentioned. Throughout the ancient geological eras and ice ages, the land along the east bank of the Hudson River at its lower end was undergirded by extremely hard rock strata that resisted the Ice Age's worst scouring. An arm of the geological region to the north, it is known as the Manhattan Prong of the New England Province, and it forms the backbone of New York's central island, Manhattan. It is this durable underpinning that has made possible the city's profusion of skyscrapers, for it is easily reachable by excavation both in the middle of the island and in the Wall Street area, where the tallest buildings have therefore been erected. Only in recent years have engineering techniques made high buildings practicable in areas without firm bedrock.

But more than the sheer size of the port was responsible for boosting New York past all rivals in the New World: it was also intricate. The highly indented shorelines and the profusion of islands permit extensive wharfage; at the height of the port's commercial shipping activity a few decades ago it had no less than 578 miles of functioning waterfront, and experts estimated that the figure could have risen to 771 miles if all wharfage sites had been developed. Although the harbor is readily accessible from the open sea, it is amply protected from the worst oceanic storms and wave action first by Sandy Hook and its nearby shoals (which are nevertheless fully passable) and, second, by the ridge line formed by Long Island and Staten Island, a line broken only by the Narrows, an opening barely a mile wide. The harbor, at least forty feet deep in many places, tends to be scoured efficiently by tidal action and so needs little dredging; the Hudson itself drops most of its silt far upstream of New York. And the port has always been able to operate throughout the year: the harbor's salty waters rarely freeze, and floating ice is generally a problem only in the Hudson itself—and today infrequently. The East River has not frozen over since the early nineteenth century.

More important still, the harbor has always had unexampled connections with overseas points as well as with much of the United States. It lies closer to Europe than any other major American port except Boston, while because of the slanting eastern coastline it is almost as close to South American ports as are ports below it on the coast. Within the United States, the Hudson again is the key, as it leads efficiently to the Mohawk Valley and thus to the Great Lakes and the heart of the continent. No port hoping to compete with New York ever had anything like this advantage. Finally, as an added fillip, New York has always possessed a "back door," a second entrance by way of Long Island Sound and the Hell Gate, so that ships unable to approach the harbor via the usual frontal entry because of storm conditions could take refuge in the Sound route and deliver their cargoes to the city with only minor delays. For coastal traffic from New England, in the old days an important source of revenue, the Hell Gate was the most efficient route by far, and the resulting easy access enabled New York to dominate the economy of southern New England.

Ironically, New York's overwhelming financial power, whose origins are directly attributable to the port, is no longer dependent on the port at all. Indeed, the port no longer holds a commanding lead over other American ports in terms of annual tonnage; and most of the Manhattan shoreline, which used to echo the deep-throated whistles of ocean liners and throb with the loading and unloading of ships, is now virtually bereft of docks and shipping. But the strength that grew out of the city's importing and exporting success had the effect of establishing it as a money center, which led to its becoming the nation's premier headquarters town. And that status, never really challenged, is a mainstay of its continued economic health. Power, in other words, begat power.

Right from the very beginning, New York's unusual site impressed all those who saw it. What is surprising is that it was not settled by

Europeans any earlier than it was. The first known European visitor to the harbor was the Florentine navigator Giovanni da Verrazano, who arrived in 1524 while exploring the North Atlantic coast for France's King Francis I. Ostensibly searching for the fabled Northwest Passage that Europeans believed would provide a shortcut to the Orient, Verrazano was actually on a mission to claim all of North America for France. He anchored the one-hundred-ton *Dauphine* in the Lower Bay just below the Narrows (today the site of the bridge bearing his name), peered north past the hills of Staten Island and Brooklyn, and liked what he saw. "At the end of a hundred leagues [along the coast]," he reported, "[lay] a very agreeable situation located within two small prominent hills, in the midst of which flowed to the sea a very great river [i.e., the Narrows], which was deep within the mouth ... Within the land about half a league [was] a very beautiful lake with a circuit of about three leagues."[6]

Although he had thus sighted the more-than-ample Upper Bay, he chose not to explore it further—a good indication that he was not really interested in the Northwest Passage at all. Nor did he sense the presence of the Hudson River, for it lay out of sight on the other side of the bay. A boatload of Indians put out from the land and "came toward us very cheerfully, making a great show of admiration," and Verrazano set off in a small boat to follow them ashore.[7] Just then, however, a sudden storm blew up, and "we were forced to return to the ship, leaving the said land with much regret because of its commodiousness and beauty, thinking it was not without some properties of value."[8]

Verrazano dutifully conferred names on what he had seen, calling the Upper Bay the Gulf of Santa Margherita (for Francis I's sister) and the "very great river" the Vendôme (honoring a French prince). He named the immediate area Angoulême, the title Francis had held before he became monarch. Francis himself dubbed the entire North American continent New France. But with other things on his mind the monarch decided to ignore the possibility of "properties of value" and did nothing further about his new overseas holding.

The next player to take a tantalizingly brief look at the harbor was a black Portuguese mariner in the employ of Spain, Esteban Gomez, who stopped by in 1525. He saw no Indians (they lived elsewhere in winter) and no evidence of gold or silver, his principal object. But he sailed up the Hudson far enough to encounter ice floes, which dismayed him so much that he turned around and sailed away. So much for Spain's interest.

There is evidence that Dutch sea traders were aware of the harbor and river by 1600 and presumably paid visits, but they made no claims on the territory at that time. In 1607 an Englishman whose name unfortunately is not known appears to have entered the lower Hudson and made the acquaintance of some Indians, as he left a map with that date on it that labels the island to the east of the river as Manahatin and that to the west as Mannahata. Both may have been variants of the Indians' tribal name, Mahican,[9] or they may have been Indian words for "island" or "island of the hills"—no one knows for sure. Despite the unknown visitor's provocative map and his having come up with a name that, with a slight alteration, has lasted to our time, his exploit did not persuade the English crown to become involved.

Instead, the Dutch beat them to it. Two years later another English navigator, Henry Hudson, under contract to the Dutch East India Company for the purpose of accomplishing the now-familiar mission of locating the Northwest Passage, arrived in the *Half Moon* and liked what he saw even more than had Verrazano. When he reported back to Holland, he put an end once and for all to the isolation of the great harbor.

1

The Businesslike Dutch

Not long after the first Jews arrived in New Amsterdam—the future New York—in the summer of 1654, the settlement's controversial director general, the harsh and irascible Peter Stuyvesant, petitioned his superiors back in the Netherlands for permission to deport them. The fact that the immigrants were beleaguered refugees from a Dutch colony in Brazil that had recently been taken over by the Portuguese, and that they had barely survived a harrowing nine-month voyage during which their ship had been captured by Spanish pirates before being mercifully set free by a French privateer—none of this interested Stuyvesant. Nor was it relevant to him that New Amsterdam had already acquired a deserved reputation for tolerance of beliefs other than the strict Calvinist tenets of the ruling Dutch Reformed Church; even Roman Catholics, Puritans, and Lutherans were allowed to worship in the privacy of their homes. But they, of course, were Christians. To the stern, bigoted Stuyvesant, the Jews were a different story. He could hardly contain his scorn for these "blasphemers of the name of Christ" who should not be allowed "to infect and trouble this new colony."[1]

But across the ocean, in the thriving, powerful city of Amsterdam, the lordly commissioners of the Dutch West India Company did not see it that way. Rejecting his request, they pointed out that the hardworking Brazilian Jews had suffered serious losses in the fighting there and, furthermore, that it was impossible to ignore "the large amount of capital which [the Jews of Amsterdam] still have invested in the shares of this company."[2] Besides, Stuyvesant's colony needed all the industrious immigrants it could get. So the commissioners decreed that under certain restrictions, and providing they took care of their own poor, the Jews should be allowed to stay. (The resulting Congregation Shearith Israel, still active, is the oldest existing Jewish congregation in North America.) The message was clear. Commerce took precedence over conformity, profits had priority over vague and disputable moral principles. Money was the ultimate measure.

The ruling was not an isolated one. During the forty-year period in which the Dutch held Manhattan and the surrounding region, the policies of the Dutch West India Company, which managed the holding under the Netherlands' relatively weak parliamentary states general, were based purely on commercial considerations, a vital factor in shaping the future city. The company was a trading organization, and overseas possessions existed primarily to enrich its stockholders. Ironically, the whole Dutch experiment in North America was a commercial failure, for the amount of trade generated was never great, and the assets of the port area that are now known to be incomparable were ignored at the time. The magnificent harbor and the unequaled access to the interior, which would one day enable New York to achieve a power far in excess of anything ever achieved by the Dutch Empire, availed hardly at all in the seventeenth century, for even a small harbor could handle all the shipping at the time and the interior was still largely unknown. But the company's record in North America was not helped by the fact that until Stuyvesant came along, the resident directors were, to a man, inept or not to be trusted, and that the company's money-minded policies fluctuated confusingly. So the fledgling colony went broke. But despite their signal lack of success and their eventual surrender to the English, the Dutch, to their everlasting credit, set the tone of the New York-to-be in ways that are unmistakable—as in the ruling concerning the Jews. New Amsterdam was a kind of microcosm of the colossus that was to come.

It was no fluke that brought the Dutch to this part of the world. Newly independent from Spain (though still fighting their erstwhile overlords), the Dutch were trading all over the globe—they dominated the spice trade and had exclusive access to Japan—and were accumulating such riches as would cause them to look back in later times and call the seventeenth century their golden age. It was the time of Rembrandt, Hals, and Vermeer, and Amsterdam could claim to be among the most cultivated cities in the world. Directing their commercial activities in the Far East was the immensely profitable Dutch East India Company. Like all self-respecting profitable organizations, however, the company desired even greater profits; and the key to such profits, they felt sure, as well as to clear-cut superiority over the hated Spanish, was a shortcut to the Orient, either via the Arctic Ocean above Russia (the so-called Northeast Passage) or through a hoped-for gap in North America (the Northwest Passage). So it was that in 1609, as a twelve-year truce with Spain was just beginning, the company dispatched the Englishman Henry Hudson in the eighty-ton *Half Moon* to seek a passageway around the northern tip of Norway.

He set sail from Amsterdam on April 4. But a month later, blocked by ice and confronted by a mutinous crew, Hudson discarded his orders and turned around and headed west, across the Atlantic: maybe he could find the elusive Northwest Passage instead. Sailing south along the coast past Newfoundland, he somehow missed the harbor that we now associate with him and continued on to Virginia. Then he retraced his course and on September 3, 1609, stumbled onto the Lower Bay. It was "a great lake of water," wrote the master's mate Robert Juet, but they could detect the current of the massive river that emptied into it, "a great streame out of the bay."[3]

A few days later they nosed into the Upper Bay where, again in Juet's chronicle, "the people of the Countrey came aboord of us, seeming very glad of our comming."[4] There was a skirmish and one officer was killed by an arrow through his throat, but aside from that the Indians seemed intrigued and delighted by the newcomers.

The shores appeared entirely forested with "great and tall Oakes." As Hudson worked his way up the wide river, gifts were repeatedly exchanged with the Indians, and Juet noted that while those near the sea wore deerskins, the Indians farther up "brought us Bevers skinnes, and Otters skinnes, which wee bought for Beades, Knives, and Hatchets." On another occasion Hudson invited some Indians to partake of wine and aqua vitae with the result that "they were all merrie" and one of them passed out.[5] But after sailing past what is now Albany, Hudson discovered that the river, while broad and deep, petered out—it was no Northwest Passage after all. So he sailed back downstream and departed these shores.

The Dutch East India Company officials who had sent him out deemed his trip a failure—he had, after all, flouted his instructions —and declined to follow up. Other Amsterdam merchants, however, kindled at his report of trading with the Indians for furs, a commodity much in demand in Europe. A great opportunity existed in an area not previously preempted by either the French (who controlled Canada, and whose explorer Samuel de Champlain had already penetrated as far south as the lake that now bears his name) or the English (ensconced in Virginia). Soon a number of enterprising Dutchmen were investigating the territory and bringing back furs. Hendrick Christiaensen retraced Hudson's route up the river and built a fort near present-day Albany. Adriaen Block, who lost his ship to fire while stopping off on Manhattan Island, spent the winter here with his crew among the Indians, built another vessel, sailed it through the treacherous strait in the East River (naming it Hellegat, or Hell Gate), and discovered Long Island Sound—including the island that he justifiably named for himself.

For a time, the merchants who had dispatched Block and the others banded together to form the United New Netherland Company, which was granted a trading monopoly in the region. The monopoly expired in 1617 and trade was once again thrown open to all, but clearly a more effective control mechanism was needed. (It was during this period, incidentally, that the English Pilgrims, then in the Netherlands, asked for permission to settle in the area now coming to be called New Netherland; but the states general turned them down and they ended up in Massachusetts.) To unify the Dutch effort, and also to help renew hostilities against Spain (the truce was expiring), the brand-new Dutch West India Company came into being in 1621.

It had the makings of a very powerful organization. Designed to complement its East India equivalent, it was given a monopoly on all Dutch trade and navigation in the Americas and West Africa; it could maintain its own military and naval forces and make war or peace; it was granted administrative and judicial powers; and it was empowered to "advance the peopling of those fruitful and unsettled parts."[6] In other words, it was a state within a state. Just how seriously it was expected to "advance the peopling" is argued among historians, but certainly its main thrust was trade, plus injury to Spain wherever possible. Specific responsibility for North American matters was entrusted to a committee of the company's Amsterdam chamber, its members to be known as the Commissioners for New Netherland.

It was all very neat and promising, but there were two problems. One was that revenue from other regions was expected to be far greater than what North America could generate, so that New Netherland never loomed large in the company's overall picture. The other was that neither the states general nor the company staked formal claim (with boundaries firmly designated) to what Henry Hudson had discovered, with the result that England, for one, never accepted the Dutch presence. This seemingly insignificant detail would come to bedevil the protocolony.

Nevertheless, a bold start was made with the sending of thirty families in 1624 to set up trading posts. More than half were placed in the Albany area (the fort had deteriorated but was to be rebuilt); others went to an island in the Delaware River and to a post on the Connecticut River; and a few were stationed not on Manhattan but on an island in the Upper Bay known as Nut Island for its trees. Most of the newcomers were actually not Dutch but Walloons, French-speaking Protestants from the largely Catholic southern Netherlands. Therein lay the seeds of yet another difficulty with the new venture: the company was having trouble interesting Dutch citizens in pulling up stakes in their prosperous country and serving in the wilderness. It was a difficulty that would never be surmounted.

The following year an engineer and surveyor, Cryn Fredericks, arrived with plans for a fort and a rudimentary town, and a newly appointed director, Willem Verhulst, decided to consolidate the immigrants in one central spot. With commendable perspicacity he chose the southern tip of the largest island in the harbor, Manhattan (also sometimes called Manhattes or other variations). The settlement was to be called New Amsterdam in honor of the company chamber supervising the outposts. By early 1626 most of the original group had regrouped on Manhattan, land was being cleared, and the fort was well under way, surrounded by modest huts. That year a permanent director, Peter Minuit, took over from Verhulst, who had been caught diverting company goods to his own use—the first of several directors to depart in disgrace. One of Minuit's first accomplishments (though there is evidence it may have been Verhulst's) was the purchase, on May 6, 1626, of the entire island of Manhattan—14,000 acres of excellent timbered land—from the Indians for an estimated sixty guilders' worth of merchandise. A nineteenth-century writer estimated that to be about $24, and while it would surely be a much bigger sum in today's economy, the transaction has to be reckoned one of the major steals in history. (Manhattan real estate is estimated to be worth a total of $30 billion.) In the luckless sellers' defense it should be noted that to the Algonquin Indians who peopled the area, as to most Indians, land never belonged to any person or group, and all "purchases" were regarded as temporary. The trouble was, the Indians never got a chance to renegotiate.

Although the fort, made of earthwork and located just below what is now Bowling Green (the shoreline has since been built out far beyond what then existed), was the principal feature of the town, most of the houses were built along the East River as its shore was more protected from the prevailing winds than that of the Hudson. The riverfront path was called Pearl Street, from the glistening sea-shells deposited there by the tides, but the main street was a former Indian path leading north from the fort. First known as the Beaver's Path, it was soon renamed Heere Straat, or Gentlemen's Street; but the settlers came to call it Breede Wegh, and so it has remained— today's Broadway.

Before long, some thirty houses and other structures clustered around the fort and along the shore, providing a look of solidity and permanence. But it was a peculiar kind of permanence, for although the town was expected to remain, its inhabitants were not. All the newcomers had been signed on as employees of the company—over-seas laborers who would put in their stint and then return home, to be replaced by other sojourners. Those engaged in trading were to be supported by others who raised crops (on a series of farms or *bouweries* north of town) and performed maintenance tasks, but there was no plan to establish a permanent colonial population. The outpost was thought of as an integral part of the Netherlands itself, not as a colony. It was an interesting scheme, but it didn't work.

First of all, the fur trade was not measuring up: in 1628, more than 7,500 beaver skins were shipped to Europe, but that was not up to the company's projections. Second, not enough people were coming: New Amsterdam had only about 300 inhabitants and needed many more. And third, those who did come were far more interested in making quick profits, even at the expense of the company, than in building up its position. Even some officials were accused of profiteering—including, as it turned out, Minuit himself.

So, in the first of several shifts that would mark their stewardship of the area, the company's commissioners changed the rules. They decided not to pump any more of the company's funds into the colony—money was better invested, they felt, in South America and the West Indies—but, rather, to see what a little private initiative might yield in New Netherland. Issuing a Charter of Freedoms and Exemptions, they invited a number of wealthy Dutchmen—all of whom happened to be big stockholders in the company—to establish patroonships, large feudal landholdings that would be granted the right to trade independently with the Indians. In return the owners, or patroons, would be responsible for recruiting settlers. The patroonships were all located outside Manhattan (which the company kept for itself), and the most prepossessing was established along the upper Hudson River by Kiliaen van Rensselaer, a rich Amsterdam diamond and pearl merchant. Although he never visited his patroonship, van Rensselaer sank a great deal of money into it and monitored it closely, and it became a success; his sons came here and stayed, and the holding prospered. All the other patroonships failed. But while they lasted they had a stultifying effect on the town of New Amsterdam, siphoning off promising settlers and valued livestock. As one historian has remarked, the system "virtually destroyed the agricultural underpinnings" of the Manhattan community.[7]

Though undernourished, the settlement carried on. In 1631 Peter Minuit was dismissed following charges that he had helped some of the patroons smuggle furs in contravention of company policy; after an interim appointment the colony received as its new director a short, stout, fat-faced young man with the redoubtable name of Wouter van Twiller. Previously a clerk in the company's Amsterdam offices, he was a nephew of Kiliaen van Rensselaer, who had engineered his appointment, and he arrived accompanied by 104 steel-corseted soldiers carrying half-pikes and wheel-lock muskets—New Amsterdam's first military force.

Van Twiller's inexperience as well as his fondness for alcohol soon undermined his authority. Barely eight days after his arrival an English ship, the *William*, entered the harbor, and its captain announced his intention of sailing up the Hudson to trade for furs. It was his right, he said, since all the land hereabouts belonged to the English monarch. Van Twiller blustered a protest but was unable to prevent the ship from sailing on. A Dutch trader named David de Vries, who owned land on Staten Island (the name honors the mother country's states general), described the ensuing scene. "Commander Wouter van Twiller assembled all his forces before his door, had a cask of wine brought out, filled a bumper, and cried out for those who loved the Prince of Orange and him, to do the same as he did, and protect him from the outrage of the Englishman, who was already out of sight sailing up the river. The people all began to laugh at him; for they understood well how to drink dry the cask of wine . . . and did not wish to trouble the Englishman, saying they were friends."[8] De Vries advised the director to send a Dutch vessel to apprehend the intruder, which van Twiller did, but the damage was done.

On another occasion a landholder named Cornelis van Vorst came to visit van Twiller carrying a bottle of claret "of which article he knew he was fond." Somehow the two men got into a violent argument. But they quickly made up, and to celebrate their renewed friendship van Vorst fired a small cannon that happened to be handy. A spark from the cannon ignited the roof of a nearby house, which burned to the ground in half an hour.[9]

Van Twiller's regime was not without its benefits, however. Fur shipments increased, and the director put into effect a new policy known as a staple right, which required all vessels outbound for Europe from anywhere along the Atlantic coast to stop in at New Amsterdam and pay a toll; sea captains who balked were required to unload their cargo and sell it on the shore. Legally questionable, the statute brought in much-needed revenue and was a harbinger of similar lucrative ploys in the future New York.

Thanks to these and other schemes, the town grew. Houses now were built more solidly and had a genuinely Dutch look, with a step-gabled end facing the street and a front door whose top and bottom halves opened separately. On some houses steps led up to a raised front door, a feature not necessitated here but derived from Holland, where flooding can be frequent. At the top of the steps there would be a landing called a stoop (from the Dutch *stoep*, a front veranda), which remained a staple of New York houses until the twentieth century. Many houses had vegetable or flower gardens out back. The fort's walls were now lined with stone, although individual blocks were constantly being swiped by citizens who felt they could help themselves to these good building materials; within the fort van Twiller built himself an official residence of brick. The town still had no dock, but New Amsterdam sported a church, a bakery, a blacksmith's shop, a barrel maker's shop, a shed for boatbuilding including a sailmaker's loft—and of course a brewery. Pigs ran everywhere—people liked them because they ate up the garbage. Manhattanites were already acquiring a reputation for heavy drinking, a trait that no amount of regulation could ever quite control.

What would much later become the city's outer boroughs were beginning to be settled. In addition to a handful of properties on Staten Island, there were some farms in the Flatlands area of what would later become Brooklyn; the town of Breuckelen itself, named for a community in Holland, would be founded in 1646. Settlers were moving into the Gowanus area immediately across the East River and could get there by blowing on a conch-shell horn to summon the rowboat ferry. In 1641 a highly cultivated gentleman farmer from Denmark, Jonas Bronck, moved into the area immediately

18

above Manhattan and acquired such a reputation for good citizenship that his name has endured. His property became known as Bronck's and is now the Bronx.

When not imbibing, van Twiller assiduously feathered his nest by buying up any property he could lay his hands on. He purchased Nut Island—where the first settlers had encamped—and renamed it Governor's Island, bought two other East River islands (one is now called Roosevelt Island), and acquired extensive acreage in the Flatlands on Long Island. But whatever else one can say about him, he did make sure that relations with the Indians, on whom the fur trade depended, remained placid. That changed, however, when the company finally caught on to his inadequate ways and dismissed him in 1637. His successor, a small fussy man named Willem Kieft, had other ideas.

Kieft was not very endearing. Shortly after his arrival he decided the town needed a new stone church. Funds for construction, however, were short. Seizing upon the occasion of a wedding party, Kieft waited until everyone had had a few drinks, then rapped for order and announced he was accepting pledges of financial support for the church project. The guests, by now in a giddy mood, pledged handsomely, but the next day most of them had indignantly changed their minds. The company ended up footing most of the bill.

It was not a good time for the colony to have a director who lacked public support, because pressures were mounting. In 1638 the erstwhile director Peter Minuit, who was still angry at being rejected, hired himself to the Swedish government and led an expedition of Swedes to establish an outpost on the Delaware River, threatening the company's position there. More serious, however, was the threat to the colony's other flank: more and more English were moving into territory that it claimed in western Connecticut as well as onto the eastern end of Long Island, for example founding the town of Southampton in 1640. The truth was that a great many more English than Dutch were coming to America, partly because their emigration was effectively organized under religious auspices. Thousands were coming, in fact, for every few hundred Dutch. Once here, moreover, large numbers of English newcomers were becoming dissatisfied with the strict Puritanism of the New England authorities and were moving into Dutch territory, where policies were more relaxed.

The Dutch West India Company soon became aware that if something were not done soon the English might overrun their colony, and in 1639 it pulled yet another switch. In effect abandoning the patroon system in an effort to spur immigration, it opened up the fur trade to any and all who wished to partake, and began allowing the sale of company-owned land—even on Manhattan—to individuals with only modest resources. The move markedly increased the flow of immigrants, but because many of the new landowners were capable, well-educated men who felt no particular allegiance to the company, it ironically produced a body of independent-thinking citizens who did not hesitate to criticize Kieft's actions, thus greatly complicating his task.

What they objected to most vociferously was his handling of relations with the Indians, which could hardly have been worse. Soon after taking office he had come up with the asinine idea of taxing them. After all, he said, if the company has to spend money to fortify itself against them, why shouldn't they contribute? The proposal soon sank without a trace, but problems with the indigenous Americans were indeed getting ticklish. Originally hospitable toward the white man, the Indians were learning that the intruders were out to displace them. There were many sources of friction. Indian dogs killed European livestock; the settlers' cattle frequently strayed into the Indians' fields, but when the Indians killed the strays there were reprisals. And while the Indians had been equipped only with bows and arrows when the Dutch arrived, many settlers had sold them firearms illegally in return for furs, and they now were as skilled in the use of guns as the whites.

The first real bloodshed came in the summer of 1641 when an Indian approached a company wheelwright named Claes Swits and asked for a piece of cloth. When Smit turned to get it, the Indian grabbed an ax and smashed the man's head open, then fled. It turned out that he had committed the deed to avenge the killing of his uncle by a group of Dutchmen sixteen years earlier. Kieft demanded that the perpetrator's tribe hand him over for punishment, but the chief refused; the young man, he said, had merely done his duty. A few weeks later a group of Raritan Indians on Staten Island fell upon some farmers working for David de Vries, killing them outright. Kieft could do nothing to apprehend them either.

Early in 1643 he got his chance for revenge. Indians from the Mohawk Valley had moved south to attack the tribes around Manhattan, who thereupon congregated across the Hudson in what is now Jersey City (then known as Pavonia). On the night of February 25–26 a detachment of Kieft's soldiers crossed the river and fell upon the unsuspecting Indians, murdering some eighty men, women, and children. David de Vries, who happened to have dined with Kieft that evening, wrote that "about midnight I heard a great shrieking, and I ran to the ramparts of the fort, and looked over to Pavonia. I saw nothing but firing, and heard the shrieks of the savages murdered in their sleep."[10] The soldiers on their return to Manhattan were congratulated by the director general.

It did not take the Indians long to retaliate, and the next several months saw one bloodbath after another as they swooped down on the Europeans' outposts, killing immigrant farmers and their families, burning houses, and destroying livestock. One family virtually wiped out was that of Anne Hutchinson, a religious dissenter who had come from New England to what is now the Pelham Bay area; the only survivor was Anne's daughter Susannah, taken prisoner by the attackers. Of the company's forty-odd *bouweries* or farms in the New Amsterdam area, only four or five were spared. The following year Kieft sent an expedition of soldiers to an Indian encampment back of the Connecticut community of Greenwich; the entire camp of more than 500 Indians was slain. That was the last major incident, however; and in 1645 the two sides, exhausted, signed a peace treaty.

Although Kieft had expected to be praised for his presumed decisiveness, he was condemned for his brutality—and principally by the recently arrived landowners, so many of whose properties had been devastated. A number of them had been appointed advisers to Kieft during the hostilities, had counseled moderation, and were incensed when he ignored their recommendations. They had banded together to form "the commonalty," which was in effect a political party, and they proceeded to complain loudly to the company directors in Amsterdam about what they called Kieft's suicidal policies. Their plea was heard, and Kieft was summoned home to defend himself (he never got there; his ship was sunk on the way and he drowned). The man sent out by the company to succeed him arrived in May 1647. He was to be the first of many effective, strong-willed men who through the centuries would dominate the community on the Hudson.

Peter Stuyvesant had been governor of Curaçao and had lost a leg during a military campaign there—his wooden leg was bound with silver bands—and he was every bit as harsh and brutal as Kieft. But he was very different from the man he replaced. Though stubborn —his gruff face looks out defiantly from his portrait—he was both highly intelligent and scrupulously honest. The colonists disliked and feared him at first, but in the end he won their admiration for his efforts to make New Amsterdam a viable, successful community.

The town that he inherited had been built up considerably since the genial days of van Twiller. Pearl Street was now a busy commercial area with a number of four-story warehouses, each equipped with a hoist for raising bundles of skins to the storage rooms. One section of the street was set aside as a weekly marketplace—farmers brought their produce in rowboats from *bouweries* across the East River, spreading the food out on the ground—while near the southern end of it was the newly constructed city tavern, where visiting dignitaries could be put up and which would presently be made over into the town's first city hall. Just beyond the tavern was a narrow canal, reminiscent of old Amsterdam itself, which led in from the East River; in time it would be filled in and become today's Broad Street.

New Amsterdam's most popular bar, however, was the Wooden Horse, on Stone Street; its name had been bestowed by its owner, Philip Gerard, as a kind of good-natured jibe at authority. The French-born Gerard had come to New Amsterdam as a member of the military guard but had taken to supplementing his pay by bartending. Soon he was charged with being too frequently absent from his duties at his own unofficial tavern, and like other offenders he was sentenced to ride the wooden horse, a sawhorse with extra long legs that the guilty person was required to straddle for an hour or two with weights attached to his feet. Gerard's sentence was embellished with the requirement that he dramatize his predicament by carrying a sword in one hand and a pitcher of beer in the other. He handily survived the ordeal, resigned from the service, and thumbed his nose at his accusers by displaying a brand-new sign of the Wooden Horse outside his establishment.

With Frenchmen like Gerard and other non-Dutch immigrants, New Amsterdam was rapidly becoming a polyglot town, and as early as 1643 a visiting Jesuit missionary, Father Isaac Jogues, who had come to town after being held captive by the Mohawk Indians, was told that eighteen different languages could be heard on its streets. (The claim, difficult to verify, was made by Kieft, who may thus qualify as New York's first certified booster.)

Among the ethnic mix was a group of African slaves who had been brought in by the company in 1626 to work on construction projects, and in 1646 another shipment arrived, this time from Brazil. Although the lot of a slave was unpleasant if not frightful, the West India Company did allow slaves to earn their freedom and assured them the same status as whites in the courts; and in general blacks in New Netherland were probably treated more humanely than those in any other colony. By far the most famous of these early slaves was Manuel Gerrit, known as the Giant. In 1641 he was one of a group of slaves who had killed another near the fort. As none of them knew who had struck the fatal blow and none would confess, they were ordered to draw lots to determine who should be punished on behalf of all; on this basis, Gerrit was chosen. He was sentenced to be hanged, but when the ladder on which he was standing was pulled away the ropes around his neck broke and he fell, stunned but alive, to the ground. The crowd that had gathered to witness the execution yelled for his release, which was granted, and three years later Gerrit became a free man.

Confronted by this busy though outwardly carefree community, Stuyvesant moved swiftly to establish his authority. Residents of New Amsterdam got a preview of what was in store upon his inauguration as director general. He remained seated while the town's prominent citizens stood, and he kept his hat on while they respectfully doffed theirs. Finally condescending to speak to them, he intoned with a magisterial air, "I shall govern you as a father his children, for the advantage of the chartered West India Company, and these burghers, and this land."[11] The order in which he ticked off these entities was important: the company came first. Above all it was necessary to bring the community to the straight and narrow. He ordered bars closed at 9 P.M. and levied heavy penalties against drinking on Sunday, proclaiming that "We see and observe by experience the great disorders in which some of our inhabitants indulge, in drinking to excess, quarreling, fighting . . . even on the Lord's day of rest. Whereof, God help us!"[12] Within a few months he had also decided to impose taxes, not on the Indians but on the colonists themselves, a move virtually unheard of among Dutchmen. To soften the blow he agreed to grant the citizens representation, but when the newly chosen body tried to act he paid them no heed. None of this was to make him popular.

A needless but serious error caused his acceptance to be even more unlikely. Among the new landowners who called themselves the commonalty were two who had suffered severely during the Indian wars, Cornelis Melyn and Jochem Kuyter. Not long after Stuyvesant's arrival they moved to bring charges against the soon-to-depart Kieft for misgovernment, claiming that his errant ways had caused their suffering. To most citizens, they had good cause for bitterness. Stuyvesant had no sympathy for Kieft, but in a kind of knee-jerk reaction he immediately saw their suit as demeaning the office of director general and ordered them arrested for rebellion and sedition. The trial was short, with Stuyvesant presiding; and both men were found guilty, banished from New Netherland, and shipped back to the home country (ironically they sailed on the same boat that carried Kieft, but while he died in the sinking, they survived). They appealed to the states general, which suspended their sentences and granted them safe-conduct back to America. In a gentle rebuke to Stuyvesant, the Dutch body said that while it did not dispute the "correctness" of his judgment, "We desire only to say that sometimes a careful consideration and prudence may prevent great trouble."[13] When Melyn arrived back in New Amsterdam he was welcomed as a hero, much to Stuyvesant's annoyance and embarrassment.

Worse still, Melyn brought with him a writ from the states general calling upon Stuyvesant to send an envoy to Amsterdam to explain his conduct in the Melyn-Kuyter affair. While the writ was being read at a civic meeting, the furious Stuyvesant stomped across the room to the man reading it and tore it from his hand. He was about to crumple it when he regained his composure and quietly handed it back. He would honor the states general's demand, he said.

All this gave encouragement to the commonalty, who had transferred their enmity from Kieft to Stuyvesant because of the director general's taxes and other moves that hurt them financially. They decided to issue their own petition and remonstrance to the states general and entrusted the writing of it to one of their most able and ambitious colleagues, Adriaen Van der Donck. A lawyer and historian, Van der Donck had been granted a large tract of land in the area now constituting much of the northern Bronx and lower Westchester; he was known as the *jonkheer*, or young lordship, and so his land was the *jonkheers*—later known as Yonkers.

Van der Donck's document, viciously (and for the most part unreasonably) attacking Stuyvesant, demanded that New Netherland be governed by the states general instead of the West India Company and that New Amsterdam be granted its own municipal government, supplanting one-man rule. The Dutch parliamentary body declined the first but said yes to the second: New Amsterdam was to have a burgher system of government such as ruled the home country's own cities, with burgomasters (or city magistrates) and schepens (or aldermen) advising the director general. What's more, the Dutch authorities, noting the Melyn-Kuyter affair, seriously considered removing Stuyvesant. Only the outbreak of hostilities between England and the Netherlands in 1652 persuaded them to retain their strong man at the helm of the small overseas colony.

So it was that on February 2, 1653, the new city government was proclaimed with a parade down Broadway to the fort, led by the peg-legged Stuyvesant—resplendent in brass-buttoned regimental coat and sulfur-colored breeches—and with formal ceremonies in the fort's church. With a politician's instincts, Stuyvesant was perfectly happy to take credit for what had been forced on him. But the major credit for bringing about what was, in effect, the first municipal council in America should really go to Van der Donck and the other stalwarts of the commonalty, who may thus be counted among the true founders of the city's government.

What had persuaded the states general to keep Stuyvesant was the very real threat to New Netherland itself—dramatized by the war —from the expanding English of New England. A major difficulty was that no boundary between the Dutch and the English territories in America was recognized by either side; the West India Company assumed rights to all the land between the Delaware River and Cape Cod, while the English would not accept Dutch control even over the Connecticut River Valley. Yielding to the reality of New England's far greater population—the English now outnumbered the Dutch of New Netherland by a whopping sixteen to one—Stuyvesant journeyed to Hartford in 1650 and worked out an agreement whereby the boundary would be fixed along a line roughly the same as that now separating Connecticut and New York, with Long Island split between the two parties. The Dutch government ratified the treaty, but the English never did. When war broke out in 1652 there seemed good reason to suspect that New England's forces might invade, and New Amsterdam tensed. Stuyvesant ordered a fortified wall built at the northern edge of town stretching from the Hudson to the East River, a total of 2,340 feet.

The attack never transpired—hostilities between the Dutch and the English ceased in 1654—and the wall was never tested. (The path that ran along inside it would become well known in another context, however, as Wall Street.) But the pressure was still there, and New Amsterdam's citizens were beginning to note the greater prosperity of the New England farmers and townsfolk, whom they called "Johnnies," or *yanikens* (the probable origin of "yankees"). Stuyvesant's town was beginning to seem more and more like a tiny island in the midst of a vast English sea. That sea, furthermore, kept encroaching, especially on Long Island. By the mid-1650s the only Long Island settlements that were still truly Dutch were clustered at the western end of the island, just across the East River from Manhattan.

Stuyvesant's 9 P.M. curfew had brought little change in the town, and tavern brawls were frequent. But the director general continued to impose necessary rules on the citizens. To control reckless driving, a hazard to pedestrians, he ordered drivers to dismount from their wagons and lead their horses on every street except Broadway, where they could remain mounted but must drive slowly. The streets themselves were largely meandering affairs; he ordered them properly aligned and, where necessary, given names. He appointed fire wardens to inspect the flimsy chimneys on houses with thatched roofs and arranged to buy ladders and leather buckets from the Netherlands for fire fighting. In 1658 he established the rattle watch, a force of volunteers who patrolled the streets at night, sounding alarms by waving wooden clappers that made a loud rattling noise. But in many ways the community was still a kind of frontier town. It had gotten its first dock in 1648, on the East River. But there were few doctors, and medical facilities were rudimentary. As for the poor, of whom New Amsterdam was seeing more and more, the city fathers appointed "orphan masters" to care for children but otherwise were content to leave the poverty problem to the attention of the Dutch Reformed Church.

A more serious concern, at least to Stuyvesant, was the influx into New Amsterdam of people whom he considered religiously unsuitable. The first he denounced were the twenty-seven Jews who came from Brazil in 1654, and only the direct orders of his superiors in the West India Company persuaded him to accept them—if only grudgingly. More outrageous was his persecution—again until stopped by orders from above—of the Quakers, who arrived in 1657 by ship after being expelled from Boston. The director general, viewing their beliefs as heretical and thus intolerable, forbade them to come ashore, but two young women managed to evade detection and began preaching in the streets. In the account of two Dutch clergymen who witnessed the incident, the women "began to quake and go into a frenzy, and cry out loudly in the middle of the street, that men should repent, for the day of judgement was at hand. Our people not knowing what was the matter, ran to and fro, while one cried 'fire' and another something else."[14] Stuyvesant clapped the women in prison and kept them there for eight days, then marched them down to the waterfront with their arms pinned behind them and put them on a boat for Rhode Island.

But three other Quakers had also gotten ashore, and one of them, Robert Hodgson, made his way to Heemstedt (today's Hempstead), Long Island, where he announced he would hold forth on Quakerism in an orchard. There he was arrested, after which he was tied for twenty-four hours in a painful position. Stuyvesant sent a deputation of soldiers to bring him back to Manhattan, lashed facedown in a cart, and swiftly brought him to trial. Convicted and sentenced to hard labor, Hodgson protested his innocence and said he would not perform the work. He was thereupon beaten, not just that day but a second and a third. Brought again before Stuyvesant, he would not yield. He was suspended from the ceiling by his wrists, a heavy log tied to his feet, and was again lashed. By now word of the director general's actions had gotten out, and public sentiment was turning against him. At length Stuyvesant's sister (who had come to New Amsterdam shortly after he had and married a company official) persuaded him to cease the torture, and Hodgson was shipped out as the two women had been before him.

But the story was by no means over. Quakers were now preaching openly throughout the English villages on Long Island, and a group of them began meeting in homes in Flushing. Stuyvesant ordered the owners of the homes arrested, but Flushing's sheriff, Tobias Feake, balked. After all, Flushing's 1645 charter had specified that its citizens were "to have and enjoy liberty of conscience, according to the custom and manner of Holland, without molestation or disturbance."[15] In this light, Feake and others felt, it was Stuyvesant himself who was breaking the law. Feake wrote out a statement of principles that was signed on December 27, 1657, by thirty-one Dutch and English residents. Known as the Flushing Remonstrance, it declared that if any persons of any faith "come in love unto us, we cannot in Conscience lay violent hands upon them, but give them free egress into our town and houses as God shall persuade our Conscience."[16]

Feake was arrested and then dismissed as sheriff. The arrests continued. But another Quaker, John Bowne, who as a result of allowing meetings to be held at his home was banished from the colony, went to the Netherlands and made an appeal to the West India Company's Amsterdam chamber, calling attention to "that liberty promised to us in our Patent."[17] The chamber took months to come to a decision, but on April 16, 1663, it wrote Stuyvesant and voiced once again the notion that discrimination is, in effect, bad for business. "You may therefore shut your eyes," they wrote, "at least not force people's consciences, but allow everyone to have his own belief, as long as he behaves quietly and legally, gives no offense to his neighbors and does not oppose the government."[18] It is because of this outcome that the Flushing Remonstrance has been called a precursor of the Declaration of Independence. Locally, it has a further meaning, as it contributed decisively to the spirit of toleration that has become so deeply ingrained among the citizens of New York City.

Even as these disturbances were testing Peter Stuyvesant, there had been other threats of a more tangible and clear-cut nature to New Amsterdam. In the early 1650s Stuyvesant became increasingly irritated by the continued existence of Swedish forces on the Delaware River, that outlying southern territory that the company still claimed for itself. As a counter-measure he had built a fort in 1651 on the site of what is now New Castle, Delaware, but the Swedes had captured it. So in 1655 he led an expedition of soldiers in seven sailing craft to retake the fort and dislodge the interlopers. The mission was a success, and New Sweden disappeared from the map. But just as Stuyvesant was savoring his triumph he learned of a far greater peril: in his absence, the Indians had once again attacked New Amsterdam.

The short, bloody conflict, known as the "peach war," stemmed from the shooting of an Indian woman by a Dutch farmer, Hendrick van Dyck, who saw her stealing a peach from his orchard. Upon hearing of the shooting, the Indians were outraged and, aware that Stuyvesant had taken most of the town's soldiers with him, they crossed the Hudson, 500-strong, and swarmed through New Amsterdam's streets ransacking homes, though at first not killing anyone. A truce was arranged, but by the time Stuyvesant got back the Indians had spread their attack to outlying areas. This time their behavior was different. Communities on the west shore of the Hudson and elsewhere were decimated, some 100 whites were killed and 150 taken prisoner; 28 plantations were torched and 500 head of cattle slain or driven away. About 60 Indians were killed. The entire affair lasted only three days but left New Amsterdam's residents in a state of shock. Stuyvesant coolly moved to improve the town's defenses, negotiated the release of many prisoners, and stood as a bulwark of competence and calm among the townsfolk. One citizen urged him to continue the war to get revenge, but the director general said no. "The recent war is to be attributed to the rashness of a few hotheaded individuals. It becomes us to reform ourselves, to abstain from all wrong, and to guard against a recurrence of the late unhappy affair."[19] As it happened, the Indians never again posed a threat to the European settlement on the Hudson.

By the late 1650s a feeling of well-being and almost of security enveloped New Amsterdam. Business was good and the town's affairs seemed in proper order. But the colony's position was precarious and not improving. To the English, the Dutch were disrupting their own trade with the English colonies; New Netherland was an annoyance that should be removed. Stuyvesant was well aware of the danger, and among other things he moved to establish a defensive outpost, a new village located in the general area of today's East 125th Street. Stuyvesant named it New Harlem, after the Dutch city, which had fought a valiant defense against the Spanish.

But there was a greater danger from the east. Many of the villages on western Long Island heretofore considered solidly pro-Dutch were being encouraged by English adventurers to pull away from Dutch rule. Stuyvesant journeyed to Boston in an attempt to get the 1650 Hartford treaty reaffirmed, only to hear the Puritan leaders renounce it. He appealed to the West India Company to send money and troops. The answer was negative. Indeed the company itself, suffering from commercial setbacks worldwide, was virtually bankrupt. It could hardly have provided help even if it had wanted to.

Early in 1664 King Charles II of England, in a lofty demonstration of monarchical arrogance, gave his brother James, duke of York, a truly handsome present. Making no mention of any prior Dutch (or English) claims to the territory, he bestowed on James parts of Maine, all of Martha's Vineyard, Nantucket, and Long Island, and "all the land from the west side of the Connectecutte River to the East Side of De la Ware Bay."[20] The lucky recipient soon dispatched a fleet of four warships under Colonel Richard Nicolls to nail down the prize, and after a stop in Boston the ships appeared just below the Narrows on August 26. Nicolls disembarked 450 soldiers at Gravesend, directing them to march to the Brooklyn shore opposite Manhattan. Then, in response to Stuyvesant's inquiry as to his intent, he demanded that the Dutch surrender.

His terms were generous: everyone in the community would be guaranteed security of life, liberty, and property. Stuyvesant's position was hopeless; he had perhaps 150 soldiers, the English in excess of 2,000. But he refused to submit and tried to conceal the Englishman's terms from the people. Very well, said Nicolls, if you do not yield I shall approach the city in forty-eight hours. Now pressure began to build up on Stuyvesant to surrender. Word of Nicolls's terms had leaked out, and city officials to a man were urging their director to accept the inevitable and thus avoid bloodshed. He would not yield. Nicolls sailed his ships through the Narrows, anchored two of them off Governor's Island, and sent the others toward the Hudson to post themselves above the city. As they approached, Stuyvesant stood atop the fort and prepared to give a fire order to the gunner, who stood by with lighted match in hand. Then, as a huge crowd looked on from below, two Dutch Reformed ministers quietly walked up to the director general, conversed with him for a few moments, took his arm, and led him away. The next day he was presented with a petition from ninety-three eminent citizens requesting that he give in. Among the signers was his seventeen-year-old son. He could do no more.

On the morning of September 8 the formal surrender was signed. Two hours later the Dutch troops marched to the dock and boarded Nicolls's flagship, and shortly thereafter English troops came ashore. Dutch rule of the city on the Hudson was at an end, and Nicolls announced that it would henceforth be named in honor of the duke who had sent him and be called New York.

2

The British Overlords

The day after the English took over the city and its colony, the citizens of what was now New York conducted business as usual. The burgomasters and schepens who had governed the municipality convened as if nothing much had happened—for had not their conqueror, Richard Nicolls, said he would honor all existing property rights? True, the flag fluttering over the fort at the foot of Manhattan was now the English ensign, not the Dutch one, and the following Sunday in the fort an Anglican chaplain conducted the first Church of England service ever observed openly in the city. But most citizens felt relief that the crisis was over and sustained no rancor against their conquerors. Nicolls offered to transport free of charge any Dutch resident back to the Netherlands; there were no takers. Even Peter Stuyvesant, though grumbling, retired without protest to his country estate at what is now Second Avenue and 10th Street.

Because the transition was so smooth, and because the ensuing 119 years of English rule have in some respects seemed uneventful, the period has been called New York's forgotten century. The label is highly misleading. The time was far from uneventful; indeed, it was pivotal in the city's long-term development. Some of the problems were brought about by English bungling. The new English governors, with a few exceptions, were insensitive, domineering, and more interested in amassing private fortunes than in ruling justly. Furthermore, the duke of York's ardent Catholicism became a serious and divisive issue after he acceded to the throne in 1685 as James II; the resulting eruptions were to change the city in significant ways. Then too, many of the Dutch came to resent the gradual diminution of their culture and way of life, and this affected the city's mood.

31

Newly arrived English merchants began elbowing aside their Dutch counterparts, causing bad feeling that helped instigate a full-scale rebellion before the seventeenth century was over. Finally, the cosmopolitan city's reputation for tolerance was severely tested on more than one occasion, with lasting effects.

Even the outward fabric of the city changed. Although the enterprising Dutch mercantile spirit survived and prospered, a new set of English governmental and legal institutions was imposed on top of it: New York became an English city, though with the Dutch down-to-earth profit-seeking attitude at its heart. At the same time, the city's special kind of freewheeling politics was decisively shaped under the English, taking on the essential cast that has characterized it to this day.

Most important, however, New York in effect grew up during these years. At the outset of the period it was still essentially a beleaguered outpost outstripped commercially by Boston. By the middle of the next century it was a city on the make. It had surpassed Boston in population and was threatening the Bay City's mercantile dominance as well; flexing its muscles, it was furthermore about to challenge Philadelphia—which, although not founded until 1681, had swept past it in population and trade activity around 1700. By the 1760s New York was not only ready for its time of travail during the American Revolution but was also poised for its explosive growth in the nineteenth century, the rocketlike rise that would astonish the world.

The first sign that things would not be the same under the English came two months after the city's capture, when Nicolls, now officially the governor, informed a group of leading townspeople that, while not renouncing Dutch citizenship, they would all have to swear allegiance to the British crown. He quietly added that all property owners must renew title to their lands in the name of the duke of York, for a fee that would be instantly collectible. A modest outcry was followed by lively discussion, but Nicolls held firm. A few months later, at the duke's urging, Nicolls removed the burgomasters and schepens and substituted an English system consisting of a mayor, a sheriff, and a set of aldermen each representing a section of town. All of them would be appointed by the governor. He softened the blow slightly by naming as New York's first mayor Thomas Willett, who though English-born had been a New Amsterdam merchant and was popular with the Dutch. But the office would be largely ceremonial, and the governor retained the all-important power to levy taxes and impose laws. Things were shifting.

So much for the city; the colony surrounding it was no better off. Nicolls, an otherwise charming and capable man who despite these severities ranks as one of the few superior English governors, outlined the new setup in 1665 to a gathering of citizens of Westchester and Long Island. The towns would send representatives to a provincial council, but this body would have few powers; almost all key decisions would be made by the governor. And while each town would have its own courts, there was no provision for town meetings, those gatherings to which the residents of New England—oriented eastern Long Island had long been accustomed, and no elected assembly. The new statutes became known as the Duke's Laws, and the towns had to obey them. Any expectations of democracy would have to be laid aside.

Circumscribed politically, New York City also found itself hemmed in commercially. The Netherlands had allowed its American colony considerable latitude in trading with other countries, but England was not so lenient. Its Navigation Acts, first enacted by Parliament in 1651, decreed that all goods from the colonies be transported in English-owned ships and be routed through the mother country; in theory this meant that New York's Dutch merchants could not trade even with Holland except via Britain. All manufactured goods also must be obtained from England; none could be produced in the colonies. Such rigid strictures were hard to enforce and invited defiance, and before long New York merchants were carrying on a brisk and clandestine trade with French and Spanish holdings in the West Indies and elsewhere. But the city's commercial growth was undeniably hobbled.

New York City even had its own backyard sliced up. It seems the duke of York felt his proprietary holdings in America were unwieldy, and so in 1665 he summarily awarded what is now New Jersey to an English group headed by Lord John Berkeley and Sir George Carteret. With that one epochal move he separated New York City from some of its most promising farmland and cut the future great port in two, defying the logic that decrees both banks of a river to be a natural economic unit. Not until the twentieth century, with the creation of the Port of New York Authority, would the harbor's two halves be united; in the meantime there would be endless bickering between New York and New Jersey over customs duties and other divisive matters. At one point New Jersey tried to establish a competing port at Perth Amboy, though with no success.

Not surprisingly in view of these restraints, the city for some time failed to prosper. Although its polyglot population—the Dutch base was interlarded with English, French, Swedes, Finns, Portuguese, and blacks, among others—was growing slightly, it brought scant revenue to the duke. It was an unimposing community. Only three of its streets were paved, and hogs still ran about everywhere. Most livestock grazed where they could, causing confusion that prompted Nicolls to order all horses and cattle branded; whereupon bulldogs were imported that were trained to seize a bull by the snout and hold it steady until it could be tied. The governor's house was still inside the fort, which remained in poor condition. Although there was little settlement north of Wall Street, Nicolls extended New York's boundaries out to encompass all of Manhattan Island. He also made formal claim on behalf of the duke to Staten Island; it became Richmond County, named in honor of the duke of Richmond, who was Charles II's illegitimate son. Other counties were designated as well, the area around Brooklyn becoming Kings County in honor of Charles II and the land north of it Queens in honor of his wife, Catherine of Braganza. Manhattan, for governmental purposes, became New York County.

But the governor did feel that life here could be pleasant. Some fine English horses were imported, and Nicolls chose a grassy area in Hempstead to serve as a racetrack, "not so much for the divertisement of youth as for encouraging the bettering of the breed of horses which, through neglect, have been impaired."[1] It was a quaint concept and one that is still in vogue.

In 1673 the city came in for a rude shock. War had broken out between France and the Netherlands, and England's Charles II decided to come to the aid of his friend Louis XIV of France. So English men-of-war began attacking Dutch vessels, and in retaliation the Netherlands decided to strike swiftly and retake New York. A fleet was secretly readied, and that summer it suddenly appeared in the Narrows. "We have come to take the place which is our own," announced Admiral Cornelis Evertsen, Jr.[2] Francis Lovelace (Nicolls's successor as governor) was out of town, but his deputy asked to see Evertsen's commission; the admiral replied that it was in the barrel of his cannon and they would soon see it if they did not surrender. The following day gunfire was exchanged between the two sides with no clear outcome, but when the Dutch landed 600 soldiers and marched on the fort, New York gave up. The city was renamed New Orange (honoring the new Dutch monarch William of Orange), and the province once again became New Netherland.

The English were furious. They ordered the governor home, confiscated his estates, and deposited him in the Tower of London, where he soon died. There was much talk of mounting an expedition to oust the Dutch, but it came to naught. As it happened, there was no need for concern. The Dutch before long sued for peace, and in the swapping that accompanied the negotiations New York was returned to the English.

Not long thereafter the duke of York was lamenting the lack of revenue from his colony. Someone—it may have been his friend William Penn, the Quaker who was shortly to come to America to found Pennsylvania—said the answer was to name an elective assembly. According to this theory, a modicum of self-government might make New Yorkers shape up. The duke went along with the notion, and the governor he sent out in 1683, Thomas Dongan, was directed to bring it about. A liberal Catholic who was another of that minute band of good English governors, Dongan gave New York City a charter that, with some modification, was to be the foundation of the municipal government until modern times. It set up a city corporation consisting of a mayor and a recorder (both appointed by the governor) plus aldermen and their assistants who were elected by the city's six wards or districts. These fourteen officials constituted the lawmaking Common Council, the ancestor of today's City Council.

Dongan also provided for the election of a provincial assembly, and when this new body met it proceeded to draw up a Charter of Liberties and Privileges that must have surprised even the governor. Calling for cooperation between the governor, the governor's council, and "the people," it asserted the people's rights to self-government, freedom of worship, trial by jury, and other privileges normally accorded only to Englishmen at home. It even contained a paragraph protecting New Yorkers against taxation without representation. In a way the document presaged the great revolutionary tracts of the next century. Dongan, to his credit, approved it and sent it along to the duke.

He was no longer the duke, however. His brother Charles had died in 1685, and James was now James II of England. And this gave him a different slant on matters. The charter would have allowed the New York legislature more power than that of any other colony, and this seemed to him unwise. He refused to accept the document.

New Yorkers were already hurting from hard times, and they had never been fond of James, but this decision brought them genuine anger; his refusal showed that he was not to be trusted. Matters were hardly helped when the new monarch, in an effort to consolidate his colonial power, decided in 1686 to combine New York, New Jersey, and New England into a single unit to be called the Dominion of New England and to be ruled from Boston, of all places. It seemed the ultimate outrage. Exacerbating the situation was the fact that the predominantly Protestant citizens of New York City, still to a large extent members of the Dutch Reformed Church, were sorely troubled by James's ardent Roman Catholicism. Rumors began circulating that the king—no doubt aided by Dongan, who was imagined by extremists to be an avowed papist—was behind a Catholic plot to subvert provincial liberties. Something had to give.

It did, in England. There the king had actively promoted an increase in Catholic power, and the people in 1688 forced him to abdicate. He and his family fled to France. The upheaval, known in the home country as the Glorious Revolution, sparked a number of subsidiary revolts in the American colonies. None was more dramatic than the events in New York, which brought to the fore an unlikely leader named Jacob Leisler.

A stocky, rough-spoken man in his late forties, Leisler was the son of a German Calvinist minister and had come to New Amsterdam at the age of twenty, had married the widow of a wealthy Dutch merchant and, partly through these family connections, had become a prosperous businessman. He was a deacon of the Dutch Reformed Church and was known for his hearty distrust of Catholicism. And although he was no politician, he had come to represent the older Dutch elite, who were gradually being edged out by the town's well-to-do English aristocracy. He was also a captain in the militia.

The news of James's abdication and the accession to the throne of James's nephew William and his wife, Mary, brought joy to the city; William, after all, was Dutch and, more to the point, Protestant (as was Mary although she was James's daughter). But it also produced a power vacuum: who was in charge in the remote colony? Some people thought no one was. It happened that Leisler, who was an importer of liquor among other things, received at this time a consignment of wine on which a duty had been charged. He refused to pay the duty on the ground that the customs collector was Catholic and therefore unqualified to act under the new regime. Other merchants followed suit, and the city's trading business began to come to a halt. Meanwhile, wild rumors grew, and reports circulated that James and the French were about to invade from Canada.

Responding to the supposed threat, Lieutenant Governor Francis Nicholson (Dongan had since resigned) proposed that the militia help guard the fort. This was agreed to, but one night while responding to a dispute over who was in command, Nicholson made a chance remark that was interpreted to mean he would set fire to the city; and the infuriated militia leaders moved to take over. Leisler was asked to assume their command, and after some hesitation he did so. On May 31, 1689, the militia seized the fort. Nicholson fled the colony, and the Leislerians were in charge.

They immediately sent a message to England declaring loyalty to William and Mary and stating that they would remain in control only until a proper representative of the new monarchs arrived. Leisler set up an interim government, called for an elected assembly, and otherwise governed sensibly—at first. There is evidence that a majority of New Yorkers admired and supported him. But over the next several months he appears to have lost control of himself, for he gradually became dictatorial. He denounced the well-to-do English "grandees" who were opposing him, railed against Romanism, likened himself to Oliver Cromwell, and began jailing his opponents. Learning that the town of Albany disapproved of him, he sent a military force to capture it; the upriver community gave in only when it learned that a French and Indian force was advancing on it from Schenectady (the invaders got no farther).

By this time even some of Leisler's former supporters were concerned about his extremism and were beseeching London to send a new governor. William did so in early 1690, but the new man's arrival was delayed. When a deputy showed up and demanded Leisler surrender the fort, Leisler refused to recognize his authority and ordered the fort's soldiers to fire on the interlopers; several soldiers were killed or wounded. The new governor, Henry Sloughter, finally arrived, but Leisler held out for hours before giving up, on March 20, 1691. He had ruled the city of New York and its province for almost two years.

Leisler and his staff were arrested and charged with treason. Their trial was swift and all were found guilty, and Leisler and his chief deputy, Jacob Milbourne, were sentenced to death. On May 16 they were brought to the gallows near what is now the Manhattan end of the Brooklyn Bridge. Leisler was calm, and when given an opportunity to speak he said, in part, "So far from revenge do we depart this world that we require and make it our dying request to all our relations and friends, that they should in time to come be forgetful of any injury done to us."[3] Then he and Milbourne were hanged.

This was, to say the least, a miscarriage of justice, for with the exception of the few soldiers killed some months back, the rebellion had cost no lives and Leisler had never claimed to be anything more than an interim custodian of power. The error was eventually righted, in a way, when some of Leisler's supporters successfully petitioned Parliament in 1694 to clear his and Milbourne's names and restore their estates to their proper heirs. But bitterness lingered in the city as many New Yorkers felt Leisler had been the victim of the local English elite's vengeance. As for the Dutch citizenry, they were discredited by the outcome of the rebellion and saw their influence further declining; they can be viewed, as one observer has noted, as "the first European group to confront the pressures of English culture and society in North America."[4]

In addition, the affair had two immediate and highly significant repercussions. One was that the split in the city between Leislerians and anti-Leislerians brought about the formation of opposing political parties that would hold center stage for more than a generation. The anti-Leislerians were essentially aristocratic and represented the successful English merchants (along with a handful of Dutch businessmen who sided with them), while the other faction had a popular base and summed up the aspirations of the middle class, farmers from out of town, and the older, less successful Dutch families. This was the first such division in colonial America, whose communities elsewhere tended to be politically homogeneous. The alignments would change over the years, but party politics was here to stay.

The other result was that the Crown, though victorious, was chastened. The new governor soon called for the election of a representative assembly, which met for the first time on April 9, 1691, in a tavern on Pearl Street. The concession was significant. Never again would representative government be absent from the city or its surrounding region.

There was an upturn in the city's trading fortunes at this time, too, as merchants sought new markets. Harbor facilities had been improved by the completion in 1679 of the Great Dock along Water Street—two enclosing piers that provided both shelter and wharfage—although most ships were anchored offshore in the East River and had their cargoes brought in by lighter. Merchants had a lucrative new commodity to trade in: wheat. Imported wheat had been found to thrive in local soil, and it now supplanted corn as New York's principal crop. Seeking to improve New York City's position within the colony, successive governors in the 1680s had enacted the so-called Bolting Acts, which gave the city's merchants the exclusive right to bolt (or process) and ship the region's grain. They also gave the city control over all transport on the Hudson River and declared New York the province's sole port of entry. Although farmers in outlying districts resented the city's monopolizing their produce, and other ports (like Southampton on Long Island) were unhappy at losing business, New Yorkers argued that centralized control resulted in higher overall sales and consistent quality standards.

At any rate, the city prospered. Becoming for a while the granary of America, it enjoyed its first business boom, and the principal merchant families in town—the van Cortlandts, Bayards, Beekmans, and their ilk—benefited mightily. Even though the Bolting Acts were annulled in 1694, the spur to the port's development helped it immeasurably. It was at this time, incidentally, that the lower tip of Manhattan began to be called the Battery. The old fort was in poor repair but the city still needed protection, and so in 1693 a gun emplacement was constructed on the rocks at the foot of Greenwich Street. No fewer than ninety-two cannon were mounted there, truly a formidable array. The guns are today long gone but the name perseveres.

Most of the flour that New York produced went to the West Indies, although not all of it was sent legally. "The Trade . . . ," wrote one governor, "consists chiefly of flower, and Biskett, which is sent to the Islands."[5] Peas and pork were also shipped there, and in return the West Indies sent New York rum and molasses—which, it was said, "serves the people to make drink."[6] New Yorkers sent furs, whale oil, and tobacco to England and received back all manner of manufactured goods like household furnishings, silver, and linens. By 1699 a governor was saying he believed that New York was "the growingest town in America."[7]

Well, not quite. That honor would more rightly be claimed at this moment by Philadelphia. Although founded as recently as 1681, it had by 1690 surpassed New York City in population and a decade later had leaped past it in trade. It had not only captured the Delaware Valley's tobacco output, it also was reaching out to control the furs and farmlands of the entire Susquehanna River Valley region, an area previously dominated by New York.

Furthermore, Boston was still number one and growing. The Bostonian supremacy had been based on its early aggressiveness and greater proximity to England than other ports. Up to the end of the seventeenth century it was the chief trading port in the New World and distributed the products not only of New England (whose total population in 1689 was still more than double that of New York and New Jersey combined) but of all the other colonies as well. Both New York and Philadelphia had to obtain most of their imported manufactures by way of Boston, and as a result gold and silver flowed into the pockets of the Bay City merchants. New York traders were constantly galled by the arrogance of the Bostonians, who insisted on being paid in solid pieces of eight for the manufactured goods they brought in to transship; they then chipped a third of the silver from each coin as their profit and sent the damaged remainder back to New York to pay for grain.

But in the mid-1690s an unusual and dazzling flush of wealth began coming to New York. For a time, it seems, the city became the privateering and pirating capital of America, if not the world. The odd situation resulted at the outset from the fact that England was at war with France and thus determined to sweep French ships from the sea. To promote its campaign it began authorizing private ships to prey on the enemy, legitimizing them by issuing them letters of marque (from a French word meaning "reprisal"). A number of New York shipowners proceeded to engage in privateering, which was perfectly legal, and profited handsomely from it. But some privateers, not only English and American but from other countries as well, found they could do far better by not noticing whether the prey was enemy or not. If it was not, their action was outright piracy. Huge treasures were there for the taking. And the taking was particularly lucrative in the Indian Ocean, as England's navy—which would normally be able to police that part of the world—was tied up in the war nearer home.

Once loaded down with their illegally gotten gains, pirate ships headed for New York, which was open to their suspect trade. Normally the city's customs officials would have declared such cargoes contraband, but the current governor, Colonel Benjamin Fletcher (one of the greediest of the fortune-seeking governors), was happy to accept protection money from pirates. In return, he persuaded the authorities to close their eyes at the appropriate time. So the city became the world's leading market for pirates' booty, its streets thronged by swaggering buccaneers in colorful pearl-buttoned, lace-trimmed coats, its shops bulging with all manner of exotic wares from oriental rugs to ivory fans to teakwood tables—clearly not produced in the colony. New York merchants were glad to trade in such goods, and it is believed that the gleanings formed the basis of more than one New York fortune.

One name that has acquired legendary status as a result of all these shenanigans is that of a seemingly proper New York ship's captain at this time, William Kidd. The son of a Scottish Presbyterian minister, Kidd went to sea and eventually did well enough to acquire several ships of his own. He had come to New York in 1691, married a beautiful and well-to-do widow, and purchased a waterfront mansion on Pearl Street (then the best part of town); it was luxuriously furnished, and Mrs. Kidd owned the first large Turkish rug ever seen in New York. Universally deemed a solid citizen, Kidd was happy to help out in the building of the first Trinity Church (then as now at the head of Wall Street) by lending a block and tackle from one of his ships.

Among Kidd's well-placed acquaintances was the respected New York merchant and landowner Robert Livingston. In 1695, while both Kidd and Livingston were in London, Livingston learned that King William was planning to send a frigate to the Indian Ocean to halt the piratical activities there and protect legitimate English shipping. Through a third party Livingston suggested to the king that Captain Kidd, "a bold and honest man," would be an ideal choice for the ship's command. His proposal was accepted, an agreement was signed dividing the prospective profits (the king was to get 10 percent), and Kidd, resplendent in the uniform of a Royal Navy officer, sailed away on his thirty-six-gun warship.

It is not known for sure what happened after that, but the newly-minted captain appears to have been beset by problems of disease and a mutinous crew. In addition, reports began filtering back to London and New York that Kidd, perhaps unable to resist the temptations before him, had turned pirate. Finding no French vessels, he had allegedly attacked and plundered ships of other countries, and stories were rife of his raising the skull and crossbones, setting fire to homes, pillaging, torturing, and amassing an incredible store of treasure. If little of this actually took place—the jury is still out on Kidd's guilt—one thing is certain: learning that there was a warrant out for his arrest, he acted like a guilty man. Abandoning the frigate, he sailed one of his prizes to the West Indies, deserted that one too, sailed north in a sloop (presumably still in possession of much of the loot), and took refuge on Gardiner's Island, at the eastern end of Long Island. There he was arrested, but not before allegedly burying all or part of his treasure (it has never been found). Taken to London, he was found guilty of piracy and was hanged there in 1701. By that time a new governor had put a stop to New York's partiality toward pirates, and the city had more or less returned to normal.

It was a bigger city by 1700, its population having doubled since 1664 until it was close to 5,000. Streets below Wall Street were now lined solidly with houses, and the newer houses were generally built in the English style, square and three stories high, sometimes with a balustrade on the roof or with corner chimneys. Wall Street, its barrier having been demolished, was no longer the northern limit of town. Broadway and other avenues had been laid out above it and some new side streets as well, one being Maiden Lane, so called because a stream that ran along it was used by young women for washing their clothes. The old Heere Gracht, or canal, that had pierced the lower part of town had been filled in and the resulting thoroughfare named Broad Street. At its head, where it met Wall Street, a new city hall was built in 1699 partly using materials from the old wall, now demolished. New York was getting wider, too, as its shoreline was gradually inching out; the spaces between wharves and slips tended to fill up with silt and refuse, and over the years instead of dredging them the city simply filled in the gaps and built a new waterfront street beyond. Thus, along the East River, first Water Street, then Front Street, and finally South Street were added beyond Pearl Street, and to the west Washington Street and then West Street along the Hudson.

The city's leading families at the turn of the century still were mainly Dutch, but they were intermarrying with well-to-do English as well as with their own kind. Thus Alida Schuyler van Rensselaer, daughter of a Schuyler and widow of a van Rensselaer (both solid Dutch names), married the Scottish-born merchant Robert Livingston; her sister Gertruyd had married Stephanus van Cortlandt, a member of another prominent Dutch family. And by the 1720s the English had become the wealthiest citizens and had the best houses in town. Their dress was elegant: a gentleman might wear green silk breeches, a gold-embroidered blue coat, a lace shirt, and a powdered wig (Bostonians, much more staid, habitually adopted more subdued colors). But such elegance was spotty. Not even the well-to-do owned coaches or carriages, and the only wheeled vehicles in town were farm carts that plodded through the unkempt streets or carters' wagons specially licensed to carry goods to and from the waterfront. There were still few sidewalks, and the only street lighting consisted of lanterns placed in front of every seventh house and lighted on nights when there was no moon.

New York's reputation as a drinker's and carouser's town was undiminished. Its residents seemed to spend a great deal of time in taverns and wolfed down huge amounts of food. A visiting Anglican chaplain, John Miller, was scandalized by the place. " 'Tis in this country a common thing," he wrote, "even for the meanest persons, so soon as the bounty of God has furnished them with a plentiful crop, to turn what they can as soon as may be into money, and that money into drink."[8] One historian notes that the otherwise respectable Stephanus van Cortlandt, while being feted at a dinner in his honor, "became so intoxicated and merry that he snatched off his hat and wig, skewered them on the tip of his sword, set fire to them, and waved them happily over the banquet table."[9] The Reverend Miller was also shocked by the townsfolk's morals: "There are many couples live together without ever being married in any manner of way; many of whom, after they have lived some years so, quarrel, and, thereupon separating, take unto themselves . . . new companions."[10]

Anti-Catholic bias, which had helped foment the Leisler Rebellion and was fueled by continuing fears of invasion from French Canada, was still strong. The city in 1691 had banned all "Romish forms of worship," and five years later only six Catholics remained in town; nevertheless, in 1700, in response to new rumors of invasion, all Jesuits, Catholic priests, and other ecclesiastics ordained by the pope were ordered to leave the province. The sentiment was to remain a part of the New York scene for another century.

It was in marked contrast, however, to the city's more relaxed attitude toward other faiths. In 1707 a distinguished Irish dissenter, Francis Makemie, who had recently been elected moderator of the Philadelphia presbytery, came to town and was startled to have his right to preach blocked by the governor, Lord Cornbury, who felt that Makemie was a "disturber of governments." When Makemie insisted on conducting services in a private home, Cornbury had him arrested. At Makemie's trial the minister was defended by three of New York's best lawyers, one of whom declared, "We have no established church here. We have liberty of conscience by an act of assembly made in William and Mary's reign. This province is made up chiefly of dissenters and persons not of English birth."[11] The visiting divine, who has been called the father of American Presbyterianism, was acquitted. Cornbury, an odd figure who incidentally seems to have been a transvestite, was subsequently recalled to England, his actions disavowed.

Although the banning of the Jesuits and the acquittal of Makemie were certainly known to most New Yorkers, they were not reported in the press, for the city up to this time had no newspapers. The town was an aural society: news was spread by word of mouth. That would soon change, however, giving rise to a famous court case whose long-term import was to be felt far beyond the city.

Back in 1693 Governor Benjamin Fletcher had hired one William Bradford to be the city's official printer. The job called for Bradford's printing the city's laws, but he was free to do any other publishing that he wished. (A young apprentice printer from Boston named Benjamin Franklin called on him in 1723 looking for work, but Bradford had no spot for him and—unfortunately for New York—advised him to move on to Philadelphia.) By 1725 there seemed a need for some kind of newspaper, and Bradford founded the weekly *New-York Gazette*. Because he was the royal printer, his paper was largely a governmental organ. There was no opposition paper until 1733, when the *Weekly Journal* came into being with John Peter Zenger as publisher. Zenger's paper had been founded to combat what its backers saw as a threat to their liberties, and Zenger soon proved himself quite up to his assignment.

The dispute had arisen over the question of pay for the governor of the colony, a touchy political matter ever since the colonial assembly in 1708 had won the right to control annual appropriations for officials' pay and other expenses. During a thirteen-month period in 1731–32 when no governor was on the scene the office had been filled by Rip van Dam, a prominent local shipowner who was the head of the provincial council. But the new governor, Colonel William Cosby—a petty, grasping official whose greed exceeded even that of Fletcher—had the effrontery to demand on his arrival that van Dam turn over to him half the salary he had drawn as stand-in. Van Dam indignantly refused, and because he was a popular figure the stage was set for a brawl between the "court" party—those in the English establishment who sided with the governor—and virtually everyone else.

To get what he felt was due him, Cosby created a special chancery court whose chief justice was Lewis Morris, a respected citizen. The court heard the case and refused to grant the money, whereupon Cosby removed Morris from office and appointed another justice more friendly to him, James De Lancey. Morris turned around and ran for the assembly and won, and because he felt his cause was not being reported accurately by Bradford's *Gazette*, he and his friends founded the *Journal* and hired Zenger.

A onetime apprentice to Bradford who had quit because he felt the *Gazette* was filled with "dry, senseless and fulsome panegyrics,"[12] Zenger began printing all sorts of satires, parodies, and diatribes against Cosby and his circle. Many of these were written by Morris's friends, but Zenger himself turned out others and took responsibilty for all of them. One article, for example, stated that "A governor turned rogue does a thousand things for which a small rogue would deserve a halter." Another contained a mock advertisement concerning "a monkey of the larger sort" that had "lately broke his chain and run into the country"; readers had no trouble recognizing the "monkey" as one of the governor's henchmen.[13] Cosby was outraged and had copies of the paper burned in public. Zenger continued, and so Cosby arrested him, charged him with seditious libel, ordered him jailed, and set bail so high that the publisher could not be freed. Dictating articles from his cell, Zenger kept up the attack.

When Zenger's lawyers argued that Chief Justice De Lancey was not qualified to preside over the trial, De Lancey disbarred them. For a while it looked as if the defendant would not be adequately represented. But when the trial began on August 4, 1735, Morris and his associates produced their master stroke: they had hired as an associate attorney Andrew Hamilton of Philadelphia, nearly eighty years old and perhaps the top barrister in all of North America. In a defense that was nothing short of brilliant, Hamilton turned the case on its ear.

While the prosecution held the traditional legal view that the mere publication of a damaging statement constituted libel, Hamilton argued that it was up to the jury to decide whether the statements were true; if they were, the defendant could not be held guilty. When De Lancey proclaimed, "The law is clear. You cannot justify a libel," the barrister responded that it was a question of the intent of the statements, and this was up to the jury to determine. In the course of the long trial he carefully demonstrated that Zenger's allegations were true. And in his closing remarks he said, "The question before the court—and you, gentlemen of the jury—is not of small or private concern. It is not the cause of a poor printer, nor of New York alone, which you are trying. No! It may in its consequences affect every freeman that lives under British government on the main of America! It is the best cause. It is the cause of liberty!"[14]

The jury took only about ten minutes to reach its verdict: not guilty. There were cheers in the courtroom, followed by celebration throughout the city. The landmark case was the world's first in the struggle for freedom of the press. It also affirmed the need for open criticism of an executive's prerogatives, and henceforth newspapers would feel free to criticize governors and other officials.

It was a shining moment in New York's history. Unfortunately the city's record was also marred during these years by two far from admirable events. Both had to do with the attitude of New Yorkers toward blacks. The first in a series of agonizing incidents, they showed that although New York was a markedly cosmopolitan community and relaxed in its relations with many kinds of peoples, lenience did not at the moment extend to blacks any more than it had extended to Catholics.

Slaves had been a fixture of New York life since Dutch times. The Dutch had imported blacks purely for economic reasons and had thought of slavery as an expedient with no stigma attached. This changed under the English. As an investor in the slave-trading Royal African Company, the duke of York had profited from increased shipments of slaves to the North American colonies; he even issued instructions to governors and provincial councilmen concerning docking facilities for slave ships and warehousing for their cargoes. Slaveholding as a result increased markedly in New York until the colony had the largest black population north of Maryland; probably as much as a fifth of the city was black, and although some of these were free, the great preponderance were slaves. So great was the demand for slaves that a market for them began operating in 1711 at the foot of Wall Street. And blacks were now considered a distinctly lower breed of humanity. Although many of those freed were engaged in skilled trades and thus drew respect, blacks in general (most were domestics) became more and more poorly treated. They were whipped or branded for committing minor crimes, and they were not encouraged to adopt Christianity, as most whites believed they lacked souls.

One night in April 1712, a group of twenty-three blacks armed with guns, hatchets, and knives gathered in an orchard on Maiden Lane and discussed plans for a revolt. Then two of the group split off, ran to the home of Peter Van Tilburgh (the owner of one of them), and set it afire. When the flames awakened nearby residents, the entire group of blacks advanced on them and killed nine men, wounding five or six others. Alerted to the crisis, the governor dispatched soldiers to find the rebels, and by early the next morning all had been captured (except six who killed themselves). For two weeks the city was gripped by fear of further revolt, and the authorities decided a strong response was in order. The seventeen survivors were tried and found guilty, and although a few were simply banished from the province the rest were tortured and killed. Two were burned alive, and one was broken on the wheel in full public view.

No further racial violence occurred for almost three decades, but in 1741 there was a far more serious outbreak. Early that year a series of fires broke out in the city, and while most could be explained as having been started by accident, their frequency led people to suspect they were the work of black arsonists. Responding to the alarm, the city recorder, noting that there must be "some villainous confederacy of latent enemies amongst us,"[15] issued a proclamation that offered rewards to informers who could shed light on the mystery. At this point a sixteen-year-old white indentured servant named Mary Burton, who had previously been implicated in a theft, came forward—presumably to escape prosecution for her own offense—and began making wild charges against blacks. A number of them had plotted to set fire to the entire city, she said, and to massacre all the white people.

A prostitute named Peggy Carey joined in the accusations, and although there were suspicious gaps in both girl's stories (Carey later tried to recant, but by that time no one listened), blacks were rounded up right and left and the city was gripped by hysteria. It was New York's equivalent of the Salem witchcraft trials. New York's trials continued for more than a year, by which time more than 150 slaves and 25 whites had been imprisoned, 18 slaves and 4 whites hanged, and 13 slaves burned at the stake. In addition, some 70 slaves "confessed" and were deported to the West Indies. Ironically, the trials came to an end only when Mary Burton began directing her accusations against large numbers of white citizens, thereby discrediting the entire campaign. Today it is generally agreed that no conspiracy existed. One historian has called the long episode the "crowning perversion of criminal justice in the annals of American history."[16]

Despite such dismaying and divisive events, New York City continued to grow and develop, and by the 1760s it had become distinctly urban and genteel, a provincial metropolis that was almost a small-scale replica of a moderate-size community in England. In 1744 a visiting Maryland physician, Alexander Hamilton, noted that "The women of fashion here appear more in public than in Philadelphia and dress much gayer."[17] Brick houses, often with tiled roofs, were by now edging out wooden ones, and London was evoked by Ranelagh Garden, a watering spot just north of town. St. Paul's Chapel, completed in 1766 at Broadway and Fulton Street at the northern end of town (and today the oldest large-scale structure in the city), could well stand comparison with any of the finest churches in London. The built-up part of New York stretched a whole mile from the southern tip of the island, reaching about as far as Chambers Street. And although the city's first expansion had been northeast, along the East River and just inland, the western sections were now being settled, though the process was slower because much of the land was owned by Trinity Church, which was more interested in leasing its properties than selling them. Farther out toward the northwest was the new and fashionable village of Greenwich. The city's population, which had grown to 9,000 by 1730, had exactly doubled thirty years later. New York had now passed Boston and was within reach of overtaking Philadelphia.

Surprisingly, it was now a clean city. Visitors marveled at the neat and virtually spotless cobblestone pavements and the well-scrubbed flat-stone sidewalks; never again would New York have such an immaculate look. But the city fathers were finding it necessary to provide an increasing number of social services. Up to 1762 police protection had been limited to citizen patrols, but in that year the Common Council established a paid standing force. Most of the streets had acquired oil-lamp posts. Fire protection, a do-it-yourself affair with homeowners supplying leather buckets, was vastly improved in 1731, when the city obtained two fire engines from London (each required twenty men to work it); unfortunately the first time they were summoned to a fire the house burned down. Fire engines would continue to be manned by volunteers for another century.

The town was big enough now, too, to have a sizable indigent population, and an almshouse had been opened in 1735 in what is now City Hall Park not only to shelter paupers but to house beggars and tramps as well. Nearby, in 1759, a jail was erected, although it cannot be claimed that the city treated its prisoners better than any other eighteenth-century community. Admittedly New York had a special problem in the large number of sailors on leave who roamed the streets, as well as in press gangs who were on the lookout for prospective seamen and sometimes clashed with residents.

In 1733 the city acquired its first park when the Common Council leased a small plot at the foot of Broadway "to make A Bowling Green thereof with Walks therein, for the Beauty & Ornament of the Said Street as well as for the Recreation & delight of the Inhabitants of this City";[18] Bowling Green is still there today. Other amenities included ferries across the East River to Brooklyn and across the Hudson to New Jersey. At least five markets operated in lower Manhattan, some offering specialized foodstuffs—the Meal Market at Wall and Pearl streets offered grain, and the Oswego Market at Broadway and Liberty Street sold both grain and meat. But the city still had no centralized water supply. Householders drew water from their own wells—its taste was horrendous—or purchased it from street vendors who carried it from the Tea Water Pump, a relatively deep well just north of town. And medical care was rudimentary; not until 1791 was New York Hospital opened, the first public institution of its kind in New York.

Although full of pretension, New York was not yet very cultivated. As one historian has put it, "The merchants were far more concerned with their pocketbooks than with their souls."[19] In this regard the city lagged far behind Boston, whose Puritan society, socially more homogeneous than New York's, had produced voluminous writings, mostly religious in nature. For this reason and others, Bostonians looked down on New Yorkers and would for a long time. During a visit to the city in 1774 John Adams recorded in his diary that "with all the Opulence and Splendor of this City, there is very little good Breeding to be found. . . . They talk loud, very fast, and all together. If they ask you a Question, before you can utter 3 Words of your Answer, they will break out upon you, again—and talk away."[20]

But a start was being made. In 1754 the New York Society Library began operating out of a room in City Hall; today it is still going strong at an uptown address. New York's first theater had opened in 1732 in a converted warehouse owned by Rip van Dam, its makeshift auditorium decorated with a sign admonishing spectators not to spit and its performances interrupted by stagehands snuffing out smoking candles in the footlights. But performances were irregular and the city's first full-scale dramatic season was not attempted until the early 1750s. Painting, limited to portraiture, had been of little consequence until 1749, when three portrait artists of future renown began sojourning here—John Wollaston, Benjamin West, and John Singleton Copley. Wealthy merchants were eager to have their portraits done by these artists, and Copley painted no less than thirty-seven in one five-month stay. Scientific thought was rudimentary, New York's chief claimant in the field being the Irish-born Cadwallader Colden, a noted physician, physicist, mathematician, and botanist who corresponded with Benjamin Franklin and English scientists and served five times as the province's lieutenant governor in the 1760s and 1770s.

Education was poor for most children. In 1732 the provincial assembly had founded a public school in the city, but it closed after six years. Most children from middle- or lower-class families thereafter could go only to charity institutions; one of these, started by the Dutch Reformed Church during the Dutch period, still exists today as the Collegiate School. Children from wealthy families attended private schools or were tutored. A concerted effort to upgrade education was made in 1754, when the assembly authorized the founding of King's College (renamed Columbia after the Revolution). The founding was not without controversy; most of the trustees, who were Anglicans—members of the Church of England—insisted the charter state that the college's goal was to "prevent the growth of republican principles"[21] and that its president must be Anglican. Non-Anglicans on the board protested, arguing that the college should be nondenominational and supported by the state, but the Anglicans won out. As it was, the college was held in poor repute by most New Yorkers for many years, largely because its students were so ill-prepared upon entering that they were hard pressed to excel academically. Its mediocre reputation may also have been diminished by the college's location: the street traversed by students to enter its campus, a block from today's City Hall, was inhabited by the town's most notorious prostitutes.

The fact that non-Anglicans were almost able to derail the college's charter was symptomatic of the tenuous hold exercised in New York by the Church of England. Attempts at the end of the seventeenth century to make it the colony's official religion had largely been ignored, for Anglicanism never attracted more than about a tenth of all adult New Yorkers. In fact no one denomination was firmly in control. The Dutch Reformed Church's influence was declining, many of its younger members leaving it out of impatience with its services conducted in Dutch. The Presbyterian Church was in the ascendant, not only luring converts from other faiths but also gaining members who had immigrated to New York from New England. But also present in the city were French Huguenots (who had come mainly as refugees from persecution at the end of the seventeenth century), Quakers, Anabaptists, Jews, and even Catholics—who attended mass in private homes. No one group was yet dominant.

In this shifting scene, the city's economic base also showed signs of widening. There were a few manufacturing operations now, the beginning of a steady expansion that would in due course make New York the nation's leading manufacturing city. It all started with the processing of foods, timber, and furs for export and the servicing of ships calling at the port. Furs led to the making of fur hats, for example, and the outfitting of ships required sails, ropes, and casks. New York's first shipyard was opened in 1720 by William Walton, presaging the development of ship construction that was to make the city the top American producer of fine sailing craft in the nineteenth century. The first smelting furnace began operation in 1730, and in 1760 a visitor noted the production of "a small quantity of cloth, some linen, hats, shoes, and other articles of wearing apparel."[22] It was an inauspicious beginning for what was to be New York's immense and fabled garment industry.

But the city was still—and would be for some time—essentially a trading center, and the merchant was at the top of the heap. Docking facilities had been improved and enlarged in the 1750s as the British, who remained at war with the French, began to take advantage of the harbor to make New York their base of military operations. By the 1770s the city was probably the most important commercial center in British North America. It now traded directly with London rather than by way of Boston; between 1720 and 1750 its exports to Britain had doubled and its imports had tripled. Its merchants had opened up the Hudson Valley hinterland, exchanging farm products, flax, hemp, and the like for manufactured goods. And partially overcoming the necessary restrictions between colonies, they were also trading profitably with their neighbors. For as one observer noted, "Connecticut on the East, and New Jersey on the West, are fertile and well cultivated Colonies, and thro' natural Necessity, must always contribute their Aids in rendering this City a plentiful Mart, because their Exports cannot with equal Ease be conveyed to any other Port of considerable Traffick."[23]

There was now a kind of triangular trade between New York, London, and the West Indies similar to that associated with Boston at this time. New York ships reexported to London such items from the West Indies as cotton, hardwoods, and sugar; carried British goods to Africa; and then brought slaves, gold, and ivory from Africa to the West Indies or New York. All of this was thoroughly legal and highly lucrative; but New York's merchants were still restive under the restraints established by the empire and sought every means to evade them. Dutch tea, gunpowder, and arms (for the Indians) were smuggled into Manhattan in large quantities, while French and Spanish goods were obtained illicitly in the West Indies. A ship captain from New York would arrive in Jamaica declaring that he was there to pick up produce from that island; he would take on empty casks while obtaining affidavits saying that they contained sugar, molasses, rum, and the like. Then he would sail to Hispaniola and load up with contraband items that he could bring into New York, covered as they were by false affidavits. Many customs officials in smaller Atlantic ports were happy (for a small consideration) to look the other way. They would observe closely, for example, as a vessel theoretically bound for New London on the Connecticut coast unloaded there—but would not notice as the goods were immediately reloaded back on board for transfer to New York. Sometimes New York merchants advised ship captains on how to evade detection. Letters to the master of the brig *Brilliant* from its New York owners Elias Desbrosses, John Waddell, and John Ludlow in 1755 instructed him on what hideaway coves to seek out on Long Island Sound and what port of embarcation to report if halted by the authorities: "If spoak with by any Vessells you may answer from the Isle of May."[24]

Although a few merchants specialized in particular products, like dry goods or hardware, most handled a wide range of items, and the prevailing type of retailing operation was the general store. John Foster & Company, on Cruger's Wharf, for example, advertised "A parcel of choice Irish Beef and Pork, Cork rose butter, dipt Candles, fine green and Bohea tea, Silk, Cotton and Kenting handkerchiefs, Muslin Cravats and Scotch Gauze, choice old Claret in Bottles and Hogsheads, with the following Scotch Goods imported in the Barrington from Glasgow, Tartans, Bonnets, Women's Stays, shoes, printed and Broad Cloths, silk and Hair Button, Oznabrigs, Camblets and Frizes of all sorts. Damasks of sundry color for vests etc. Poplin, Stock Tape, Cardinals, Cloaks, Cotton Allapeens, Flowered Dimity Plaid Forrest Cloths, Kersey, duffils, Baize, Horn and Ivory Combs, Metal and Steel Buckles, Knives and Forks, Hinges and a parcel of choice Barley."[25]

The merchants' newfound status was partly due to the fact that they not only handled many kinds of goods but performed many functions as well. Colonial regulations forbade banks in North America, and so the merchant acted as his own banker (and was thus frequently short of cash). Because the Crown had granted empirewide marine insurance monopolies to two London concerns, the merchant acted as his own insurance broker, often combining with other merchants to arrange coverage if a large property was involved. He was also his own advertiser, transporter, and warehouser: he seemed to be everywhere. Most prominent merchants belonged to the Merchant's Exchange, a kind of club where insurance needs and bills of exchange could be negotiated. The exchange did not deal in stocks, however, as there were no corporations (all companies were privately held) and therefore no securities to sell.

Profits from supplying the British forces fighting the French between 1756 and the early 1760s further benefited the merchants, and the most successful of them constituted a small elite. It was purely an aristocracy of wealth and open to anyone of energy and talent. Uriah Hendricks, for example, came to New York in 1755 as an eighteen-year-old Jewish youth, opened up a small shop, and did well; selling supplies to the British military forces and investing in privateering ventures, he built a small fortune, then sold out and became an importer of metals; he ended up as one of the first copper kings in America. The well-to-do had town houses on Broadway, Wall, or Pearl streets and country estates north of town; among the latter were those of the Quaker merchant Robert Murray (remembered today in Murray Hill) and James Beekman (today's Beekman Place). Furnishings were imported from England, and dress followed the latest fashion: just coming into style was the "macaroni," which called for short waistcoats, outsize wigs, cocked hats, and sticks bearing long tassels (much too expensive, evidently, for Yankee Doodle). Reflecting the new affluence, the first local coachmaker, James Hallett, had begun advertising his deluxe carriages in 1750.

Intermarriage had by now fused the original Dutch, English, and French families; among the well-to-do only the Jewish merchants remained distinct socially. The top families were thus interrelated or at least very familiar to each other, and they also made up the leadership of the political parties, shifting allegiances as issues changed. As one of them remarked, "We Change Sides as Serves our Interest best."[26] The two sides that had revealed themselves in the John Peter Zenger case, the Morris faction versus the De Lancey faction, remained similarly split over later issues, but at times either one might oppose the governor. Such fluid political combinations would become a hallmark of city politics from this time on, as would other electoral practices in use at this time—pamphleteering, slates of candidates, slogans, catchphrases, and the election-day roundup of voters.

The times were thus very good for New York's merchant elite in the middle of the eighteenth century, and for the substantial middle class of the craftsmen and shopkeepers as well, who profited from all the moneymaking. But with the winding down of the French and Indian War after 1760 the boom was over and a recession hit the colonies. Though victorious in the war, England emerged burdened by a huge debt, which it hoped to recoup partly from its colonies. At the same time, the permanent acquisition by the Crown of French Canada necessitated the stationing in America of some 10,000 British troops, who were headquartered in New York City and whom New Yorkers were expected in large measure to support—a huge burden. In 1764, to help gather the needed revenue, Parliament told New York's business community that the colony could no longer issue its own paper currency. Local merchants were enraged. The following year the Stamp Act produced an even more violent response. New York was about to enter its most dangerous and difficult time.

3

The Cataclysm
of Revolution

"What is the reason that New York must continue to embarrass the Continent? . . . Are their people incapable of seeing and feeling like other men?"[1] The questioner, speaking from the Second Continental Congress in Philadelphia, was John Adams of Massachusetts, and his indignation burst forth as New York's Provincial Congress in the early days of July 1776 persisted in withholding approval of the Declaration of Independence. Its hesitation prevented New York's delegates to the Philadelphia meeting from joining the others in acclaiming what by then seemed inevitable. When the critical vote was taken on July 2, New York was the only colony to abstain. When it belatedly gave its assent seven days later, its change of heart appeared almost perfunctory.

Its reluctance seemed especially annoying because little more than ten years earlier, when the Americans in 1765 had protested the Stamp Act, no colony had been more vociferous than New York in denouncing it and no rioting more frenzied than that which took place in New York City in opposition to the distribution of the stamps. The reasons why the colony, dominated as it was by its vital city at the mouth of the Hudson, gradually shifted its stance in response to the onrush of events are still debated. But there is no question that what happened underscored the city's role as a merchant-oriented community as well as its sensitive but exposed strategic position on the great harbor. There were pro- and anti-independence factions in every colony; it happened that in New York those whose moderate views led them to advise reconciliation rather than revolt were in the ascendant, and their reasoning can in retrospect seem justifiable or at least pardonable. Their stance mirrored the hesitancy and doubt that were felt by a great many American colonists, if not by the Sam Adamses and Patrick Henrys who blazed the trail to rebellion.

New Yorkers were not "incapable of seeing and feeling like other men"; they saw and felt all too well. The city's merchants, landowners, lawyers, and other influential citizens, who made up the dominant elite, were realists. While to varying degrees they were dead set against the mother country's policies that had so inflamed all the colonists, they had prospered under English rule and were not sure that independence was the solution to their difficulties. England had given ground before; might it not once again? The more cautious of them were also fearful that "the mob," as they termed those who took to the streets, might sweep away their fragile world. And almost everyone could agree that New York City was critically vulnerable. As the debate heated up in 1775 and early 1776, residents were very much aware that a single broadside from one of His Majesty's warships lying offshore in the East River could demolish them.

It is particularly ironic that, in a way, the worst fears of the cautious were justified, though not exactly as they had envisioned. No city suffered anywhere near so brutally as did New York during the Revolution. Captured by the British in a series of battles that almost wiped out the revolutionary forces, it was occupied for more than seven years—longer than any city of its size in modern times—and suffered major depredations. Its population was almost completely replaced three times: first when all but a few thousand fled before the start of hostilities and were supplanted by colonial troops, then again when the revolutionary forces were routed and the city filled up with Loyalists during the British occupation and became a Tory stronghold, and, finally, when the majority of defeated Loyalists were forced out at the war's end, to be superseded by their erstwhile neighbors, the revolutionists. On top of all this, a large portion of the city was destroyed at this time by two major fires. In short, the critical period from 1765 to 1783, when the war ended and New York was free again, were years of upheaval, drama, and despair.

It would have been hard to predict in 1765 that New York City would later be hesitant about independence, for its merchant community had willingly orchestrated the overall colonial response to the Stamp Act. New York's outrage was presaged, as with other colonies, by its reaction to the Sugar Act in 1764. At first glance the Sugar Act seemed innocuous: Britain was actually lowering the duty on molasses brought to American ports from the British West Indies. But while the previous duty had been so high that it was ignored, this one was to be enforced rigorously, as was a prohibition against importing molasses from French and Spanish possessions. Merchants who had imported from the British islands saw their profits wiped out, and those who had traded with the now prohibited islands—sending them flour, beans, Indian corn, and other foods and returning with sugar, cotton, and indigo with which they purchased manufactured goods from England—faced ruin. For if they resorted to smuggling, their ships might be confiscated by royal revenue officers. Word of the new regulations arrived in the city just as it was entering a severe business downturn, which New Yorkers blamed on the Sugar Act. It did not help the Crown's cause that the revenue raised would go largely toward supporting British troops stationed in the colonies.

Coming on the heels of this toll, the Stamp Act provoked even more widespread anger because it affected a much larger segment of the population. Fees, imposed through the purchase of stamps, were to be levied on a bewildering assortment of daily transactions from the purchase of newspapers to marriage licenses, newspaper advertisements, ship sailings, and even drinks in a tavern. Again, the revenue was to help pay for British military forces in America, which the Americans felt were not needed: France, having been defeated, was no longer a threat. There was no question that this was a hidden tax, and the outcry was vehement. New York's Provincial Assembly, currently controlled by moderates, sent a petition of protest to Parliament in London that was so strong no M.P. dared introduce it.

The assembly also entered into communication with its counterpart in Massachusetts, and together they issued a call for a Stamp Act Congress, which convened in New York on October 7, 1765. New York's representatives included the merchants John Cruger and Leonard Lispenard. Out of the meeting came a proclamation asserting that Americans were entitled to the "same inherent rights and liberties" as the citizens of England and so could not be taxed without consent. Thus was born the rallying cry of the revolution: no taxation without representation. At the same time New York's merchants agreed to stop importing English goods until the act was repealed.

Parliament did not budge, and as the city waited for the first shipment of stamps townspeople took to wearing mourning and draping their buildings with black crape. There was much haranguing in the streets, prompted by the feeling that if the congress could not head off enforcement of the act, something more momentous would have to come about. When the stamps arrived on October 23 a crowd of 2,000 gathered at the Battery to prevent their being unloaded. To circumvent such protests, the British authorities waited until the crowd had dispersed and had the stamps secretly unloaded at night and brought to the fort at the southern tip of Manhattan, currently known as Fort George. The commandant of the garrison, Major Thomas James, let it be known that he was prepared to "cram the stamps down the throats of the people" with the end of his sword.[2]

On November 1, when the stamps were due to be distributed, all business came to a halt and ships in the harbor lowered their flags. No stamps were sold, as no one could be found to issue them. That night another crowd assembled in what was known as The Fields (the area now occupied by City Hall Park) and prepared to march on the fort. Feelings were running high. An effigy of the lieutenant governor, Cadwallader Colden, had been prepared. An elderly scientist who was filling in pending the arrival of a new governor, Colden was an inept and shortsighted politician and cordially disliked by the multitude. An effigy of the devil was placed next to his so that it seemed to be whispering in his ear. Hooting and jeering, the crowd placed the figures in a cart and tramped down Broadway by torchlight. Coming upon Colden's coach house just outside the fort, they broke in, hauled out Colden's gilded coach, and transfered the effigies to it amid much yelling and cheering. They then resumed their advance on the fort.

Inside the fort, Colden cowered in terror. Atop the ramparts Major James watched the mob approach and stood ready to order his soldiers to fire. Shouting defiance, the crowd lunged at the doors of the fort. The doors held, and the troops withheld their fire. The mob slowly withdrew. Still enraged, however, they pulled Colden's coach to the middle of the Bowling Green and set it afire. Finally, some of them marched off to Major James's house, on Warren Street near King's College, broke in, and wrecked it. As a bystander recounted, "In less than 10 Minutes they had the windows and dores the Looking Glasses Mehogany Tables Silk Curtains a Libiry of Books all the China and furniture the feather Beds they cut and threw about the streets and burnt books and tore the Garden drank 3 or 4 Pipes of wine destroyed the Beef throo the butter about and at last burnt the whole."[3]

Over the next few days a chastened Colden decided to yield, and so he turned the stamps over to city officials, who deposited them in the City Hall. A week or so later the new governor, Sir Henry Moore, arrived and announced he would suspend his power to issue the stamps. The crisis was defused.

The actions of the mob might have appeared spontaneous, but they were not. The crowds were adroitly directed by the Sons of Liberty, a new radical organization with branches in several cities, which was to play a major role locally in the events of the next decade. Led by a triumvirate that included Isaac Sears, a New York merchant and shipmaster who was popular along the waterfront, the group was made up principally of "mechanics"—artisans, sailors, and shopkeepers—plus a sprinkling of liberal-minded lawyers and merchants. They were sometimes referred to as "leather aprons" from the garb of most of their members. Most of them did not have the vote, and their protest was not only against British arrogance but against New York's propertied classes. For the moment, the city's merchant elite was happy to ally with them against a common foe. But that confidence would not last.

In the spring of 1766 Parliament at last relented and repealed the Stamp Act. It also reduced the duty on sugar and molasses. New York rejoiced, as did every other colony, and the Provincial Assembly commemorated the event by ordering statues erected in the city to William Pitt, who had argued in Parliament for repeal, and to King George III. The monarch's statue, of gilded lead and portraying him as a Roman emperor wearing a wreath, would be erected in the Bowling Green. For their part, the Sons of Liberty commemorated the occasion by erecting a Liberty Pole in The Fields with a large board fixed to it bearing the inscription GEORGE III, PITT AND LIBERTY. As of 1766, the young king was riding high in America.

Marring the sense of triumph, however, was a feeling of unease among the city's most prominent merchants. They were frightened by what they had seen on November 1. "The mob" had been effective, all right, but what if later it got out of hand? As the young Gouverneur Morris, a moderate who would in time become a staunch patriot and help draft the Constitution, wrote not long afterward, "I see, and I see it with fear and trembling, that if the disputes with Great Britain continue, we shall be under the worst of all possible dominions; we shall be under the domination of a riotous mob."[4] Men of Morris's ilk resolved that they would try to restrain or control the Sons of Liberty's more violent elements.

As for the British government, it appeared to have learned little from the crisis. In 1767 it issued the first of the Townshend Acts, which imposed duties on a wide variety of substances from glass and painters' colors to tea. Again colonial merchants protested and stopped importing British goods, and in 1770 most of the duties were canceled. Rejoicing in this new victory and noting that business conditions were generally improving, New York's merchants dropped out of the nonimportation campaign. Their counterparts in Boston and Philadelphia disagreed with them; this was no time, they felt, to ease up on the pressure and they were indignant, a harbinger of their later feelings. A group of merchants in Philadelphia wrote to their friends in New York wryly suggesting that they send them the Liberty Pole, "as they imagine they can, by their late conduct, have no further use for it."[5]

The pole, however, had already occasioned a succession of incidents involving the Sons of Liberty. It had become a rallying point for the Sons, who met at its base periodically to pledge themselves to freedom. British redcoats whose barracks were nearby found this annoying and disrespectful, while New Yorkers resented the Britisher soldiers who, having little to do, often took odd jobs around town (at low pay) that could have been performed by locals. Three times in 1766–67 the soldiers crept out at night and cut down the Liberty Pole, and each time the Sons of Liberty replaced it, girding it with iron bands for good measure. Once the British fired shots toward a tavern frequented by the Sons, but no one was injured.

In January 1770, however, the redcoats attempted to raze the fourth pole. They were discovered and routed, but a few nights later they succeeded, depositing the pieces at the door of the Sons' tavern. The following day the Sons held a mass meeting and vowed revenge. Isaac Sears and a band of colleagues later came upon some redcoats who were putting up posters that mocked the Sons. Sears seized them and marched them to the mayor's office, whereupon twenty more redcoats hastened there and a large crowd gathered. Sensing real trouble, the mayor persuaded the soldiers to return to their barracks. On the way back they were joined by other troops at a spot on John Street near Gold Street, where it ascended a rise called Golden Hill. There they turned on the crowd following them and shouted taunts. A lively fight ensued, the redcoats wielding swords and bayonets against the townsfolk's fists and brickbats. A number of New Yorkers were wounded, as were several soldiers, before officers arrived and ordered their men off.

The confrontation has come down in history as the Battle of Golden

Hill and is acclaimed as "the first blood of the Revolution" (the Boston Massacre occurred more than a month later). Whether or not the episode deserves to be called a battle, it did have considerable significance on the local scene. Once again New York's elite noted uneasily how close to the surface lay the rage of the Sons of Liberty and how readily it could erupt. The British recognized it too and ordered that henceforth their soldiers walk the streets only in pairs.

Three years were to pass before the city witnessed further incidents of this nature. And so great was the temporary feeling of goodwill that when the statue of George III in the Bowling Green was dedicated with elaborate public ceremonies in August 1770, not even the Sons of Liberty objected. But in 1773 trouble arose, as elsewhere in the colonies, because of tea.

Faced with the near-bankruptcy of the British East India Company, Parliament gave it a monopoly on shipping tea to the colonies and levied a small duty on it. Again there was an outcry from New York's merchants who had profited from the tea trade. But the real problem was the duty. It was another hidden tax, and it reopened the dispute that in theory had been settled with the repeal of the Stamp Act and the Townshend Acts. Americans resolved not to drink the imported tea, and a tea-bearing ship that arrived in Boston in December 1773 was boarded by Bostonians dressed as Indians who dumped it in the harbor—the celebrated Boston Tea Party. When Paul Revere, who was already acting as a messenger of the incipient rebellion, arrived in New York to spread the news, the Sons of Liberty resolved to do their part.

Their chance came on April 22, 1774, when the *London* on arrival in New York was suspected of carrying boxes of tea. The captain denied having them, but a delegation of Sons of Liberty—in Indian garb like their cohorts in Boston—searched the craft and found eighteen boxes. They opened them up and poured the contents into the harbor. Unlike the Boston party, which was carried out secretly, the New York affair was witnessed by hundreds of people who cheered from the wharf. The following day church bells rang, vessels in the harbor ran up their colors, and the Sons of Liberty hoisted an extra-large flag to the top of the Liberty Pole.

Given such confrontations, there was now a decided quickening of events in the American colonies as a whole and a feeling that some kind of turn in the road vis-à-vis Britain was in the offing. In New York the merchant community began to feel it must make a move soon. But it would have to proceed with the utmost care, lest its

61

control appear to falter; and to a large extent the city's story over the next two years revolves around the struggle of the merchant elite—some of them more moderate, others highly conservative and pro-British—to contain the radicals. If they did not succeed in steering the protest, they might be out of it altogether.

The first overt act came from Britain. George III and his ministers decided they were fed up with their colonists' insolence and resolved to punish the Bostonians for the Tea Party by closing the Boston harbor to all commerce until the tea owners were compensated. Boston's Committee of Correspondence wrote to the other colonies urging united action opposing the measure. New York's Sons of Liberty, who still had allies among some of the more moderate merchants and lawyers in town, proposed to reconstitute the city's own Committee of Correspondence, which had been formed years earlier; the new body could press forward with acts of resistance.

To their surprise, the Sons at this point found themselves outmaneuvered by the conservative merchants, who recommended forming a larger body that would represent all political factions. And when the new Committee of 51 came into being it was chaired by a merchant who was moderate-to-conservative, Isaac Low.

But what action should be taken to satisy all shades of opinion? There was much debating and speechmaking. (Among those who attracted attention in The Fields calling for support for Boston was a seventeen-year-old student at King's College named Alexander Hamilton.) Low and his colleagues eventually decided that only an interprovincial body could act with any force and without getting mired down in local disputes. So it was that New York's merchant-controlled, moderate Committee of 51 was the first colonial group to propose, of all things, what turned out to be America's instrument of rebellion, a continental congress.

Note that the proposal had not come from New York's Provincial Assembly. That body, which had gained a significant measure of home rule by winning control over the governor's salary, and which had helped thwart the Stamp Act, was at this point controlled by the most conservative of all the merchants, the party led by such wealthy families as the De Lanceys, and it was unable or unwilling to act. The key decisions from now on would be made by extralegal bodies, and New York over the next two years would be in the odd position of having two parallel governments, one legal but ineffectual, the other impromptu but in control.

Not only had the moderates and conservatives co-opted the Committee of 51; by judicious politicking they had also picked the delegates who would go to Philadelphia to the First Continental Congress in the fall of 1774. All were moderates: one was John Jay, a tall, bookish young lawyer who would become the first chief justice of the Supreme Court, but who shared the merchants' concern about mob rule; the others included the merchants Isaac Low and John Alsop. It was Jay who wrote the Declaration of Rights adopted by the Congress.

But the Congress also voted to cease all importing from or exporting to Britain until American rights were restored. It furthermore set up the so-called Continental Association to enforce the agreement. Local bodies like the Committee of 51 would administer the association, identifying and sometimes even taking action against those who balked.

This "peaceful coercion" forced people to take sides, thereby bringing the radicals into greater prominence. Unsuited to the role of enforcer, the Committee of 51 dissolved, and a new and more radical Committee of 60 came into being. The grip of the conservative merchants was weakening.

Indeed, the merchants were now splitting into two distinct camps that reflected earlier political alignments but were based largely on their attitude toward the Crown and British officialdom. Although there were exceptions, those merchants who favored stronger action and who would eventually (though belatedly) come out for independence were those who had been engaged in sugar refining or distilling (like Leonard Lispenard and the Roosevelt and Livingston families) and thus had been hurt by sugar restrictions; or those who had resorted to smuggling or other illicit trade (the Beekmans and van Zandts and the radical merchant Francis Lewis); or those who had been privateers (like Isaac Sears and Rem Remsen). Most of them had little to lose from a break with England, and they came to be labeled Whigs; most of them also were Presbyterians. The other camp consisted of those with close ties to Britain or British officialdom or who were of English birth; most were Anglicans; the best known among these were the De Lanceys. Such families had much to lose from a break with the mother country; they made up the core of the Loyalists and also came to be known as Tories.

As the De Lancey faction still controlled the Provincial Assembly, it was no surprise during the winter of 1774–75 that the assembly refused to approve the work of the First Continental Congress or appoint delegates to the Second. Once again the extralegal body, the

Committee of 60, got it done, and this time the delegation was less conservative; among other changes, Isaac Low was replaced by the more radical Francis Lewis. However, even at this late date, in New York at least, almost no one spoke of independence. The word would not be heard until another year had passed. Even to the radical leaders the idea was politically too risky. As the colonies began sending delegates to the Second Continental Congress, which would end up declaring independence, a member of the Sons of Liberty advised a colleague, "You must not utter the word independence, nor give the least hint or insinuation of the idea, either in Congress or any private conversation; if you do, you are undone; for the idea of independence is as unpopular in Pennsylvania, and in all the Middle and Southern States, as the Stamp Act itself."[6]

The actual outbreak of hostilities, at Lexington and Concord in April 1775, nevertheless pushed the colonies a decided step farther toward that unlikely goal. When news of the battles reached New York City on April 23, a crowd led by Isaac Sears and other Sons raided the city arsenal, seized muskets, and organized a militia. Within a few days the Committee of 60 had enlarged itself to 100 and in turn elected delegates to a new provincial body to supersede the Provincial Assembly; it was called the Provincial Congress. The Committee of 100 was now in effect the government of the city, the Provincial Congress that of the colony; and on May 3 the old Provincial Assembly adjourned, never to meet again. The extralegal had superseded the legal, and the province of New York was in the hands of an unmistakably revolutionary body. Even so, that new body was not yet fully committed to armed resistance. Its leaders were for asserting American rights to the utmost. But they were not for rebellion or for independence.

That spring another element intruded onto the New York scene. The British warship *Asia*, carrying sixty-four guns, sailed into the harbor and dropped anchor in the East River near Governor's Island. Her presence was an acknowledgment by the British of the supreme importance of the city and its harbor, which gave access to the river that led northward toward Canada and thus lay athwart the American colonies. New York was the key to America; whatever happened in the unfolding crisis, Britain did not intend to yield the city. In the coming months, too, New Yorkers could never ignore those powerful guns or the possibility that one false move could result in their city being shelled and burned.

So caution was in order. And although the Provincial Assembly was defunct, the city still had its British government. The peculiarity of New York's status was demonstrated on June 25, 1775, when two important welcoming ceremonies threatened to collide. General George Washington, just appointed commander in chief of the new Continental Army, was to arrive in town on his way to Cambridge, Massachusetts, to join his troops there. He was to be feted with ceremonies including a parade and a reception. But by coincidence another august figure, William Tryon, was returning as governor of the colony and official representative of the Crown after medical leave in England. He too required a ceremony. To forestall a painful confrontation, members of the Provincial Congress worked out an artful plan. Tryon was asked to delay his arrival by a few hours (he was waiting on board a ship offshore), and he tactfully agreed. General Washington's party, in turn, was asked to land not downtown but up the Hudson a bit, near what is now Canal Street. The general came ashore in midafternoon, attended a reception at the nearby mansion of Leonard Lispenard and then accompanied a parade in his honor down Greenwich Road and Broadway to his overnight lodging. A little while later, promptly at 8 P.M., Tryon landed at the foot of Broad Street and was greeted by a substantial throng of citizens and militiamen, many of whom had hurried there direct from Washington's parade. He then proceeded to his lodging a scant few blocks from that of the general. Both dignitaries handled the delicate situation well, as did the city. But New York was relieved when Washington—who had seen and heard enough to conjure up a dislike for what he considered the city's low moral standards—departed the next day.

As news arrived of Bunker Hill and the city awaited the next moves in what had clearly become a continental struggle, peaceful coercion against "non-Associaters" was stepped up. Citizens were notified they must swear to support the Continental Association; if they refused, their names were published on handbills and in the press, and they faced ostracism. Their businesses could be ruined. Meanwhile the Sons of Liberty and local militiamen staged small raids on British arms caches and provoked other incidents. Responding to one raid, the *Asia* let loose a broadside that gave off a thundering roar, lit up the sky, and damaged some buildings in town. It did not stop the raid, but New Yorkers were duly alarmed. Tryon had previously withdrawn the royal garrison from the city to ships in the harbor. He himself moved to an offshore vessel in October.

Others were leaving, too. Among the first were Loyalist merchants like John Watts and John Cruger, both of whom had helped lead protests against the Stamp Act but could not stomach the thought of rebellion against the Crown. Watts moved to London, Cruger to his estate out of town. But plenty of well-to-do people on the other side were moving out, too, for safety's sake, to protect their families during what seemed to be shaping up as a dangerous time.

In November 1775, Isaac Sears overstepped himself, damaging the radical cause. Seeking to disarm notable non-Associators, he led a pickup group of Connecticut cavalrymen through Westchester and into New York City, victimizing two well-known royalist sympathizers. One was the Anglican clergyman Samuel Seabury, who had written a number of anti-Association pamphlets signed "A Westchester Farmer" that were both admired and hated for their caustic wit ("If I must be enslaved, let it be by a King, at least, and not by a parcel of upstart, lawless committeemen");[7] he was taken prisoner. The other was James Rivington, publisher of the rabidly pro-British *New-York Gazetteer*, New York's largest and most successful newspaper; he could not be found, but Sears's men wrecked his presses and took away his type, putting him out of business. The Provincial Congress, of which Sears was a member, was profoundly embarrassed by these acts and expressed strong disapproval. Discredited, Sears moved to New Haven. By chance several other leaders of the Sons of Liberty became inactive at this time. As a result, when New York came to its decision time in June and July 1776 the radicals were no match for the moderates and conservatives.

As early as March 1776, after Washington had ousted Britain's General William Howe from Boston, New Yorkers felt sure the British would move to recoup and would soon arrive in force to attack them. So did George Washington. The general might personally mistrust New York, but he could not abandon it to the enemy. "Should they get that Town and the Command of the North River," he wrote, "they can stop the intercourse between the northern and southern Colonies, upon which depends the Safety of America."[8] He had already sent one of his top lieutenants, General Charles Lee, to the city to begin military preparations; and although there was general agreement that the city would be extremely difficult to hold for any length of time without control of the water around it, Lee set to with alacrity. A vast network of barricades, redoubts, earthworks, and trenches was built around the Manhattan shoreline and in many of its streets, as well as in Brooklyn, and guns were emplaced at strategic points. The feverish activity prompted large numbers of people to flee the city. Everywhere was noise and confusion as the rumbling of carts loaded with household belongings mingled with the shouts of men hauling cannon or directing the diggers. Members of one church recalled that their preacher's voice could hardly be heard over the din from without. The city's population, which had exceeded 25,000 in 1775, would shrink to around 5,000 by midsummer.

Howe did not come—yet. Instead of heading directly for New York he had detoured to Nova Scotia, to rest his troops. But Washington arrived with the major part of the Continental Army, and the fortification work was redoubled. Empty houses, of which there were by this time a great number, were taken over for billeting, and among these were many splendid mansions of departed Tories. "Oh, the houses in New York," wrote one observer, "if you could but see the insides of them, occupied by the dirtiest people on the continent!"[9]

Amid the heightened activity any remaining Loyalist was suspected of being a spy or at least a potential one, and many suffered. Theophilus Hardenbrook, an architect and builder, "was taken from his house by a desparate mob, who tore all his clothes from his body, rode him round the city in a cart, pelted and beat him with sticks in so cruel and barbarous a manner that he . . . very nearly had lost his life."[10] Actually there was genuine cause for concern, for in June a conspiracy was uncovered whereby colonial soldiers were being paid to desert and come over to the British. The city's mayor, a Crown appointee named David Matthews, was arrested for being tied to the ring—which included no less than a member of Washington's own bodyguard, Thomas Hickey. There were even rumors, never proven, that Hickey and others conspired to poison Washington and other American leaders and take over New York. For his participation in the recruitment scheme, Hickey was hanged.

Under such circumstances the notion of independence was bound to surface, and suddenly it was on everyone's mind. On June 7 in Philadelphia, Richard Henry Lee, a member of the Virginia delegation to the Continental Congress, introduced a motion declaring the United Colonies independent of Britain. It caught the New York delegates by surprise; they had not expected the issue to come up so soon. And although some of them might have wanted to support it, they could not act without instructions from the Provincial Congress. That body, despite its almost radical composition in comparison with the departed assembly, continued to shy away from the idea. But a potent influence was the appearance of a number of British ships in New York's Lower Bay at the end of May; concerned that their lives might be in peril if they stayed in the city, the provincial legislators made plans to move to White Plains. Another factor was that they had scheduled an election for mid-June to decide whether to declare New York a state instead of a province, and they were uncertain how to include the question of independence in the voting. So they omitted it. Perhaps most important, however, many of them were fearful that the rebellion was shaping up as a losing cause—as indeed it seemed to many Americans in those dark days. If Britain won the war, everyone would be ruined. They withheld their approval. Their representatives in Philadelphia could do nothing. While not objecting to the Declaration, they abstained.

Those ships at the end of May had been a false alarm, but there was no mistaking what turned up on June 29. At daybreak the first vessels of a huge British fleet began arriving in the Lower Bay, and by midmorning more than forty ships had shown up. Daniel McCurtin, a Continental Army private who spied them from an upstairs window in Brooklyn, said they resembled "a wood of pine trees trimmed. I declare, at my noticing this, that I could not believe my eyes ... I thought all London was afloat."[11] By the end of the day more than 100 vessels had arrived, and that was only the beginning. Two weeks later another fleet, this one comprising 150 ships, arrived from London under General Howe's brother, Admiral Richard Howe. It was followed by a third fleet, from Charleston, South Carolina. In all, nearly 500 ships—frigates, transports, ships of the line—had come carrying 32,000 soldiers, including 9,000 German mercenaries, all under the command of Sir William Howe. It was the largest expeditionary force Great Britain had ever assembled. On July 2 Howe put 10,000 men ashore on Staten Island.

Given everyone's conviction that attack was imminent, it is remarkable that the news on July 9 of the Declaration of Independence's final passage was received with relative calm. That afternoon Washington ordered his troops to assemble in The Fields and nearby locations and had the document read to them. Following its completion, the chaplain read parts of Psalm 80. The regiments in The Fields gave three cheers and were dismissed. Many soldiers thereupon strolled down Broadway accompanied by a crowd of civilians, and when they got to the Bowling Green they decided something ought to be done about the statue of George III. Ropes and crowbars were found, and the crowd went methodically to work pulling it down. It cracked as it hit the ground, and soon it was in pieces—from which

42,088 bullets were later fashioned. The statue had been in place less than six years.

The same day, acting from its new venue in White Plains, the Provincial Congress did its best to wipe out the embarrassment of New York's abstention by voting unanimously to "join with the other Colonies in supporting" the Declaration.[12] It also declared that the province of New York was now a state.

Howe delayed his attack—he was severely criticized by his countrymen for this—and while he procrastinated Washington deployed his limited forces. With only some 18,000 men to Howe's 32,000 he was woefully outnumbered, but worse than that he had no control over the waterways. Hoping to close the Hudson River, he had ordered some ships sunk to form an underwater barrier just north of today's George Washington Bridge, but a couple of Royal Navy vessels sailed right over them. Obviously the British would be able to land anywhere they chose. Washington kept a small part of his force in New Jersey and split the rest between Brooklyn Heights and Manhattan; holding the Heights, the general felt, was essential to Manhattan's defense. The Brooklyn troops occupied entrenchments from the Heights along a range of hills to the northeast.

The British started their conquest on August 22 as Howe ferried a large force of foot soldiers and artillery from Staten Island across the Narrows to Gravesend Bay at the southern end of Brooklyn. (Washington felt he had too few troops to oppose the landing.) Three days later Howe added a detachment of Hessians, as the German mercenaries came to be known, until he had some 20,000 troops ready to advance. On the night of August 26 came his main attack. Sending a token force straight ahead to engage General Israel Putnam's troops on Brooklyn Heights, Howe dispatched his main body of more than 10,000 men to the east in a classic flanking maneuver. The Americans had troops guarding all the breaks in the line of hills except the easternmost, the Jamaica Pass, through which the invaders poured. At daybreak an American scout at the far end of the line saw a long column of British advancing like a red ribbon on the horizon to attack the colonial troops from the rear. The American line folded back as 2,000 men fled toward Brooklyn.

It was a rout; some 1,000 Americans were taken prisoner. Luckily, Howe did not follow up, and on the night of August 29–30 Washington evacuated his remaining troops to Manhattan as boats manned by regimental units from the seafaring towns of Marblehead and

Salem, Massachusets, brought them across under cover of darkness and fog.

There was a pause now as General Howe, feeling he had a decided advantage, put out peace feelers. On September 11 he received a delegation from the Continental Congress consisting of John Adams, Benjamin Franklin, and Edward Rutledge at a mansion on Staten Island. But after a three-hour meeting accompanied by excellent wine and tasteful food it was clear he had no real power to negotiate and that no meaningful settlement was possible. The war would continue.

Two decisions confronted Washington: how to position his troops and whether New York should be burned to the ground—assuming the British could capture it. Believing the island basically untenable, he was disposed to abandon it except for one overriding concern: he felt his troops were so demoralized by their Long Island defeat that further withdrawal might well break their spirit. He decided to leave 3,000 men in the city proper, in lower Manhattan; to post a line of brigades along the East River; to station a moderately large force on the river near Hell Gate (at approximately today's East 125th Street) where he thought Howe might land; and to concentrate the rest of his force in Harlem Heights, a hilly spot north of what is now West 125th Street. As to burning the city, Washington felt it might be advisable—few inhabitants were left, much of the property belonged to Loyalists, and there was no sense providing the British with a headquarters town intact. But he checked with the Continental Congress, which directed him to spare it. Not only was the idea of putting it to the torch shocking to the delegates but, in a remarkable display of optimism, they also expressed their conviction that the city, if taken, would soon be recaptured.

Washington had guessed correctly that Howe intended to land in northern Manhattan, but because of the turbulence of the Hell Gate currents the Britisher decided instead to invade farther south. On the morning of September 15 a phalanx of eleven powerful British warships let loose a devastating bombardment of the shore of Kip's Bay, where today's 34th Street meets the East River, and shortly thereafter British redcoats and Hessian grenadiers stormed ashore. The undermanned American line broke and the defending troops took off. Alerted by the sound of the British guns, Washington and his staff had hastened down from Harlem Heights, and the general took up a position in an open area at approximately the location of today's Fifth Avenue and 42nd Street, attempting to rally his troops. He could not. The terrified men paid little attention. He cursed, yelled at them to take cover and regroup, tore off his hat and threw it to the ground, and even took to slashing the soldiers with his riding crop. They continued to run away. Finally an aide, concerned that the commander in chief was exposed to enemy fire, took the bridle of Washington's horse and led him to safety.

Washington knew that disaster loomed. If Howe merely marched across Manhattan to the Hudson he could cut off the entire American force down in the city itself. Such a coup might well mean the end of the rebellion.

But a stroke of good fortune was at hand. Howe, ever the procrastinator, did not move immediately beyond his Kip's Bay beachhead. His delaying was arguably correct in a tactical sense, though conservative, for he believed he must bring his entire force ashore before proceeding. The legend has grown up that he was really delayed by Mrs. Robert Murray, who invited him to take refreshments at her mansion on what is now Murray Hill (near today's Park Avenue and 37th Street) and who is therefore credited with saving the colonial effort. But in fact Mrs. Murray could not have known how precarious the American position was, and Howe had decided to pause anyway.

At this point the Americans were also the beneficiaries of a fluke. When Howe did move out, toward the end of the afternoon, he directed his troops not to the west, across the island, but to the north, up the Post Road, a track leading up the eastern side of Manhattan. Meanwhile General Putnam, commanding the colonial forces in the city, was seeking desperately to extricate his men from their potential trap. Acting on the advice of young Major Aaron Burr, who knew New York's terrain well, Putnam led his men up Bloomingdale Road (roughly the route of today's Broadway) on the island's west side. The two routes were not much farther apart than the width of today's Central Park, but because of the wooded, hilly terrain between them the two armies proceeded on parallel tracks unbeknownst to each other. The British, unaware of what they had missed, halted in the vicinity of today's East 110th Street, and the Americans safely joined the rest of their army on Harlem Heights.

The following day an engagement occurred that, though inconclusive, went a long way toward restoring the morale of Washington's troops. Early in the morning, to feel out the enemy, the general sent a scouting party under Major Thomas Knowlton down from Harlem Heights and up the neighboring rise to the south (known today as Morningside Heights). At what is now West 112th Street Knowlton ran into British pickets. Gunfire was exchanged, and kilted Black Watch soldiers advanced to turn back the Americans. Knowlton retreated, and as the British came on toward the Hollow Way (through which West 125th Street now leads) one of their buglers sounded a hunting call signaling that the quarry is at bay. Washington, furious, ordered a counterattack. His troops pushed the British back to a buckwheat field near the present site of Barnard College, where a fierce two-hour battle ensued, after which the British gradually withdrew, pursued by yelling and whooping rebels. Then Washington ordered them to break off lest Howe's superior forces be brought into play. As they returned to the Heights the colonial soldiers were exultant. They had shown that in a fair fight they could not only hold their own against the enemy but even get the better of him. The British were not invincible after all. As Washington's adjutant general, Joseph Reed, wrote to his wife, "You can hardly conceive the change it has made in our army. The men have recovered their spirits and feel a confidence which before they had quite lost."[13]

Unfortunately, the American position was still basically untenable. With his control of the water Howe could at any time land troops behind Washington's forces and cut them off. In due course, therefore, Washington withdrew to Westchester, leaving only a detachment of 2,800 men at Fort Washington near the northern end of Manhattan. Howe pursued the Americans to White Plains (from which the Provincial Congress had departed) and defeated them there, forcing Washington to retreat again, westward to New Jersey. On November 16 Fort Washington, the last colonial bastion on the island of Manhattan, fell to the British after a fierce and protracted fight. New York City was lost. Its unsuccessful defense had cost the Americans several hundred lives and more than 4,400 prisoners.

The city they left behind had been semideserted, its streets torn up by the fortification work and its lovely shade trees ruined. But otherwise it was intact. Now, as the British took over, a major calamity occurred. In the early hours of September 21, barely four days after the colonial troops had left, a fire broke out in a small wooden house on a dock near Whitehall Slip. A brisk southerly wind fanned the flames, and because the city's fire companies were undermanned and disorganized and their engines inoperative the fire could not be contained. The flames leapt from block to block, consuming the wooden houses of rich and poor alike. British soldiers and sailors dispatched to fight the blaze were able to stop its spread to the northeast, but after a couple of hours the wind shifted and the fire raced to the northwest up Broadway, consuming Trinity Church along the way. "The steeple, which was 140 feet high," wrote an onlooker, "the upper part of wood, and placed on an elevated situation, resembled a vast pyramid of fire and exhibited a most grand and awful spectacle."[14] Only the desperate work of a crowd wielding fire buckets saved St. Paul's Chapel, several blocks above Trinity. Finally the open land around King's College checked the fire's spread. A total of 493 houses had been destroyed, about a quarter of the city, and a path of desolation a mile long had been cut through the heart of town. It was a first-class disaster for the British and their American partisans, the Loyalists.

Naturally the British suspected arson by colonial sympathizers. Loyalists claimed that holes had been cut in fire buckets, and there were reports of men caught with rosin-tipped matches and of others scrambling across rooftops. Howe's investigation came to naught, and the cause was never determined. But as Washington remarked wryly after learning of the fire, "Providence, or some good honest fellow, has done more for us than we were disposed to do."[15]

The day following the blaze another kind of event occurred, this one dispiriting to all those on the revolutionists' side. A blue-eyed, fair-complexioned young man named Nathan Hale was brought to General Howe's headquarters. He had been arrested as a spy and had confessed. A captain in the Continental Army, Hale had undertaken to enter the city disguised as a teacher to sketch fortifications and obtain other military information, and had been apprehended with incriminating papers on him. He was swiftly tried by the British, and on September 22 he was hanged, having declared, "I only regret that I have but one life to lose for my country."

Howe swiftly established New York as Britain's principal military and naval base. It became a garrison town, subject to martial law, and trial by jury was suspended. For most people the occupied city was not a pleasant place. Hessian soldiers and members of the Light Horse cavalry patrolled the streets, but their main assignment was to protect the British military effort. Civilians robbed, beaten, or otherwise abused by the military would have no redress; even a soldier convicted by court-martial of murder might be set free within weeks.

Besides being a military center, the city rapidly assumed its role of Tory capital of America. Every citizen who wished to avoid suspicion of favoring the revolutionary cause wore a red ribbon on his hat signifying loyalty to George III. Loyalists issued a "counterdeclaration of independence" proclaiming all powers of the Continental Congress and provincial congresses to be null and void. Pro-Britishers who had fled the city in 1775 and early 1776 now flocked back, and their numbers were augmented by sympathizers who made their way to New York from other areas controlled by the rebels. By early 1777 the city's population had climbed back to 11,000.

Where to put them all? The fire had wiped out a quarter of the houses, and in addition to the increasing number of Loyalists several thousand soldiers had to be billeted. Many of them were accompanied by their wives and children (by 1779 the military dependents came to 1,550 wives and 968 children). The result was a colossal housing shortage that continued during the war. All unoccupied houses of rebels were marked GR (i.e., dedicated to the king's service) and taken over by the military, but this was not nearly enough. When all the existing houses were filled up, the military permitted the construction of shacks and huts in the burned-out areas. This makeshift section became known as Canvas Town because of the shelters erected by placing spars or other beams between the exposed walls and chimneys and stretching canvas over them. When a second great fire swept the city in August 1778, wiping out an additional 100 houses, the lodging problem became even more acute.

Food was a constant concern. Although farmers on Long Island, which was controlled by the British, were able to supply part of New York's food, other areas like Westchester and New Jersey, which had previously provisioned the city, were held by the Americans. Large amounts of food therefore had to be brought all the way from Great Britain and Ireland. And as English vessels were subject to seizure by American privateers and by the French navy after France entered the war in 1778, and as much of the food spoiled in transit, shortages were frequent. At least once the city ran out of food entirely. Prices skyrocketed and a flourishing black market in foodstuffs developed. By the end of the war the cost of living in New York had tripled.

A related problem was the shortage of fuel. Firewood became extremely scarce, and residents began burning furniture, outbuildings, fences, and any other woodwork they could get their hands on. Systematically they cut down Manhattan's trees, working their way to the northern end of the island. They also deforested much of nearby Long Island and Staten Island. The relentless search for wood affected everyone, and no one who owned a stand of trees could save them, not even prominent Loyalists. Mrs. Roger Morris, a staunch Loyalist,

New York's purchase was recorded in a 1626 agreement between Peter Minuit (whose signature appears at lower right) and the Manhattan Indians, by which Manhattan was bought from the Indians for the sum of 60 guilders (about $24). Collections of the Municipal Archives of the City of New York

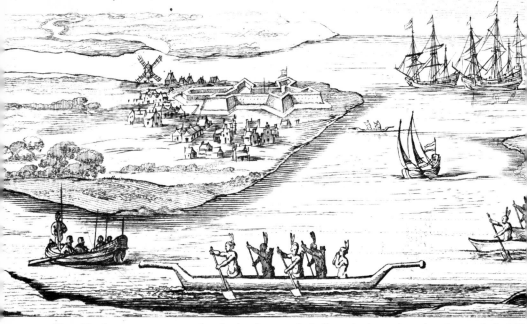

t' Fort nieuw Amsterdam op de Manhatans

How Manhattan was expected to look when partly built up is shown in a drawing made in 162(?) probably by the engineer Cryn Fredericks, who laid out the town. By a fluke the drawing was reversed when it was printed; Manhattan should be pointing to the left, not the right, and the la(?) on the right is Governor's Island, which should appear on the left. Beyond is the land that is no(?) New Jersey. Print Collection, New York Public Library

New Amsterdam's strong-willed director general, Peter Stuyvesant, glares out of a portrait made by an unknown artist.
Courtesy of The New-York Historical Society

Opposite: *This bird's-eye view of N(?) Amsterdam in 1660, though origin(?) drawn by a surveyor named Jacq(?) Cortelyou, is known as the Castello p(?) for the villa in Italy where it was l(?) discovered. It shows the town all ne(?) laid out and inhabited as far as fortified wall on its north side, erecte(?) repel an expected invasion by the Eng(?) from New England (which n(?) occurred); the adjoining lane later bec(?) Wall Street. At left are the fort, with(?) church, the governor's house, and barracks. Below it, on the water's e(?) near the two large ships, is the large ho(?) of Peter Stuyvesant. Broadway is the l(?) street at the top leading in from the f(?) and the canal in the center, leading in fr(?) the East River, is the Heere Gracht, wh(?) in 1676 (after the British takeover) (?) filled in to become Broad Street. Along bottom in this view runs Pearl Str(?) which today lies several blocks from river.* Print Collection, New York Public Lib(?)

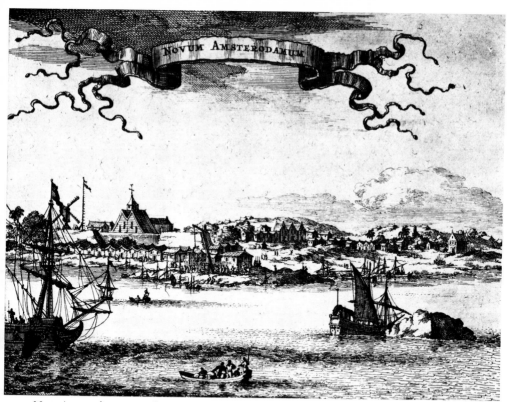

New Amsterdam around 1643, as seen from Brooklyn, was dominated by its fort, which contained the church. Print Collection, New York Public Library

An elaborately decorated notice of a meeting of the Hand-in-Hand Fire Company, one of New York's first, in the 1760s is embellished by a scene of the company in action. Firemen pass buckets from the well at left to fill the engine, at center, where three men on each side work the pump propelling water onto the fire. The operation is directed by a chief, just beyond the engine, who shouts into a megaphone. Print Collection, New York Public Library

Tiny houses and a Methodist church line the south side of John Street, between William and Nassau streets, in 1768. The steeple in the distance is that of the Middle Dutch Church, on Nassau Street. Museum of the City of New York

A detailed map, or plan, was made of New York and surroundings in the 1760s by a British army officer named Bernard Ratzer, who included at the bottom a view of the city from Governor's Island. Manhattan, at the top, is now built up for well over a mile from its southern tip. Prominent features include the Common (also known as The Fields), a triangular open area about ten blocks up from the Battery and today occupied by City Hall, and, just above it, a small lake known as the Collect Pond (here labeled Fresh Water). The main road out of town to the north is the Bowery, which at the top of the map becomes the Bloomingdale Road. The rest of Manhattan is mostly farmland or woods. Brooklyn (here called Brookland), lower right, is still only sparsely settled, as are the areas across the Hudson River in New Jersey.
Print Collection, New York Public Library

A South Prospect of ye Flourishing

Captain Henry Hudson discovered this Countrey designed and led to ye Hollanders ye Indies Ships being projected to come March ye 9 Aug...

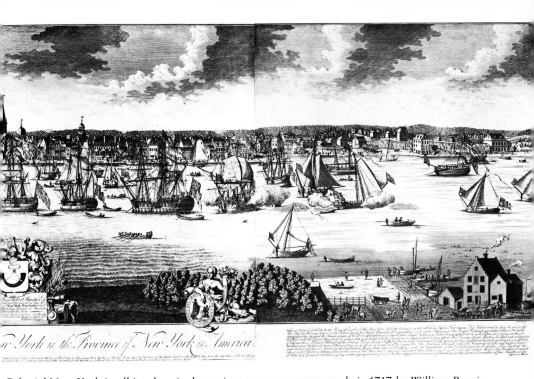

r York in the Province of New York in America.

Colonial New York in all its glory is shown in a great panorama made in 1717 by William Burgis and printed in London on four copper plates. Although Burgis called it "A South Prospect," it is actually drawn from Brooklyn Heights, to the east. The presence of a large fleet hints that the view was made to commemorate some special event, and two of the ships are firing salutes. At the far left, Peter Stuyvesant's former house is now a burned-out shell. To the right of it is the enclosed berthing area known as the Great Dock. At the far left of the third picture is the steeple of the first Trinity Church, built in the 1690s and now the tallest structure in town. As with many such views, the buildings are largely accurate representations; in the second picture, the large structure with three gables and very tall chimneys is the abode of Robert Livingston, who had taken it over from its first owner, Captain William Kidd. In the foreground of the final picture is the Brooklyn landing of the East River ferry. Beyond the entire scene rise the hills of New Jersey.
Print Collection, New York Public Library

The vanguard of a vast British invasion fleet of nearly 500 ships lies at anchor in the Narrows, between Staten Island (foreground) and Brooklyn, at the end of June 1776. Print Collection, New York Public Library

Celebrating the news of the Declaration of Independence, New Yorkers on July 9, 1776, after marching to the Bowling Green, pull down the statue of George III that had been erected there following the successful resolution of the 1765 Stamp Act crisis. Museum of the City of New York

British redcoats are shown parading through newly captured New York on September 19, 1776, in a European engraving that gives the city an undeservedly Continental look. Print Collection, New York Public Library

In triumph, General George Washington enters an exultant city on November 25, 1783, the event becoming known as Evacuation Day in commemoration of the departure of British forces. Print Collection, New York Public Library

The hustle and bustle of mercantile New York after the Revolution is seen in Francis Guy's painting of the intersection of Wall Street (which leads off to the right, to Coffee House Slip) and Water Street around 1797. At the left is the Tontine Coffee House, which at that time housed the fledgling New York Stock Exchange. Courtesy of The New-York Historical Society

Another painting by Francis Guy, made between 1817 and 1820, shows neighborhood activity on snowy Front Street in Brooklyn, which at that time was scarcely more than a village. Museum of the City of New York

The more sedate upper end of Wall Street is shown in an engraving made in 1820 looking up from Broad Street (foreground) toward Broadway. The second Trinity Church, in the background, replaced the first edifice, which had been destroyed by fire in 1776. This one was in turn replaced in 1846 by a third Trinity, Gothic in style, which remains today. Courtesy of The New-York Historical Society

The rural outskirts of the city were sketched in 1798 by Archibald Robertson, who looked south from a point around today's Canal and Centre streets to show the Collect Pond and the buildings of lower Manhattan. Within two decades the scene had changed drastically. The pond had been drained and filled in, and hills like that at left had been removed to create the undeviating terrain that marks Manhattan today. Print Collection, New York Public Library

The crowded, hectic Five Points neighborhood, one of the most crime-ridden districts in the city (near today's Chinatown), is shown in a delightful drawing made in 1827. Museum of the City of New York

Maritime New York during its first great flush of prosperity is shown in a drawing of the East River and lower Manhattan made from Brooklyn Heights in 1836. The large white building in the center background is a hotel at the corner of Fulton and Water streets, near the Fulton Market.
Print Collection, New York Public Library

Although this photograph of South Street (opposite) *with its abundance of square-rigged merchant ships was made late in the nineteenth century, it conveys the air of energy and romance that had made New York's mercantile center so distinctive earlier in the century.*
Courtesy of The New-York Historical Society

After the advent of steamships, for which the East River was too cramped, the center of commerce shifted to the Hudson River, as shown in this engraving of the west side docks that appeared in Harper's Weekly in 1869. Museum of the City of New York

toward the Loyalists who were leaving, and many harsh words were uttered, but there were few incidents of violence. (It was different outside the city, where gangs who came to be known as Levelers viciously attacked Loyalists who had fled to the city during the war and now tried to return home.)

One source of contention was the status of former slaves. Many blacks had gone over to the British side on being promised their freedom, and hundreds had joined Burgoyne's labor battalions in his Hudson Valley campaign. Now, ironically, many returning patriots insisted that blacks sheltered by the enemy should be returned to slavery. One man sought to return to New York with his slave, who refused to accompany him. When the man tried to force him, the slave was rescued—by a detachment of Hessians, of all people. Many onetime slaves chose to depart with the Loyalists, while others managed to merge with the city's free black population and start new lives.

Plans for the formal transfer of the city to American hands had been made in the spring, but the day when control would actually change was set for November 25, 1783. Known as Evacuation Day and celebrated for decades thereafter, it was a highly formalized affair. First, British troops on duty in upper Manhattan pulled back to the city and began embarking for England. As they marched downtown, the Americans followed at a respectful distance, gradually taking over the city and finally moving down Broadway to the fort. Then, when the patriot troops had completed their occupation, a procession got under way headed by General Washington and the governor of New York State, George Clinton (once an anti-British member of the provincial assembly—and a distant cousin of the British general), as well as other military and civilian dignitaries. As it came down the Bowery and Broadway and past the burned-out remnants of the prewar town, cheers rang out loudest for Washington, back after seven years.

Two minor but humorous incidents stood out during the day. Many New Yorkers who had hidden their American flags during the occupation were anxious to display them in honor of Washington's return. But the British provost marshal, William Cunningham, felt it was his duty to defend the Crown until the final moments and roared around the city demanding their removal. When he got to Day's Tavern on Murray Street he was met at the door by Mrs. Day, a stout and spirited woman, and she was his match. As he tried to remove the prematurely displayed Stars and Stripes from her establishment she began beating him with her broom until his nose bled and the powder flew from his wig all over his red coat. To the applause of bystanders, he retreated. Some chroniclers have called this the last conflict of the American Revolution.

Later that day, as the American troops arrived at the fort, they discovered that the British flag was still flying over it, nailed in place, and that someone had not only removed the halyard and cleats but greased the pole. Attempts to shinny up it were unsuccessful. Finally someone ran to an ironmonger's store and returned with a saw, hammer, and nails. After a board had been split into cleats, a sailor tied the halyard around his waist, nailed some cleats to the pole, climbed up, nailing cleats as he ascended, reached the top, pulled the offending flag down, and affixed the rope to the pulley. This done, the Stars and Stripes was raised amid cheers and the firing of guns. It was the last time a national flag would change over New York City.

More than independence had been gained. The revolutionary aspect of the American Revolution had also been demonstrated in New York. An entire stratum of society—the most conservative and pro-British of the merchant families and their allies—had been ejected, political alignments had shifted and would continue to change, and a new economic structure would come into being. Cleansed and chastened by its difficult experience, the city was ready to start anew.

4

The City Reborn

New York was in ruin. Its streets were torn up and in disarray. Its entire lower section was still a charred shambles from the disastrous wartime fires of 1776 and 1778, and those houses which had been fortunate enough to escape destruction were dilapidated and shabby. Shacks and other makeshift shelters dotted the landscape. Almost all public buildings had been wrecked from their use as barracks, jails, or military hospitals. Wharves and slips had been left to rot, and stores and warehouses were decaying. New York in the closing months of 1783 was not a prepossessing sight.

Almost more damaging, one would have to suppose, was the loss of much of the city's elite, the experienced Loyalist merchants and other entrepreneurs who might have helped lead the way to recovery but who had recently departed in the massive Tory exodus to Canada. The remaining populace was divided by bitter memories of the long war and the British occupation; known Tories who remained in the city were deprived of the right to vote and forbidden to hold public office. From all outward signs, New York City would take a long time to recover.

But anyone making such a prediction would have to consider three other factors, each prompting a more optimistic view: the city's reputation for commercial enterprise was intact, its cosmopolitan atmosphere stood a good chance of attracting new immigrants, and the superb harbor was unimpaired. So it was that New York's rebound was swift and sure. Over the next couple of decades buildings were restored and new ones constructed. Trade, which had come to a standstill, resumed and multiplied. Returning patriots were joined by arrivals both from elsewhere in the United States and from Europe.

81

In less than four years the city's population, which had sunk to 10,000 in 1783, had surpassed its prewar figure and stood at 23,614. New streets were laid out and the city began expanding to the north. By 1810 the population had jumped all the way to 96,000, a fourfold increase in a single generation, a spurt that swept New York past Philadelphia and made it the nation's largest city. Even before that time—by the end of the century, in fact—New York had overtaken Philadelphia in the dollar value of both its imports and its exports and was thus also the number one port. A widespread assumption exists that the city owed its newly found dominance in the early years of the nineteenth century to the building of the Erie Canal. Certainly there is no denying the extraordinary benefits that the canal brought. But the city was already in first place and extending its lead before the canal had even been started.

Such achievement did not come about by chance. It was wrought by energetic and creative individuals, who would be increasingly in evidence in the city as the commerce born of the port widened the scope of personal opportunity and attracted talent. Aggressive merchants—some established, some newly on the scene, but all operating as if their old Loyalist colleagues had never existed—led the economic resurgence. But workers in other fields also helped shape the city. Now for the first time, figures whose accomplishments helped change New York were also known on a national scale—men as disparate as Alexander Hamilton and Aaron Burr.

Soon after being rid of the British, as if hastening to get rid of the past, the city tore down the aged and decrepit Fort George, which had stood at the foot of Manhattan and undergone so many name changes since the earliest days of the Dutch. The site was leveled, and the dirt that had formed the walls was dumped into the water to form the beginnings of Battery Park, another chapter in New York's endless drive to create more land. At about the same time the city acquired a new government. Although New York was no longer a British colony, it did preserve, for the moment, the English tradition that the mayor would be appointed by the governor of the state. And so in 1784 Governor George Clinton (who had held office ever since the state government had been formed upstate in Kingston in 1777) appointed a respected lawyer, James Duane, as the city's first postwar chief. The post was unsalaried, which did not bother the wealthy Duane, but the mayor was entitled to collect a number of fees from the sale of licenses and excise stamps, and these constituted a tidy income. The mayor was assisted in his duties by a city recorder, the chief legal officer, and by a number of aldermen, who made up the City Council. Both the city and the state governments were lodged in City Hall on Wall Street. The following year the so-called Articles of Confederation Congress, the new nation's governing body, moved to New York from Trenton, New Jersey, where it had been meeting temporarily. Having three echelons of government coexisting in the limited space of downtown Manhattan made for a certain amount of congestion, but New Yorkers were proud that their city was recognized as the country's preeminent center.

Another effort to make a new beginning was reflected in the changing of street names. Queen Street became part of Pearl; King George Street, part of William; King Street was renamed Pine; and Crown Street was now Liberty. King's College was reopened as Columbia College and was removed from the aegis of the Anglican Church (which in the United States was metamorphosed into the Protestant Episcopal Church, a branch of the Anglican community).

Trade took a little while to recover. Although New York's ties to the London business community were still strong, the new nation no longer enjoyed the protection of Britain's trade system, and not only England but also France and Spain at this time barred American vessels from trading with the West Indies, formerly a key market. Luckily, France and Spain both revoked their ban in 1785, and New York merchants managed to evade the British restrictions by trading (illegally) through Dutch and Danish ports in the Caribbean, until by the late 1780s trade with the West Indies was as brisk as ever. Merchants also moved aggressively to build up the city's share of coastal trade between the states, and soon they were transshipping cotton from the southern states to England, a practice that was to develop into the celebrated and lucrative "cotton triangle" in the nineteenth century.

It was clear, however, that new markets would have to be developed. Of surpassing significance, therefore, was the sailing from New York in February 1784 of the *Empress of China*, a small craft barely 103 feet long laden with 2,600 fur skins, 1,270 woolen garments, a load of pig lead, and some 30 tons of ginseng, a root grown in East Coast forests that was known to be an "alterative tonic, stimulant, carminative, and dimulcent"[1] and in great demand in China. The ship's destination: Whampoa, on the Canton River, where merchants from Britain, Holland, Spain, Denmark, and Sweden were already trading with the Chinese and where American merchants hoped to gain a foothold. The *Empress*—the first American ship to sail to the

Far East—was something of a cooperative American venture. She had been built in Baltimore, her affairs were administered by a Bostonian, and there was Philadelphia money in her; but the bulk of her financing had been arranged by a New York syndicate, so she was a New York ship. In May 1785 she was back in New York bearing a cargo of tea, fine silks, cinnamon, and chinaware. On a total investment of $120,000 she had made a profit of $30,727. Merchants up and down the East Coast rushed to emulate her performance. It was the beginning of the fabled China trade, which brought immense riches to both Boston and Philadelphia but even more to the merchants of Manhattan.

About the time the *Empress of China* was departing on her epochal voyage, a twenty-year-old German youth from Waldorf, a small village near the Black Forest, arrived in New York carrying $25 in English coin, a spare set of clothes, and seven flutes. His name was John Jacob Astor. He had been preceded here by his older brother Heinrich, who had come with the Hessian troops, decided he liked the Americans, and was now a butcher in lower Manhattan. Jacob, as he called himself, had no desire to join Heinrich as a butcher; that was what their father had been. A tall, blond, friendly fellow with a deceptively impassive demeanor, Jacob wanted to strike out on his own, and he had purchased the flutes in London with the thought of setting up a musical instrument shop. To get himself established he worked briefly for a baker on Pearl Street and then for a Quaker fur merchant, where his job was to beat the furs to rid them of moths. The Quaker was impressed enough with his diligence to send him on fur-purchasing trips upstate, and before long Astor was in business for himself, tramping alone (carrying a seventy-five-pound pack) through the wilderness of northern New York and Ohio and into Canada buying the skins of beavers, muskrats, raccoons, and foxes. He happened to be in on the ground floor of a lucrative trade: beaver skins bought from the Indians for $1 sold in London for $6.25. He opened a small store in which he sold flutes and other instruments, advertising that he also "has for sale a quantity of Canada Beavers and Beavering Coating, Raccoon Skins, and Raccoon Blankets."[2] The furs were soon crowding out the flutes, and business boomed. Astor was on his way to becoming the possessor of America's first superfortune. It was a fortune that had special meaning for New York City as Astor invested most of it in real estate. He was to make his first purchase of land in 1789, buying two small lots on the Bowery for $625. He paid for them in cash, of which he had plenty. In time he would own much of Manhattan Island.

Another young man of promise, not yet known to Astor but destined to play a critical role in shaping the new nation and thereby in the development of New York, was Alexander Hamilton. In 1784 he was just twenty-seven years old, but he was already someone to be reckoned with. Like Astor, he had come from another land. Born on the West Indies island of Nevis, the illegitimate son of a wellborn Scotsman and a local planter's estranged wife, he had as a youngster gone to work for a merchant on St. Croix who was so impressed with his industry and sharp mind that he made it possible for him to attend King's College in New York. Hamilton arrived in the city in 1773, and the following summer he attracted sudden attention with his eloquent speech at a rally in The Fields urging the American colonies to unite in resistance to Britain's taxation policies.

A slight, sharp-featured, elegant-looking youth with reddish hair tied loosely with a ribbon, Hamilton looked even younger than he was. But his actions belied his appearance. During the following year he wrote a number of highly influential pamphlets attacking the Loyalist point of view, and when fighting broke out he soon came to the attention of General Washington, who made him one of his aides. Hamilton ended up one of Washington's most trusted advisers. When the fighting ceased, he studied for the law, was soon admitted to practice, and opened an office at 56 Wall Street. His wife, the former Elizabeth Schuyler, was a member of one of New York's richest and most prestigious families. Hamilton could thus be considered not only a political light but a social one as well. Dinners at the Hamiltons' house, next door to his office, were society events.

His views were well known: the new nation must be strong both governmentally and financially. As early as 1780 he had expounded on the need for centralized federal authority; he also felt money must be made readily available both to governments and to private concerns for their security and useful growth. Banks, he said, are "one of the surest foundations of public and private Credit."[3] Philadelphia, still the financial capital, already had its own bank; and in 1784 Hamilton used his influence to bring about the chartering of the first bank in New York. He even purchased a share of its stock (which, despite his successful law practice, he could barely afford). The Bank of New York is still going strong.

Hamilton also believed that the time for bitterness toward former

Tories had passed. Reconciliation would benefit the commonweal. A large segment of the public disagreed vigorously, but Hamilton pleaded for moderation in a series of essays signed "Phocion." He also risked public odium by defending a former Loyalist in a pivotal court case, *Rutgers* v. *Waddington*, in which a patriot landowner who had fled the city in 1776 sued a Loyalist (who had used the property during the occupation) for back rent. Hamilton argued that because the Loyalist had paid rent to the British authorities he owed nothing further, and this view prevailed. A few years later, as a member of the state legislature, Hamilton worked to restore the voting rights of all Loyalists, and in 1788 the bill passed. Slowly New York's anti-Loyalist resentment was dying down.

Although New Yorkers were becoming more prosperous, full-scale recovery from the war was hobbled by the weakness of the Articles of Confederation, and Hamilton in 1787 led the drive to call a constitutional convention. Gratified by the resulting document, which set up the strong state he had long envisioned, he applied himself to the campaign for ratification, joining with James Madison and John Jay to write *The Federalist Papers*, which have been called the most notable contribution to political thought ever made in America (Hamilton himself wrote the majority of the papers). Ironically, New York State almost failed to ratify the Constitution and probably would not have done so had it not been for Hamilton's vigorous efforts. But this time it was not the merchants (the group that had expressed such strong reservations about independence) who dragged their heels. In this cause they were solidly behind Hamilton and already formed the core of what was becoming known as the Federalist Party, which espoused his views and saw the Constitution as benefiting their interests. The opposition, made up largely of delegates from the rural upstate areas, was led by Governor Clinton, a believer in states' rights who felt the document gave far too much power to the federal government; this view would eventually develop into the set of anti-Federalist beliefs espoused by the followers of Thomas Jefferson.

It may or may not have been Hamilton who started the rumor at New York's ratifying convention (held in Poughkeepsie) that the city might secede from the state and join the United States if the delegates did not back the Constitution; John Jay actually voiced the threat. But Hamilton was surely the inspiration behind a mammoth parade staged in New York City on July 23, 1788, after the news had come that New Hampshire had become the ninth state to ratify, thus making the Constitution the law of the land. A milelong procession down

Broadway included floats honoring all the states that had voted for ratification as well as the city's major skilled trades (the bakers, the coopers, the hatters, and so on), and was highlighted by a twenty-seven-foot replica of a thirty-two-gun frigate under full sail pulled by ten white horses—and appropriately named *Hamilton.* That evening 5,000 revelers attended an open-air banquet near what is now Lafayette and Grand streets. Anti-Federalists were miffed but could do nothing; New York's sentiments were plain. Three days later the delegates took the hint and voted to ratify the Constitution.

The following spring, on April 30, 1789, George Washington was inaugurated as the nation's first president in a ceremony on the balcony of Federal Hall, the former City Hall on Wall Street, which had been rebuilt to serve the national government. (A statue of Washington designates the site today, at Broad and Wall.) Hamilton did not take part in the proceedings, as he was still a private citizen, but within weeks he received the ultimate accolade that a man in his position could hope for: he was chosen by Washington to be the first secretary of the treasury. He was thirty-two years old.

For the next fifteen months, while the federal government remained in New York, the city was a heady place. More than ever, it seemed to be the center of everything. The president at first resided in a house on Cherry Street (the site is occupied today by an approach to the Brooklyn Bridge) and then, when it proved too constricted, in the more commodious McComb house on Broadway not far from Bowling Green. He and Mrs. Washington observed an elaborate schedule of levees, receptions, and formal dinners, and for official occasions the president moved around town in virtually regal splendor in an ornate coach drawn by four or sometimes six horses and accompanied by liveried outriders, postilion, and driver. The John Street Theatre was packed every evening, formal balls and other entertainments abounded, and fox hunting flourished on the country plains of Jamaica, on Long Island. The Schuylers, Verplancks, Livingstons, Duanes, Bleeckers, Beekmans, and Bayards among other grand families presided over a social life that was distinctly aristocratic. Taverns ran full blast. And anywhere on the streets of Manhattan one might suddenly come upon Vice President John Adams, Chief Justice John Jay, Leader of the House James Madison, or Senators James Monroe or Robert Morris—or of course Alexander Hamilton—scurrying about the nation's business. Secretary of State Thomas Jefferson, who had only recently arrived back from diplomatic service in France, got to town some months after the others.

Of all these dignitaries, Hamilton was preeminent inasmuch as his task, that of putting the new government on a sound financial footing, was more demanding than that of any other cabinet officer; in addition, all the other departments looked to him for funding. Hamilton relished the challenge and frankly enjoyed being in effect the country's prime minister. Within just a few months he submitted to Congress a massively detailed brief entitled *Report Relative to a Provision for the Support of Public Credit*. In it he proposed that the government take over and manage all debts accumulated by the states and other bodies during and since the war, and that it raise tariffs to pay them off while establishing a central fund for promoting private commercial and industrial development. This was the foundation of the country's national debt.

Parts of the program passed Congress easily, such as the government's assuming the obligation of paying off all the soldiers who were still owed back pay. But the takeover of state debts did not sit well with the southern states, whose obligations were relatively light. Why should they submit to taxation to bail out northern states like Massachusetts and New York? Seeking a way to break the deadlock, Hamilton decided to approach Thomas Jefferson, the most influential of the southerners, and the resulting agreement has come to be known, with admirable simplicity, as "the deal."

Quite by chance, the two men met one day on the sidewalk in front of the McComb house as Jefferson was about to enter to confer with the president. The normally elegant Hamilton, looking (in Jefferson's words) "sombre, haggard & dejected beyond description,"[4] asked to have a few words with the Virginian. He said the fate of the new government hung on the debt question, and he hoped they could compromise. For half an hour the two men—Hamilton short, wiry, and intense, Jefferson tall and self-assured—strolled and discussed the situation, and finally they arrived at a meeting of the minds. The details were ironed out the following evening over dinner at Jefferson's rooms on Maiden Lane, with Madison present. One issue that was bothering the southern states, said Jefferson, was the location of the national capital. They did not want it here in New York, as the city's interests differed too much from theirs. If it could be promised for the South he could persuade his colleagues to switch their votes on the debt issue. Hamilton was agreeable, and so it came to pass. He got his federal debt package, which was immensely beneficial to the interests of merchants like New York's, and the capital moved (after a ten-year intermediate period in Philadelphia) to the shores of the Potomac. Thus it happened that the United States became one of the few major nations of the world with its central government located elsewhere than in its biggest, most important city.

For New York City, the establishment of a federal debt had another result of immense long-term significance: it created a securities market. Hamilton funded the government's debt by issuing stock, an easily transferred medium that could be bought and sold by individuals. Shortly thereafter bank stocks became available as well, and both types of securities sold briskly in New York's moneyed atmosphere. The stocks were at first handled by auctioneers, who transacted their sales on the sidewalk near Federal Hall on Wall Street. But a group of independent brokers, finding the auction system too haphazard, set up a more formal operation under a buttonwood tree down the street at 68–70 Wall, meeting daily to exchange quotations and make whatever sales presented themselves. On March 21, 1792, they agreed to abide by a number of rules and to have no dealings with the auctioneers, whom they soon put out of business. Although they moved their operation the following year into the newly built Tontine Coffee House at the northwest corner of Wall and Water streets, and although the New York Stock Exchange did not itself come into being until 1817, the 1792 "buttonwood agreement" is recognized as the Exchange's true origin. Wall Street's history as a money center dates from that time.

Meanwhile, in 1790, the federal government had departed to Philadelphia. Many of those leaving had a twinge of regret; Abigail Adams, the vice president's wife, remarked that while she was prepared to make the best of Philadelphia, "When all is done, it will not be Broadway."[5] In the city itself there was a fear that the loss of both the government's official business and its social glow would throw the city into a slump. (Compounding the loss, the state government decamped to Albany in 1797.) There was no need for concern. The last decade of the eighteenth century saw the city growing faster than ever.

A contributing cause was the outbreak of war in Europe in 1792: with England and France fighting each other, the West Indian trade lay open to American shipping, and tremendous profits accrued to the merchants of all the eastern ports, but especially to those in New York. Observed a French visitor to the city in 1801, "New York is particularly able to furnish provisions to the southern colonies of the belligerent powers. Sugar, cotton, coffee, indeed all the provisions that they receive in payment, are transported on their ships to Europe and exchanged for territorial products or manufactures, which they carry to the colonies or to the United States." New York was bustling, he said. "Everything in the city is in motion; everywhere the shops resound with the noise of workers . . . one sees vessels arriving from every part of the world, or ready to depart, and . . . one can not better describe the opulence of this still new city than to compare it to ancient Tyre, which contemporary authors called the queen of commerce and the sovereign of the seas."[6] In 1796–97 New York's port drew ahead of Philadelphia's in both imports and exports, and from then on it continued to extend its lead.

The city's population in the first federal census of 1790 was officially pegged at 33,131, and by that time some 4,000 new houses had been built. All the old public buildings had been rebuilt or replaced; a new Trinity Church, for example, had been consecrated. But by the end of the following decade, in 1800, the population had reached 60,489, almost doubling. For the first time, immigrants were coming to New York from Europe in considerable numbers. Some were refugees from the political turmoil in France, but there were also Germans (following the lead of their compatriots like Heinrich Astor) and large numbers of Irish—who incidentally had been delighted by England's comeuppance in the American Revolution. Many immigrants were merely passing through, for example to recently opened lands in upstate New York. But a significant number remained in the city, establishing a pattern that would hold into the twentieth century. Manhattan's population was also boosted by the arrival of a great many New Englanders, who sensed that New York offered greater scope for their talents than they could find at home and who were to play a prominent role in the city's commercial expansion.

But as the merchant class prospered and grew, the number of the poor also increased. Many of the recent immigrants, especially those from abroad, were penniless and required public assistance. New York had always had a poor population, but the underclass was now increasing substantially, putting a strain on the rudimentary relief facilities. By 1800 a third of the city's white population is believed to have been destitute. More poverty inevitably brought an increase in crime, and the city's jails—there were two in The Fields plus a state facility near today's Christopher Street—were chronically overcrowded. Although Wall Street and Broadway (which were now the best residential addresses) presented an elegant appearance and gave the impression that all New York was prospering, there were also slums, especially in the region next to the Collect Pond just west of today's Chinatown.

Sanitation was almost nonexistent. Pigs still rooted among the piles of garbage that were everywhere, and the city's water supply was still inadequate. In consequence New York suffered from repeated epidemics. An outbreak of yellow fever in 1795 claimed more than 700 lives; three years later another outbreak killed three times as many. Those who could fled to the village of Greenwich, northwest of town, or to Brooklyn Heights across the East River. The only institutions capable of treating the sick were New York Hospital, which had reopened in 1791 after being wrecked from its use as a barracks in the war, and the New York Dispensary, which served the sick poor. To alleviate the shortage of beds, the city in the mid-1790s purchased a farm known as "Belle Vue" located on the East River near present-day 25th Street, and began lodging yellow fever patients in its buildings and some others nearby. Thus did New York's famed Bellevue Hospital come into being.

Despite the epidemics, the city continued to expand. By 1800 streets had been laid out all the way to Houston Street, though settlement had not reached that far. Houses of the wealthy were being built in the Georgian style, or in the new Federal style, which was more homegrown, and city law now required any building more than two stories high to be constructed of brick or stone, with a slate or tile roof. Smaller structures could still be built of wood.

Partly to make new land for housing, but also in an attempt to eliminate low-lying, wet areas that were becoming contaminated and thus breeding grounds for disease, plans were laid in the late 1790s to drain the Collect Pond, the sizable body of water just north of The Fields, and also a swampy area to the west of it known as Lispenard Meadows. The Collect had long been a popular place for fishing in summer and skating in winter, and its water was used by breweries and tanneries along its banks; no matter, it would have to go. Both it and the Meadows drained through small streams to both rivers. Shortly after the turn of the century the streams were straightened out and run into a single canal stretching across the island, and in the ensuing years both the Collect and the Meadows were gradually filled in. Later the canal was covered over—but water still flows beneath today's Canal Street.

The city's political picture was changing, too, thanks to the machinations of Aaron Burr, one of the strangest but most brilliant figures ever associated with New York. The man who would become Alexander Hamilton's nemesis was in some ways very much like him: he was of slight stature with sharp features, had won distinction in the war, and was an expert attorney. Both men were highly energetic and politically ambitious. Burr was just one year older than Hamilton, and they were well acquainted. But while Hamilton was very much a man of principle, dedicating himself to bringing his strong Federalist beliefs to fruition, Burr (who was from a distinguished family, his grandfather having been the noted theologian Jonathan Edwards, his father the president of the college that would become Princeton) was a psychological oddity, an engaging and attractive person bereft of conscience. He simply did not know right from wrong, and if a scheme seemed to further his interests he unhesitatingly adopted it without regard to its moral implications. Neither of the two major ploys for which he is best known in New York annals was evil, but in both he deliberately masked his intent in order to achieve political gain.

One ploy was political. Shortly after the Revolution, a patriotic organization called the Society of St. Tammany had been formed with branches in major cities, its members made up principally of former enlisted men. Named for a Delaware Indian chief who allegedly welcomed William Penn and possessed superhuman powers— he had created the rapids of Detroit and the falls of Niagara—the group had begun in opposition to the Society of the Cincinnati, an elitist officers' organization founded and led by George Washington and Alexander Hamilton. Aristocrats, the Tammany people felt, had gotten control of the government and were not to be trusted. They also opposed Hamilton's efforts to forgive Loyalists, who they believed had sinned against America. But in New York City, at least, the Tammany Society was more a social and fraternal organization than a political one.

Burr in the late 1790s was momentarily out of office, having just completed a term as senator from New York—in which he escaped voting on every controversial issue (some of Hamilton's supporters referred to him as the Eel, as he was too slippery to be caught). He was already nursing a grudge against Hamilton, whom he rightly suspected of trying to thwart his career. In 1792, for example, when Burr had tried surreptitiously to line up votes to displace John Adams as vice president, Hamilton had penned a barrage of letters to well-placed friends attacking Burr's probity and honesty ("He cares for nothing about the means of affecting his purpose ... In a word, if we have an embryo-Caesar in the United States, 'tis Burr").[7]

Searching for a political base from which to challenge the Federalists and get back at Hamilton, Burr set out to control the Tammany Society. While careful not to become a member, he ingratiated himself among its leaders and quietly took over its affairs. Tammany was best known for its stirring parades; Burr saw that a parade could garner a lot of votes. He and his henchmen developed techniques that would become staples of American politics: they reported to the newspapers, for example, that their candidate had spoken eloquently to a series of well-attended gatherings at which his remarks had been lustily cheered—whereas in actuality the meetings had been attended only by the candidate and two friends or had not taken place at all. Such maneuverings produced quick results. In the 1800 presidential election, with Tammany men behind him, Burr captured New York State's electoral votes and even came within a whisker of gaining the presidency. And Tammany, with Burr as its first "boss," was well on its way to becoming a New York City fixture, surviving well into the latter half of the twentieth century.

Connected with this ploy was a companion move of Burr's to counteract Federalist financial power in New York. Again his tactics were devious. The inadequacy and impurity of the city's water supply had long been suspected of helping to cause the epidemics that were becoming so destructive, and in 1799 Burr, then a state legislator, sponsored the chartering of a utility company to be called the Manhattan Company. Its purpose would ostensibly be to establish a centralized water system. Imbedded in its charter, however, was a clause permitting the company "to employ all such surplus capital ... in any other monied transactions or operations not inconsistent with the constitution and laws of this state."[8] Questioned about this during hearings, Burr cheerfully admitted that it would enable the company to speculate in stock, open a bank, or engage in any other activities benefiting its investors. No one objected, and the bill passed.

But opening a bank was actually Burr's main purpose. It was the only way, he reasoned, that a bank not dedicated to Hamilton's principles could be chartered in New York. And there was surely a need for such a bank. The Bank of New York, which thus far had exercised monopoly control over New York banking, did business only with moneyed, propertied New Yorkers. This was bad enough, but it had political ramifications, as the right to vote was restricted to property holders. If the Manhattan Company's bank loaned money to less affluent citizens, like members of the Tammany Society, their vote-getting power (and Burr's) would increase and Hamilton's sway would be counterbalanced. So while the Manhattan Company proceeded in a desultory way to dig wells and lay wooden water mains under the streets, its main energies and resources went into its Republican (i.e., anti-Federalist) banking operation. Providing mortgage loans to good men of democratic persuasion, it gave substance to Burr's 1800 presidential bid. Within a decade or two the company itself had become little more than a shadow, while its stepchild, known by the odd name of the Bank of the Manhattan Company, prospered for a century and a half. Finally taken over in the 1950s by the Chase National Bank, it lives on in the combined name of Chase Manhattan, a lingering twitch of Burr's legacy.

Although Burr had blunted Hamilton's power, he had not removed him as a political obstacle, and it was partly due to Hamilton's intervention that Burr was forced to bow to Jefferson in the 1800 election. Four years later, after an unimpressive stint as vice president, Burr tried to run for governor of New York. Again Hamilton barred the way, and when Burr learned that Hamilton had uttered some uncomplimentary remarks about him at a New York dinner party he challenged him to a duel. Hamilton would have hoped to avoid the confrontation and heartily disapproved of dueling, but his honor was at stake; Burr for his part was desperate to avenge what he considered his opponent's unceasing smears. Because New York State forbade dueling, the affair took place on a bluff overlooking the Hudson in Weehawken, New Jersey, on the morning of July 11, 1804. Hamilton had no desire to do more than draw blood, in accordance with dueling custom; but Burr, who fired first, is believed to have shot to kill. His ball entered Hamilton's right side, mortally wounding him, and the former aide-de-camp to General Washington, apologist of the Constitution, and master architect of the government's financial structure died the next day in a friend's house in Greenwich Village.

On the evening after the duel, Tammany members meeting at their favorite tavern drank toasts to Aaron Burr. But the next day, when Hamilton's death was announced and they found the city reacting in shock and horror, they were aghast and quickly proclaimed their official sorrow. In one of the most impressive funerals the city had ever witnessed, Hamilton was buried with full honors in Trinity churchyard. Burr, accused of murder, fled the city, his political career at an end and his reputation destroyed. (Ironically, he lived on for thirty-two years. Tried for treason for conspiring with persons in the western United States to overthrow the government, he was acquitted but left for Europe. On running out of funds he returned in 1812, found New York was willing to drop the murder charge, and reentered law practice. He died in 1836 on Staten Island at the age of eighty.)

Into the void left by the death of Hamilton and the banishment of Burr stepped an equally dynamic personality, De Witt Clinton, another of those outsize figures who keep turning up in the city's history. The nephew of former Governor George Clinton (and therefore a distant cousin of the English Clintons who produced the British general, Sir Henry Clinton), he had entered Columbia College when it reopened after the Revolution and graduated at the head of his class at age seventeen, delivering a commencement address in Latin. He was a commanding figure, well over six feet tall, heavily built, with a broad forehead, a Grecian nose, wide-set eyes, and curly hair. Strong-willed and possessed of a keen intellect as well as an awesome dignity, he was also noted for his intransigence and stubbornness. After being admitted to the bar he served as secretary to his uncle, the governor, whose anti-Federalist views he shared. For a time he belonged to the Tammany Society, but its leaders turned bitterly against him after he voiced his suspicions of Burr's motives after 1800. After a turn as state legislator and then U.S. senator, Clinton became mayor of New York in 1803, serving on and off for more than ten years.

In response to the city's accelerating growth, New York that year was just starting construction on a new City Hall, to replace the old Federal Hall on Wall Street that had become inadequate. It was to sit in The Fields, the common just below Chambers Street that had seen so many stirring events. A competition for its design had been won by John McComb, Jr., and Joseph Mangin; their plans called for a graceful structure blending French Renaissance and Federal elements. In an odd mixture of pride and caution, the builders decided to use white marble for the front, which faced south, and also for the sides, but to use a less expensive red sandstone for the rear facade, which they presumed would never be noticed—after all, the building was on the north edge of town. Completed in 1812, City Hall is still in use, one of America's loveliest public structures. But less than ten years later, by 1820, New York had extended itself as far north as 14th Street, and City Hall was in the middle of town. Many years later the rear facade was redone in marble.

De Witt Clinton presided over the city with a firm but creative hand. As ex officio head of the local militia, he was not afraid to maintain law and order. One day, upon hearing that a fight had broken out between a crowd of sailors and the local watch, he rode forth with a group of civilian volunteers to investigate. Meeting up along the way with militia officers returning from a parade along with their marching band, he commandeered them, ordered the band to play a charge, and galloped full speed toward the rioting seamen, putting them to rout. Improvements to the city were a high priority. Voting rights were extended to include certain rent-paying citizens in addition to property owners. The number of docks was increased, a move that pleased the merchants. The mayor helped found both The New-York Historical Society and the American Academy and Institute of Arts and Letters. The first black congregation was formed by members of the Methodist Episcopal church, and Clinton drew up a bill removing all remaining political disabilities from Roman Catholics and pushed it through to enactment. Catholics were rapidly becoming a significant part of the population. Under the British their worship services had had to be performed secretly, in private dwellings. In 1785 there had been only 2,000 of them in the city, but they formed a benevolent organization, the Friendly Sons of St. Patrick, and started construction that year of their first church, St. Peter's, at Church and Barclay streets. By 1806 their numbers had increased to 10,000.

Clinton's finest contribution to the internal welfare of the city, however, was the introduction of public schooling. Up to this time New York's schools were either private or church-run, and many poor children got no education at all. To help them, the mayor in 1805 helped found the Free School Society and made sure it would be supported by public funds; the following year the society started classes "for the education of such poor children as do not belong to or are not provided for by any religious society."[9] In 1809 the society dedicated its first schoolhouse, Free School No. 1, on Park Row opposite the new City Hall. Teachers were hard to find, and so the society adopted the Lancasterian system of instruction, which used older and more advanced student monitors to instruct younger pupils. Discipline was also rudimentary, punishment being meted out by shackling students to their desks or by placing six-pound logs on their shoulders. But a start had been made. By 1824 more than 5,000 pupils were enrolled in the society's classes, and the following year it changed its name to the Public School Society of New York. It would continue to direct publicly supported education in the city until the 1850s.

Although cultural activity had come to almost a halt during the Revolution and resumed only slowly in the 1780s, the city experienced a minor literary renaissance in the 1790s that gathered momentum in Clinton's time and gave New York reason to call itself the nation's literary capital. More than a dozen newspapers flourished in the 1790s; their number was increased in 1801 with the first publication of the *New-York Evening Post*, founded by Alexander Hamilton and two partners to present the Federalist viewpoint, and today the oldest newspaper in New York. There were several literary journals, and New York in the first decade of the nineteenth century could claim such distinguished writers as Noah Webster and the essayist and commentator Washington Irving.

With his brother William and James Paulding, Irving collaborated on the *Salmagundi* papers, a series of humorous essays poking fun at New York City. In these writings the city was usually referred to as Gotham, after a proverbial thirteenth-century English village whose inhabitants took to acting like idiots to persuade King John (whom they loathed) not to buy a castle there. "More fools pass through Gotham," said the villagers, "than remain in it."[10] The nickname is still used. In 1809 Irving published *A History of New-York from the Beginning of the World to the End of the Dutch Dynasty*, by Diedrich Knickerbocker, in which he lampooned historical writing and happily made up all sorts of facts about the city's origins. He was astonished to find that most of his readers believed every word. It gave New York one of its most durable symbols, that of Father Knickerbocker. The word means "baker of marbles."

A glimpse into the future was afforded New Yorkers in August 1807, when Robert Fulton fired up his pioneering steamboat, the *Clermont*, and piloted her all the way from the foot of Amos (now West 10th) Street to Albany and back, carrying a load of dignitaries. No one knew what to make of the hissing, thumping, smoking craft, and a farmer along the way ran to announce to his wife that he had seen "the devil on his way to Albany in a sawmill."[11] But the era of faster and more reliable transportation was imminent, and it would bring still greater potential for growth to the city. Among the optimists was De Witt Clinton, who predicted in a speech that New York within a century would be built up solidly all the way from the Battery to the northern tip of Manhattan. (Hearing this, a Quaker turned to the man next to him and asked, "Don't thee think friend Clinton has a bee in his bonnet?")[12]

Another optimist was John Jacob Astor, who by now was wealthy and on cordial speaking terms with the city's top merchants and aristocrats, having done extremely well shipping furs to China and bringing back tea. Between 1800 and 1818 he invested an average of $35,000 in land each year. One canny purchase involved a farm covering the area from today's Times Square all the way west to the Hudson (which includes today's theatre district). Having heard that its owner was in financial difficulties and had taken out a mortgage, Astor rode up and looked around. He liked what he saw, and in two installments bought the mortgage for $25,000. The owner soon went bankrupt, and Astor foreclosed. Astor liked to hang on to his land, preferring to rent rather than sell, and made many such purchases.

With growth on everyone's mind, the state in 1807 appointed a three-man commission to devise an orderly program for developing Manhattan's land. The resulting proposal, known as the Randel Plan for the commission's surveyor and announced in 1811, made no attempt to realign streets already in place; thus downtown and Greenwich Village streets were left in their sometimes odd configurations. But the rest of Manhattan was laid out in a gridiron pattern that was to become a cardinal feature of the city. Cross streets were numbered in sequence above Houston Street all the way to 155th Street, while north–south avenues were numbered from east to west. Only the Bloomingdale Road, a rambling route that later took the name of Broadway as it led above 14th Street, was allowed to deviate from the rigid grid, cutting across avenues and thus forming a series of open spaces like the future Times Square. No circles or diagonals were permitted, said the commissioners, as "a city is to be composed principally of the habitations of men, and . . . straight sided, and right angled houses are the most cheap to build, and the most convenient to live in."[13] No parks were allowed along the rivers: the waterfront was too valuable and was reserved for commerce. Furthermore, the number of avenues was skimped in favor of cross streets, which were seen as playing a critical role in facilitating the transfer of goods to and from the docks. A major flaw in the plan, the paucity of avenues, was to cause much tooth-gnashing congestion once the horse and cart was replaced by the automobile and the importance of the piers declined.

Inevitably, the gridiron plan also brought the unfortunate leveling of Manhattan. There was little room for unusual features in the grid: hills were inconvenient and had to go. After some debate, for example, a popular eminence called Bunker Hill, east of Broadway on what is now Grand Street, which had been a favorite picnic ground and was for a while proposed as an ideal site for an observatory, was simply carted away—there is no sign of it today. Rocky outcroppings throughout Manhattan were blasted away and depressions filled in, and the shoreline was straightened out as needed. Only in Central Park—an area saved at the last moment in the mid-nineteenth century—and at the northern tip of Manhattan can the island's original appearance be glimpsed. The gridiron did, however, produce one special benefit: it enabled the city dweller to see open sky, or open land, at a distance at all times; for with few exceptions the streets led the eye straight to the edge of town, a pleasing antidote to claustrophobia.

The confidence brought on by the boom of the 1790s suffered a jarring blow after 1807 as American commerce began to feel the effects of hostilities in Europe. Earlier, the war had benefited New York; but in its latest phase both England and France were enforcing blockades, and American ships were subject to seizure by both sides. In one local incident, an American ship was fired on by a British warship just a mile or two off Sandy Hook and the helmsman was decapitated; New Yorkers cried out for revenge. Meanwhile, British sailors were jumping ship to sign on to American craft, which paid higher wages, and this gave Britain additional cause to apprehend American vessels. Fearful that war was imminent, Jefferson in 1807 asked Congress to pass the Embargo Act, which shut down all international trade to and from American ports. A handful of vessels sneaked out of New York harbor to beat the deadline, but thereafter shipping came to a halt. Business slumped, unemployment rose, and grass began to grow on the wharves. New Yorkers took to calling the crisis "O Grab Me"—embargo spelled backward.

On the basis of some artful deception, one New York ship was given permission to leave during the shutdown. Her departure was announced in the *Commercial Advertiser* in a single line: "Yesterday the ship *Beaver*, Captain Galloway, sailed for China."[14] Seeing the notice, New York shippers were incensed, for it was common knowledge that the *Beaver* belonged to none other than John Jacob Astor. They demanded that federal authorities explain this display of rank favoritism. The reply: special permission had been given by President

Jefferson so that the *Beaver* could transport back to China a venerable merchant named Punqua Wingchong, whose grandfather had just died. The merchants scoffed, claiming there was no such person. Oh, yes, said the authorities, we saw him in the *Beaver*'s cabin, dressed in his silken coat and drinking tea. An imposter, cried the merchants. "The great Chinese personage was no mandarin," one of them wrote Jefferson, "not even a Hong Kong merchant, but a common Chinese dock loafer, smuggled out from China, who had departed from that country contrary to its laws, and would be saved from death on his return only by his obscure condition."[15]

It seemed that this "personage" had asked New York's Senator Samuel Mitchill to petition the president in his behalf; Mitchill believed his story, and so did Jefferson. The president then directed the secretary of the treasury, Albert Gallatin, to issue the necessary permits. When Gallatin learned that Wingchong would like to sail on the *Beaver*, he had misgivings, for although he was a good friend of Astor he wondered what was going on. However, an order from the president could not be ignored, and Gallatin complied. When Jefferson learned he'd been had, he was embarrassed but ignored the protests—anyway, the *Beaver* was by now out of reach. When she reached China she found its waters bereft of American ships, and when she got back to New York in 1809 the market for Chinese tea was sharply up. On this one voyage alone John Jacob Astor, who had hoodwinked New York's port collector, the secretary of the treasury, and the president of the United States, made a profit of $200,000.

By that time Congress had rescinded the embargo, and for a time prosperity returned to New York. The population in 1810 was counted at 96,373, surpassing that of Philadelphia and making New York for the first time the nation's biggest city. But the good times were short-lived as relations with England continued to deteriorate, and on June 18, 1812, the United States declared war against Great Britain.

Fearing a repeat performance of the 1776 debacle, New York looked to its defenses. In preceding years several large forts had been constructed at strategic spots around the harbor; one of them was Castle Clinton (named for the mayor) just off the Battery, which despite some changes of identity—it would later be used as a music hall and an aquarium—is still there. Other strongpoints were added now on Brooklyn Heights and at Hell Gate. Swift vessels sailed forth as privateers to prey on British shipping around the globe. In retaliation, the British in 1813 clamped a blockade on the harbor, and once again all sea trade came to a halt. In August 1814, after news arrived that the British had burned the city of Washington, New Yorkers began digging trenches in the streets. A huge naval steamship designed by Robert Fulton, the *Demologos*, was launched as a floating fort to guard the city. But the expected invasion did not occur. On February 11, 1815, a vessel arrived with tidings of the Treaty of Ghent ending the war. New Yorkers celebrated with a lavish succession of balls, dinners, and illuminations. Now perhaps the city could really begin to flex its muscles.

Quite soon, indeed, construction would begin on a project that would make New York's muscle flexing especially impressive, and it would be spearheaded by the man who had already done so much for the city, De Witt Clinton. It was the Erie Canal. Although New York had already achieved its number one ranking, the canal would put it far ahead of its rivals, providing it with a virtually unbeatable advantage before railroads made other cities similarly accessible to the West. It would also start New York on its road to becoming a true metropolis, assure its position as the country's biggest port, and confirm it as the gateway for large-scale European immigration. It would, in short, bring greatness to the city.

Clinton did not think up the canal; the idea had been around for a long time. Back in 1724 Cadwallader Colden, the scientist-turned-public servant who would later suffer ignominy during the Stamp Act crisis, had urged that a route be opened up between upper New York and the Mississippi Valley; in 1784 an Irish-born mathematician named Christopher Colles proposed a canal linking Albany with Lake Ontario. Nothing came of these proposals; the idea seemed too farfetched. In 1807 a flour merchant from Geneva, New York, named Jesse Hawley argued for a canal that would bypass Lake Ontario and lead all the way to Buffalo on Lake Erie. This route, he claimed, would be practicable and also far superior to the Lake Ontario route, which was dangerously exposed to potential disruption from unfriendly forces in Canada. His essays were regarded as the emanations of a lunatic. Someone around this time approached President Jefferson with a similar scheme, suggesting that federal help might be appropriate. Nothing doing, said the president; he pointed out that George Washington had proposed a canal stretching only a few dozen miles along the Potomac, but Congress had never come up with the money to complete it. "And you talk of making a canal three hundred and fifty miles through the wilderness! It is little short of madness to think of it at this day."[16]

But Clinton had read Hawley's essays and was sold. Not only could the canal be built, it had to be. The interior of the country was rapidly being settled, but the produce raised by the new homesteaders was going down the St. Lawrence to Montreal, down the Delaware to Philadelphia, or down the Mississippi to New Orleans. Shipping by any of these routes, though expensive, was cheaper than shipping overland via wagon roads to the Hudson, a slow and dangerous process. A canal from Lake Erie would be the most efficient and cheapest route of all. It would be a boon to all the towns along the route, like Rochester and Utica, and it would open up the West to New York City.

In 1810 Clinton, who happened to be between mayoral terms, was visited by two Federalist party leaders who asked if he would take over leadership of the drive to build the canal. He said he'd be glad to, and from then on he and the canal project were inseparable. The state legislature appointed a commission to study the project and he dominated it. The canal could be built, the commissioners said, for $5 million, and should follow the Lake Erie route. Clinton and another commissioner went to Washington to ask for federal aid. Unfortunately the Madison administration was preoccupied with the prospect of war and said no. Then war did come and the canal project was shelved. Clinton went back to being mayor (and ran unsuccessfully for president against Madison in 1812).

With the war over, Clinton renewed the drive. He was no longer mayor and could devote full time to it. The legislature now balked. Clinton noted that opposition was coming mainly from New York City, whose merchants were unconvinced. He convened a great meeting of the merchants in the City Hotel, appealed to their self-interest by describing the benefits they would derive from the canal, and won them over. Copies of his speech were distributed throughout the state; mass meetings were held and a petition in favor of the canal received more than 100,000 signatures. Clinton also worked out the finances: the project would be funded by a tax on salt produced within the state and by state bonds to be paid off by canal revenues. His eloquence not only produced a final endorsement from the legislature but also catapulted him into the governorship. On July 4, 1817, just three days after taking the oath of office as governor, he turned the first shovelful of earth at Rome, New York, and construction got under way.

The canal took eight years to complete; and especially during the first few years, before any section had opened, many people began to feel it was all a mistake. Jingles ridiculed the project: "Clinton, the federal son of a bitch / taxes our dollars to build him a ditch."[17] But Clinton was undismayed, and the extraordinary engineering marvel gradually took shape.

On October 26, 1825, it was declared done. The total cost: not quite $8 million, still a bargain. At 10 A.M. the canal boat *Seneca Chief* entered the waterway at Buffalo with Clinton (who was still governor) and other officials aboard and headed east. Nearby at the same moment a cannon was fired, the sound of it serving as a signal to another cannon down the canal to fire, and so on for 500 miles all the way to New York City, which thereby got the news eighty-one minutes later. Nine days later the *Seneca Chief* arrived in New York harbor, towed down the Hudson by the steamer *Chancellor Livingston*. A flotilla of forty-one boats escorted the craft down through the Narrows and Lower Bay and out to sea, where Clinton emptied a keg of Lake Erie water into the Atlantic.

It was "the longest Canal in the world, built in the shortest time, with the least experience, for the least money, and to the greatest public benefit."[18] Before it was built, moving a ton of freight from Buffalo to New York had taken three weeks and had cost $120. Now it took only eight days and cost just $6. The heartland of America was open to New York.

5

The Heyday
of the Merchants

It was snowing hard on the morning of January 5, 1818, as the 424-ton square-rigger *James Monroe* made ready to sail from Pier 23 on the East River. Few other ships had ventured forth that bleak morning, and it seemed an unlikely moment for a vessel to start a long voyage across the boisterous, wintry Atlantic to Liverpool. The three-masted vessel was not even fully loaded: only eight passengers had signed on (there were accomodations for 28), and her cargo of 71 cotton bales, 860 barrels of flour, 200 barrels of apples and other assorted items was well below capacity. A small crowd had gathered on the South Street dock to see whether she really would depart as advertised, and there were plenty of skeptics. After all, common sense and maritime tradition held that a trading vessel would not sail until fully loaded and certainly not under such unfavorable conditions—better to stay snugly in port. Yet promptly at 10 A.M., as the bells of St. Paul's Chapel sounded through the snow, Captain James Watkinson gave the order to cast off, the sails were trimmed, and the *James Monroe* slid out into the murky river, right on schedule. By four in the afternoon she had cleared Sandy Hook and was headed east toward Liverpool, and into history.

The prompt departure was critical to her owners, for the service she was inaugurating was unprecedented. The *James Monroe* was one of four vessels of the recently formed Black Ball Line, owned and operated by a consortium of Quakers engaged in importing

British goods. Known as packets, the blunt-bowed, trim ships were readily identifiable by the large round black insigne on their fore-topsails. They were to sail on a rigidly set schedule, regardless of conditions and loads throughout the year. The daring concept, never attempted before, was the brainchild of one of the partners, the English-born New York merchant Jeremiah Thompson, an importer of British woolens as well as an exporter of raw cotton from the southern states. Thompson reasoned that even though many of the vessels might initially carry only a fraction of their freight-earning capacity, their punctuality would persuade increasing numbers of travelers and merchants to use them, and they would end up capturing the most lucrative and desirable cargoes from the "regular traders" whose sailing times could not be relied on.

And he was right. After a couple of money-losing years the Black Ball packets caught on and were soon drawing the quality freight and most demanding passengers on the North Atlantic run. New York was getting the top-of-the-line traffic. By 1822 the Black Ballers had competition from other New York shipping firms, to which the owners responded by adding more vessels and expanding the service. Outdistancing its competitors, the line flourished for sixty years, and to it can be credited the principle of scheduled ocean transit that has long since been considered standard throughout the world. More important for New York, the Black Ball liners set the tone of bold, innovative mercantile leadership that would bring tremendous new wealth to the city and carry it to new heights of power during the first half of the nineteenth century, putting it so far ahead of its rivals that they would never catch up. By 1860, for example, New York was handling more than three times as much tonnage as its nearest American competitor.

For Robert Greenhalgh Albion, whose definitive *The Rise of New York Port* is a classic, it was the packet service rather than the Erie Canal (whose opening did not occur until 1825, seven years hence) that clinched New York's leadership and made it the entrepôt, or commercial emporium, to which all other American ports would be secondary.

"It was by developing the entrepôt function," Albion wrote in another work, "that Amsterdam and London had grown powerful. They were not primarily interested in creating new wares; they gathered together from all directions the products of others, distributed them to those that wanted them, and grew rich from the accumulations of profits, commissions, freight money, insurance premiums, interest and the other forms of collecting toll on the volume of trade which passed through their hands. The accumulated wealth derived from this business gradually made them the principal sources of surplus capital and the centers of financial power. New York was to follow them in that lucrative role, thanks to its timely efforts in attracting trade."[1] And it was a few dozen potent merchant firms clustered along and around the South Street docks that led the way to the top. Their hard-nosed, aggressive moves brought the United States to its zenith as a maritime power and helped give the city an economic dominance it retains to this day.

Their leadership, moreover, produced a side effect that is often overlooked. The rapidly expanding commerce gave rise to extensive manufacturing in the city as entrepreneurs began increasingly to produce goods for sale not only in New York itself but also in all those communities to which it was so fortuitously connected. Most of the entrepreneurs operated on a small scale, at least at first, but their production grew so rambunctiously that by 1860 New York was America's leading manufacturing city, a primacy it was to enjoy for many decades.

As it happened, a fluke in 1815, three years before the Black Ball packets were introduced, had helped establish the city's new central role. The War of 1812 was just over. During it, the British had accumulated huge surpluses of manufactured goods, which they were unable to export under wartime conditions. They now proceeded to dump them on the American market, partly to cut their losses but also to snuff out the new American industries that had grown up during the hostilities. "It is worth while," intoned a member of Parliament, "to incur a loss upon the first exportations in order, by a glut, to stifle in the cradle those rising manufactures in the United States which the war has forced into existence contrary to the natural course of things."[2] The port they chose to receive the avalanche was New York. While the blow staggered it (and did cause many new businesses to fail), the city paradoxically benefited as buyers flocking to snap up bargains began to rely on New York—if they were not already doing so—as the nation's key marketplace. They would come back later, rather than to Boston or Philadelphia, for repeated orders. As the nation's market center, furthermore, New York came to be known for its access to British capital, and this helped solidify its position as the nation's financial center.

The city's merchants responded to Britain's dumping by putting into effect an effective auction system that enhanced the efficient handling of goods. Many imports went for trifling sums, but the New York customhouse earned almost $4 million in duties. Then the city proceeded to consolidate its advantage. By 1817 there were signs that the market might be glutted and the British might divert their trade to other ports like Boston or Philadelphia—whereupon the city got permission from New York State to reduce its customs duties radically. As a result British textiles and other items continued to pour into the port. During this entire process, of course, the auctioneers profited hugely; one of their number, Philip Hone, amassed such a fortune that he was able to retire from business in 1820, at the age of forty, and devote himself to good works. He subsequently served as mayor and is remembered for a wonderfully detailed diary that chronicled city events during the 1830s and 1840s.

The Black Ball packets had established New York as the prime port for serving both demanding shippers and well-to-do ocean passengers; the city's response to Britain's dumping had strengthened its position as the prime import center. The culminating move made by the South Street merchants to draw trade to their counting-houses—one that was similarly in place well before completion of the Erie Canal—was an outrageous device that came to be known as the cotton triangle. What the merchants did, in effect, was to divert the South's cotton production so that it would be transshipped through New York on its way to England—and to charge for this seemingly unnecessary detour.

Thanks to the invention of the cotton gin, cotton had become a boom crop in the South by the early nineteenth century. Southern planters, however, were for the most part too engrossed in producing their crops or too unschooled in business techniques to handle distribution. Mostly, they did not want to be bothered. Agents representing New York shipping firms were only too happy to help them out—for a fee. Circulating quietly through the southern states, they offered to arrange loans (planters were always strapped for cash and frequently in debt), take care of insurance, and handle all of the other disagreeable details involved in getting the cotton bales to market in England or France. Some of the cotton would be shipped direct to Europe from Charleston, Savannah, Mobile, or New Orleans (in New York bottoms, of course), but most of it went via coastal packets to New York, where it was painstakingly unloaded onto the docks (for a fee) and reloaded onto Black Ball and other liners for the transatlantic trip.

This scheme not only earned the New York merchants handsome

a one-room countinghouse. Henry, the older, "stood up at a little pine desk, not even painted, in the back part of the store; John worked at a table nearby. Once Henry went down to the dock to oversee the unloading of a cargo of coffee, noticed that coffee was coming out of small holes in some of the bags, and carefully picked up all the scattered grains and put them back in the bag, and ordered a man to sew up the holes."[4] The silk jobber Arthur Tappan believed that visitors to his countinghouse should be discouraged from hanging around, and so he was careful to provide no chair for them. He would "rise and receive [the caller] with much economy of speech, and as no seat was at hand, the person, whoever he was, soon took his departure from the taciturn and busy merchant."[5]

Considering their constantly expanding business, it is surprising how unvarying was their typical daily routine. For the merchant Schuyler Livingston, said Scoville, every day was much the same: "To rise early in the morning, to get breakfast, to go down town to the counting house of the firm, to open and read letters—to go out and do some business, either at the Custom House, bank or elsewhere, until twelve, then to take lunch and a glass of wine at Delmonico's; or a few raw oysters at Downing's; to sign checks and attend to the finances until half past one, to go on change; to return to the counting house, and remain until time to go to dinner, and in the old time, when such things as 'packet nights' existed, to stay down town until ten or eleven at night, and then go home and go to bed,—this for forty-three years had been the twenty-four hour cycle for Mr. Livingston, as it is for thousands."[6] (To "go on change" was to drop in at the Merchants' Exchange on Wall Street to catch up on the latest news or gossip and possibly transact some business.) As late as the 1860s the eighty-two-year-old dry goods merchant John Robbins, who was probably worth well over $1 million, still lived an austere life. "Every morning, as early as the light, he is in his store," recounted Scoville. "He opens it, sweeps it out, and makes the fire ... Mr. Robbins has never been a slave to luxuries, or felt their necessity. He never had a fire in his sleeping compartment, and he never had a wash-stand there."[7]

The Coster brothers were so unyielding in their ways that even in the 1830s and 1840s they continued to wear the traditional merchant costume of knee breeches, white stockings, and old-fashioned shoes with buckles. They were not the last of that breed. As late as 1860 a fishmarket merchant on Coenties Slip, Oliver Cobb (who was then in his eighties and is the great-great-great-grandfather of this writer), still wore not only knee breeches but also a powdered wig with a queue. When he strode down the street he was followed by a crowd of children delightedly calling attention to his garb.

But any merchant expecting to get ahead in a competitive world had to be alert to the most recent news and the latest ways. Ocean-going ships were the sole source of news from Europe, which could have a marked effect on New York prices, and so their arrival was an event. Many merchants arose at dawn and strolled down to the Battery to see if any of their ships had appeared in the Narrows; they were known as "peep o'day boys." Other shipowners might send a small boat out to intercept the incoming liner as it arrived off Long Island so as to get advance word of market conditions in Liverpool or London. The news would be relayed by swift horsemen to the home office on South Street. Then, while the ship pointedly dawdled off Sandy Hook, the owner could act on his exclusive tip and get the jump on his competitors in town. He would also be ahead of competing merchants in Boston or Philadelphia, where ships from Europe arrived far less frequently.

The ranks of the merchants, moreover, were constantly swelling, as enterprising newcomers kept arriving to take advantage of New York's manifest opportunities. The city had always been a melting pot, even in the merchant world. John Jacob Astor had come from Germany, Archibald Gracie was of Scottish descent, Jeremiah Thompson was a Yorkshireman, and Philip Hone was of German and French descent. Western Europeans continued to enter the business arena throughout this period; a key newcomer was a German Jewish financial wizard named August Schönberg who arrived in 1837 as a representative of the Rothschild banking interests, changed his name to August Belmont, and proceeded to make a fortune. He and another immigrant, Joseph Seligman, were the first of a wave of German Jewish bankers who would become prominent fixtures of the New York financial scene. But the mightiest influx of business talent during the early 1800s was not from abroad but from New York's neighboring states to the northeast, in New England.

The New Englanders came partly because the talent market in Boston was glutted, but more because New York offered far greater scope for their skills than they could find at home. "The tales of ships and skippers," writes Albion, "leave the impression that New England enjoyed a virtual monopoly of America's seagoing enterprise. The arid tables of imports and exports, however, show that the center of commercial activity lay not in New England but thirty miles beyond its frontiers in New York City. By the eve of the Civil War, the foreign commerce of New York was nearly six times that of all New England. The answer to this apparent conflict between tradition and statistics is that the New Englanders captured New York port about 1820 and dominated its business until after the Civil War."[8]

One early transplant was Anson Greene Phelps, who had operated a general store in Hartford, Connecticut. He began buying and selling cotton and then branched into shipping. Presently he was importing metals, and in 1815 he moved to New York, where he opened a commission warehouse in Burling Slip. Three of his daughters married well, and Phelps took in his three sons-in-law—William Earl Dodge, James Stokes, and Daniel James—as partners. Eventually Phelps, Dodge & Company became one of the premier metals companies in the United States, and it is still flourishing. Anson Phelps was a devout churchgoer, and he and his extended family and descendants gave large sums to all manner of charitable causes like the YMCA; the Dodges were instrumental in founding what is now the American University of Beirut. Ansonia, Connecticut, is named for Phelps, who established a plant there, and one renegade descendant built a grandiose luxury apartment house on the Upper West Side that he thoughtfully named the Ansonia. Today the ebullient structure is a designated landmark.

From Old Lyme, Connecticut, came George Griswold and his older brother Nathaniel, who under the company name N. L. & G. Griswold shipped flour to the West Indies while bringing back sugar and rum. Business proving good, they extended their trading to South America and then to China, importing tea sold throughout the United States with such success that their company initials were said to stand for "No Loss and Great Gain." The Griswolds were stern taskmasters. When a captain in their employ balked at sailing at the designated hour because snow was falling and there was no wind, his request was denied. "Go and find wind," he was told.[9]

An even larger fleet of vessels was operated by Grinnell, Minturn & Company, whose founders had come from New Bedford, Massachusetts, and included a former whaling captain with the odd but actual name of Preserved Fish. Dealing at first in whale oil, the company responded to the success of the Black Ball Line by founding the competing Swallowtail Line, and in due course they owned more than fifty ships including the celebrated clipper ship *Flying Cloud*. Like other New Englanders the Grinnells gave special attention to employing young errand boys and clerks from back home, finding them far more diligent and willing than New York boys. As Scoville imagines a scene in their counting room, "Moses H. Grinnell comes down in the morning and says to John, a New York boy—'Charley [sic], take my overcoat up to my house on Fifth Avenue.' Mr. Charley takes the coat, mutters something about 'I'm not an errand boy, I came here to learn business,' and moves reluctantly. Mr. Grinnell sees it, and at the same time, one of his New England clerks says, 'I'll take it up.' 'That is right. Do so,' says Mr. G., and to himself he says 'that boy is smart, will work,' and gives him plenty to do. He gets promoted—gets the confidence of the chief clerk and employers, and eventually gets into the firm as a partner."[10]

The New England newcomers (who also counted among their later number J. Pierpont Morgan, who would dominate New York finance toward the end of the century) decided at an early date to stick together; and in 1805 they founded the New England Society, whose members met regularly to "promote friendship, charity and mutual association." Toasts at their annual dinners were raised to "the rich and precious cargo of the *Mayflower*—Yankee capital—the real wealth of nations." Understandably, locally born New Yorkers did not applaud such sentiments. One of them, the writer Washington Irving, organized his friends to found the rival St. Nicholas Society in 1835, made up of steadfast Knickerbockers. At their annual dinners, Albion reports, they adopted the custom of "turning the head of the society's gilded rooster to the eastward so that it might crow back at the Yankees."[11]

Whether sparked by New Englanders or Knickerbockers, New York's maritime burgeoning had a significant spin-off: a flourishing shipbuilding industry. The port had always had shipbuilders, notably the firm founded by William Walton in the eighteenth century, but locally built ships had not been outstanding; now they were. Although again the popular impression is that the great sailing ships of this period were built mostly in New England, in point of fact New York yards turned out as many craft as those of any other port. Most important, those built in the extensive yards located along the shores of the East River were generally acknowledged to be the finest and best constructed of all.

Indeed, New York's vessels were more expensive than those built elsewhere, as labor tended to be higher and materials had to come from afar (tall "sticks" for masts from Maine and extrafine live oak for key sections of the hull from Georgia or Florida). But the city's potent commercial leaders were demanding the best ships, and they

114

were glad to pay a premium for the privilege of inspecting the work at every stage. So the waterfront from just above the present-day Williamsburg Bridge all the way around Corlear's Hook (the easternmost bulge of Manhattan Island) and up to about East 13th Street rang with the banging of hammers and the whining of saws, while all around the yards were ranged the sailmakers, riggers, blacksmiths, ship chandlers, painters, block makers, small-boat makers, and such specialists as carvers of figureheads and fine woodwork. New York had the nation's first dry dock—eliminating the need to "careen" or tip over a vessel to clean or repair her hull—and, for the steamboats that were appearing on American rivers and bays, the first ironworks for constructing steam engines.

Three yards provided the nucleus. One was founded by Henry Eckford, a Scot who came to New York via Quebec in 1796 and, among other craft, built John Jacob Astor's celebrated *Beaver*, the ship that eluded the 1807 embargo. Eckford later turned out warships, helping to build the vessels that won control of the Great Lakes in the War of 1812, and in 1817 he took over direction of the just completed Brooklyn Navy Yard, across the East River from his own yard. He died in 1832 while organizing a navy yard for Turkey's sultan (and was returned to New York preserved in a cask of wine). His successor, Isaac Webb, maintained the high reputation of the original shipyard and among other young apprentices trained the brilliant Nova Scotian Donald McKay, who was to win fame as a clipper ship producer in East Boston. Webb produced more tonnage than any American shipbuilder up to his time.

A second great shipyard was that of Christian Bergh, a formidable six-foot, four-inch descendant of Palatine Germans who had come to the Hudson River Valley in 1710. Bergh specialized in smaller craft—schooners and brigs that excelled as privateers—and in swift merchantmen, and his eye was unusually exacting. One day while working in his office he happened to glance out and saw some of his men 150 feet away shaping a timber. Something about it seemed not right to him, and he called out that it was out of line by three-quarters of an inch. The workers at first thought he was joking but finally appealed to two of Bergh's partners who were standing nearby. The timber was measured, and Bergh was proved right.

The third pioneering yard was that of Adam and Noah Brown, who had grown up on the New York upstate frontier and learned the shipbuilding trade in New York City in the first decade of the nineteenth century. The Browns built the pioneering Black Baller

James Monroe and many other of the trim packets, and their firm (renamed Brown and Bell in the 1820s) had the honor of launching the first clipper ship, the *Houqua*, in 1844. In the ensuing decade, which is known as the clipper ship era, New York yards produced many of the most notable of these lovely sleek vessels.

The notion that a large merchant sailing ship might be designed with speed alone as a consideration was hatched by one of New York's most outstanding mariners, Captain Nathaniel B. Palmer. Like many another autocrat of the quarterdeck at this time, he was a product of the small port of Stonington, Connecticut. The idea occured to him in 1843 while he was returning from China in command of a vessel owned by one of the city's top merchant firms, A. A. Low & Brothers. As a result of the Opium War four new treaty ports in China had been opened to foreign commerce. Palmer felt that a ship that sacrificed cargo space to achieve great speed would pay for itself handily, and he whittled a model that he showed to one of his passengers, William Low of the Low company. Back in New York, William passed the scheme along to his brother Abiel; the result was the *Houqua*, named for a prominent Chinese merchant. As the *New York Herald* rhapsodized following her launching in 1844, "One of the prettiest and most rakish-looking packet ships ever built in the civilized world is now to be seen at the foot of Jones Lane on the East River . . . She is about six hundred tons in size—as sharp as a cutter—as symmetrical as a yacht—as rakish in her rig as a pirate —and as neat in her deck and cabin arrangements as a lady's boudoir."[12] On her maiden voyage, with Palmer in command, she reached Canton in the very fast time of eighty-four days.

A spate of China clippers followed. The first "extreme clipper" was the *Rainbow*, designed by the naval architect John Willis Griffiths for the South Street commission merchants Howland and Aspinwall. Her revolutionary bow had a concave profile instead of the conventional bluff-bowed configuration, and her masts were unusually tall, a prized feature to captains who liked to pile on extra sail for bursts of speed. She was a money-maker: on one voyage she earned a 200 percent return. Shortly after this ship, also for Howland and Aspinwall, Griffiths designed the *Sea Witch* to be commanded by Captain Robert H. Waterman, one of the most notorious "drivers" of his day. At the height of the monsoon season in 1846 Waterman brought the *Sea Witch* back from Canton in eighty-one days, a record.

With so many clippers already commissioned, the South Street merchants were well situated to take advantage of the California gold rush of 1849. Heretofore ships had run out eastward to China and back again by way of South Africa's Cape of Good Hope; now vessels like the *Houqua* beat their way to San Francisco by way of Cape Horn in South America, carrying provisions so desperately needed in the gold country. Bearing the specie earned by these provisions, they would then run across the Pacific to Canton, pick up tea, and head for home via the Cape of Good Hope, circumnavigating the globe. It was a heady time, and New York shipyards were hard put to keep up with the demand. Indeed they really could not, since their raw materials had to come from so far away. Maine shipyards, close to the forests, pulled ahead, as did the Boston yards under the guidance of Donald McKay. Nevertheless, more clippers cleared New York harbor for the run around the horn than departed from any other port, and this was especially true of the fastest and best equipped of them. The financial returns were so splendid that New York's banks were hard pressed to contain them, and between 1851 and 1853 twenty-seven new banks were created, more than doubling the number that had existed in the 1840s.

Interestingly enough, the greatest clipper of them all, the *Flying Cloud*, though built in East Boston by McKay, was sold by her intended owner (a Boston packet operator) to Grinnell, Minturn in New York and thus became yet another spectacular caller at the South Street piers. On her maiden voyage in 1851 the 1,782-ton ship sped out to San Francisco in 89 days and 21 hours and, on one day alone, logged a total of 374 miles, the fastest run ever made by a sailing ship up to that time. Three years later the clipper beat her own record from New York to California by 13 hours, to set a mark never surpassed.

Not all swift New York sailing ships, to be sure, were commercial carriers. The East River yards turned out many a superb pleasure boat. In 1850 the newly formed New York Yacht Club received an invitation from England's Royal Yacht Squadron to enter a boat in a forthcoming race to be held off the English coast, and they ordered up a rakishly designed schooner that they christened the *America*. New York's entry proceeded to drub the opposition, and she sailed home in triumph with the cup that has ever since carried her name.

Sadly, the dazzling clipper era ended almost as quickly as it had begun. By 1854 there were simply too many clippers, and their speed no longer made up for their lack of cargo space. Besides, the Cape Horn route was being bypassed by steamers that took passengers and freight to the Isthmus of Panama, where they could be brought overland to the Pacific and sped by other steamers to San Francisco. But the New York shipyards adapted, at least for a time. They had long since constructed steam vessels alongside sailers, and now steam began to take over. On a single day in 1851, for example, Isaac Webb launched no fewer than three ships: a packet for the run to Le Havre, a clipper ship, and a sidewheel steamer destined for the isthmus trade. New Yorkers were nothing if not versatile.

And shipping was directly responsible for most of the city's new manufacturing enterprises. Shipbuilding itself had been a major factor in New York's economy ever since the early eighteenth century, and during the South Street era another great undertaking rose up beside it, the clothing industry. The making of ready-to-wear garments started with providing clothing for sailors—crudely stitched, cheap items that could be turned out during the winter when tailors were not busy fashioning custom garments for well-to-do patrons. In the 1820s, with so much cloth being imported and with the cotton triangle in full swing, New York carried on a brisk trade supplying clothing for slaves on southern plantations. With the completion of the Erie Canal the city's clothiers were able to sell dungarees, flannel drawers, and the like throughout upstate New York and the Midwest; California's gold rush gave further impetus to this activity. Most of the garment making took place in small shops or in the lodgings of seamstresses, most of whom were newly arrived immigrants. The respectable firm of Brooks Brothers, founded in 1818 in lower Manhattan, employed only seventy workers directly but kept between 2,000 and 3,000 people stitching for it on the outside. Another offshoot of the shipping business was provisioning, so that by midcentury New York had become a key meat-packing center. And because of the port's links with the West Indies that dated back to the previous century, New York was the nation's principal sugar refiner.

As the city grew, it saw the development of a great many small-scale industries that took advantage of the availability of both skilled and unskilled labor, with many workers fresh off the boat from Europe. Skilled artisans made carriages and furniture, while others less skilled turned out such routine items as soap, cigars, and hats. As a communications center the city supported many printing concerns, each one employing engravers, bookbinders, and a host of other specialists. Musical instruments, especially pianos, were turned out in quantity, one of the most prominent makers being Henry Steinway, who arrived from Germany in 1850, along with many other educated Germans in the aftermath of a failed revolutionary uprising.

During these decades the city continued to attract innovators like Steinway who would leave their mark on the local—and often the national—scene. From Baltimore came the sons of the Scottish-born Alexander Brown, who had founded a flourishing linen-import business in that city in 1800. Desiring to expand, the firm opened branches in Philadelphia and then (1825) in New York, but the New York office was soon outstripping the others in volume and was moving into merchant banking. Its head, Alexander's son James, finally sold off the dry goods part of the business entirely, and Brown Brothers & Company began operating solely as a private bank serving the booming merchant community. It became a Wall Street fixture and thrived as the local and national economy expanded. In 1930, it merged with W. A. Harriman & Company, Inc., and as Brown Brothers, Harriman & Company remains one of the world's most prestigious private banks.

Less enduring but noteworthy as the first of a colorful breed was Jacob Little, a tall, slender, slightly stooped man whose pictures make him look as if he could be played by Gregory Peck on a gloomy day. He was Wall Street's first true speculator and the bane of more conservative operators, who kept trying to oust him from the market. Little's favorite technique was the short sale, which benefits from a falling market. The purchaser contracts to sell stock (which he does not own) at a certain price but to deliver it at a later date; after its price goes down he proceeds actually to buy it at the lower figure, delivering it and collecting the amount he had contracted for—which provides him with a handsome profit. Little's first big chance to make a killing came during the panic of 1837, a severe downturn that forced great numbers of New York firms, including many organizations along South Street, into bankruptcy ("The prospects in Wall Street are getting worse and worse," wrote Philip Hone at the time).[13] Somewhat new on the investment scene were railroad securities, and Little decided to sell large blocks of Erie Railroad stock on sellers' options that would mature six or twelve months later.

Many of his fellow brokers had already become aware of Little's unorthodox methods, and they banded together to try to corner him, buying up all available Erie stock so that he could not find shares to deliver. Unbeknownst to them, however, he had secretly purchased on the London market a number of convertible bonds that were exchangeable for common stock. On the appropriate day he made the swap and delivered the securities to his surprised (and humbled) foes. Operaters like Daniel Drew and Jay Gould would later become famous for utilizing on a much larger scale techniques that Little pioneered—and by trading in Erie stock, at that. (Ironically, twenty years later Little found himself unable to cover a short-sale position in Erie stock, and his resulting losses forced him finally from the field.)

Operating in a totally different field, but one that likewise was to become a feature of New York City, was the Irish-born Alexander Turney Stewart, America's first department store magnate. He had come to New York in 1821 and, after working for a year or two as a teacher, opened a small store near City Hall where he specialized in Irish lace. Business proved uncommonly good, and in 1846 he built a retail palace on Broadway just above City Hall Park that forever changed purchasing habits. It was America's first department store and, covering a good portion of a whole block, one of the biggest retail establishments in the world. Up to this time women had bought ready-made clothing and household objects at specialty stores up and down Broadway; now they could take care of most of their shopping needs under one roof. The store was built of white marble in the newly fashionable Italianate style, and Stewart's clerks cultivated a quiet, refined manner that pleased his customers. "There is nothing in Paris or London," remarked Philip Hone, "to compare with this dry goods palace."[14] So confident was Stewart of his store's pulling power that he deliberately left his name off it—after all, everyone knew it was his. His policies paid off, and A. T. Stewart became one of the richest men in the United States.

Not quite so dazzling as yet, but destined for later fame, was Captain Rowland H. Macy, a member of a prominent whaling family of Nantucket, Massachusetts, who had spent years at sea and then operated a succession of small dry goods stores in and around Boston and in California, most of which failed. In 1858 this stocky, bearded New Englander opened a tiny store with an eleven-foot front on Sixth Avenue and 14th Street. His prices were rock-bottom and he kept adding new and unorthodox items like books and toys to his inventory, and soon he had expanded into nearby properties. In the 1890s, after his death, the store was bought and further enlarged by the Straus family and soon moved to Herald Square, where it is still thriving, a household word.

Yet another New Englander who staked out a special place in New

York's changing economic scene was Edward Knight Collins, a Cape Codder who had come to join his father in the shipping business and had operated packets first to Mexico and then to Liverpool. He became the city's main contender in the race to establish transatlantic steamship service. The achievement was long in coming. Despite South Street's tremendous expertise in and success with sailing ships, and although the first successful steamer had been developed in New York by Robert Fulton, the conversion to steam for ocean travel was fraught with difficulties and with doubt. There were steamers on sheltered bays and on rivers like the Hudson, but nothing on the all-important route to Europe. New York merchants in 1818 had turned down the chance to back a proposed transatlantic steamer, and so the ship was financed in Savannah, Georgia, and named for that city; but the *Savannah* was really a sailing ship with standby steam power, and when she failed to attract passengers her engines were removed and shortly thereafter she was wrecked. In 1835 Captain Nathan Cobb, a part owner of the Black Ball Line (and a cousin of this author's quaint forebear), raised money for a steamship line and began building a vessel that would be commanded by Cobb himself, "to whose energy and perseverance," a newspaper reported, "will the publick be indebted for the first steamboat to run between this port and Europe."[15] But the panic of 1837 erased his venture. For several years thereafter no plans were made in any American port for ocean service. With money being coined by sailing ships, why gamble on something so risky and marginal?

The British, however, were soon ready with a viable steamer, and in 1838 the 1,340-ton *Great Western*, built by a British rail company, arrived in New York to begin regularly scheduled service. Other English steamships presently joined her. Then in July 1840 Samuel Cunard, a Nova Scotian of American descent (his Loyalist father had fled Philadelphia after the Revolution), established regular steamship service between Liverpool and Boston. Cunard's venture was more promising than the others because he had obtained a substantial mail subsidy from the British government; he had chosen Boston as his western terminus because of business connections there. His four vessels were well built, and their captains were instructed to stress safety over speed.

New York was startled to be bypassed. The federal government for its part agreed that it too would have to offer a subsidy of some kind if our ships were to compete on the transatlantic run, but the first subsidized American attempts were unpromising. Meanwhile

Cunard finally conceded that he could not justify serving only the second most important American port, and so he extended his line to New York. Now it was doubly vital to mount a viable American endeavor. At this point, in 1847, Edward Collins entered the picture. Obtaining a mail subsidy, the suave former packet owner won financial backing from Brown Brothers and announced the formation of the United States Mail Steamship Company, more popularly known as the Collins line. His first ship, the *Atlantic,* went into service in 1850, to be followed soon by three others.

Collins had already acquired a reputation for luxury service with his sailing packets, and his new steamships not only were larger and faster than the Cunarders but also offered the ultimate in comfort. Rich carpeting covered the saloon floors, cabin doors were of satinwood, and the food and wines were top-grade. A special device called an annunciator provided the staterooms with bell service. For the moment, Cunard was outclassed. New York newspapers gloated over the faster times racked up by the Collins liners. And Collins was carrying 40 percent more passengers than Cunard. While the American mail subsidy lasted, New York—and the United States—rode high in transatlantic steam travel.

Unfortunately, the speed of the Collins liners proved their undoing. All were plagued by engine troubles; one ship suffered a collision with a small French steamer and another simply disappeared, having perhaps hit an iceberg. The government abruptly reduced its subsidy, and Collins was finished.

By coincidence, one prominent steamship operator was left in the transatlantic field after Collins's demise, and he is a major ornament to this period in New York's history. He operated without a subsidy and did not offer regular service (shutting down during the winter months), but his ships were large and fast and for a while they attracted passengers who had good reason to feel their owner knew what he was doing, given his reputation. Indeed he did, and his remarkable career spans the entire South Street boom period and leads directly into New York's next economic era. This upstart was not an immigrant or a New Englander but a local boy named Cornelius Vanderbilt.

The second son of an unambitious Staten Island boatman who ferried vegetables to Manhattan, Vanderbilt in 1811, at the age of seventeen, borrowed $100 from his mother to buy a small sailboat and was soon operating three passenger and freight ferries across New York harbor. During the War of 1812 he acquired a reputation for dependability and daring. Once when an army officer on Staten Island demanded to be taken to Manhattan during a raging storm that frightened every other ferry captain, Vanderbilt told him, "I'll carry you across, but I'll carry you under water half the way."[16] He forthwith delivered his drenched passenger to the Battery. Such exploits, together with his penchant for expressing himself in extreme profanity, prompted his competitors to call him Commodore, and so he was known for the rest of his life.

Wearying of sailboats, he entered the employ of Thomas Gibbons, a renegade steamboat operator who was challenging an 1808 monopoly of steamboat service between New Jersey and New York that dated back to Robert Fulton and New York's Chancellor Robert Livingston. Vanderbilt took over command of a boat running between Elizabeth and New York and along the Raritan River, and he gloried in the chance to help fight the monopoly, which New York authorities were trying to enforce. Inspectors tried over a two-month period to arrest him when his ferry docked in the city, unaware that he hid from them each time in a secret compartment that he had constructed in the cabin. Gibbons eventually won his fight. Triumphing in a celebrated lawsuit that went all the way to the Supreme Court in 1824, he broke the monopoly, with Chief Justice John Marshall issuing a landmark opinion that invoked the power of Congress to regulate interstate commerce.

The Commodore cared little about law. "The law?" he once allegedly remarked to a friend. "Why, I have the power already."[17] But he liked Gibbons and remained in his employ. In 1830, however, he went out on his own, running steamboats on the Hudson River and Long Island Sound. He soon became known for providing excellent service at low rates, which he did not hesitate to reduce further to drive out a competitor. At one point his fare from New York to Hartford was one dollar. On another occasion, when competing with the steamboat operator and former cattle drover Daniel Drew, with whom in due course he would battle often, he cut the fare to Peekskill to 12½ cents. Such low rates impoverished others, but the efficient Vanderbilt prospered and by the age of forty was worth $500,000.

Racing was a frequent diversion among steamboat men, and the Commodore was only too happy to oblige. In 1847 a celebrated race was held between the *Cornelius Vanderbilt*, with the owner at the helm, and the *Oregon*, owned by a burly, bewhiskered operator named George Law. The boats were to steam up the Hudson to Sing Sing and return. At the turn the *Oregon* was slightly ahead, though

Vanderbilt had bumped her and damaged her wheelhouse. On the way downstream the *Oregon*'s coal gave out, and her captain ordered everything burnable tossed into the engine. As thousands watched from the banks, furniture, doors, decorative woodwork, and all other detachable items were fed into the flames, and the *Oregon* barely won. Vanderbilt's loss was due to his having made too wide a turn at Sing Sing. It was one of the few contests in his entire career that he failed to win. In any event, such events helped business. In 1845 the Commodore was said to be worth $1.2 million, and about that time he moved his family to a comfortable mansion on Washington Place in the city.

When California's gold rush suddenly made steamboat service to Central America a lucrative opportunity, Vanderbilt jumped in and soon had fast ships shuttling back and forth on both the Atlantic and the Pacific legs of the route. Again his fare-cutting capers made competitors gasp: for a while he was charging only $100 for first-class transit from New York all the way to San Francisco and just $50 for steerage. Vanderbilt's route was via Nicaragua rather than Panama, and his presence in that troubled country led to one of his more memorable remarks. In 1853, while he was away in Europe on an extended vacation trip, two underlings whom he had left in charge of the company began manipulating company stock to their advantage and then, worse still, began plotting with the American soldier of fortune William Walker in his efforts to seize Nicaragua's government. If the plot succeeded, Walker was to shift the trans-Isthmus franchise away from Vanderbilt and award it to them. Walker did indeed capture the government, and he fulfilled his promise by transferring the franchise. Vanderbilt got back from Europe and gave vent to some of his more expressive profanity. Then he wrote his two former associates a letter that is unique in business annals. "Gentlemen," he declared, "you have undertaken to cheat me. I won't sue you, for the law is too slow. I'll ruin you."[18] And four years later he did.

With the California trade declining, the Commodore decided to move on and began sending steamers to Europe in competition with Collins. The withdrawal of the mail subsidy finished Collins, but Vanderbilt kept his ships going to Southampton and Le Havre. As usual, his methods could be brusque, especially with respect to labor. Once as a Vanderbilt liner headed out to sea her crew staged a mutiny for higher wages. The captain immediately reversed course and deposited his crew on the dock. Within an hour he had a new crew, which one observer described as "cosmopolitan."[19]

The Civil War brought a halt to this effort, but by then the Commodore was ready for new ventures anyway. In his late sixties this irascible figure had begun to move into the arena for which he came to be best known and in which he made his most substantial contribution to New York City, railroads.

Although one of America's first working rail lines, the Camden & Amboy, had been chartered in nearby New Jersey as early as 1830, New York City had not kept up with its rivals in the development of the new mode. It is easy to see today that while the Erie Canal had been a critical force for solidifying New York's commercial leadership in the first half of the nineteenth century, further progress and development in a country as big as the burgeoning United States would depend on good connections by railroad. But New Yorkers were perhaps understandably slow to recognize this truth. To be sure, geography in this instance did not favor Manhattan. For while rails could easily be laid to the heart of Boston, Philadelphia, or Baltimore, the Hudson and other waterways that made New York such a superb port were also barriers to western access by land. In addition, the phenomenal success of the Erie Canal and the plentiful returns earned by South Street's mercantile wizards may have induced a feeling of complacency among the city's leaders. Just as they had lagged in the development of transatlantic steamers, putting their trust in sail, now their attention wavered while other cities quietly laid plans to outflank the Erie Canal and breach the Appalachians by rail. If such plans succeeded, these cities could connect to the heartland via a swifter and more reliable means of transportation than canalboat. For a while it seemed as if Baltimore or Boston might actually succeed.

Baltimore was the first city to envisage a through rail link to the west when a group of its business leaders in 1830 began operations on the fledgling Baltimore & Ohio Railroad. Heading west along the Potomac River, the line was planned to cross the Alleghenies somewhere south of Pittsburgh to enter the Ohio Valley. It would need the consent of either Virginia or Pennsylvania to make the connection, and unfortunately this took so many years that the B&O was unable to make off with the prize.

A bigger threat was mounted by Boston. Rankled by New York's coup in building the Erie Canal, Bostonians in the 1830s noted that several small rail lines were coming into existence parallel to the Canal, potentially linking Albany and Buffalo. If Bostonians could build a railroad across the Berkshires to Albany to connect with them, they might put it all together and steal freight from New York. (No railroad had as yet been constructed along the Hudson south of Albany.) And this they proceeded to do. Their line (the future Boston & Albany Railroad) went via Worcester all the way to the Hudson, and by 1842 they could offer through rail service to Buffalo.

Abruptly New York woke up. Boston's stroke, together with Cunard's initial decision to ignore New York as a steamer terminus, demanded a response. Two routes came to mind. One was represented by the Erie Railroad, chartered in 1832, which was to follow a series of valleys and low areas along the southern edge of New York State to reach Lake Erie south of Buffalo. But construction problems had slowed its development. Now investors pumped money into it (bringing it to the attention of Jacob Little, among others). The other, more promising route lay along the Hudson. An existing line, the Hudson River Railroad, led north from the city but went only as far as Poughkeepsie. In 1847 its extension to Albany was begun, a formidable project involving cutting through many solid headlands along the river that had previously blocked the way. Finally in 1851 the line was completed, and that year the full length of the Erie Railroad was opened. New York now had two rail links to the west, and Boston's challenge had been checked.

The only hitch was that the more logical water-level route up the Hudson and west to Buffalo was made up of several independent rail lines, involving delays and inefficiencies. Enter Cornelius Vanderbilt. In the mid-1860s he first acquired control of the New York & Harlem Railroad, which led north from the city through central Westchester; then he managed to take over the Hudson River line. Eyeing the upstate rail companies, which had been combined under the name of the New York Central Railroad, Vanderbilt exerted pressure by denying them the use of the Hudson line for access to New York City. Swiftly the Central's directors caved in, and on December 11, 1867, Vanderbilt became president of the Central. Now it was no trouble to consolidate the three lines, and under his aegis the rail mammoth was born. A few years later the Commodore was able to extend the New York Central all the way to Chicago. New York City now had a superlative water-level route to the west that was more efficient than that of any other city.

The great new link to an expanding America signified more than continued prosperity and dominance for New York; it exemplified a shift to the industrial age. The old mercantile way of doing things, personified by the idiosyncratic South Street trading firms, was no longer relevant. No longer could the merchant in his countinghouse be in total control; business had become too complex. From now on, the banker and the industrialist would direct a larger commercial world, with higher stakes. Simultaneously, as the West continued to open up, the nation was beginning to turn its attention inward, to its own internal development and progress. Thus Congress's decision to halt the Collins line's mail subsidy signaled a declining concern for the merchant marine, and so American-built shipping at this time went into a tailspin from which it essentially never recovered. From now on, foreign carriers like Cunard and its French and German counterparts would ply the key North Atlantic route and others, essentially unchallenged by American flags.

But the aggressive tactics of the South Street merchants left a permanent mark. As the United States grew and other cities came into prominence, the superior position of the port of New York would gradually recede in relative terms, though not in actuality. For the port itself would keep developing and enhancing its entrepôt function, dwarfing the old South Street dock area as new and bigger piers lined the Hudson to berth the ever larger merchant fleets of other nations—and bringing ever more impressive returns to the city. By 1860 the port was handling two-thirds of a growing nation's imports and fully a third of its exports, and this would not change for a long time. The city's economic suzerainty, firmly established by the wily and creative merchants in lower Manhattan, would be greatly enhanced during the coming decades, although new kinds of leaders would be calling the shots.

6

Expanding and Changing

As the superb port flourished and grew, and as South Street's merchants and other entrepreneurs were building so energetically on New York's strong economic base to make the city the dominant business center of North America, their ships and others entering the harbor were, more and more, carrying another kind of cargo whose implications would be immeasurable. That cargo was people. But these were not transplanted merchants or go-getting individuals, come to try their hand at commerce in the new country and fitting in easily. Many of them were farmers, manual laborers, or factory workers, fleeing economic distress, political upheaval, or religious persecution in the Old World and not at all certain where they would end up in America. New York had always accommodated newcomers, even if it did not always welcome them outright, and had always benefited from the added zest and drive they brought to the already cosmopolitan mix. This new influx, however, was different.

For one thing it was far bigger than anything that had come before, and it was growing. The great transatlantic displacement of Europeans that got under way in the second decade of the nineteenth century and continued and increased for almost 100 years was the most phenomenal migration of modern times. And because New York had established itself as the nation's premier port, immigrants by the thousands came ashore in lower Manhattan. (Or even by the millions—during the 1850s more than two million alien passengers debarked in New York.) Most of them passed through the city on their way to other parts of the country, but many stayed, either because they had no place else to go, or because they had relatives already here, or because in time they found employment in one or another of New York's expanding industries. But in their sheer numbers they virtually swamped the city.

More to the point, they changed New York. Not only did they help it to grow physically, enabling it to expand northward with astonishing speed and to surge in population from a mere 123,700 inhabitants in 1820 to 312,000 in 1840 and an incredible 813,000 in 1860. They also altered it socially and ethnically (and politically, as will be seen), with long-term significance for the future. Despite all the changes New York had gone through, even as late as 1820 it was still essentially an eighteenth-century municipality, made up mainly of Protestants and dominated by a Protestant elite of English, Scottish, or Dutch ancestry. As late as 1820 only about 11 percent of the population was foreign-born. Although the city would continue to attract great numbers of New Englanders and other Americans who did not affect the ethnic balance, by 1860 almost half of a far bigger population was foreign-born, and of these a substantial number were Roman Catholic, creating a strong minority that had no hesitancy voicing its disagreement with the formerly secure Protestant majority on a number of critical issues—such as education, for example. On more than one occasion immigrants would be the critical factor in a dispute that ended in violence.

New York would still remain fixated on trade and money and characterized by its cosmopolitan, fluid society. But the ingredients at this time were shaken up markedly, and the city would never be the same.

The first large wave of newcomers was made up of Irish, many of them leaving their homeland because of famine or because of appeals for laborers on the Erie Canal. The earliest were predominantly Protestant, from Ulster, but later on Catholics were very much in the majority. Ireland's potato blight in the mid-1840s brought great numbers to this country. By 1860 some 200,000 New Yorkers were Irish-born. In the 1830s they had been joined by large numbers of Germans, whose homeland had been racked by crop failures and changes in land use; many Germans also were departing in the wake of failed revolutions, most notably in 1848. By 1860 there were 100,000 German-born in the city.

So swiftly did the newcomers arrive that all sorts of prejudices, jealousies, and enmities grew up between ethnic groups—between recently arrived Irish, for example, and the city's struggling black population, or between immigrant groups and native-born Americans—and there were frequent ugly clashes in the streets. Many of the old guard feared the worst. Philip Hone, the well-to-do diarist, observed in 1836, "All Europe is coming across the ocean; all that part at least who cannot make a living at home; and what shall we do with them? They increase our taxes, eat our bread, and encumber our streets, and not one in twenty is competent to keep himself."[1]

He was wrong about their competence, of course, for the majority of immigrants were nothing if not industrious. But a great many found life in their new world discouraging and sometimes harrowing. Just getting here was horrendous. The ships were overcrowded (rudimentary bunks wedged into steerage holds with headroom that rarely exceeded four and a half feet) and unsanitary (toilets poor or lacking). Food was meager at best, and the crew could be tyrannical. Many passengers arrived sick or disabled. Although they were likely to be unabashedly thrilled by their first view of the city with its many church spires as the ship emerged through the Narrows and made its way up the bay, the scene at the dock in the years before the city got around to systematizing the process was chaotic. "Runners"— agents of boardinghouses near the docks or of transportation lines offering to carry immigrants to inland areas—set upon the weakened, unsuspecting passengers and in many cases swindled them out of whatever savings they happened to have. Often the culprits were themselves recent immigrants, so that, as one chronicler put it, "Irish runners preyed on the Irish, Germans upon the Germans, English upon the English, and Americans upon them all."[2] In no time at all many newcomers were destitute.

Unable to afford even the cheap, decrepit boardinghouses near the docks for more than a few days, immigrants perforce moved into whatever permanent housing was available, usually in rundown areas already inhabited by people of their own nationality. Many of them crammed into ramshackle dwellings that had once served the needs of a quiet seaport town but had recently been abandoned by their former owners, who were moving uptown with the expanding city. For the most part such buildings were now overcrowded firetraps.

The Irish in particular gravitated toward the Five Points, a shabby and crime-ridden neighborhood that had once been covered by the now-drained Collect Pond just up from City Hall and that now was marked by the intersection of five streets. It was a warren of dark and dirty passages, with backyards filled with shacks and with one privy often serving dozens of families. The most notorious structure was the old brewery, formerly famed for its beer when it stood on the shore of the Pond but now housing several hundred Irish and blacks including, reported one observer, "thieves, murderers, pick-pockets, beggars, harlots, and degenerates of every type."[3] Charles Dickens, on a visit to New York in 1842, was repelled: "Such lives as are led here, bear the same fruit here as elsewhere. The coarse and bloated faces at the doors have counterparts at home and all the world over. Debauchery has made the very houses prematurely old . . . From every corner, as you glance about you in these dark streets, some figure crawls half-awakened, as if the judgement hour were near at hand, and every obscure grave were giving up its dead."[4]

Compounding the difficulties faced by the Irish were their Catholicism, which aroused deep distrust among Protestant New Yorkers, and their propensity for strong drink, which gave them a reputation for unreliability. "NO IRISH NEED APPLY" appeared frequently on signs listing job opportunities, and a large portion of the Irish were dependent on charity or on the already overburdened almshouses. What work they did find was likely to be as laborers, carters, dock workers, domestic servants, or seamstresses, and this brought them into frequent conflict with blacks who had long held such jobs. The luckiest of them found employment in the burgeoning garment industry, working either at home or in sweatshops, and in the building trades, where their leaders helped found some of the nation's first (albeit abortive) labor unions. But such jobs were often insecure or seasonal, and many observers like the diarist George Templeton Strong remarked on the monotonous daily drudgery of "our swarms of seamstresses."[5] Children were likely to be forced out into the streets at any early age, young girls all too frequently turning to prostitution.

The German immigrants, if perhaps more likely to qualify for semiskilled work than the Irish, had to learn a new language; and most of them were Catholic. They congregated in a district north of the Five Points extending up from what is now Chinatown all the way to Houston Street, the area coming to be known as *Kleindeutsch-land,* or Little Germany. Within its confines all the stores were German, and there were hundreds of beer parlors (among local German brewers were the Schaefer brothers). Sunday for most Germans was a day dedicated to having a good time—a habit that scandalized many a native New Yorker who felt the sabbath should be observed quietly. But the Germans were adept at making themselves useful and at learning skilled trades, and by 1855, as the historian Edward K. Spann has pointed out, they "constituted more than one-half the city's bakers and confectioners, cabinet-makers, tobacconists, shoe-makers, tailors, and woodworkers."[6]

Linking the Five Points and *Kleindeutschland* was the Bowery, the onetime lane that in Dutch days had led to Peter Stuyvesant's farm. By the 1820s the enlarged thoroughfare had become a shopping and amusement center chockablock with taverns, dance halls, theatres, clothing stores (whose clerks would forcibly pull unsuspecting passersby inside and then overcharge them), brothels, and pawnshops. Its sidewalks were jammed all day long and for much of the night. The Bowery Theatre, which opened in 1826, seated 3,000 and attracted top-ranking stars. In the 1840s a number of Bowery theatres staged Garden of Eden tableaux portraying "living men and women in almost the same state in which Gabriel saw them . . . in the first morning of creation,"[7] but after a year or so the police closed them all down—a frequent turn of events in the city ever since.

Among the street's most flamboyant denizens were the Bowery Boys (or B'hoys), young Irishmen who toiled at ordinary jobs during the week but on weekends strutted about the neighborhood decked out in elegant attire including a high beaver hat, frock coat, and full pantaloons tucked into heavy boots. The Bowery Boy's hair would be clipped close, but his temple locks were elaborately curled and anointed with bear grease. On his arm was his Bowery Girl, equally showy with a beribboned hat on the side of her head, a long skirt reaching to her ankles, and colorful gaiters. Most Bowery Boys belonged to one of the many volunteer fire companies, which competed for the honor of dousing a blaze. If a boy reached the scene of a fire before his company mates, he would grab a barrel, upend it over the nearest fire hydrant, and sit on it until his buddies arrived, resolutely denying access to all others. The greatest Bowery Boy, it was said, was a legendary figure named Mose who was eight feet tall with ginger-colored hair and who liked to demonstrate his prowess by lifting a horsecar off its tracks, carrying it several blocks on his shoulders, and laughing uproariously at the panic of the passengers as he set it down.

While the Bowery Boys generally meant no harm, other groups—especially those from the Five Points—were essentially gangs of hoodlums. With names like the Dead Rabbits, Roach Guards, and Plug Uglies, they were quick to foment disorder or even start a riot in order to get even with some other group or to advance a particular political view, and so vicious were their methods that for the first time in the city's history the streets became unsafe for ordinary folk. In the so-called flour riot of February 13, 1837, several gangs protesting unemployment and high food prices combined to break into a flour warehouse and empty its contents into the street. For several hours they held off the police and even attacked the mayor with stones and bricks when he tried to intervene. In the aftermath, forty of them were sent to prison. Such incidents were frequent over the next quarter of a century. Admittedly, gang members had reason to feel contempt for the police, who were habitually paid off to ignore such community blights as gambling dens, criminal hideouts, and brothels but were quick to arrest poverty-stricken immigrants for the slightest misdemeanor.

Amid all the turmoil, New York's black population, which still numbered only a few thousand, was not improving its situation. Although all slaves remaining in New York State had been legally emancipated in 1827, discrimination both legal and otherwise remained. Blacks faced far greater restrictions on voting than whites did, were frozen out of most well-paying working trades, and could sit only in certain sections in public assemblies and churches. They now faced bitter competition from the Irish for the menial jobs on the docks or as domestics that they had heretofore regarded as safe for them. As with other ethnic groups, they tended to live in certain well-defined areas, for example on the side streets west of Broadway in today's Tribeca and Soho districts. In the 1850s they began moving uptown to the West 30s, which remained a black enclave for several decades. Many lived in shanties on the edge of town.

Although the slavery issue nationwide aroused many a New Yorker, few white residents related it to the plight of the blacks locally. The abolitionist cause was spearheaded in the city starting in the 1830s by the dry goods merchants Arthur and Lewis Tappan—known for their disinclination to provide chairs for visitors to their office—but while much money was raised, none of it went to alleviating local ills. Arthur Tappan in 1827 had founded the *New York Journal of Commerce* and used its columns to preach abolitionism, but he was forced to sell the paper (it is still published today), and the new owners were proslavery.

To help alleviate some of the problems occasioned by the avalanche of immigrants, each ethnic group had its benevolent society, such as the Friendly Sons of St. Patrick or the German Society of the City of New York, which tried to help the newcomers find housing or jobs. But all these well-meaning organizations were soon overburdened, as were such charities as the Society for the Relief of Poor Widows with Children and the New York Orphan Asylum. The crux of the matter was that too many of the immigrants were, as Philip Hone had remarked, simply unable to cope, being ill, mentally disturbed, or otherwise unemployable. Many had had their passage paid for by their home communities in Europe, who wanted simply to be rid of them. Hospitals and almshouses were overrun: poverty had become a first-class public issue. The famed editor Horace Greeley wrote in the *New York Herald* in the 1840s that "there are Fifty Thousand People in this City who have not the means of a week's comfortable subsistence and know not where to obtain it."[8] In 1843 a group of civic leaders founded the Association for Improving the Condition of the Poor, and under the aggressive direction of Robert Hartley, a social worker who set up a network of volunteer "visitors" to work with individual families, some headway was made. But the problem persisted—and indeed plagues the city to this day.

Some New Yorkers, shocked by the rise in pauperism, the decline in public safety, the increase in rioting, and the willingness of immigrants to work for substandard wages (thus taking jobs away from homegrown Americans), formed supersecret nativist organizations with names like the Supreme Order of the Star-Spangled Banner, which distributed anti-Catholic tracts and backed political candidates who stood for policies curbing the rights of immigrants. That such groups enjoyed only limited success and generally ended up being discredited by the great mass of city dwellers was due to the overriding fact that, for the most part, the city was booming.

The speed with which New York was expanding uptown during the 1830s, 1840s, and 1850s was awe-inspiring. With both money and people pouring in, the city kept bursting its bonds. "New York never saw such days as the present since it was a city," said the *New-York Evening Post* in 1825. "The streets are so obstructed by the great number of buildings going up and pulling down, that they have become almost impassable, and a scene of bustle, noise, and confusion prevails that no pen can describe, nor any but an eye witness imagine."[9] Gas lighting had been introduced to the city's major streets in the 1820s, appreciably brightening their nighttime aspect. Broadway, once exclusively residential, was becoming the busiest and most opulent shopping street in America; its lower reaches, from Bowling Green to Trinity Church, had yielded completely to banks and countinghouses. Farther uptown, while the thoroughfare still boasted some of the finest mansions in town, these were increasingly being replaced by deluxe stores (for example A. T. Stewart's magnificent emporium at Chambers Street) and hotels, as homeowners pulled up stakes and relocated farther north. Wall Street was by the 1830s exclusively commercial—and busy. "The hurry-scurry of the Broadway and Wall-Street," said a British visitor in 1835, was replete with "driving, jostling, and elbowing . . . Add to this the crashing noises of rapid omnibuses, flying in all directions, and carts (for even they are driven as fast as coaches are with us), and we have a jumble of sights and sounds easy to understand but hard to describe."[10]

By far the finest hostelry in town after 1836 was the Astor House, built by John Jacob Astor at Broadway and Vesey Street overlooking City Hall Park. With 309 rooms it was larger than any hotel in London or Paris, and it not only provided its guests with gaslight but also offered bathing and toilet facilities on every floor, something few mansions at the time possessed. One of the poshest residential districts lay just to the west of the Astor, on Greenwich Street and along Park Place; and a dozen or so blocks uptown was perhaps the choicest area of all, St. John's Park, between Hudson and Varick streets (in today's Tribeca). Modeled on the residential squares of London's West End and lined with elegant houses, the felicitously landscaped park was dominated by St. John's Chapel on its flank, whose architecture was similar to that of St. Paul's downtown. Property owners around the park had exclusive entry by key to the park itself, and some of the city's most distinguished families resided there. (Today the spot carries exit traffic from the Holland Tunnel.)

In the 1840s, the center of fashionable living and shopping had shifted northward on Broadway ten or twenty blocks. "The spirit of pulling down and building up is abroad," proclaimed Philip Hone. "The whole of New York is rebuilt about once in ten years."[11] After 1853 the most splendid hotel was the St. Nicholas, on Broadway between Broome and Spring streets (in today's Soho), with 600 rooms, and even bigger and more elegant than the Astor; a stately Italianate structure, it presented a dazzling interior replete with gaslit chandeliers, black walnut wainscotting, and satin damask window curtains. Its opulent bridal suite was called "one of the newly invented institutions of hotel life."[12] Broadway itself was lined with buildings as far north as 14th Street, and to its shoppers and residents the poverty of the Five Points seemed far away. "Broadway is New York intensified—the reflex of the Republic," wrote one newspaperman. "No thoroughfare in the country so completely represents its wealth, its enterprise, its fluctuations, and its progress."[13] The street had its

"Broadway dandies," its more cultivated answer to the Bowery Boys. "What horn-like moustaches!" marveled a magazine writer. "What hyacinth curls! What delicately kidded little hands! . . . Who else can boast of such glossy hair, with such a very small quantity of brains beneath it?"[14]

Joining in the move uptown was Tiffany's, which had been founded as a gift and bric-a-brac store on lower Broadway in 1837 by Charles Lewis Tiffany, a newcomer from Killingly, Connecticut. Ten years later, its owners having decided to concentrate on jewelry, fine china, and silverware, the store moved up to 271 Broadway, diagonally opposite A. T. Stewart's. But only five years after that, having prospered from sales of jewelry made from gold from California, Tiffany's relocated again, to its own opulent five-story marble-fronted building at 550 Broadway, a block above the St. Nicholas. Its main floor, reported one shopper, was a "blaze of glittering temptations."[15] Ladies strolling along Broadway or being delivered in their carriages to one or another of the sumptuous stores could have lunch at Taylor's, on Broadway at Franklin Street, which was proclaimed the world's largest and most elaborate restaurant. Serving some 3,000 persons each day on two floors, Taylor's was lavishly adorned with mirrors, gilt, frescoes, and fountains, its central drama provided by a twenty-one-foot-high silver and crystal fountain whose splashing waters were visible to all the diners. On busy days customers cheerfully waited in line for an hour or more to be seated.

Philip Hone himself typified the northward transplanting of society when he moved his family in the mid-1830s from their mansion at 235 Broadway, in the same block as the uncompleted Astor House, to the corner of Broadway and Great Jones Street, more than a mile uptown. His new neighborhood, between Houston and 14th Streets, was just coming into vogue, and the side streets off Broadway— Bleecker, Bond, and East 4th in addition to Great Jones—were already lined with stately Federal and Greek Revival houses. Some of New York's most eminent citizens, including former secretary of the treasury Albert Gallatin and General Winfield Scott, hero of the Mexican War, were buying houses on Bond Street.

But ambitious residential development was being pursued even farther up. On a long blockfront several blocks above Bond Street that had belonged to John Jacob Astor, a speculative builder named Seth Geer erected a stately row of houses in 1832–33 linked by Corinthian columns and now known as Colonnade Row. The houses were described as "the most imposing and magnificent in the city," and much of the row still stands today. (Astor did not live in the row, residing instead a few blocks down Broadway, but his son William B. Astor maintained a large mansion across the street from it.) And several blocks to the west the former potter's field and parade ground that in 1826 had become known as Washington Square was being enclosed on its north side by a splendid series of Greek Revival houses with high front stoops and white doorways that have remained among the most distinguished dwellings in New York.

The most foresighted pioneer in the luxury-housing field, however, was the landowner Samuel B. Ruggles, who in the 1830s set about leveling hills and filling in swamps on his farmland east of Fourth Avenue above 14th Street to create Gramercy Park. Laid out between 20th and 21st streets and modeled on St. John's Park, it too was a private enclosure to which the sixty surrounding property owners had exclusive access by key. Ruggles's scheme caught on, even though the land was distinctly on the edge of town. Not all such concepts were successful. A campaign in the 1840s to develop Tompkins Square, a presumably inviting area a few blocks east of Lafayette Place between Avenues A and B, never attracted enough wealthy buyers. Evidently it was a shade too far east. Before very long it had become a working-class neighborhood in common with much of the Lower East Side.

The new fashionable stretch of Broadway was just as rackety during the day as the environs of City Hall had been. "The rumbling noise of the omnibuses' wheels along the iron rails," notes Charles Lockwood, "the shouts and curses of their drivers, the sharp sounds of hundreds of iron horseshoes striking the stone pavement, and the rattling of boxes and building materials in the wagons" made it less than inviting. Most people got used to it. As Walt Whitman, at that time a newspaperman in Brooklyn, asked in 1842, "What can New York—noisy, roaring, rumbling, tumbling, bustling, stormy, turbulent New York—have to do with silence?"[16]

But in the evening Broadway was quiet and magical, its storefronts illuminated, its sidewalks echoing to the sound of music from its theatres and saloons and to the pleasant voices of strollers. Prominent at night were also the streetwalkers, invariably got up in style. "Their complexions are pure white and red," reported one observer, "and their dresses are of the most expensive material, and an ultra-fashionable make. Diamonds and bracelets flash from their bosoms and bare arms."[17] It was estimated that roughly 10,000 women in New York were prostitutes, many of them recent immigrants who had been unable to find other work. The most successful prostitutes operated out of expensive brothels just west of Broadway on Mercer and Greene streets, whose front doors with their twinkling red lights gave the streets an eerie nighttime glow.

Customers in these establishments could be assured of safety and discretion. It was not so in other parts of New York. In an age-old ruse, a young prostitute might invite a man to her own room in some dingy backstreet building, whereupon her outraged "father" would suddenly burst in on them, obliging the unfortunate customer to pay a far larger sum than he had counted on, before escaping to the street.

As rapidly as stylish new houses and stores were put up on and around the northward-pushing Broadway, immigrants and other less fortunate people moved into the previously fashionable downtown houses. And in other developing districts, like the Lower East Side, smaller and less expensive housing went up, including buildings designed specifically for the poor; these were New York's first tenements. All this put tremendous strains on the city's municipal facilities. There was a desperate need, above all, for a new water system. The vaunted Manhattan Company, founded in 1799 by Aaron Burr ostensibly to supply fresh water to the city, had always been more interested in its bootleg banking operation than in laying pipes, and it served only a fraction of New York's homes. Anyone not fortunate enough to be so connected had to get water the traditional way, from public pumps or from hawkers peddling casks on the street. The shortage of potable water was thought by some residents to be behind the great rise in public drunkenness, thirst being theoretically quenchable only by beer. But there were far more serious consequences. Outbreaks of disease continued to hit New York, a cholera epidemic in 1832 taking 3,500 lives and another in 1834 exacting an even higher toll; doctors warned that a decent water supply, to improve sanitation, was essential if recurrences were to be prevented. Fire, too, was an ongoing threat.

After much study, the city in 1835 finally voted $12 million to dam the Croton River some forty-five miles north of Manhattan and import its water via aqueduct to reservoirs on the edge of town, from which it would be piped all over the city. Some observers feared that the huge cost of the undertaking would bring delays, but then fate intervened to speed the project. Just a few months after the vote, on the evening of December 16, 1835, a fire broke out in a warehouse near Hanover Square and rapidly spread out of control. With the temperature hovering around zero degrees Fahrenheit, water froze in all the available outlets, which in any event were inadequate. The blaze could be seen from Philadelphia some ninety miles away (prompting firemen there to turn out, thinking it was in their suburbs), and it continued for three days, wiping out a seventeen-block area below Wall Street that had contained some 700 structures. It was by far the worst fire in the city's history and destroyed the last of New York's old Dutch houses and stores.

Philip Hone, who at that time still lived opposite City Hall, heard the alarm bells not long after the fire started and ran out to track it down. "When I arrived . . . the scene exceeded all description; the progress of the flames, like flashes of lightning, communicated in every direction, and a few minutes sufficed to level the loftiest edifices on every side . . . At this period the flames were unmanageable, and the crowd, including the firemen, appeared to look on with the apathy of despair, and the destruction continued until it reached Coenties Slip, in that direction, and Wall Street down to the river, including all South Street and Water Street."[18] The loss was estimated at $17 million, forcing a number of large insurance companies into bankruptcy (and helping to bring about the panic of 1837).

Now there was no question about the urgency of the Croton water project. Work proceeded over the next several years, and the completed system—which included a distributing reservoir at Fifth Avenue and 42nd Street, where the New York Public Library now stands—was celebrated on October 14, 1842, with a mammoth parade and celebrations all over the city. New York now had the nation's most up-to-date water system. Fountains splashed in Union Square, in City Hall Park, and at Bowling Green, and indoor plumbing was soon being installed in the finest homes. Although the new system did not remove the threat of big fires—a great blaze in 1845 caused almost as much damage downtown—it became indispensable to the city's new manufacturing concerns and permitted New York to handle a population that doubled between 1845 and 1855.

A water shortage could be solved with money, but other problems were not so easily addressed. Education was one, and it was given immediacy by the fact that so many of the recent immigrants, especially the Irish, were Catholic. To them, the instruction provided by the city-sponsored Public School Society, a private corporation founded as the Free School Society back in 1805 with the help of De Witt Clinton, was unacceptable: it did not provide the religious teaching they considered essential to a person's upbringing. Worse yet, in their view the official schooling was strongly biased; daily

Bible readings, for example, were read from a translation that the Roman Catholic Church abhorred. Nor were Catholic New Yorkers about to desert their church, for it was a strong source of comfort and help to most of them. And so over the years Catholics began to start their own schools, in which their children would at least receive what they considered a proper moral education. But these schools were both strapped for funds and unable to accommodate more than a fraction of the city's Catholic children, and in 1839 it was estimated that more than 12,000 youngsters—almost half the children in the city—were receiving no schooling at all.

Into this quandary stepped a vigorous, imaginative bishop, Irish-born John Joseph Hughes, who holds a secure place as New York's first high-ranking Roman Catholic cleric. In 1840 Governor William H. Seward had suggested to New York's legislature that schools be set up in which the children of immigrants might be "instructed by teachers speaking the same language with themselves and professing the same faith."[19] Hughes, whose admirers called him "Dagger John," seized on this presumed opening and formally requested that the City Council grant funds for the support of parochial schools.

The council turned him down, saying the proposal was unconstitutional, but Hughes persevered. Demanding an appeal, he harangued the council for more than three hours, attacking the Public School Society's pro-Protestant textbooks and claiming that its actions violated the principle of freedom of speech. Losing again, he decided to demonstrate the potential power of Catholics by running an all-Catholic ticket in a city election. His slate lost, but its presence on the ballot split the vote for the majority Democrats, who thereby lost too. He had made his point: the Catholics must be heard. In 1842 the state legislature attempted an interim solution to the bitter controversy by setting up a nonsectarian publicly elected Board of Education, and by August 1853 the Public School Society had passed out of existence. Hughes's nemesis was gone—but he had not really won either, as the new arrangement forbade all schools from teaching any religious doctrine whatsoever. The bishop responded by expanding the church's parochial school system, thus bringing about the arrangement of two parallel, mutually wary organizations that is still in existence. The relationship between religion and public education—the issue of the separation of church and state—provokes controversy in New York City to this day.

A problem that seemed at times to be without a solution was housing for the city's poor, the majority of whom were immigrants.

Although many of the old dwellings that the poor had taken over might have been habitable if they were not overcrowded, most contained scores of people and some gave shelter to more than a hundred. Landlords, who saw no reason to keep such buildings in good repair, found they could squeeze in still more tenants by erecting another structure in the backyard; the courtyard between the front and back buildings was usually filled with garbage. Then cellars were rented out; though damp, unventilated, and foul-smelling, rooms in such quarters might house two or more families. The new tenement buildings were, if anything, worse still. One sympathetic New Yorker, a Quaker named Silas Wood, resolved with the best of intentions in 1850 to attempt a solution and built a "model tenement" on Cherry Street, just a few blocks from the Five Points district. Called Gotham Court, the structure was solidly built, and the *New York Evening Post* commented that it was "a praiseworthy enterprise and well worthy of imitation." Alas, just six years after it opened an inspection team found the experiment to be a failure. The building was filthy, and nearly half the apartments contained not one family but two. In that short span it had become one of the worst tenements in its neighborhood.

A different kind of dilemma was presented by the class and cultural conflicts resulting from the disparity between the affluence of New York's merchants and other business leaders and the poor circumstances of so many other citizens. When conflicts arose, the existence of gangs, whose members resented the upper classes, surely made things worse, and gangs were a prime component of the famous Astor Place Riot of 1849, which arose out of a rivalry between, of all things, two actors.

The scene of the dispute was the Astor Place Opera House, a stately theatre on Broadway at Astor Place, just below 8th Street. The hall had been built with funds provided by John Jacob Astor and other wealthy New Yorkers. To less fortunate city dwellers, the theatre symbolized the privileged elite who had backed it, and they called it the kid-glove opera house, as it purportedly restricted entry to persons wearing kid gloves. It happened that in May 1849, a well-known English actor named William Macready was booked into the house for a performance of *Macbeth*. By unfortunate coincidence, an American actor named Edwin Forrest was also performing the role at another theatre downtown. The two actors, both highly popular, detested each other and had not been above attending the other's performances and hissing him. To many lower-class residents, Mac-

142

ready represented the Anglophile upper crust, while Forrest was a man of the people. Forrest was also popular among the Irish, who had no love for things English.

As Macready's appearance neared, an unprincipled political propagandist named Edward Z. C. Judson, who wrote nativist tracts under the pseudonym of Ned Buntline, began issuing broadsides with inflammatory messages like "Workingmen! Shall Americans or English rule in this country?"[20] Sentiments of this sort were guaranteed to incite the gangs of the Five Points area, and when Macready first appeared at the Opera House on May 7 gang members infiltrated the audience and pelted him with rotten eggs, old shoes, and other missiles.

Mortified but also irate, the actor announced he was going home. But a group of prominent New Yorkers, among them Washington Irving, implored him not to retreat. Reluctantly he agreed to appear again on May 10. That evening an enormous crowd of more than 10,000, liberally spiced with gang members, filled the streets around the theatre, while 200 policemen supported by some 300 militiamen stationed themselves nearby hoping to preserve order. When Macready made his entrance in the first act the heavily hostile audience drowned his words with shouts and whistles. He nevertheless continued. Soon the crowd outside began throwing bricks and paving stones at the theatre. Streetlights were smashed and hydrants opened. The police counterattacked with clubs and with difficulty managed to contain the onslaught. Amazingly, Macready completed the play, though he had to race through the last two acts and was barely heard over the din. His triumph in doing so served only to inflame the crowd outside, and they stormed the building. Hoping to dissuade them, the police fired a volley into the air; the crowd responded with jeers. Finally the militia moved in and, on orders, fired directly into the onrushing crowd. The desperate move succeeded in dispersing the attackers, but as a result of it 22 persons lay dead, another 5 died over the next few days, and 150 were injured. The police arrested more than 100 troublemakers, including Ned Buntline, who was sent to prison for a year for inciting to riot.

New Yorkers of every stripe were deeply disturbed by the affair. The rioting had been curbed; but what did it all mean? Had the once-peaceful city somehow developed an underlying culture of violence? Was this the result of allowing in all those paupers from abroad? The well-to-do were convinced that poor immigrants were at fault. But Horace Greeley, in the *New York Tribune*, felt the blame lay equally at the door of the rich, whose "unbridled lust for money" stoked resentments that fomented radical action. Whatever it was, New York had tasted violence—and not for the last time.

While thoughtful residents pondered the meaning of the riot, the city continued to accept more people and to grow. America was booming in the 1850s—one authority estimated that the national wealth went up by 90 percent between 1850 and 1857 alone—and the city boomed right along with it. Former president John Tyler waxed ecstatic over New York. "Look at that city," he said, "and see her extending streets, her palatial mercantile establishments, with her vast congregation of vessels at her docks bursting forth like a crab from the shell, and expanding itself until it covers the adjacent shores of the beautiful roadstead and rivers with cities and villages."[21] With so many thousands of immigrants pouring into the port each year, it did seem to some onlookers as if Europe had captured the city. But rural America was contributing plenty of people too. "The crowd in Broadway ... seems to have come from out of town," remarked the editor George William Curtis. "It has a strange, wondering air. And the population of the city itself is so incessantly reinforced by those who come from the country that the city has always a little air of novelty to its own citizens."[22]

By the late 1850s Manhattan was solidly built up all the way to 36th Street on the East Side and 50th Street on the West. An especially telling statistic was that between 1846 and 1858 the area north of 14th Street gained 290,000 persons, which was almost as much as the city's total population had been in 1840. The city's epicenter and most fashionable district had moved up almost a mile from the Spring Street area and was now located at Union Square (between 14th and 17th streets, east of Broadway), a park that had been laid out as recently as 1831. Large mansions surrounded it. A particularly impressive one, owned by James F. Penniman, was one of the first houses in the city to be built of brownstone, a dark sandstone that in the next half century would be used all over New York.

As fast as new areas came into fashion, others declined, not only because they were no longer considered socially acceptable but also because commerce and trade were moving uptown right behind the residential procession. Suddenly the Bond Street area was in a decline; a magazine in 1853 declared that "Bond and Bleecker Streets, that were then the *ultima thule* of aristocracy, are now but plebian streets."[23] Several fine dwellings on Bond had already become boardinghouses for immigrants, and Broadway below 14th Street was becoming almost totally commercial. The word went out in polite society that it was necessary to live above 14th Street. In 1859 a new uptown outpost of fashionable living came into existence with the opening of the Fifth Avenue Hotel on the corner of Fifth Avenue and 23rd Street, opposite Madison Square. With accommodations for 800 guests and a new mechanical contrivance called a passenger elevator (known as a "vertical railroad"), the grand establishment eclipsed the St. Nicholas Hotel, just as the St. Nicholas had earlier outshone the Astor House.

Even sadder than the decline of Bond Street, because it had shown such promise as a gem of urban living, was the gradual deterioration of St. John's Park down below Canal Street. Again commercialism was a contributing cause. Waterfront activity along the Hudson River had brought warehouses to Greenwich Street just west of the park in the 1840s, and a rowdy element began appearing on nearby side streets. So the well-to-do families began to feel they were really too far off the approved social track, and they began to move out. The situation worsened in 1851 when Vanderbilt's Hudson River Railroad laid tracks along Hudson Street right past the park to carry passengers down to their terminal on Chambers Street. Before long none of the former residents wanted any part of the area, and its death knell was sounded barely fifteen years later when the Commodore purchased the park and erected a massive train shed on it. (The handsome St. John's Chapel survived in lonely splendor until 1918, when it was torn down to make way for the widening of Varick Street.)

Just as St. John's Park may have seemed a bit too far west, so did Broadway itself above 14th Street. For some reason there was a desire among the moneyed classes to stay reasonably close to a central axis; and as Broadway above 14th Street veered west on its way uptown (following the route of the old Bloomingdale Road), society abandoned it. Fifth Avenue, which had been little more than a dirt track as recently as 1840 but which headed straight uptown, was now the best address. Mansions had begun to arrive north of Washington Square in 1834 when the millionaire Henry Brevoort moved into a house at the northwest corner of 9th Street. He was presently joined in nearby blocks by the banker August Belmont and the merchant Moses Grinnell.

Confidence in Fifth Avenue's future was nowhere summed up so convincingly, perhaps, as by John Hughes (by then New York's Roman Catholic archbishop) when he decided in 1850 to construct a new St. Patrick's Cathedral for his diocese far uptown at Fifth Avenue and 50th Street, an area still only barely settled. He bought the land from the city for $83. Hughes's move had been sparked partly to symbolize the growing respectability of his flock but also to emulate, if not to upstage, the new Trinity Church recently completed at Broadway and Wall. The Trinity edifice consecrated in 1790 (replacing the structure burned during the British occupation) had deteriorated by the 1830s and was demolished; and to design the new building, which would be the third on the site, the vestry hired the architect Richard Upjohn, who came up with a Gothic Revival structure that won universal praise—as it still does. Not to be outdone, Archbishop Hughes took on thirty-two-year-old James Renwick, Jr. (an Episcopalian) to design St. Patrick's; and Renwick's building, whose cornerstone was laid in 1858, can certainly claim to be the aesthetic equal of its rival downtown—indeed they are two of the city's finest churches. St. Patrick's was completed in 1879.

(On a different level entirely, Fifth Avenue received another endorsement when Ann Trow Lohman, an abortionist who said she was a "female physician" and "professor of midwifery" and who called herself Madame Restell, arrived on the scene. She had conducted her profitable business for many years at 148 Greenwich Street downtown, but in the 1850s she vaulted all the way up to Fifth Avenue and 52nd Street. Carrying on her trade from a handsome brownstone mansion that she had financed herself, Madame Restell resisted all attempts to dislodge her and delighted in taking an afternoon carriage ride each day in her stylish equipage driven by liveried coachmen. It was suggested that she chose the site largely to annoy the Catholic hierarchy.)

With so many of the well-to-do moving uptown while their places of business remained in lower Manhattan, New York acquired a new phenomenon, the commuter. Merchants had traditionally lived above their stores or countinghouses, or else close by, and could walk to work. Now it was too far to walk. While artisans and storekeepers —the middle class—still resided near their places of work, factory workers and the elite commuted, and the city's transportation system was sorely overloaded. Omnibuses, which were really large carriages, had been introduced in the 1830s but had soon proved inadequate, and so in the 1850s the city tried horsecars, much larger horse-drawn vehicles that ran on tracks. Although they, too, soon became overcrowded, and traffic jams produced frequent episodes of "dead-lock" (the ancestor of today's gridlock), the horsecars were the beginnings of a mass transit system, and by 1860 they had helped extend the city limits to 59th Street.

While Manhattan had been enjoying its mind-boggling expansion, its neighbor across the East River had been growing at an equally astonishing rate. Brooklyn until the early part of the nineteenth century had been essentially a collection of small towns and villages. But when steam ferry service from Manhattan went into operation in 1814, Brooklyn Heights (immediately opposite the Wall Street area) and the environs of the ferry dock around Fulton Street both became suburbs and underwent rapid development. Many prominent merchants built substantial homes there. Closeness to Manhattan was a distinct asset, and Brooklyn not only acquired its own shipyards, rope walks, and other maritime endeavors associated with New York shipbuilding but also became an industrial center with distilleries, tanneries, and lead factories among other enterprises, some of which had been banned from operating in Manhattan. Between 1820 and 1830 Brooklyn's population doubled, going from 7,000 to 15,000. It had been incorporated as a village in 1816, but by 1834, with 24,000 inhabitants, it had grown so fast that it was able to obtain a charter as a city—over the objections of New York, which insisted it should be combined with Manhattan (as of course it eventually was).

From that point on its rise was spectacular. A large portion of the immigrants who flooded into the port in the 1830s and 1840s settled in Brooklyn, where there was plenty of room, and shipping (notably in the Red Hook section) and manufacturing concerns also proliferated. Thousands of Brooklynites commuted by ferry to downtown New York. By 1840 Brooklyn's population was 36,000; by 1850 it had almost tripled, to 96,000; and in 1860, with the annexation of Greenpoint and Williamsburg, it had leaped to 267,000. Brooklyn had passed Boston, New Orleans, and Baltimore and was the third largest city in the United States, surpassed only by New York itself and Philadelphia. The combined population of Brooklyn and New York, in fact, exceeded one million.

But Manhattan alone could by now with confidence call itself a metropolis. A great urban center, it not only was the nation's commanding commercial capital but also was rapidly achieving cultural and artistic leadership, though Boston might still disagree. Its role as the nation's premier importer gave it control over the dissemination of news from Europe and helped establish it as the nation's journalism center as well as the advertising capital; in 1857 there were no fewer than 104 newspapers in the city with a combined annual circulation of 78 million. New York could be said to be enjoying a golden age of newspapers. The poet William Cullen Bryant was editing the *New York Evening Post*, which had been founded back in 1801; Benjamin Day had started publishing the *New York Sun* in 1833, James Gordon Bennett founded the *New York Herald* in 1835, and Horace Greeley inaugurated the *Tribune* six years later; and in 1851 Henry J. Raymond started the *New York Daily Times*, which shortly dropped the "Daily" from its name. Among magazines, perhaps the most promising was *Harper's Monthly*, which got under way in 1850 and was to become one of the most important periodicals in the country. A few years later it would add its pictorial edition, *Harper's Weekly*. Another magazine that had begun publication was *Scientific American*.

The proliferation of newspapers and magazines attracted writers, and New York had drawn Herman Melville and Edgar Allan Poe among many others to its precincts, while Washington Irving was still writing from his home at Sunnyside, near Tarrytown north of the city, and Walt Whitman was in residence across the river in Brooklyn. The naturalist and writer John James Audubon lived in the upper stretches of Manhattan. And New York had established itself as the nation's great supplier of books. Charles Scribner and G. P. Putnam were already in New York by 1850, but the city's oldest and largest book publisher was Harper & Brothers, which also owned the monthly and weekly periodicals carrying its name. In 1853 alone Harper published no fewer than 733 books, of which almost 400 were by American authors.

Although the city had its share of artists, like Samuel Morse (who was to win greater fame as the inventor of the telegraph), Thomas Cole, and Asher Durand, its most significant artistic role was that of the nation's leading purveyor of art. By dint of its position as a money center it was a lodestone for collectors. The National Academy of Design, organized in 1826, staged an annual show that was recognized by artists all over the country as the critical event at which to exhibit their latest works; while the American Art-Union, which flourished briefly in the 1840s and 1850s, pioneered in mass marketing art. Private art galleries catered to the tastes of wealthy art buyers like the department store magnate A. T. Stewart.

Theatre and music were well established in the city. The oldest theatrical house, the Park Theatre near City Hall, had functioned ever since the 1790s, and although it was destroyed by fire in 1848 there were many other houses along Broadway to take its place. Furthermore, interest in the stage was keen, as the Astor Place riot demonstrated, and New York theatres drew top talent. Appreciation of serious music was beginning to be discerned, and the Philharmonic Society, founded in 1842, regularly presented concerts by prominent foreign musicians. But it was in opera that the city's musical strivings took firmest root, in part because opera's expensive (and thus exclusive) nature attracted the new rich. As it happened, the Astor Place Opera House was not a success, quite apart from its notoriety brought about by the riot; the hall was not big enough to pay its way, and it closed in 1852. But the following year a number of prominent New Yorkers banded together to build the Academy of Music on East 14th Street. Seating 4,000, it was the largest opera house in the world, and with a mixed fare of opera and concert performances it was a focal point of New York's cultural life for the next generation. Its success may have been foreshadowed by the coup pulled off in 1850 by the showman P. T. Barnum when he presented the "Swedish Nightingale," Jenny Lind, to a sellout crowd as part of the singer's nationwide tour. The concert was staged at Castle Garden, the former fort previously known as Castle Clinton off the Battery. (In 1855 the round fort was once again converted, this time to serve as an immigration center; in the 1890s it would become New York's aquarium.)

The enormous turnout for Jenny Lind said something else about New York's enthusiasm for culture. No matter how "American" the city truly was, for generations to come its cultural leaders and wealthy art and music patrons would be more excited by European artists and musicians than by American ones. Because the city was a gateway for European ideas (as well as people), its cultural aspirations would tend to focus on works and personalities across the ocean and to scant homegrown works of art. Only in the twentieth century would New York begin to view American arts and artists with the seriousness they deserved.

In higher education, New York had failed to distinguish itself by midcentury. Columbia College, although it moved from its downtown campus in 1857 to a new site on East 49th Street, was still small and bereft of adequate funds; New York University, on Washington Square, had started classes in rented rooms in 1832 but was still struggling; and the laudable Cooper Union, founded (near the Astor Place Opera House) by the businessman and inventor Peter Cooper to provide free technical schooling to the disadvantaged, was never intended as a general educational institution. New York for many years would have nothing to compare seriously with top New England institutions like Yale or Harvard.

With all its achievements, the city felt so sure of itself that in 1853 it staged America's first world's fair. Modeled on an exposition held in London two years earlier, the fair took place in what was called (emulating its English predecessor) the Crystal Palace, a huge iron and glass structure on the site of today's Bryant Park at 42nd Street. Tremendously popular, the fair ran for two seasons, and part of its attraction was due to a 350-foot tower across 42nd Street called the Latting Observatory (after its builder, Waring Latting), from which visitors could get an unexampled view of the entire city and its environs. Sadly, both the Crystal Palace and the tower burned to the ground just a few years after the fair closed.

Some observers looking out from the tower might have noticed an odd thing about the developing city: except for a few open spaces downtown and Union and Madison squares farther up, New York had set aside very little of its land for public parks. The lack was partly a result of the city's relentless mercantile drive, whose adherents would doubtless have argued that any property not commercially useful was a waste. The Randel plan of 1811, which set up Manhattan's grid system, had made little allowance for parks. But in recent years a number of influential residents had increasingly predicted that New York would soon become unfit for decent habitation if it did not set aside land to serve as the "lungs of the city." The first public figure to do so was William Cullen Bryant, who warned in the *New York Evening Post* in 1844 that "Commerce is devouring inch by inch the coast of the island, and if we would rescue any part of it for health and recreation it must be done now."[24] Joining Bryant in the plea was Andrew Jackson Downing, a young landscape architect from Newburgh, New York. Arguing for parkland as a civilized amenity, Downing said that the city needed spaces where people of all classes could meet together for enlightenment and enjoyment.

Thanks to the lobbying of Bryant and Downing, government officials began to take notice. Bryant urged the city to set aside as a potential park a 153½-acre tract called Jones's Wood, on the eastern edge of Manhattan north of 66th Street, and legislation was planned. Downing, however, objected, claiming the plot was nowhere near big enough: "Five hundred acres is the smallest area that should be reserved for the future wants of such a city, now, while it may be obtained."[25] His argument won out, the Jones's Wood plan was dropped, and in 1853 the city got permission from the state to buy the site of what would become Central Park—originally some 624 acres between Fifth and Eighth avenues and stretching from 59th Street up to 106th. Six years later the site was extended to 110th Street, for a total of 843 acres. The cost of the land came to about $5 million.

If Downing had lived he would probably have been the designer of the park, but he was killed in a steamboat accident on the Hudson River in 1852. A nationwide competition for the design was then held, and the winners were Frederick Law Olmsted and Calvert Vaux. Olmsted, a New Englander, was a writer and nurseryman who had never designed anything; the London-born Vaux (pronounced vox) was a little-known architect who had worked in Downing's office. Despite these unprepossessing credentials their design was brilliant. The park they envisioned was to be picturesque and restful but also efficient; traffic was to flow around and through it without endangering its serenity. Completed over a twenty-year period, the park is universally deemed a triumph of urban planning. Olmsted and Vaux later designed Prospect Park in Brooklyn, while Olmsted planned Riverside Park on the Upper West Side of Manhattan and was responsible for a number of other noteworthy American parks.

Providing a handsome open space for future generations did nothing, of course, to relieve the problems of the 1850s, which remained vexing. And anyway, the new park was to be uptown, where the rich were moving, not downtown where the slums were. The city was acquiring a homeless population, most of them presumably immigrants who had become destitute. Public health was poor, epidemics kept occurring despite the new water system, and infant mortality was shockingly high—more than half of all children under the age of five died. A severe business downturn in 1857 threw thousands out of work, and when great numbers of unemployed marched on the Sub-Treasury and the Custom House that year to demand jobs, troops had to be called out to maintain order.

The antagonisms that had given rise to the Astor Place riot had furthermore not been dispelled. Just how deep-seated they were would be shown in the infamous Draft Act riots of 1863.

Although there had been strong feeling, especially in the merchant community, during the months before the outbreak of the Civil War that New York should not turn against the South, with which it had established such cordial trading relations, the city's response to actual hostilities was enthusiastic. Rallies were held and New York's two

151

regiments, the Seventh and the Sixty-ninth, marched down Broadway to the cheers of thousands as they went off to the front. Volunteers enlisted in the Union forces at an impressive rate, and New York financiers loaned the federal government more than $200 million for war expenses.

By 1863, however, it was clear that volunteering was not going to produce enough troops to win the war, and President Lincoln reluctantly instituted the draft. The measure was not popular in New York City, and the most vociferous opponents were the Irish. For while many Irish had supported the fighting—the Sixty-ninth Regiment was made up largely of sons of Erin—tremendous numbers of them felt the war was not in their interests. Not only did they feel no loyalty to the United States, since they had not prospered here, they also resented the provision of the draft act that allowed a man to buy exemption for $300, a sum they could not possibly afford. It was a rich man's war, they said, but a poor man's fight. Even more important, they resented the war's allegedly being fought for the rights of blacks, with whom they competed for hard-to-get jobs. Blacks, they said, were strikebreakers, and on more than one occasion striking Irish workers had been dismissed and replaced by blacks willing to work for lower wages. The Irish in such instances retaliated by beating up the blacks, with the police unable to intervene. To an overwhelming extent, the mobs who brought about the Draft Act riots were made up of Irish Catholics, many of them members of the celebrated gangs of lower Manhattan. The mobs were ably led, though it never became clear by whom.

In early July 1863, when the first names were to be drawn for induction, there was a dearth of militiamen in the city: almost all available troops had recently been sent to Gettysburg, just now the scene of a critical campaign. On Saturday, July 11, a sullen crowd watched as more than 1,200 names were picked out of a drum at the draft office on Third Avenue and 46th Street. But the number was insufficient, and authorities announced that the drawing would continue the following Monday. Saturday's evening papers listed the names already drawn, and over the weekend popular anger built up markedly.

On Monday morning, a well-armed mob of several thousand marched on the draft headquarters, bullied aside the 800 policemen stationed to guard it, stoned the building, and surged inside, wrecking the lottery wheel and setting the structure ablaze. Prominent among the rioters were a gang called the Black Jokers. Presently a detachment of Invalid Corps soldiers—men recovering from battle wounds—attempted to relieve the police and were savagely attacked, a score of them killed. Elsewhere mobs halted all public transportation, looted and burned houses, and plundered stores. One crowd at City Hall threatened to capture the mayor, George Opdyke, but he was able to escape and find refuge at the St. Nicholas Hotel.

That afternoon the first move against blacks was made as a massive crowd surrounded the Colored Orphan Asylum, a large building on 43rd Street west of Fifth Avenue, and shouted their intention to burn it. The 233 youngsters were hastily evacuated out the back door before the building went up in flames. An advance on the central police headquarters on Mulberry Street was turned back only after a fierce battle, as were attempts to sack the offices of the *Sun* and the *Times*, both of which had supported the draft. By this time the mobs were in control of New York. As Carl Sandburg observed, "Never before in an American metropolis had the police, merchants, bankers, and forces of law and order had their power wrenched loose by mobs so skillfully led."[26] Late Monday evening, Mayor Opdyke wired Washington to request the return of New York's troops from Gettysburg.

Monday night a black man was hanged in a downtown street; Tuesday morning another was assaulted and killed not far away. The rioting and destruction continued, and every citizen who was able to do so had left town. Around noon that day New York's governor, Horatio Seymour, who had been vacationing on the New Jersey shore, arrived in town and declared the draft suspended. The announcement had no effect. Mobs destroyed a bridge over the Harlem River, a hotel near City Hall, and a ferry terminal on the Hudson. More homes were looted. On Wednesday three blacks were lynched at 32nd Street and Eighth Avenue, and homes of blacks on Staten Island were wrecked. Finally at 10 P.M. Wednesday evening National Guard troops began to arrive. By early Thursday morning there were 10,000 soldiers on hand, and they soon restored order. A kind of calm settled over the bewildered city. The following month the draft was resumed. It went off without any stir.

The four-day episode, in which some 1,500 to 2,000 people were killed and property worth millions of dollars was destroyed, has been called the most brutal, tragic, and shameful in the city's history. Citizens were shocked and unbelieving. Wrote the diarist George Templeton Strong: "This is a nice town to call itself a centre of civilization!"[27]

His despair was rightly felt. Yet if some of the immigrants had been the cause of the trouble, the great preponderance of recent arrivals had taken no part in the disorder and were doubtless as ashamed as everyone else of what had happened. The terrible event had a kind of cathartic effect: nothing anywhere near so ugly would ever take place in New York City again. The city's diversity, sorely challenged, would in time be again seen as its greatest strength.

7

The Bosses

George Washington Plunkitt, a bluff, mustachioed man who was a highly effective cog in the Tammany political machine in the early years of the twentieth century, took great delight in expounding on the benefits of boss rule in New York City, and his remarks occupy a prized place in the literature of machine politics. Garbed in his usual severe black coat and tall silk hat, he was happy to express his views to any audience that might collect around his "office," the bootblack stand in the New York County Courthouse. "See how beautiful a Tammany city government runs," he said on one occasion, "with a so-called boss directin' the whole shootin' match! The machinery moves so noiseless that you wouldn't think there was any. If there's any differences of opinion, the Tammany leader settles them quietly, and his orders go every time."[1]

He particularly liked to defend the big-time Tammany pols, whom he referred to as "statesmen," against the charge that they were corrupt. "The papers and some people are always ready to find wrong motives in what us statesmen do," he remarked. "If we bring about some big improvement that benefits the city and it just happens, as a sort of coincidence, that we make a few dollars out of the improvement, they say we are grafters. But we are used to this kind of ingratitude. It falls to the lot of all statesmen, especially Tammany statesmen. All we can do is to bow our heads in silence and wait till time has cleared our memories."[2] And again: "Some papers complain that the bosses get rich while devotin' their lives to the interests of the city. What of it? If opportunities for turnin' an honest dollar comes their way, why shouldn't they take advantage of them, just as I have done?"[3] Indeed he had. Though born to a penniless family

155

in the shantytown north of the city that later gave way to Central Park, Plunkitt had done very well for himself in politics. By the turn of the century, conducting his business solely from the bootblack stand or on the sidewalks of his district, he had extensive holdings in contracting, transportation, and real estate, and in addition to wielding extensive power in the Tammany machine, and thus throughout the city, he was a millionaire.

Plunkitt was actually a minor if colorful member of a special breed, the Tammany bosses who rose to prominence in New York City in the latter part of the nineteenth century, and who for extended periods exercised virtually ironclad control over the city's political life. They left a lasting imprint on New York and on its image. One of them, William M. Tweed, achieved such notoriety that to many Americans "Boss Tweed" automatically connotes grandiose corruption—and justly so, for the Tweed Ring is believed to have stolen well over $50 million from the city. (Tweed's crowning outrage, his fabled courthouse behind City Hall, ended up costing more than $13 million—most of the excess went into the Ring's pockets —and stands today as a monument to civic greed.) But Tweed, though wicked, was not the most potent of the bosses; that honor goes to a successor, Richard Croker, who in the 1890s exercised more power and exhibited more swagger than any other city boss before or since.

The Tammany bosses rose to such heights because they fulfilled a need that was not being met by anyone else: that of catering to the vast horde of newly arrived poor from Europe and elsewhere, as well as to the poor already on the scene. Their rise, like so much else in the city's history, was due to the confluence of the two major forces that have continued to shape New York: the city's formidable financial prowess and its role as a cosmopolitan port of immigration. The city's potent economic muscle, as symbolized by the South Street merchants as well as the Wall Street bankers, meant that there was plenty of money around—New York was a prosperous place. At the same time, the massive wave of immigrants pouring into the city formed a new constituency that demanded to be served but was not. The newcomers needed food, clothing, jobs, help in adjusting to the city, and protection against discrimination and persecution. But the city's government was unequal to the task. Indeed, New York's old-time governing elite shrank from the prospect. Into the vacuum stepped Tammany Hall, as opportunistic as it had been in the days of its early mentor, Aaron Burr. Alexander Callow, in his biography of Boss Tweed, sums up the situation: "As the old ruling class abdicated from practical politics, visiting the lower wards only to deliver moral manifestoes, the professionals moved in."[4] In exchange for votes, Tammany professed to see to the needs of the newcomers. And from that power base the most capable and unscrupulous of its leaders, the storied bosses, vaulted to command of the city. With all that money to be manipulated, with financial buccaneering the order of the day, and with few effective election or conflict-of-interest laws to hem them in, they also profited handsomely in the process.

One other key element contributed to their power: the arrival of universal suffrage. Up to the 1820s only property owners had been able to vote. But the state had extended voting rights to all male citizens during that decade, and in 1834 New Yorkers for the first time could vote for mayor. It was the era of the common man, Andrew Jackson was in the White House, and the Jacksonian spirit demanded that the people control their government. Tammany Hall and other political organizations saw the opportunity and, seeking more voters, rushed to naturalize as many of the new immigrants as they could. Courts presided over by pliant judges became naturalization mills, in many cases speedily conferring citizenship before the mandatory five-year waiting period was up. In Boss Tweed's time, one judge boasted that he could examine two witnesses (testifying to an applicant's character) every minute, although a review of the records showed he was being modest; his average was actually three per minute. Immigrants on whom citizenship had been so handily bestowed would of course show their gratitude by voting as directed on election day. If they did not, Tammany found a way to school them properly.

Tammany Hall, with its arcane officialdom who carried exotic Indian titles like Sachem (the chief was called the Grand Sachem) and Wiskinsky, had never been above condoning a certain amount of graft. As early as 1806 one grand sachem, Benjamin Romaine, had been indicted for fraud while serving as city comptroller. Two decades later another Tammany chieftain, Samuel Swartwout, managed to flee the country to avoid being apprehended for having borrowed from the city, in his job as collector of the Port of New York, the sum of $1,225,705.69; to "swartwout" came to mean to line one's pocket with government funds.

But Tammany had originally been opposed to foreigners. That changed as the potential of the immigrant vote became clear, and before long the Irish in particular—well versed in political tactics from centuries of combating English oppression back home—had become loyal troops of the Hall. ("The Irish was born to rule," said Plunkitt, "and they're the honestest people in the world.")[5] Tammany politicians instructed them in tactics and helped many of them to own or operate saloons, which became party rallying points. Young Irishmen were especially active in the political gangs that were useful in controlling nominating conventions and swaying elections; one gang, the Empire Club, led by a tough former Mississippi riverboat gambler named Isaiah Rynders (who obviously was not Irish), was adept at breaking up meetings of Whigs and anti-Tammany Democratic groups.

Immigrants of every sort, but especially the Irish, were happy to be of service to Tammany, for a fee, as "repeaters," persons who voted over and over again on election day, sometimes using the names of legitimate voters who had not yet shown up, other times impersonating people long dead. Many stories attest to the good-humored skepticism with which some voting clerks viewed these transgressions. On one occasion a repeater stated that he was William Croswell Doane, a prominent Episcopalian clergyman. "Come off," said the clerk. "You ain't Bishop Doane." Back came the indignant response: "The hell I ain't, you ———!"[6]

Because New York's aldermen, as members of the City Council, controlled all city jobs (there was no civil service), and because the same aldermen owed their own election to Tammany or one of its lesser rivals, Tammany was soon staffing New York's government with immigrants, especially the Irish. The handing out of jobs to diligent party workers was known as the spoils system, from the famous remark made by New York's Senator William Marcy in the early 1830s. New York's politicians, he said, do not complain if they lose an election, but they expect to reap the appropriate rewards if they win, for "They see nothing wrong in the rule that to the victors belong the spoils."[7]

Most notably, New York's police force acquired the Irish cast that it retained until only recently; by 1855 more than a third of the police were recent immigrants, and of these three-fourths were Irish. The Irish police were generally assigned to Irish districts, while well-to-do districts got American-born patrolmen. For recreation and good fellowship many of the politically minded Irish who were not policemen joined the volunteer fire companies, whose members could be counted on to vote as a bloc and which therefore became key units in the Tammany apparatus. To make political transactions, firemen, gang leaders, and ward politicians met at the neighborhood saloon, whose keeper was likely to be Irish too; and if a fight broke out between rival factions the keeper could be confident the cop on the beat would not interfere—for he was Irish and therefore part of their world.

Here were all the makings of a corrupt political apparatus, from malleable voters to thugs ready to beat up the opposition to cops who would look the other way. Yet during the entire first half of the nineteenth century no true boss arose to control the scene. City politics were chaotic, riven by splinter parties. The Whig party was in a decline (the Republicans were not yet on the scene), and other groups like the nativists came and went. Tammany itself did not yet dominate the Democratic party and was itself frequently torn by dissension. It would take a strong and assured leader to unify the Democrats under Tammany's banner and go on to control the city. Such a man, in the late 1860s, was William Tweed. Yet Tweed himself might not have aspired to such a lofty achievement if he had not learned from the exploits and errors of one of the most elusive and dangerous characters ever to become mayor of New York, Fernando Wood.

The son of a failed Philadelphia merchant who had moved to New York, and named for the hero of a romantic novel that his mother happened to be reading just before she gave birth, Wood was a tall, slim, debonair charmer who somehow did not appear totally on the level. There was a coldness to his impassive, calm features. "Were it not for that pitiless eye and those closely compressed lips," recalled one observer, "you might mistake him for a moral reformer or a Home Missionary Society Agent."[8] As the diarist George Templeton Strong wrote, after noting Wood's superior political capabilities, "Pity he's a scoundrel."[9]

At various times an actor, a wine dealer, a cigar maker, and the proprietor of a waterfront grocery and grog shop, Wood joined Tammany Hall in the 1830s and in 1840 was elected to Congress, where he served one term. He then made a fortune as a merchant shipper and by 1850 felt secure enough to return to politics, running for mayor with Tammany backing. Even by this time, however, his record was clouded by allegations of deceit and dishonesty. There were reports that he had cheated a local bank, and a partner in his shipping concern claimed that Wood had swindled him out of profits from the California trade. Wood evaded these accusations. But he was also known to have engineered his nomination for Congress by directing a group of friends to infiltrate delegations to the nominating convention, then suddenly declare for Wood and stampede the meeting, a tactic that turned out to be successful. Opponents also alleged (he denied it) that he was a secret member of the Know-Nothing Party, a virulently nativist group.

He lost the 1850 race; but in 1854, with three other candidates also running, he narrowly won—partly because the Tammany-controlled Sixth Ward racked up 400 more votes for him than the total number of registered voters in that district. Wood proceeded to astonish his detractors by championing a wide range of civic reforms. He ordered saloons to close on Sunday, as the law required, and directed that Broadway be cleansed of streetwalkers and that hackmen not overcharge. He championed the cause of Central Park. He proposed upgrading the city's higher education system by establishing a municipal university, and he instituted a "complaint book" in City Hall where citizens could register gripes about municipal services. He also advocated giving the mayor more power so that even greater advances could be achieved. Reformists were ecstatic and began calling him the "model mayor," and his fame spread across the nation. Was he in earnest, or was he simply trying to buy respectability?

To further his cause—whatever it was—he insisted on making the police directly responsible to him. He soon possessed, in effect, a quasi-military force loyal solely to him, and people began to question his motives. Presently it became apparent that the "model mayor" was more interested in personal power than in the good of the city. When his Tammany backers complained about the closing of saloons he allowed the bars to stay open; arrested prostitutes were back on the street the next night. Throughout the city it was once again business as usual.

Seeking reelection in 1856, Wood ordered his policemen to contribute to his campaign fund, then used them to bar voters opposed to him and to allow supporters to make off with ballot boxes. On narrowly winning, he abandoned his earlier posture of rectitude. City offices were sold to the highest bidder with the assumption that the buyer would get his money back later by any means of subterfuge available. Bills to the city were padded, with the excess going to the Mayor, although one inflated transaction backfired. When the city was revealed to have purchased a $60,000 real estate parcel for $196,000 and felt compelled to cancel the deal out of embarrassment, the realtor sued the city and, to collect, arranged to have City Hall sold. An anti-Wood alderman thoughtfully stepped in and bought it for $50,000, then sold it back to the city.

Luckily for New York City, Wood soon ran into difficulties that cut short his corrupt reign. First he tangled with the state over the police. State legislators, responding to outcries that the city was as lawless as ever, voted to abolish Wood's municipal force and substitute a Metropolitan Police—responsible for an area greater than the city—to be run by five commissioners appointed by the governor. The mayor refused to recognize the new force or to disband his own, and for some time the city was blessed with two rival forces that spent more time fighting each other than catching criminals. One day a dispute over the naming of a new street commissioner brought large numbers of both groups to City Hall, where Wood's men prevented the state-appointed commissioner from entering the building to take office, and the Metropolitans battled to turn them aside. Other state officers tried to enter to arrest the mayor on charges of inciting to riot and were repulsed. For a while a full-scale donnybrook raged, the blue-clad Municipals clubbing and hacking away at the frock-coated Metropolitans and getting the same in kind. Wrote a reporter for the *New York Times*, "The scene was a terrible one. Blows upon naked heads fell thick and fast, and men rolled helpless down the steps, to be leaped upon and beaten until life seemed extinct."[10] A crowd in the park joined in, tearing branches off the trees to use as weapons.

The riot was halted only by the chance arrival of troops of the Seventh Regiment of the National Guard, who were marching down Broadway on their way to embark for a ceremonial trip to Boston. Seeing the state's authority jeopardized, their commander ordered his soldiers to disperse the mob and storm City Hall on behalf of the Metropolitans—which they promptly did. He thereupon entered and arrested a crestfallen Fernando Wood. A month later the courts upheld Albany's authority to impose the Metropolitan Police (and to name the street commissioner). Wood never stood trial, but his authority had been severely compromised by the episode, and he had become a source of civic shame.

The second blow to Wood's tenure was his abandonment by the sachems of Tammany Hall. They had never forgiven him for striking out against the saloons, and they were also irked because he had gone back on a number of promises made to party regulars for city offices—Tammany did not break its word. He was allowed to run again but received only lackluster support and went down to defeat. Indignant, he led his supporters out of Tammany and formed a rival known as Mozart Hall (for the building where it met). In 1859, with Tammany unable to come up with a strong candidate, Wood somehow made it back into City Hall under the Mozart aegis, but the following year he made a fool of himself by sponsoring the idea, in the months preceding the Civil War, that New York should befriend the southern states—and thereby protect its commercial interests— by seceding from the Union. That was his swan song on the local scene, although he went on to serve nine more terms in Congress, to no ill effect.

One of the Tammany leaders who had engineered the shunting aside of Fernando Wood was a great strapping alderman named Bill Tweed. At this stage Tweed, a minor Tammany sachem, was far from achieving his eventual prominence. But he had learned much from Wood's rise and fall. He saw the power that could accrue to someone who could centralize control of city departments, as Wood had attempted with the police. More to the point, he saw that before anyone could control the city government he would have to possess absolute control of Tammany Hall and unify the Democratic party. It was a prospect worth considering.

Because of the overwhelmingly Irish tone that Tammany was acquiring during these years, it comes as something of a surprise to learn that Tweed himself was not Irish at all or Catholic (neither was Fernando Wood, for that matter). Tweed's family, solidly Protestant, hailed from the River Tweed region in Scotland and had come to New York in the eighteenth century. Bill was born in 1823 on Cherry Street, in a respectable middle-class neighborhood near what is now the Manhattan end of the Brooklyn Bridge. He was the youngest of six children. His father was a chairmaker, and it was assumed young Bill would embark on a business career as he had a good head for figures. He grew to immense size, almost six feet tall and weighing well over 250 pounds, a bluff and brawny fellow known for his amiable smile and his unusual memory for faces and names. By his late twenties he was involved in both chair and brush manufacturing and was doing moderately well.

But the business world lacked excitement. What absorbed him most was the volunteer fire company he had helped start and whose name he had personally chosen: the Americus Engine Company Number 6. He had also dreamed up its symbol, a snarling tiger—which many years later the cartoonist Thomas Nast, in his series attacking Tweed, swiped to symbolize Tammany Hall (and whose subsequent leaders adopted it officially). Nothing was more exhilarating to Bill Tweed, the company's foreman, than to don his bright red shirt and white fire coat and trot alongside his red-shirted buddies and the company engine (despite his size he was fast on his feet) as they raced to beat competing companies for the honor of dousing a fire.

Heading up a fire company also meant getting into politics, and, because he was foreman, Tweed controlled the seventy-five votes represented by the members, not to mention the votes of their friends and relatives—no mean thing in the Seventh Ward. Charming and dependable, he seemed a good candidate for public office, and in 1850 he ran on the Tammany ticket for assistant alderman. That time he narrowly lost, but the following year he ran for alderman and won.

The city's Common Council on which the aldermen served was a uniquely powerful body with responsibility not only for all municipal patronage (for example, appointing all policemen) but for public franchises and civic improvements as well, of which there were a great many to be approved in the expanding New York of the 1850s. It even had a judicial function, appointing grand juries and trying election violators. Aldermen were unpaid, but the opportunities for graft were immense. Tweed later observed, "There never was a time when you couldn't buy the Board of Aldermen." But these particular aldermen approached their duties with such zeal that they became known as the Forty Thieves. City contracts were padded (Fourth of July fireworks costing $500 were billed at $4,000), with the aldermen pocketing a percentage; appointments to city jobs were available for a fee; and franchises were lucrative affairs (the franchise for a new horsecar line on Third Avenue cost the bidder $18,000 in bribes). Tweed learned about using "strike" legislation to earn a windfall. A fictitious resolution would be introduced threatening some merchant or trade, whereupon the alderman would go to the aggrieved party, commiserate with him, and say, "Give me $250 and I'll make sure it's killed in committee." The merchant would pay, never dreaming he'd been had.

Tweed also got an insight into the good life that public service could offer when the Thieves voted themselves an official tearoom in which refreshments were available. Horace Greeley in the *Tribune* once analyzed a lunch bill submitted by the group and figured that each alderman had consumed, at one sitting, eight pounds of beef, a chicken and a half, 225 oysters, a pound of sausage, two pounds of ham, and more than three loaves of bread—followed by 100 cigars.

This was heady stuff, and Tweed must have been enthralled. From then on—except for a two-year stint as a congressman in 1853–55, which bored him—his course was undeviating. There was money to be had, and he was going to have his share. He did not return to the Common Council, but in 1855 secured a position on the Board of Education, where cash could be generated from textbook contracts and kickbacks exacted from teachers. Two years later he became a member of the Board of Supervisors, whose powers had just been greatly increased by the state legislature in a move to offset those of the mayor—that dangerous character, Fernando Wood. Tweed had for some time seen Wood as an obstacle in his path, and his manipulation of the board to gain political power at the mayor's expense (as well as to bring in more money) was masterful. The supervisors wielded power similar to that of the later Board of Estimate, upstaging the Common Council (of Forty Thieves fame). The state legislature had intended the board to be bipartisan, with six Democrats and six from the Republican party (now a city fixture). Tweed outflanked this inconvenience by bribing one or another of the Republicans to be absent from key meetings, at which all the important—and profitable—business was transacted. Meetings were conducted with great efficiency, Tweed briskly ordering the voting or else moving at a strategic moment to suspend the rules. The other Democrats generally followed his bidding. All at once Bill Tweed was one of the most potent politicians in the city.

Possessing this kind of influence also enabled him to move up commandingly in Tammany Hall, whose leaders were always happy to recognize special talent. After helping to withdraw the Hall's support from Wood, Tweed in 1859 won appointment to Tammany's Council of Sachems; now he was in the charmed circle. Skilled at running meetings, he began presiding over Tammany nominating conventions, adeptly using sly parliamentary tricks to get his friends named. (Once when opponents tried to stop his railroading he ended the meeting by abruptly having the lights turned out.) In 1860 he became chairman of New York County's Democratic Central Committee, and in 1863 he took over Tammany's two top positions, becoming permanent chairman of its executive committee—the real power position—and then, later in the year, ascending to the honorific post of grand sachem. As he was still also firmly in control of the Board of Supervisors, William Tweed was now unquestionably the boss of New York.

It was during this time that he formed what became known as the Tweed Ring, the tight band of four who set an all-time record for plundering New York. Tweed masterminded the conspiracy, but each of the others had a special role. His key sidekick was Peter B. ("Brains") Sweeny, a short, ugly man whose deep-set eyes, it was said, shone "like little dollars in the night."[11] The son of an Irish saloonkeeper in the rough-and-tumble Sixth Ward, he was a lawyer and former lobbyist and an expert at political maneuvering behind the scenes. Sweeny functioned as Tweed's principal tactician. His formal post for a while was that of city chamberlain, whose purview was the selection of banks for the deposit of city funds; and he had created quite a stir by renouncing the $200,000 a year in interest payments that he could legally have pocketed from such deposits— acquiring what turned out to be a misleading reputation for honesty. Tweed eventually stated that he and Sweeny had never been close: "He is a hard, overbearing, revengeful man . . . He treasures up his wrath."[12] But the Boss found him indispensable.

The Ring's financial expert was Richard Connolly, a large, plump man whose size was exaggerated by the tall stovepipe hat he habitually wore, even indoors. Known as Slippery Dick, he had been born in Ireland and after arriving in New York had applied himself diligently to befriending his fellow Irish as a Tammany ward heeler. He had also been a bank officer and a state senator before Tweed had him appointed city comptroller in 1868. After the Ring's misdeeds were exposed, a contemporary observed that Connolly "had not an honest instinct in his nature. He lacked courage to carry through great frauds, but he was ready enough to follow the lead of bolder rogues. He was an uncertain friend and a treacherous ally."[13] But in the 1860s Connolly appeared impeccable. "Amid all the storms and whirlwind of public suspicion," the *Times* wrote after his election to the state senate, "he almost alone stands forth untainted by the breath of distrust."[14] A few years later the *Times* would feel differently. Connolly tyrannized his subordinates but cringed in the presence of Tweed.

By far the most bizarre member of the group was a slight, mustachioed, and black-bearded man who dressed with gaudy splendor and affected beribboned pince-nez, and who is fondly remembered as the Elegant Oakey. Abraham Oakey Hall was a man of wide talents, some of them formidable. He had written and acted in plays.

His magazine articles and short stories overflowed with Latin quotations and Shakespearean references. He was a sought-after lecturer and a respected drama critic. He was furthermore a skilled lawyer (serving for a while as the city's district attorney), had married well, and belonged to the best clubs. Tweed engineered his election as mayor in 1868. But it was Oakey Hall's endlessly changing wardrobe that most delighted observers. He was especially fond of custom-tailored frieze coats with velvet collars, embroidered multicolored vests, and silk bow ties, and he sported a new set of sleeve buttons every day. He could be counted on to put on a special show for great occasions, St. Patrick's Day, for example. "In 1870, when the great day came, there was a terrible snow storm," recalled a newspaperman years later. "It was an Irish snow storm, flakes as big as your fist. Well, the elegant Oakey stood on the reviewing stand dressed in a green suit, a green hat, a green tie, everything green, even green spats. He stayed all through the parade despite the inclement weather. Naturally it made a great hit with the Irish . . . after that people took to calling him Mayor O'Hall."[15] When he lit up a German gathering with a dazzling combination of the fatherland's colors, someone dubbed him the Honorable Abraham von O'Hall.

The Elegant One's political past was spotty: he had in turn been a Whig, a Know-Nothing, a Republican, and a Mozart Hall Democrat before finally entering the Tammany wigwam in 1864. His religious background was almost as confusing, for after being raised as a Presbyterian he had turned Swedenborgian and then Roman Catholic. Even Tweed had a few doubts about him. "Hall's all right," he remarked once. "All he needs is ballast."[16] But Hall performed a vital function for the Ring by giving it a cloak of respectability. And as mayor he showed no hesitancy in giving official sanction to some of the most brazen steals imaginable. If Tweed and Sweeny conceived of a new way to fleece the citizens of New York, Connolly would take care of the accounting and Hall would stamp it OK.

This, then, was the high command. But to accomplish its aims the Ring needed supporting troops. Most important were the Tammany ward leaders, who made possible Tweed's complete control of the electoral process. It was they who dispensed favors to the needy and the jobless, made sure the police went easy on gamblers, prostitutes, and saloonkeepers, sponsored clambakes and grand balls for the faithful, and on election day turned out the vote—marshaling the repeaters, standing ready to send in a few bullies to straighten out recalcitrant voters (or to wreck opposing precincts), and faking the final results as needed. Each with his own fiefdom, many ward captains were prima donnas and had to be handled with care lest they conspire to form competing organizations threatening the Ring's control. But so compelling was Tweed's aura of success from the mid-1860s to 1871 that revolts were rare and fleeting.

The Ring also needed pliable officeholders who would do their bidding. The most notable was John T. Hoffman, an engaging lawyer who preceded Hall as mayor, having been elected in 1865 under Tammany auspices. Hoffman liked to have lunch every day in the City Hall basement with Tweed (who would drop by from Tammany Hall, then located just across Park Row), Sweeny, and others, and it was out of these cordial affairs that the Ring itself evolved. Hoffman was glad to allow Tweed to provide him with so much power, and in 1868 he ran successfully for governor, thus not only enabling the Elegant Oakey to occupy the mayor's office but also providing Tweed with a staunch friend in Albany.

Finally, Tweed had to have friends in court. With its hold on Tammany, which in turn managed nominations to the judiciary, the Ring was able to stuff the city's legal system with its allies. A raft of new clerkships were created, providing jobs for Tammany minions, although some of the new attendants were imaginary persons whose salaries went straight into Connolly's coffers. Of the higher-ups, a handful of judges were respectable jurists whom Tweed allowed to function as a front. Others were hacks who could be counted on to rule in the Ring's favor.

The most notorious was George G. Barnard, a tall, soldierly man with black eyes and a black mustache who had been a gambler, an unsuccessful prospector in California, and a member of a minstrel troupe. "George knows about as much law," his brother reputedly said, "as a yellow dog."[17] Barnard was likely to enter his courtroom wearing a tall white hat that remained at a rakish angle throughout the session. He would make obscene jokes, drink conspicuously from a brandy bottle and, when bored, take to whittling the pine sticks that were provided each day by a court officer. (The shavings were swept up by a young Tammany-appointed attendant named Richard Croker.) Barnard was especially valuable in dismissing challenges entered against high-level Ring appointees, and he was adept at ruling in favor of Wall Street concerns whose leaders might be helpful to Tammany. Another Tweed judge, the scholarly looking Albert Cardozo, could be relied on to pardon criminals who were useful to the Ring. (The Cardozo name, thus besmirched, was cleared a half century later by his son, Benjamin Cardozo, who served with distinction on the Supreme Court.)

The purpose of this ramified mechanism, which seemed foolproof at the time, was to generate money for Tweed and his friends. No one has ever been able to state exactly how much was pocketed, but estimates range from $30 to $200 million. There were the kickbacks from patronage, and some of the plums benefited the Boss's family directly: two of his sons were given well-paying jobs, a brother became a tax assessor, and two of Tweed's nephews were clerks or deputy commissioners, at least on the record. But the biggest haul came from the padding of city contracts. It was assumed that all contracts would be inflated artificially, and up to 85 percent of the excess was returned directly to the Ring. A number of lofts and stables, for example, were rented for $85,000 a year to serve as National Guard armories but never used. The armories that actually were used cost $109,600—one of them being the top floor of Tammany Hall, where the available drill space was 40 by 100 feet. Whether used or not, these "armories" had to be kept in good repair, and Tweed's favorite plasterer, Andrew J. Garvey, collected $197,330 for supposedly performing this work, one of the deeds that was to win him the sobriquet of Prince of Plasterers. A plumber was paid $434,064 for the same manner of work, and a friend of Tweed's named James Ingersoll got $170,729 for chairs on which the guard troops could sit when tired—someone estimated that this was enough to supply three chairs for every soldier. Stationery supplies for the city over a two-year period came to almost $2.3 million.

In some instances Tweed could profit doubly. Back in 1864 he had bought a controlling interest in the New York Printing Company, at that time only one of several that did work for the city. Shortly thereafter he made sure that it got 100 percent of the city's printing—and overcharged for it all. So Tweed not only took a share of the firm's profits—in one year it paid $50,000 to $75,000 to each stockholder on capital stock worth only $10,000—but also enjoyed the benefits of payoffs that the firm made available on each order. Business was especially good for the company because Tweed persuaded other firms doing business with the city to throw their printing to it too. In addition to this company, Tweed was also part owner of the *New York Transcript*, an obscure newspaper to which he gave all the city's official advertising. And he had purchased, or was given by grateful businessmen, shares in a number of other companies under contract to the city.

Some of these fraudulent funds, it must be admitted, were used for what can be construed as a noble purpose: furthering the interests of New York City at the expense of the state. Tweed, in addition to his other posts, had been elected a state senator in 1867, and in Albany he proceeded to exercise all the wiles and stratagems that had worked so well in New York. Arriving in the capital, he allied himself with, and then took over direction of, the so-called Black Horse Cavalry, a group of legislators who freely sold their votes to the highest bidder. In 1870, partly with the help of his friend Governor John Hoffman but, more important, as a result of bribes to the cavalry totaling at least $600,000, he succeeded in ramming through the legislature what is known as the Tweed Charter, a new frame of government for the city. This document was a victory for all city partisans who hoped for more home rule, as it increased the authority of the mayor and got rid of the Metropolitan Police that had so vexed Fernando Wood. But it greatly benefited Boss Tweed, too, for after all the mayor was another faithful friend, Oakey Hall. More power to the mayor meant more to the Boss.

But such worthy expenditures pale beside the great sums that Ring members lavished on themselves and that Tweed in particular spent for his own comfort and amusement. He and his wife and eight children had moved in the early 1860s from a modest home on the Lower East Side to a handsome brownstone at 41 East 36th Street; but when it proved inadequate he moved around 1870 to a mansion on the corner of Fifth Avenue and 43rd Street that was reputed to have cost $350,000. In his stable a few blocks away he kept his horses, carriages, sleighs, fur robes, and gold-plated harnesses. In Greenwich, Connecticut, he maintained a country estate and a steam yacht. Andrew Garvey, the Prince of Plasterers, was said to have taken on the job of decorating the grounds of the estate with statues. Tweed asked him what a certain statue represented. "That's Mercury," replied Garvey, "the god of merchants and thieves." Tweed laughed. "Good! That's bully!" he said. "Put him over the front door."[18]

Not far away was the Americus Club, founded by Tweed and occupying a lavish thirty-bedroom clubhouse (jocularly known as the "Hôtel de Tweed") overlooking Long Island Sound. The initiation fee was $1,000 and monthly dues were $250; membership was limited to Tammany sachems and the Ring's most favored friends (which included a few token Republicans). Champagne was served at every dinner, and the food was prepared by French chefs. Tweed and the most affluent members liked to wear the official club pin, a $2,000 representation of a tiger's head with ruby eyes. While toiling in the city, the Boss stood out by virtue of a large blue-white diamond that he habitually wore in his shirtfront.

What Tweed could not manage to spend on himself he invested handsomely, and by the late 1860s he was believed to be the third largest holder of real estate in the city (after John Jacob Astor's son William and the department store magnate A. T. Stewart). He was never strapped for cash. One Christmas, it is said, he decided to donate $5,000 to the poor of his home district, the Seventh Ward. When a colleague said, "Oh Boss, add another naught to it," Big Bill was happy to oblige and made it $50,000.

In this world of make-believe numbers, nothing could approach the extraordinarily inflated spending that surrounded the construction of New York's lasting monument to Tweed, his courthouse in City Hall Park. The original design of the building, by the architect John Kellum, had called for a structure costing no more than $250,000—and the building in its present state does seem to justify that expense and not much more. When construction got under way in 1862, however, Tweed had just taken control of the Board of Supervisors, and soon costs began to escalate. The city kept pouring money into the project—$1,000,000 more, then an additional $800,000, then $600,000, until in 1870 the total approached $13 million and still the building was not finished. One observer commented that this one building had cost New York almost four times what England had recently paid for its extensive Houses of Parliament.

Some of the bills submitted by the contractors, all of them Tweed's friends, were mind-boggling, and the Ring was taking 65 percent off the top of each. Andrew Garvey received $2,870,464 for his princely plastering. A total of $5,691,144 went to James Ingersoll for furniture, carpets, and shades. (Note that an 1870 dollar would be worth about $10 today.) Lumber worth about $48,000 cost the city $460,000. Eleven thermometers, essential to any well-appointed courthouse, came to $7,500, and a number of very good brooms and other utensils were bought for $41,191. Not only was the expense exorbitant, but the work actually performed was shoddy, and the building's final cost included more than $1 million for necessary repairs.

What is most surprising about all this is that such a long time passed before the Tweed Ring's transgressions became known. Connolly's security was tight: only he and a couple of dependable sub-ordinates had access to the books. Furthermore, none of the contractors who were benefiting so egregiously had any desire to spill the beans. Beyond that, the Ring bought off potential critics by paying City Hall reporters regular stipends to keep quiet. More important still, New Yorkers at this point were not looking for anything wrong with their government, for times were good. The city was prospering as never before, and Tweed was taking credit for improving the waterfront and the water supply, hastening the completion of Central Park, and many other advances, not to mention the new charter. Later on, the Boss defended the whole system by remarking that as everyone was benefiting, how could there be any guilt?

Only two journals opposed the Boss. In 1868, *Harper's Weekly* (a sister publication of the *Monthly*) began printing the brilliant political cartoons of Thomas Nast, a German-born artist who with gusto portrayed Tweed as a lecherous, gloating, glowering oaf feast-ing off the people of New York. His caricature was understandably exaggerated—the Boss, at age forty-five, was going bald and begin-ning to look a bit weary and, with his genial look, never seemed threatening. But Nast's cartoons were both biting and humorous, and Tweed knew they could hurt him. "I don't care a straw for your newspaper articles, my constituents don't know how to read," he noted, "but they can't help seeing them damned pictures."[19]

The other critical publication was the *New York Times*, which in 1870 sensed something was wrong and began running editorials at-tacking Tweed. It had no evidence, however, and later that year Tweed blunted the attacks by appointing a blue-ribbon panel of distinguished citizens, headed by John Jacob Astor III, to examine the city's books. Inexplicably the panel found nothing wrong. (Either they were not shown the real books or, as has been alleged, they were all threatened with severe increases in their property assessments if they created a ruckus.)

The break finally resulted from one of those classic criminal oc-currences, a falling-out among thieves. A Tammany ward heeler named Jimmy ("The Famous") O'Brien, who was jealous of Tweed's power, apparently wanted the Ring to pay him $300,000 owed him for fees collected while he had served as sheriff. Unable to get the Ring to respond, he succeeded in having a protégé, William Copeland, appointed to the staff of the county auditor, James Watson, one of the handful of officials privy to the Ring's secrets. On January 21, 1871, Watson was badly hurt in a sleighing accident, and a week later he died. Copeland now had freer access to the books and began secretly copying incriminating documents that covered payments for the Tweed Courthouse. He turned these over to O'Brien. Now armed with damning evidence, O'Brien showed the Ring what he had and offered to sell them the copies if they satisfied his claim. After what seems to have been a heated discussion, they refused, calling his bluff. So O'Brien paid a call on the editor of the *Times* and presented his evidence. The jig was up.

The Ring panicked. Learning that they had been betrayed, they sent Slippery Dick Connolly over to call on the *Times*'s owner, George Jones, and offer him $5 million if he would refrain from printing the figures. Replied Jones after hearing Connolly's proposal, "I don't think the devil will ever make a higher bid for me than that."[20] The answer was no. On July 8, 1871, the *Times* began publication of the transcripts. Copeland's figures were augmented by those of another bookkeeper, Matthew O'Rourke, who also had a grudge against the Ring. By the end of the month every literate New Yorker was aware that Tweed and his cronies had perpetrated a massive fraud on them. (The Ring had also tried to buy off Nast, sending a banker around to offer him $100,000 to go on a long vacation in Europe. Nast, sensing what was going on, good-humoredly asked if the offer could be increased to $200,000. Yes, said the banker. How about $500,000, Nast pursued. When the banker assented once again, Nast threw him out of the office.)

As the *Times* continued its exposé, one horror after another was revealed—the armory scam, the payroll paddings, the corruption of the judiciary, and all the rest. A mass meeting of reform-minded citizens was held at Cooper Union out of which came the appointment of a Committee of 70 to clean up the city government. About this time Tweed, turning testy, uttered the remark forever associated with him. Confronted by a reporter who recited the charges building up against him, the Boss growled, "Well, what are you going to do about it?"[21]

What the reformers were going to do was throw the book at the Ring. An injunction was brought preventing the Ring from making further payments to anyone. Tammany tried to get Judge Barnard to dismiss it, but the jurist—jumping off a sinking ship—refused. Now the Ring was without judicial protection. Tweed, although reelected to the state senate in November (the Seventh Ward still loved him), was indicted a month later on 120 counts of deceit and fraud, and was hauled off to jail. Asked by a prison attendant what his occupation was, the Boss drew himself up and responded with the word that George Washington Plunkitt and others were to adopt with pride: "Statesman." By this time Tammany had hastily replaced him as grand sachem. Brought to trial two years later, he was convicted, sentenced to twelve years in jail, and fined the paltry sum of $12,500.

Meanwhile, his cohorts had eluded punishment. Sweeny and Connolly escaped to Europe. Indicted by a grand jury and tried, Oakey Hall conducted his own defense with such suavity and skill (he'd been too busy to pay attention to every single financial matter that came across his desk) that the jury was unable to reach a verdict. After a sojourn in Europe he returned to New York and became city editor of the *New York World*. The Ring's judges either resigned or, like George Barnard, were impeached; when Barnard died a few years later, more than $1 million in cash and securities was found among his effects. Few of the greedy contractors suffered. Garvey, for example, was granted immunity in return for testifying at the Tweed and Hall trials and never paid back a cent. In the end, the city was able to recover only $876,241 of the millions stolen by Tweed and company.

The saga of Tweed enjoyed a last twist. After he had served a year of his sentence, an appeals court threw out his conviction on technical grounds. He was thereupon slapped with a $6 million civil suit and was arrested anew. Confined to the Ludlow Street Jail, he was given certain privileges, like going for afternoon outings. On one of these he eluded his guards, escaped to New Jersey, and fled to Spain, where ironically he was picked up on the basis of a Nast cartoon in the possession of the Spanish authorities. Hustled back to Ludlow Street, Tweed tried to make a deal with the state's attorney general; in return for his release he would reveal the truth about everything the Ring had done. And he enclosed a draft of what he was prepared to say. The offer was tempting, and for a while the attorney general leaned toward accepting it. But finally he declined, saying Tweed's evidence was too sketchy. It is believed that the Boss was prepared to reveal altogether too much, hurting officeholders hitherto thought to be untainted by scandal—even highly placed members of the reform movement. So in a way Tweed had the last laugh, even if it meant staying in jail. He died there on April 12, 1878.

Tammany Hall, though severely wounded by Tweed's dramatic fall, did not die. Indeed, its greatest days were ahead, for the need was not only still there but growing: immigrants continued to flow in, contributing to a bigger New York, and the government was still far from adequately serving either them or the rest of the have-nots. Someone who could get things done was always useful. Tammany had recently occupied a brand-new clubhouse on East 14th Street and was beginning to flex its muscles for new battles. The man who rescued it and shaped its new image was a stolid, heavyset politician who has come down in history as New York's second great Tammany Boss, and the first who was a Roman Catholic, "Honest John" Kelly. As Morris R. Werner states in his study of the organization, "Kelly changed Tammany Hall from a disorganized and sociable political society for the development of the financial interests of its members into an efficient association for complete political exploitation."[22] The Tammany machine, which he truly created—it had previously been a haphazard affair, if basically predatory—was to be replicated in other American cities, and urban party organizations still carry signs of what Kelly wrought.

He was not a talker. The son of Irish immigrants, he was such a quiet fellow when young that his mother was once moved to say to a friend that John "thinks a great deal more than he talks, but be sure he is not dumb."[23] Nor was he cut out to be a conventional, plodding workman: as a young man he organized a dramatic club and cheerfully played the leads in *Macbeth*, *Hamlet*, and *Othello*. He held a variety of jobs, including office boy at a newspaper and stonecutter, but his real interest was politics. He had ways of making himself felt. Defeated in his bid for alderman on an anti-Tammany slate, he suspected foul play. At the next election, again a candidate, he visited a polling place with some of his rough-and-ready friends and found a screen set up behind the booths. He and his companions demolished it and found election inspectors who had been doctoring the tally. This time—it was 1853, the era of the Forty Thieves—he won and was invited to join the Tammany organization. Thoroughgoing and efficient, he became the leader of the foreign-born voters of the Sixth Ward and subsequently served two terms in Congress. But it was as sheriff, a post he held after completing his Washington stint, that he earned his nickname. The job carried no salary, the sheriff being expected to earn his keep through the collection of fees. Kelly did so with such success, and evidently in such a straightforward manner, that after several years he was said to be worth $800,000, all of it earned legitimately.

Kelly had been friendly with Tweed; but as the Boss ascended to his exalted state in total control of the party, Honest John began to

One of the most elegant parts of town in the 1840s was St. John's Park, on Varick Street between *Varick and Hudson streets (in today's Tribeca), which was dominated by St. John's Chapel, on Varick. Residents of the surrounding houses had exclusive use of the handsomely landscaped park, right.* But the area's grandeur was short-lived. *During the next decade the onrush of commercial activity in the area drove well-to-do residents away, and in the 1860s the park was sold to Commodore Cornelius Vanderbilt for use as a train depot. The chapel was torn down in 1918 for the widening of Varick Street.* Museum of the City of New York

In the first really large-scale flush of foreign immigrants to New York, passengers come ashore near the lower tip of Manhattan in the 1840s, disembarking directly onto the city's streets. When the flow of arrivals became too great, Castle Clinton at the Battery (left) was converted into a way station and processing center and was so used until Ellis Island opened in 1892. Museum of the City of New York

Totally restored and rebuilt after the 1835 fire, lower Manhattan was sketched from the steeple of St. Paul's Chapel, on Broadway at Fulton Street, by J. W. Hill in 1848. At the far left is P. T. Barnum's museum, while down Broadway is the steeple of the newly completed third Trinity Church. Print Collection, New York Public Library

Opposite: The most spectacular fire in the city's history occurred on the night of December 16, 1835, destroying much of the downtown area, including the columned Merchants' Exchange (left) on Wall Street. Courtesy of The New-York Historical Society

Tradesmen and storekeepers on lower Hudson Street pose for a group portrait in 1865. Courtesy of The New-York Historical Society

Lower-class suspicion of the well-to-do as well as enmity between New Yorkers of Irish and English descent led to the Astor Place Riot of 1849 outside the classical Astor Place Opera House. The disorder, which left twenty-two dead, was brought under control only by police and militiamen working together. Museum of the City of New York

The most violent disorder in the city's history, known as the Civil War Draft Act riots, took place in July 1863 as opponents of wartime conscription wrecked the city's draft headquarters and, despite aggressive police action, went on to produce mayhem all over town. Before the rioting was over, at least 1,500 people, a large portion of them black, had been killed. Museum of the City of New York

The northward expansion of the city can be sensed from a view made sometime after 1853 looking south from the Latting Observatory, a tower on the north side of 42nd Street (shown in the foreground). The 350-foot observatory, ascended by a steam-powered elevator, was erected to attract visitors who had come to a world's fair staged in the Crystal Palace (lower right). To the palace's left is the Croton Reservoir at Fifth Avenue and 42nd Street, the site occupied today by the New York Public Library. Aside from these imposing structures, the blocks in the area are only sparsely built up. A decade later they would be solid with new structures. Unfortunately, both the Crystal Palace and the observatory burned down by the end of the 1850s. Print Collection, New York Public Library

An ornate bar at the corner of Broadway and Worth Street, the Gem Saloon, is revealed in a drawing made in the 1850s to poke fun at Mayor Fernando Wood (in top hat at center, shaking hands), who first denounced all prohibition of alcoholic consumption and then reversed himself and declared he was for it. Museum of the City of New York

posite: Proceeding sedately, top-hatted inventor Charles T. Harvey demonstrates the heady ential of elevated railroad travel as he rolls along his new experimental line above Greenwich et in lower Manhattan in July 1868. Although his carriage appears self-propelled, it was ally pulled by a cable. Within a few years Harvey had extended his line to 14th Street and then to 30th, and although he went bankrupt, the city soon was spanned by a number of elevated s—using small (and sooty) steam engines for propulsion rather than cable. Museum of the City of York

TWO GREAT QUESTIONS.

Th. Nast.

"WHO STOLE THE PEOPLE'S MONEY?" — DO TELL. N.Y. TIMES. 'TWAS HIM.

One of Thomas Nast's most famous—and damaging—cartoons attacking the Tweed Ring, this one (published in Harper's Weekly in the summer of 1871) showed the bearded, portly Boss (at left) and his henchmen trying to evade blame. Next to Tweed is the mustachioed Peter ("Brains") Sweeny, then the clean-shaven comptroller, Richard ("Slippery Dick") Connelly, and the diminutive, worried Mayor Abraham ("Elegant Oakey") Hall. Courtesy of The New-York Historical Society

Topped by a statue of St. Tammany, its Indian patron saint, Tammany Hall on East 14th Street, erected in 1867, served as the society's headquarters until the 1920s, when a new building was dedicated a few blocks away. Courtesy of The New-York Historical Society

From his "office" on the courthouse bootblack stand, Tammany's George Washington Plunkitt gets ready to offer up a few words of wisdom. Photo from *Plunkitt of Tammany Hall*, by William L. Riordon

At the height of his power, Richard Croker (center, in derby) returns in 1899 from a sojourn in England. Museum of the City of New York

The young Jay Gould stands solemnly for his portrait, probably in the 1860s.
Lyndhurst, a property of the National Trust for Historic Preservation

A drawing in Harper's Weekly *shows Jim Fisk and Jay Gould, in a rowboat, almost being swamped by a ferry as they fled across the Hudson River to New Jersey on the night of March 11, 1868.* Courtesy of John Steele Gordon

Panic reigns on the New York Stock Exchange on April 13, 1872, as a result of speculation in the stock of the Erie Railroad after Jay Gould's ouster from control of the line. Courtesy of The New-York Historical Society

art of a panorama of Manhattan photographed in 1876 by John H. Beal from the Brooklyn tower of the unfinished Brooklyn Bridge shows a cityscape still lacking high buildings. The steeple at far eft is Trinity Church; the bulky building to the left of the bridge's Manhattan tower is the post office that then stood in City Hall Park. Courtesy of The New-York Historical Society

rotting enthusiasts try out their rigs on Harlem Lane (today's St. Nicholas Avenue) in a Currier ❧ Ives print of 1870 (opposite). In the center foreground, sporting a white tie, is Commodore anderbilt. Museum of the City of New York

The wily Commodore Cornelius Vanderbilt
posed for Mathew Brady around the time
of his move from shipping into his last
hugely successful venture, railroads.
Brown Brothers

Notoriously camera-shy
because of a nose ailment that
partially disfigured him, J.
Pierpont Morgan was snapped
by a passing photographer in
1908 as he waited for a
carriage. Courtesy of the Archives of
the Pierpont Morgan Library, New York

have his doubts and joined a group of Tammanyites prepared to field candidates opposed to the Ring. Then tragedy struck: within two years both his son and his wife died, and Kelly, lonely and distraught, quit politics and went to Europe. While there he learned that his two daughters had also died. Plunged into deeper despair, he considered joining a monastic order.

When the lid blew off the Tweed Ring, Kelly seemed to the dazed Tammany sachems just the man to rescue them, for he was untainted by the scandal. Locating him in the Holy Land, they persuaded him to return to New York, and in 1872 he was appointed county leader and Tammany's operating chief—in short, the new Boss.

His first move was to appoint men of unassailable integrity as sachems, like the merchant banker August Belmont and former governor Horatio Seymour. But that was window dressing. What he concentrated on was reorienting the organization toward efficiency and service. Tweed had gone too far, he believed, and had needlessly given Tammany a bad name. Tammany should not live on outright corruption, but it could flourish from the benefits of political patronage and from what was to become known as "honest graft." Dishonest graft, the new creed went, was the relentless shakedown of saloonkeepers and the like for kickbacks. This was officially to be abhorred, if in actuality it was allowed quietly to continue. Honest graft, on the other hand, was money made on the awarding of franchises, on city contracts, and the like. That was theoretically acceptable, as there were no victims—everyone benefited (except the taxpayer). As the rough-cut philosopher George Washington Plunkitt commented on the delicate distinction, "The politician who steals is worse than a thief. He is a fool. With the grand opportunities all around for a man with a political pull there's no excuse for stealin' a cent."[24]

The key to Tammany's success, Kelly said, was the link between elections and patronage. Elections were won by dispensing favors both to voters and to party workers; and winning creates more jobs, permitting more favors, and so on. To ensure that the system worked, he tightened the chain of command, with district workers held more directly accountable to their superiors. Each district had a quota for the patronage jobs allowed it, and there were no exceptions. It was vital to get the right man in the right place. As Plunkitt put it, "Every district leader is fitted to the district he runs and he couldn't exactly fit any other district."[25]

Service was vital, as it meant votes. "If a family is burned out,"

Plunkitt explained, "I don't ask whether they are Republicans or Democrats, and I don't refer them to the Charity Organization Service, which would investigate their case in a month or two and decide they were worthy of help about the time they are dead from starvation. I just get quarters for them, buy clothes for them if their clothes were burned up, and fix them up till they get things runnin' again. It's philanthropy, but it's politics too—mighty good politics. Who can tell how many votes one of these fires bring me?"[26]

Tammany Hall thrived, winning most of the city elections during Boss Kelly's forteen-year rule and gaining further strength as new ward leaders were trained. One of Kelly's proudest achievements was the election of William R. Grace as mayor in 1880, the first Roman Catholic to head the city's government since Thomas Dongan at the end of the seventeenth century. And the Boss personally benefited New York after being named city comptroller in 1876; frugal as ever, in five years he reduced New York's debt by more than $12 million.

It was only when Kelly tried to influence political events outside the city that he came to grief. He could not control the state Democratic party and lost out in some key races. His worst error was in opposing Grover Cleveland, the former mayor of Buffalo who had become governor in 1883. Reform-minded, Cleveland was unalterably opposed to taking Tammany's advice on patronage, and so Kelly vindictively tried to destroy Cleveland's campaign for the presidency in 1884. Cleveland won, while in the same election Kelly's candidate for mayor went down to defeat. On election night, after the returns became clear, he walked out of Tammany Hall and never returned. The double loss broke him. He became ill, was unable to make decisions, retired to his home, and in June 1886 died.

While Kelly was in his decline, he was visited each day by his trusted subordinate at Tammany, Richard Croker. From the big armchair in his home on West 69th Street, Kelly would tell Croker what Tammany should do, and Croker would execute his orders—or change them as he saw fit. Croker, in fact, was already in control of the Hall, although his role was not acknowledged except by true insiders. The day after Kelly's funeral, while senior sachems were pondering whether to name an interim ruling committee, Croker simply walked into Kelly's office and sat down at his desk. No one who had tangled with him would have been likely to argue. Dick Croker did not tolerate opposition.

Blunt, coarse, ruthless, and built like a prizefighter, Croker scorned the humility that had enabled Kelly to rebuild Tammany. But he was a better judge of people than Kelly and knew when he could find his enemies at their weakest and demolish them. His career was filled with setbacks that would have stopped a lesser man. He would not be swayed. As Alfred Connable and Edward Silberfarb put it in *Tigers of Tammany,* "Throughout his career he was hounded by leading educators, clergymen and publishers. He was investigated three times by special committees of the State Legislature. Twice he was defeated by reformers. Once he was tried for murder. Within his own circle of district leaders—even within his family—he was subject to sudden attacks whenever his authority appeared vulnerable. Yet for 16 years, until he committed the two unpardonable Tammany sins—pushing too hard and talking too much—he exercised more power than any Tammany leader before or since."[27]

Like Plunkitt, who was to become one of his most trusted lieutenants, Croker arose out of the shantytown north of the city. He had been brought to the United States at the age of four with his family from Ireland in 1846, the year the potato blight struck. Croker's father was a farrier, a kind of blacksmith and veterinarian, and a descendant of a soldier who had come to Ireland with Oliver Cromwell's English subjugators two centuries previous; his mother's stock was Scottish. As a boy Dick ran free, living by his wits and his fists. After his father had gotten a job courtesy of Tammany and the family moved to East 28th Street, he joined a gang. His school attendance was haphazard. Though small for his age, he was sturdily built and a natural fighter: in his teens he once knocked out his boxing instructor, and he was known to have severely tested several professional fighters. These accomplishments brought him to the attention of Jimmy ("The Famous") O'Brien, the subsequent betrayer of Tweed, who arranged for Dick's gang to be allied with Tammany Hall. Croker was promising enough, O'Brien thought, to be what he called a "comin' statesman," a good Tammany wheelhorse.

Although employed during business hours as a locomotive machinist, Croker zealously devoted himself to Tammany's needs. He became a dependable repeater, once voting for a certain candidate seventeen times in one day. O'Brien introduced him to Slippery Dick Connolly, who got Croker the job in George Barnard's court. Barnard was handling all sorts of cases involving powerful corporations and, for the most part, ruling in favor of the owners (who in gratitude contributed heavily to the Ring), and Croker was happy to sweep up Barnard's whittlings in return for this insight into the benefits of cozy arrangements between Tammany Hall and the city's powerful businesses.

Rising in Tammany's estimation, Croker won election as an alderman. When the Tweed scandal broke, he allied himself with the so-called reform faction of Jimmy the Famous and Honest John Kelly. But when a new Tammany leader was needed, Croker sided with Honest John, not O'Brien—a decision that Jimmy resented. Kelly rewarded Croker by arranging for him to win election as coroner, a post that could earn him fees as high as $15,000 a year.

By this time, at age thirty-one, Croker had married and acquired a patina of good manners and dignity, but the street brawler was still there. One election day Croker and a band of Tammany toughs were patrolling the East 30s when they came upon O'Brien and a group of West Side repeaters. Taunts were exchanged, O'Brien slugged Croker, and Croker countered with a blow to O'Brien's jaw. Then as both sides pitched in, a shot rang out and one of O'Brien's men fell, gasping out Croker's name as he died. Croker was tried for murder and, despite swearing that he'd never carried a pistol in his life, only narrowly escaped conviction when the jury split. He was never tried again, but his reputation was badly damaged and he had to relinquish his post as coroner. He was almost broke, with no job in sight.

Kelly, at some risk to his own reputation, found Croker a minor city job and later took him into Tammany Hall itself as his special assistant. Croker was endlessly grateful and learned much from the master. Lying low and working behind the scenes, he slowly acquired authority, and by the time of Kelly's death he was a power to be reckoned with. At the time of his actual takeover he was forty-four.

A quick succession of election triumphs followed his assumption of command. He backed the successful mayoral campaign of Abram S. Hewitt, Peter Cooper's son-in-law and business partner. When Hewitt proved to be irritable, opinionated, and reluctant to follow Tammany's advice on patronage, Croker dumped him and ran a close friend, Hugh Grant, who took the mayoralty in 1888 by a sizable margin. Once again Tammany was riding high, as patronage and lucrative contract deals flowed.

Enjoying his power, Croker discarded his self-imposed restraint and began playing the role of boss to the hilt. Now black-bearded and shaggy-browed and exuding confidence, the former bullyboy took to dressing with flamboyance and living the good life. His stern, glowering look mesmerized opponents and fascinated the public. Bit by bit New Yorkers realized they had a kind of homegrown celebrity on their hands. Croker played the races, betting huge sums. If he lost a big bet, that hardly mattered, because there was plenty of money where that had come from. In 1890 he bought a house in the East 70s for $80,000 and spent another $100,000 on it. The following year he acquired an upstate horse farm for $500,000. He added a plush winter home in Florida and, to top it all off, an imposing country estate in Berkshire, England, where he trained thoroughbred racehorses. Boss Croker was living like a prince and had acquired the informal title of Master of Manhattan.

The reason for all this unusual opulence—in spite of his not occupying any salary-paying office—was his stretching of "honest graft" to the limit, if not beyond. Kelly probably would have been shocked. Although Croker was careful not to steal from the public treasury, as Tweed had, he readily seized the "grand opportunities all around" later memorialized by Plunkitt. The key was Wall Street. Not only was he receiving kickbacks on franchises and city contracts, but businessmen requiring his approval or cooperation felt it prudent to make him a member of their boards or, more often, to quietly give him large blocks of stock. They also fed him speculative tips, bringing him many a windfall.

The opportunities for kickbacks and bribes were endless. A prolific source was the Ludlow Street Jail, where civil prisoners—businessmen who had gotten into difficulties, for example—were held; a cash payment of $500 or $1,000 might enable a prisoner to spend a couple of days in a hotel or to enjoy special privileges while incarcerated. All city jobs were for sale, most notably in the police force, which was controlled by Tammany. Any policeman expecting a promotion had to pay a fee according to a recognized schedule: promotion to sergeant could be had for $1,000, but it cost at least $12,000 to become a captain. Policemen who refused to pay were refused advancement and transferred from one precinct to another; many quit the force in disgust.

Most cops were glad to go along with the promotion-fee system because the rewards were so great. Kelly might have disapproved of "dishonest graft," and Plunkitt may have scorned it, but Croker allowed it to flourish as never before—and perhaps as never since. Graft of any sort was permissible as long as Tammany was cut in on it. Not for naught was the decade called the Gay Nineties—New York was a wide-open town courtesy of Tammany Hall. The richest returns came from the area stretching from Broadway west to Ninth Avenue between 23rd and 42nd streets, which had become New York's center of vice and crime. It was chockablock with bars, bawdy houses, and gambling dens all ready to be shaken down. Once known as Satan's Circus, the district came to be called the Tenderloin from the remark of a police captain, Alexander ("Clubber") Williams, who said upon his transfer into it, "I've had nothing but chuck steak for a long time, and now I'm going to get a little of the tenderloin."[28] Every police precinct had its wardman whose sole duty was to collect protection money from saloons, brothels, and even streetwalkers. Nor were legitimate businesses exempt—the wardman hit them too, as well as street peddlers. The wardman was allowed to keep a small part of the take, turning the rest over to the captain, who kept a percentage for himself and his patrolmen. The rest was sent up the line until a handsome remnant ended up in Tammany hands. If the mayor at the time knew about the process, he was content to look the other way. Tammany's view of it was a reprise of Boss Tweed's: everybody was happy, so who could object?

Some reformers objected, pointing out that while Croker and Tammany might be happy, much of the city—particularly its poor, whom Tammany professed to benefit—was not. For Tammany was feasting on the city, not using its clout to improve the people's lot. But the reformers got nowhere—a state investigating body turned up hardly anything incriminating—until a Presbyterian minister, the Reverend Charles H. Parkhurst, undertook single-handedly to shame Croker from power. A highly persuasive orator, Parkhurst in 1892 preached a sermon attacking Tammany for its corrupt maintenance of vice in New York, and when skeptics doubted the accuracy of his charges he embarked personally—in suitable disguise—on a three-week tour of saloons, vice dens, and criminals' hangouts in the Tenderloin and elsewhere. His revelations hit the city like a bombshell and led the state legislature in 1894 to appoint a second inquiring body, the Lexow Committee, which launched a thoroughgoing investigation of Tammany's ties to New York vice and corruption. Croker instantly sensed that the tide was against him. Pleading illness, he hastily resigned from Tammany Hall (leaving it in the hands of a dependable underling) and sailed for England, where he spent the next three years on his estate improving his thoroughbreds. In the fall of 1894 Tammany's candidates took a pasting, and a reform administration took office headed by a reputable Republican banker, William L. Strong, as mayor.

Did this spell the decline of Tammany? Not by a long shot. The Strong administration won praise for the work done by its zealous young police commissioner, Theodore Roosevelt, who did his best to rid the department of favoritism and other corrupt practices, and who liked to lead noctural sweeps of depraved neighborhoods testing the rectitude of his patrolmen. Strong also earned high marks for paving the way for Greater New York. But in just a few years, as they were to do often in the future, New Yorkers tired of "good government" and reform. An East Side gang member had an explanation. "These reform movements," he said, "are like queen hornets. They sting you once, and then they die."[29] Again, Richard Croker read the signs correctly. Hastening back from Europe, he recaptured Tammany Hall by marching in, summoning all the ward leaders (including some who had talked of breaking away) and announcing in no uncertain terms that he was once again the Boss. It was a personal triumph, achieved through sheer force of personality. His admirers called it the Return from Elba.

Croker was now to exercise power, and to exhibit pure braggadocio, on an unprecedented scale. He personally selected as a mayoral candidate a little-known City Court judge, Robert van Wyck, and got him elected over a field of far more capable men. (Van Wyck, who would become the first mayor of Greater New York, is remembered today in an expressway universally cursed by travelers to Kennedy Airport.) Not long after the election the Boss, with his compliant mayor-elect in tow, hosted a gathering for party leaders at a resort hotel in Lakewood, New Jersey, that New York newspapers with delight called Croker's Court. For more than a month, with regal aplomb and with van Wyck acquiescing, he doled out appointments to city offices high and low while supplicants quavered. Every evening all gathered for dinner in formal dress, a costume new and highly uncomfortable for many of those present. Some months later the Boss outdid himself, if that was possible, when he threw an opulent Jefferson Day banquet for 1,200 at the Metropolitan Opera House, whose orchestra seats were removed and replaced by lavishly decorated tables. As Croker made his entrance—with the ward leaders' wives looking on from the surrounding boxes—the band played "Hail to the Chief."

Van Wyck did as he was told, allowing the old corrupt ways to flourish without restraint. His most memorable appointment was that of William Devery as chief of police. Devery had distinguished himself during the Lexow hearings by intoning, in response to questions about police corruption, "Touchin' on and appertainin' to that matter, I disremember."[30] In fulfilling the duties of his new post, he liked to station himself by a pump at Eighth Avenue and 28th Street each evening and transact business both with his gambling friends and with city police on the take. Asked if he was aware of a saloon immediately behind him that stayed open after legal hours, he said he was not. He had seen people going in and out but did not know it was a saloon.

Spurred partly by the renewed laxity toward vice, the state in 1899 launched yet another inquiry into Croker's regime, and this one hurt. Known as the Mazet investigation, it focused on Tammany's links to big business. Croker fought it with all the vigor he could muster and was defiant on the witness stand, refusing to reveal anything about his personal holdings, which he said were nobody's business. At one point the committee counsel, Frank Moss, while cross-examining the Boss about Tammany's take from the sale of judicial offices, asked, with some sarcasm, "Then you are working for your own pocket, are you not?" Croker shot back, "All the time—the same as you."[31] The grim response made headlines. For the first time a Tammany boss had demonstrated the venality of the entire system.

More damaging still was the committee's revelation of what became known as the Ice Trust. Unbeknownst to the public, Tammany Hall had entered into an agreement with the American Ice Company that gave it a monopoly on the sale of ice; no other company was allowed to land ice at the municipal docks. In exchange for this privilege, which enabled it to keep its prices high, the company had bestowed large blocks of stock on virtually every important Democratic politician in New York, especially Croker. So Tammany was on the take not just from petty vice and political officeholders but also from the slum dwellers whom it was ostensibly befriending, for it was forcing them to pay artificially high prices for an indispensable commodity.

After retreating again to his bucolic estate in Berkshire, Croker made one final attempt in 1901 to recover his power but failed when his candidate for mayor lost heavily. The stubborn, willful boss had by now become an embarrassment even to Tammany, and there was no recapturing his former glory. For the last time he sailed away. He spent the rest of his life in England, achieving a brief notoriety in 1907 by winning the derby at Epsom Downs. Disputes with his children brought litigation that used up most of his ill-gotten fortune. He died in 1922.

By that time his successor as Boss of Tammany and the city, Charles Francis Murphy, had been in power for almost two decades. Murphy redirected the organization toward better service and won praise for espousing social legislation that would benefit the poor, a significant change from the old days. But "honest graft" in the John Kelly sense remained. So would Tammany Hall, until civil service reform and the advent of the welfare state finally wiped out its sources of power by midcentury.

Toward the end of his Tammany rule, Croker on one of his many trips across the Atlantic remarked to a fellow passenger, who was an English editor, that New York's wealthy, educated citizens could not govern because they would not touch political work—"no, not with their little fingers." And so, he said, you have to interest the masses in politics, and the only way was through the spoils system. "I admit it is not the best way," he said. "But think of what New York is and what the people of New York are. One-half, more than one-half, are of foreign birth . . . They do not speak our language, they do not know our laws, they are the raw material with which we have to build up the State . . . Except to their employer, they have no value until they get a vote . . . If we go down into the gutter, it is because there are men in the gutter; and you have to go down where they are if you are going to do anything with them."[32]

It was a viewpoint that would be widely held in New York right down to our day.

8

Wall Street
Takes Command

One of the most bizarre episodes in the annals of New York finance took place on March 11, 1868, as three speculators well known to Wall Street fled across the Hudson River to the safety of Jersey City one step ahead of the law. One of them carried $7 million in greenbacks with which they hoped to outmaneuver railroad magnate Cornelius Vanderbilt. The others carried nothing more than the clothes on their backs but, traversing at night, came close to drowning in midstream.

The fugitive trio were the craggy-faced Daniel Drew, the rotund showman and playboy James Fisk, and the small, deceptively meek Jay Gould. All three were members of the executive committee of the Erie Railroad, a benighted line whose finances had been manipulated with abandon almost since its founding—but never so flagrantly as in recent months by those who were now scampering across the Hudson. Vanderbilt had tried to purchase the Erie to protect his investment in his recently acquired New York Central line, but his adversaries simply printed more stock to dilute his holdings. He had served them with injunctions, and they had retaliated with court orders denying his right to do so. At length, the exasperated Vanderbilt got a compliant judge to issue a warrant for their arrest for contempt of court.

The three had gotten word of Vanderbilt's move while they were celebrating their latest triumph over him at the Erie's headquarters on West Street. The seventy-year-old Drew, a wily operator affectionately known as Uncle Daniel even to those whom he had fleeced in the market, panicked and resolved to get out of town immediately. Accompanied by underlings who struggled with bags and boxes stuffed with folding money, he hustled aboard the first ferry to New Jersey, which was beyond the court's jurisdiction. The much younger Fisk (thirty-three) and Gould (thirty-one) decided to luck it out in the city, but that evening while dining at Delmonico's they got word that the sheriff's deputies were closing in. Hailing a cab they raced to the foot of Canal Street, where they persuaded crewmen of a docked steamer to row them across in a small boat. Dense fog had settled over the Hudson, reducing visibility to a few yards, and halfway to their destination the crewmen lost their bearings and began rowing in circles. Twice they were almost run down by passing ferries. Finally a third ferry came splashing past them, and Fisk and Gould lunged for its paddle-wheel housing, barely caught hold, and dragged themselves aboard, to be delivered drenched to the New Jersey shore.

Luckily the three were soon able to make peace with the Commodore; and although Uncle Daniel got dealt out of the Erie, in the settlement Gould and Fisk retained command of the railroad and went on to perpetrate other outrageous deeds. Few would have expected anything else of them, given their reputations and the temper of the times. The post–Civil War United States was rife with lawlessness—and nowhere more than in the nation's money capital. Immense amounts of money were being raised to pay for all manner of new industries and above all for railroads, which were being flung across the country at a great rate and which were, in effect, the first truly modern corporations. With the United States in a relaxed and forgiving mood, a certain tolerance for freebooting was understandable. It is no coincidence that the peccadilloes of Boss Tweed were foisted on New York at the same time as were the plunderings of Fisk and Gould. Indeed, Tweed was a Gould ally and at one time sat on the board of the Erie.

For just as bossism was a feature of New York's political adolescence, flourishing in the vacuum caused by the city government's inability to cope with the problems thrust upon it, so did the wild, woolly, and sordid time of the Fisks and Goulds occur because the economic scene was changing. The old merchant economy, ruled by the importers, shippers, and wholesalers of South Street, was being superseded by a much bigger game, one that required far more capital than the South Street merchants had ever been able to command. Copious transfusions of European money were needed, and a new breed of moneyman came to the fore to raise and manage the vast sums: the investment banker. South Street, which had called the tune in the first half of the century, gave way to Wall Street, which would direct the city's and the nation's economy thereafter. So bandits like Drew, Fisk, and Gould had their day of quick killings (and losses), but after a time, as the United States adjusted to the different and larger demands of the industrial age, and as the buccaneers' excesses were seen as hurtful and began to be curbed, they yielded to more solid, sober, and prudent (but no less dramatic) actors of the nature of Jacob Schiff and J. P. Morgan.

The catalyst was the Civil War, which not only expanded the nation's industrial capacity but also required infusions of money on an unprecedented scale. The federal government, after failing to sell its war bonds on its own, appealed to the bankers of the northeastern cities—primarily New York, Philadelphia, and Boston—for help. The Philadelphia broker Jay Cooke masterminded the first successful war bond campaign, but a number of banks and brokers in New York either got their start or expanded during these years. One of the most notable cases was that of the Seligman brothers, the German Jewish family that had done well in the clothing import business. Acquiring a contract at the war's outset to supply uniforms to the Union Army, and going on from there to sell war bonds (especially to their friends in Europe), the Seligmans profited to such an extent that in 1865, just after the war ended, they set up the international banking firm of J. W. Seligman & Company with offices in many of the world's principal cities. From then on the Seligmans played a prominent role in New York's investment banking scene.

With the coming of peace the nation went on an expansionist binge, and speculators thrived on the money flowing into and out of Wall Street. Speculative techniques like selling short had been introduced three decades earlier by the first great operator, Jacob Little, but such maneuvers now came into their own. Short sellers were "bears" while long sellers, who bet on the market going up, were "bulls," and the two were forever jousting. Few rules governed the buying and selling of stocks, and it was often easy for speculators actually to control the prices of securities they had taken a position on so as to maximize their profits. Speculators could also form pools, groups of investors who would orchestrate their buying and selling so as to influence the market. The New York Stock Exchange was no place for timid souls.

Daniel Drew was not timid, and he had been feasting off the market for years. What made him especially elusive for an opponent was his

187

sanctimonious air, for he was extremely devout and much sought after as a preacher at Methodist conferences. In his business life he almost seemed to be saying a prayer while separating his victims from their money. Drew came from a poor farming family some sixty miles north of New York in what is now Putnam County, and as a young man he became a drover, moving cattle from farms in his area down to the city, where they would be sold to one of New York's wholesale butchers like Heinrich Astor, John Jacob's older brother. Drew was smart and, according to a widely accepted legend, not above playing tricks. As he neared the city in the late afternoon, it is said, he would feed his herd but give them no water. Instead he allowed them to lick plenty of salt. The following morning, driving them down the island of Manhattan, he would pause at a stream that flowed at about today's 77th Street and let them drink . . . and drink. Arriving at the market, the beasts would be bloated, earning Drew extra profits. As he later went into stocks and bonds the term "watered stock" came to mean, in his dubious honor, any security whose worth has been diluted.

By this means and others, by 1829 he had put aside enough money to purchase a country inn and tavern just beyond what were then the city limits, which at the time were around Third Avenue and 24th Street. The hostelry catered mainly to other drovers, who often had extra cash to put aside, and Drew would act as their informal banker and run down to Wall Street to put the money into investments. The Street itself was just beginning to take on its busy—even frantic—air, and Drew was soon buying and selling for his own account. For a while in the 1830s he dabbled in steamboats and competed with Vanderbilt for passenger traffic on the Hudson, but Wall Street was to remain his first love. He became adept at moving in the opposite direction from the way the market seemed to be going. Sometimes called the Great Bear, he was, as one chronicler put it, "a most robust architect of panics."[1]

Like many other Wall Street denizens, Drew took great delight in speculating in the stock of the Erie Railroad. Founded on the suggestion of De Witt Clinton, who thought the residents of New York State's southern tier deserved a transport route that would compensate them for being off the track of the Erie Canal, the railroad followed a difficult route whose development ate up money to such an extent that the line was often close to, or submerged in, bankruptcy. The unending spate of new issues was a speculator's dream, and Drew used dozens of brokers to conceal his moves in and out of the market. During the 1850s he got himself elected to the Erie's board of directors and shortly thereafter had himself appointed treasurer. As John Steele Gordon puts it in his amusing book about the so-called Erie Wars, *The Scarlet Woman of Wall Street*, "The fox of Wall Street was now in charge of the henhouse."[2]

And he was doing mighty well in the process. In the late 1850s, the Erie was showing signs of prosperity, tapping not only the lush dairy country between New York and Binghamton but Pennsylvania's coalfields as well. Drew had accumulated such wealth and prestige that he was invited to join the exclusive Union Club, a reserve not normally hospitable to country boys. But the members learned to respect the speculator's prowess. At one point they had apparently ribbed him mercilessly about having taken a loss in the market, but the Great Bear did not like to be kidded. Shortly thereafter, Gordon relates, Drew entered the clubhouse in what appeared to be a highly agitated state. He seemed to be looking for someone and kept mopping his brow. Just as he was leaving, he pulled out his handkerchief again and, seemingly without knowing it, dropped a small slip of paper on the floor. After his departure his friends pounced on the paper and read, "Buy all the Oshkosh you can get at any price you can get it below par." This puzzled them as they knew Oshkosh had been rising and was presumably a good sale. But on the assumption that Drew must be on to something, they formed a pool and bought a large block of Oshkosh. Drew had in fact sold it short, and it plummeted, so he had the last laugh.

Uncle Daniel's manipulations of Erie stock might have gone on indefinitely had it not been for Commodore Vanderbilt. In 1867 the seventy-three-year-old Vanderbilt had acquired control of the New York Central Railroad, which ran west from Albany toward Buffalo, and with his other lines along the Hudson was putting together the first water-level route from New York City to the west. Though he did not object to the Erie's existence, he was aware of Drew's reputation for slick dealings and did not wish to get into a dispute with him that might lead to a rate war. So he bought enough stock to get someone on the Erie board to represent his interests. Reports filtering back to him unfortunately confirmed his suspicions: Drew was still cheerfully playing with the stock.

Then Vanderbilt learned that another party was eyeing the Erie, the management of a New England line whose name, the Boston, Hartford & Erie Railroad, they had coined simply because they hoped to connect with the Erie and get in on the Pennsylvania coal trade.

The Commodore entered into an alliance with them in the interests of ousting Drew. Uncle Daniel, faced with dismissal, pleaded with him, promising to be good, and Vanderbilt in an uncharacteristic act of kindness permitted him to remain. It was a mistake. For presently a new board election was held that resulted in the addition of two men who would complicate matters for the Commodore. They were Jim Fisk and Jay Gould.

Good friends and staunch allies, Fisk and Gould could hardly have been less alike. Fisk, a dandy and born showman, was fat, jovial, and expansive and had virtually no enemies; the slight, intense, bearded Gould was introspective and widely disliked. Fisk was the son of a country peddler in Brattleboro, Vermont, who passed along to him the tricks of the trade with such success that at the age of twenty or so Fisk offered to buy his father out, take over the business, and put him on the payroll. (The father accepted the offer.) Such zeal was not likely to be fulfilled in the country, and before long Fisk went to work for the Boston dry goods firm of Jordan, Marsh & Company. When the Civil War broke out he went to Washington, rented a suite in the Willard Hotel, and liberally dispensed food and wine to politicians—landing the company a fat contract to supply blankets, clothing, and other goods to the armies. Now a partner in the firm, Fisk sent agents to the South to buy cotton from behind enemy lines and became a company hero. At the war's end, however, he found that the day-to-day dry goods business no longer excited him. So he left Jordan, Marsh and, saying a fond good-bye to his wife, Lucy, whom he decided to leave behind in Boston (but with whom he remained on affectionate terms), set out for New York.

There he opened a broker's office, and before long his flamboyant ways brought him to the attention of Daniel Drew, who recognized a kindred spirit and taught him the fine points of speculating. Fisk became known on the Street and also attracted attention about town, as he was fond of high living and was often seen in the company of attractive young "actresses." One in particular stood out: Josie Mansfield, a tall, buxom, dark-haired woman for whom he soon developed an infatuation. "She was tall and shaped like a duchess," wrote an admiring reporter. "Her skin was as fair in fibre and hue as the lily itself."[3] Fisk took to supporting her in grand style, while he also bought an expensive house for Lucy back in Boston.

Such grandiose ways were not for Jay Gould. Indeed, Gould never lifted a finger to ingratiate himself with anyone except members of his own family, with whom, surprisingly, he was warm and loving.

He seemed, in fact, to be without any sense of business morality and unhesitatingly turned on people who thought he was on their side. (He never turned on Fisk, however.) For this he was roundly despised, which did not bother him in the slightest. Anyone judging Gould, however, should do so with an eye to the context of the times. The late nineteenth century was rife with scoundrels, and in a way Gould was merely one of the smarter ones. He was, in fact, brilliant.

Like Drew and Fisk, Gould was also a country boy, and he hated it. Raised on a farm in Delaware County west of the Catskills, he was descended from a long line of hardworking, upstanding New Englanders, one of whom had fought with distinction in the Revolution. (Because of Gould's Shylockian manner, there was—and still exists—an assumption that he was Jewish, but in fact there is no evidence of it. He was first named Jason, which his family shortened to Jay. The family name was originally Gold; no one knows why the *u* was added.) As a boy Jay was sickly but industrious, with few friends, and he spent his spare time reading and studying. A sister remembered that he once spent three weeks, off and on, solving a problem in logarithms.

Itching to escape, Gould in 1852, just short of his sixteenth birthday, left home with five dollars in his pocket to work for a surveyor. The surveyor failed but Jay and two others completed the assignment, and he became expert at the difficult craft. A few years later he decided to write a history of Delaware County. After a fire at the publisher's destroyed the manuscript, Gould rewrote the book from memory and from the few charred fragments. It is still considered a standard work.

What happened next would later be considered by Gould's detractors to be the first instance of his duplicity, though the evidence is unclear. During his surveying Gould had met Zadock Pratt, an elderly semiretired tanner who was greatly impressed by the young man. Gould learned of a rich stand of hemlocks in eastern Pennsylvania that could yield bark ideal for tanning, and he told Pratt, who decided to set up a new tannery with Gould as manager. The business thrived and a town grew up in the vicinity named Gouldsboro (it is still there), but Gould for some reason had a falling-out with Pratt. The old man said that he would buy Gould out for $10,000 but that Gould could have the business for $60,000, never dreaming that Gould could raise that sum. Gould went to New York and found two leather merchants who agreed to back him, and so he took over the tannery with the other two as partners. One of them, who had a history of instability, soon committed suicide, and there was a disagreement over the reworking of the agreement; whereupon the other partner journeyed out to Gouldsboro with a gang of toughs and attempted to take over the tannery. Gould and a band of employees with whom he was popular repulsed the attack. But the experience soured him on the tannery business, and he resolved to get out.

With almost no money left he moved to New York and undertook a blitz study of Wall Street and the stock market. How he managed to acquire funds to start investing is not known, but in a few years he was sufficiently well off to acquire a controlling interest in a short but nearly bankrupt railroad that ran from Rutland, Vermont, to Troy, New York. Studying the railroad business with his customary intensity and applying himself zealously, he put the line back in shape, made it a paying proposition, and sold out for a handsome profit. Suddenly he was a railroad executive. As Maury Klein remarks in his biography of Gould, "From the Rutland [& Washington Railroad] he gleaned the vast potential of railroads for making money. His experience on the Street taught him a variety of ways to gain control of a rail company on a shoestring. He emerged from the Civil War period a seasoned Wall Street warrior, wise beyond his years, fired with ambitions that dwarfed those of ordinary men and possessed of the audacity to attain them."[4] It was presumably his fine record with the Rutland that got him named to the board of the Erie.

Once on the board, Gould made an ideal comrade for Daniel Drew, as did Jim Fisk. Uncle Daniel was not, as it turned out, keeping his promise to the Commodore. He just could not keep from speculating in Erie and even formed a pool of some of the board members to manipulate the market—before proceeding to double-cross them for his personal gain. This was the last straw for Vanderbilt. Trying to influence Drew did not work; he was going to have to buy the railroad. He began acquiring Erie stock.

But there was something wrong. Each time the Commodore thought he had a controlling interest in the road, new stock appeared. An 1850 law forbade railroads to increase their stock, but no matter. Drew was finding new shares that had been authorized but not issued, and with the aid of Fisk and Gould he was also issuing bonds (which was permitted) of a type that could be converted into stock. Vanderbilt, continuing to buy, got the disreputable Tweed judge, George Barnard, to enjoin the Erie from printing more shares; Drew and his cohorts found a way to do so in their capacity as members of the executive committee. More injunctions followed; Drew found judges to nullify them. Drew's brokerage, one observer remarked, "was resonant with the rustling of fifty thousand shares of fresh, crisp, Erie certificates, like the chirping of locusts at noontide in July."[5] One injunction served notice on the Erie's secretary that he would go to jail if he registered more shares. Fisk solved that one by lying in wait for the messenger who was delivering the certificates, swiping the bundle, and running off down the street with it. If no one knew where the stock was, how could the secretary be arrested for issuing it?

Vanderbilt eventually decided to have Drew, Fisk, and Gould arrested for contempt, resulting in their disorderly retreat to Jersey City. The renegades holed up in Taylor's Hotel, which the press— noting that Fisk had seen fit to guard it with three small cannon plus a detachment of Jersey City policemen—soon dubbed Fort Taylor. Fisk brought Josie Mansfield across and installed her in a suite.

All was not well, however, in the Erie high command. Uncle Daniel, who had been the first to run for cover, got homesick for Manhattan and began to sulk. Gould did not hesitate to move in and take over; from now on he was in command. More court orders were being issued, but Gould countered by having a friendly legislator in Albany introduce a bill that would, in effect, absolve the Erie management of all past sins. With the permission of Judge Barnard, he traveled to Albany carrying a suitcase stuffed with many of the greenbacks extricated from Manhattan. After most of these had passed into the possession of state legislators—and despite the counterbribe undertaken by the Commodore's men—the bill passed. Sometime thereafter a settlement was reached with Vanderbilt. The Commodore got most of his money back, Drew was ousted, and what was left of the Erie was given to Gould, who became president of the line. Fisk was installed as controller.

The line was in poorer shape than ever, for the settlement had cost the stockholders a cool $9 million. This did not faze Gould, who by various feats of legerdemain began bringing cash to its till. For reasons that are unclear he also decided to spring a "bear trap" on his former partner. This involved restricting the money supply by certain technical means, a move that caused stock prices to begin falling; inviting Drew to join him in selling short (Drew accepted with glee); watching prices drop further; and finally, just as Drew was about to cash in, releasing his large store of cash so that prices soared—and stayed there. Drew lost heavily and was never again a force on the Street.

One would have thought that a large outcry would long since have arisen as a result of such predations, for too many people were ruined by them. The state legislature was no help; its members were content with things as they were. Finally, at the end of 1868 the New York Stock Exchange revised its rules, severely restricting the issuance of new securities. Other new regulations gave it more power over those trading therein. It was a beginning.

Delighting in their success, Fisk and Gould bought Pike's Opera House, an imposing structure at the northwest corner of Eighth Avenue and 23rd Street, and converted it into a luxurious headquarters for the Erie. (Fisk bought a brownstone for Josie a few doors away and moved in with her.) But bigger things were on their minds, and in 1869 they attempted to take over the Albany & Susquehanna Railroad, which ran between Binghamton, a key Erie stop, and Albany. The object was to effect a link between the railroad and New England and once again challenge the Commodore. The Albany & Susquehanna's president, Joseph Ramsey, was having none of this, and when Gould began buying shares in his railroad the air was again filled with injunctions and counterinjunctions. Fisk, who was directing field operations this time, decided to capture the line physically. His forces seized the A&S station in Binghamton and dispatched a train up the line bearing some twenty muscular Erie employees, who took over each station as they moved north. In response Ramsey's forces sent a similar train south from Albany, and the two met near Harpursville some fifteen miles east of Binghamton, with a fine collision of locomotives and a free-for-all that was halted only by the arrival of the state militia. The result was a standoff, and in the court trial that followed Ramsey won. The Albany & Susquehanna was beyond the reach of Jay Gould. An interesting sidelight on the case was that Ramsey had retained as his chief financial adviser the promising young New York banker J. P. Morgan.

Undaunted, Gould with the help of Fisk went on to attempt a mind-boggling financial feat: to corner the gold supply of New York and, by extension, that of the United States. Wrote Henry Adams, "Of all financial operations, cornering gold is the most brilliant and the most dangerous, and possibly the very hazard and splendor of the attempt were the reasons of its fascination to Mr. Jay Gould."[6]

On the surface, his scheme was nothing more than a way to benefit the Erie Railroad. Much of the Erie's revenue came from shipping wheat and other crops from farmers in the Midwest to merchants in New York, who then sold it in Europe. The European purchasers paid in gold, for most of Europe was on the gold standard. The United States, however, because of the lingering effects of the Civil War, was not. The New York merchants therefore paid the farmers in greenbacks but were reimbursed from abroad in gold. While waiting for his gold from Europe, the merchant "borrowed" some of it in New York at the Gold Exchange, located right next door to the Stock Exchange. If the price of gold went down while he waited, he was covered by his borrowing, which was in effect a short sale. If the price went up, he was also covered, but only after the gold arrived. In the interval before the arrival, a shortage of gold would drive the price up at least temporarily; and a price rise would benefit not only the farmer waiting for his money but the Erie as well. And if the person who caused the shortage profited from the corner, that was nice too.

There was only one hitch, but it was a big one. The amount of gold normally available in New York was worth only around $20 million, a sum within reach of a Jay Gould. But the federal government maintained, at its Sub-Treasury right across Wall Street from the Exchange, a sum far in excess of that for use in emergencies. For his scheme to work, it would be necessary for Gould to somehow immobilize the federal gold and keep it out of the market.

To do this, Gould hatched an audacious plan: he would get the president of the United States on his side. Ulysses S. Grant had just been inaugurated, and though a consummate soldier and a man of great intelligence, he knew little of economics. Jay happened to be acquainted with an aging New York lawyer and speculator named Abel Corbin, who had recently married Grant's sister. Through Corbin, Jay got the president's ear and made his pitch: a rise in the price of gold would benefit the Midwest's farmers, who would therefore be grateful to the new administration. This could be brought about if the government held its own supply of gold in abeyance, at least temporarily. Grant thought the argument made sense and he agreed. Jay Gould in the spring of 1869 started buying gold contracts.

For some time the price of gold hardly changed at all, hovering between 135 and 138. The summer passed and it still did not rise. Gould did not have much more time to pull off his coup, and so he got Fisk to help him. At Gould's urging Fisk plunged in and began to buy—noisily and on a large scale. The price edged up.

Just at this point Gould made a mistake. He had been cultivating the president all summer, wining and dining him and subtly emphasizing the need to leave the market alone. Now he felt he had to be certain. He wrote a long letter to Grant urging him once again to allow gold to rise unimpeded, and he had the letter delivered by special messenger to a town in western Pennsylvania where the Grants were visiting. Grant's secretary, wondering why a messenger had come all the way from New York just to bring a letter, mentioned his puzzlement to the president. Suddenly Grant realized he was being taken.

By Wednesday, September 22, gold had risen to 141, and excitement in the Gold Exchange was building. Fisk was in his element, buying like mad. Late that afternoon Gould got an urgent call from Corbin; please see me immediately, he said. Gould learned that Corbin's wife had just received a letter from Mrs. Grant saying, "Tell your husband that my husband is very much annoyed by your speculations. You must close them as quick as you can."[7] Gould persuaded the terrified Corbin not to tell a soul about the message.

He knew what he had to do. The next day, with Fisk continuing to stampede the market, and with the price still rising, Gould began to sell in small quantities.

Friday, September 24, was the culmination and became known as Black Friday. The Gold Exchange was now in a fury, with brokers screaming and gesticulating and Broad Street crowded with concerned spectators. The price passed 150 and kept climbing. Gould sat in his broker's office tearing small bits of paper to pieces and selling in increasing quantities. At 11:40 A.M. the price hit 160. Just then Gould received word that Joseph Seligman was quietly selling gold—a sure sign that the government was ready to act, as Seligman represented the official in charge of the Sub-Treasury. A short while later a prominent broker, James Brown, shouted "Sold!" and the panic was broken. A bit later still, the Sub-Treasury pumped $4 million in gold into the supply, but the crisis was over. Soon the price was below 140 and falling.

In the wake of the panic, much anger was directed at Gould, for many brokerage houses had failed and others had suffered huge losses. Gould and Fisk set their lawyers to obtaining injunctions right and left that would hamstring suits for damages. As to the plotters themselves, Fisk repudiated many of his purchases while Gould, although he had profited considerably from the debacle, was forced to spend large sums settling up with resentful claimants. More important, he failed to help the Erie and also acquired a great many more enemies, and so the net effect was decidedly against him.

The pair returned to day-to-day operations of the Erie, but Fisk's days were numbered, all on account of Josie Mansfield. She had acquired another lover, a dashing but unstable young man named Edward S. Stokes (of the Phelps-Dodge-Stokes clan that had figured so prominently in the merchant era). Booted out of Mansfield's house, Fisk found that Stokes had been taking money from the oil refinery where he worked (and which was partly owned by Fisk) and had him arrested for embezzlement. Mansfield and Stokes countered by threatening to publish letters that Fisk had written to her. Fisk accused Stokes of blackmail, and January 6, 1872, a grand jury indicted Stokes on the charge. In a rage, Stokes got a pistol, waited for Fisk at a hotel he was due to visit, and shot him twice as he mounted the stairs. Fisk died the next day. Jay Gould sobbed openly in public, the strongest emotion anyone had ever seen in him.

Gould himself did not last long at the Erie. Its board had been increasingly vexed by his behavior, and at length it forced him out. But the ouster did not mark his departure either from Wall Street or from the railroad business. He became involved in a number of western rail lines, notably the Union Pacific and the Missouri Pacific, each of which he took over by financial maneuverings, and he later controlled the Western Union Telegraph Company. He bought a splendid Gothic Revival mansion, Lyndhurst, in Tarrytown, New York, which remains a showplace. But his deeds no longer had a marked influence on New York itself.

In his wake, the city's legal and financial leaders moved to prevent Gould-like excesses from recurring. Its Bar Association, for example, pushed through a law requiring any motion in a case to be filed in the court where the case originated; this went a long way toward preventing the judicial disarray that had prevailed where one judge could countermand another's injunction. And the Stock Exchange tightened up its rules, requiring brokers to trade listed securities only on the floor of the Exchange. It also forbade corporation directors to sell short the stock of their own company.

In the larger sense, however, Wall Street was simply getting too big for the kind of games that Drew, Fisk, and Gould had played; the stakes were now too large. The capital needed by the multiplicity of new corporations being formed dwarfed what had sufficed earlier, and the new Wall Street potentates were the investment bankers, who specialized in taking care of all the financial needs of their corporate customers, including raising funds virtually on a global scale. Many astute financiers came to the forefront during the next several decades, but by far the most powerful—so potent that he sometimes seemed almost a caricature of the breed—was J. P. Morgan.

Brusque, domineering, and supremely self-confident, Morgan was in many ways such an arch–New Yorker that it comes as something of a surprise to learn that he was yet another, if perhaps the most striking, of the long line of New Englanders who came to New York because it presented such great opportunities. He was no country boy in the mold of Daniel Drew or Jim Fisk, however. Morgan's grandfather had prospered as a hotelkeeper in Hartford, Connecticut, and had helped found the Aetna Fire Insurance Company; Morgan's father went to Boston and became a banker specializing in foreign trade transactions and then moved to London to join an international banking house that became J. S. Morgan & Company. So Pierpont Morgan grew up in a moneyed atmosphere in which it was perfectly normal for a banker to function on a grand scale. After private schooling and a year or so at the University of Göttingen, he was taken on as a junior accountant in a private banking firm in Manhattan. He was also the American representative of his father's bank in London.

Moving easily in the Wall Street world as well as in New York society, Morgan soon advanced to such an extent that he was ready to go into business on his own. His record during these years was not unblemished; one investment commitment, lending money to a man who was selling obsolete carbine rifles to the Union Army in the Civil War, was morally dubious. But he seemed to learn from such experiences, for in the latter part of his life he became a model of probity and responsibility (if sometimes insufferably so). By the late 1860s he was one of the most promising young men in New York's financial community, and so it was no fluke that he turned up as an adviser to President Ramsey of the Albany & Susquehanna Railroad.

Although it is not known just what Morgan contributed to Ramsey's victorious cause, it is possible to speculate on his reaction to the proceedings. Gould's and Fisk's dealings were competition gone wild, and Morgan did not approve of such competition; businessmen, he felt, should cooperate for the benefit of all. In the words of Morgan's biographer, Frederick Lewis Allen, "It is hardly an accident that most of the Americans who at the beginning of the twentieth century were charged with being monopolists had got a good look in their youth at competition at its savage and unbridled worst, and had decided to try to do something about it."[8] Morgan would spend the rest of his life trying to bring order and stability to the financial world, as he saw it. If his view of that world and its needs was not popular with many less privileged Americans, that was irrelevant.

A few years after the Albany & Susquehanna affair, Morgan got a break that was to bring him far greater influence over the nation's railroads. Commodore Vanderbilt's son, William H. Vanderbilt, who had taken over the New York Central system, asked Morgan if he could very quietly sell a large block of Central stock for him. Vanderbilt simply felt, he said, that he owned too much of it for propriety's sake, but he did not want to rattle the market and give the impression that the line was in trouble. Morgan skillfully placed the entire lot among English investors without attracting notice. As a result he was taken on the New York Central's board, a position of some moment. Other board appointments were forthcoming, and soon Morgan was a railroad authority. During the 1880s he successfully reorganized a number of lines, including the Reading, the Baltimore & Ohio, and the Chesapeake & Ohio.

It was on the basis of these accomplishments that he tried in 1888 to actually bring together the heads of the major rail lines in order to halt what he believed was ruinous competition. The Interstate Commerce Act had just been passed, and Morgan felt the railroads might keep the government off their backs if they worked together. So he invited them all to New York for a series of meetings at his house on Madison Avenue and 36th Street. (One of them, incidentally, was Jay Gould, representing the Missouri Pacific.) As it happened, the loose cooperative association formed during the talks did not last. The meetings were nevertheless significant in that a New York banker had acquired the status—and nerve—to assemble and knock together a large number of heads of industry, as it were, in the interests of cooperation and discipline.

Many of the men who gathered at Morgan's house, even if they represented railroads spread across the United States, probably did not have to travel far to attend, because they were already here. Gould, for example, was a confirmed New York resident, with a house at Fifth Avenue and 47th Street in addition to his Tarrytown estate. New York during these years was rapidly becoming the headquarters of American business. It had long led all other cities both commercially and financially, but now because of its role as a money market center it was the place from which the nation's industrial economy was being directed. Industrial leaders were finding that, even if their businesses for the most part functioned elsewhere, they were better off establishing their headquarters in New York. Thus the steelmaker Andrew Carnegie had moved east from Pittsburgh to be closer both to the big banks and to the railroad heads who were his best customers. Similarly, the extravagantly successful oilman John D. Rockefeller in 1883 moved to New York from Cleveland, where his operations had begun; he built a large corporate headquarters for his Standard Oil Company at 26 Broadway, not far from Wall Street, and moved his family into an imposing mansion on West 54th Street just off Fifth Avenue. Other magnates were doing the same. A newspaper survey in 1892 revealed that the New York area contained 1,265 millionaires, or 30 percent of the national total. By 1900 the city was the headquarters of 69 of the 100 largest corporations.

Along with this concentration of corporate power came a great concentration of expertise. To serve the captains of industry and finance, the city was also attracting ever-larger numbers of lawyers, accountants, engineers, architects, advertising agents, and printers. It was essential, too, that these experts be close at hand, for industrialists and financiers had to have what one observer has called "knowledge in a hurry."[9] To operate effectively they required copious amounts of information on short notice, they had to have the latest reading on "what the market is," and they had to be able to confer readily with colleagues, consultants, business acquaintances, customers, and even competitors. Today, with electronic communication so advanced, physical proximity is less vital, but a century ago it was essential. And it made for the crowding that was to mark lower Manhattan and, later on, other parts of the city too.

Morgan relished the concentration of power at the top of the corporate and financial world and felt it was good for the country. In middle age he had become a formidable figure, six feet tall and hulking, with round features. His piercing gaze could wither an opponent; his nose was disfigured by a skin disease that had made it bright red. This somewhat intimidating personage was to be found during workdays at his bank's office at 23 Wall Street, at the corner of Broad directly opposite the Stock Exchange. Morgan's alternate seat of power was his imposing home, to which he summoned those whom he wished to persuade or with whom he wished to confer privately.

From both these bastions during the 1890s and the first years of the new century he endeavored to bring about the consolidation of industry and greater cooperation among large corporations. The idea was one whose time, many businessmen felt, had come, though not every scheme was legally feasible or politically acceptable. In the 1880s the notion was hatched that a group of companies could combine by entrusting their securities to a central body of trustees, who would watch over the whole affair and pay dividends to all the shareholders as needed; but the resulting trust was deemed in restraint of trade and was ruled out by the Sherman Antitrust Act in 1890. In the 1890s a substitute was devised, the holding company, in which the supervising organ—which would hold the shares of the participating companies—was a new company registered under the laws of a state that welcomed such devices; the first state to do so was New Jersey. As the century ended, the country was enjoying prosperity, and holding companies appeared to be politically acceptable. Mammoth corporations registered in New Jersey became a fixture on the economic landscape, and Morgan played a key role in setting up many of them. Indeed, he was to be the linchpin of the biggest combination ever seen.

One group of hotly competitive concerns that seemed to cry out for consolidation and integration was the steel industry, a vast array of muscular companies whose national importance was incalculable. Some combining had already taken place. One group of companies had been brought together as the American Steel & Wire Company by John W. ("Bet-a-Million") Gates, a sobriquet he had earned by his zeal for gambling—he was reputed to have spent an afternoon betting with a friend at $1,000 a race as to which of two raindrops would get to the bottom of a windowpane first. Gates and Morgan had cooperated to form another corporation, the Federal Steel Company; Morgan had arranged two others; and there were four more, for a total of eight modestly big concerns.

One potent and immensely profitable body, however, was not part of any combination. That was the Carnegie Steel Company, of Pittsburgh. Founded in the 1870s by Andrew Carnegie, it differed from all the others in that it was a maker of crude steel (the others were almost all devoted to turning out the finished article). Carnegie had made it a model of efficiency and profitability. Anyone putting together a truly powerful consortium would want to buy it. But the cost would surely be astronomical, and, anyway, Carnegie was thought to be unwilling to sell. Only one man was believed capable of assembling the necessary capital for such a deal: J. P. Morgan. But when approached on the possibility he had replied, "I would not think of it. I don't believe I could raise the money."[10]

There was one glimmer of hope. Carnegie was almost sixty-five and might be thinking of retiring. But no one knew when he might decide to do so. In the summer of 1900 the non-Carnegie companies, fed up with having to buy from the Scotsman, decided to cut loose and set up their own crude steel works. In retaliation Carnegie announced plans for a massive new plant for making finished articles. War had been declared.

Amid all the signs of rising tension, a dinner was held on December 12, 1900, at the University Club in New York, in honor of Carnegie's young and personable chief assistant, Charles M. Schwab. Seated next to Schwab at the head table was Morgan. The reason for the dinner is not recorded, but it made history. Schwab was expected to limit himself to a short speech, but instead he launched into an hour-long discussion of the future of the steel industry and its potential for bringing about greater prosperity and improved international trade—a potential, he emphasized, that could be realized only if the industry was thoroughly integrated. When he was finished, Morgan, though he had stared at his plate impassively throughout, took Schwab aside and they talked intently for half an hour. The financier had been vastly impressed, and now he saw a way to proceed.

A week or two later Morgan got word to Schwab in Pittsburgh that he would like to confer further with him, and Schwab returned to New York to meet with the financier in Morgan's mahogany-paneled library. After much discussion Morgan asked the younger man to find out whether Carnegie might sell and, if so, at what price. Schwab arranged to play golf with Carnegie on a course outside New York, and to his surprise the small, bearded Scot gave his assent and wrote some figures on a slip of paper. Schwab returned to the city and stopped in at 23 Wall Street. The slip of paper outlined terms, adding up to a sale worth almost half a billion dollars. No one had ever paid that kind of money for a company. Morgan glanced briefly at the paper and said, "I accept."[11]

Thus was born United States Steel, the first billion-dollar corporation. There remained a great deal of work for Morgan and his partners; for one thing, the independents had to be brought in. All did so readily except for Gates's American Steel & Wire. Gates was holding out for a much higher price than Morgan was willing to pay, and he showed no signs of giving in. As the negotiations dragged on at 23 Wall Street, Morgan, who was not present, was persuaded that the time had come to issue an ultimatum. Striding into the room where Gates and the others were assembled, he announced sternly, "Gentlemen, I am going to leave this building in ten minutes. If by that time you have not accepted our order, the matter will be closed. We will build our own plant." He turned on his heel and walked out. Gates accepted.[12]

With the creation of the steel corporation, Morgan was universally recognized as the most powerful banker on Wall Street and the most potent financier in the nation. He was not without challenge, however. As the steel megalith was being put together, it was felt that it should include the Lake Superior Consolidated Iron Mines, a rich source of ore in Minnesota's Mesabi Range and the property of John D. Rockefeller. Morgan said he would not talk to Rockefeller; he disliked him. So an emissary was dispatched to the Standard Oil building to broach the possibility of a purchase. Rockefeller was evasive, but not long afterward he sent his son, twenty-seven-year-old John D., Jr., over to confer with the banker. Morgan received him in his office, made him wait for several minutes while he concluded other business, and then asked abruptly, "Well, what's your price?" Rockefeller, at first nonplussed, replied, "Mr. Morgan, I think there must be some mistake. I did not come here to sell. I understood you wished to buy." Taken aback, Morgan stared at him for a moment and then smiled. The ice was broken and the resulting talks went smoothly.[13]

If Morgan stood at the summit of the money world, one other man could claim to share it with him. Indeed it was widely known that Jacob Schiff, after Joseph Seligman died in 1880, was the only German Jewish banker whom Morgan treated as a peer. At one point Schiff almost bested Morgan. The short, trim, white-bearded controlling partner of the hugely successful firm of Kuhn, Loeb & Company had, like Morgan, made a specialty of representing major railroads and counted among his clients the Pennsylvania, the Illinois Central, and the Southern Pacific. He was also the principal banker for the Union Pacific, whose chairman was the slight, bespectacled, and mustachioed Edward H. Harriman, a genius of modern railroading (and a native New Yorker who operated throughout his life from Wall Street). Schiff and Harriman worked together closely, if warily, and in 1901 they confronted a problem. The Union Pacific, stretching west from Omaha across the Rockies, lacked access to Chicago, which Harriman naturally considered vital to his line's success. Access could be attained by purchasing the Chicago, Burlington & Quincy, which served Iowa and the surrounding states in addition to Chicago. But the way appeared to be blocked: the Burlington had just been secretly bought by Harriman's major competitor, James J. Hill, of the Great Northern and the Northern Pacific railroads. Hill's banker was J. P. Morgan. Harriman and Schiff seemed to be stopped cold.

Harriman was not one to take defeat lying down. He now undertook to bring off a preposterous coup. Unable to buy the Burlington, he decided to buy its owner, the Northern Pacific, right out from under Hill's and Morgan's noses—and Schiff backed him to the hilt.

The Hill-Morgan forces actually owned less than half of the Northern Pacific stock, although that would normally suffice to assure control. Harriman began buying the rest in large amounts. For quite a while no one noticed: the market at the time was booming because of the U.S. Steel launching, and big purchases were being made everywhere. When other brokers questioned the purchases, the Kuhn, Loeb traders would say Northern Pacific was rising because of its acquisition of the Burlington. Not until the end of April 1901 did Hill, on a business trip to Seattle, sense that something was wrong. He sped east. Morgan was in Europe, and so Hill stopped in to see Jacob Schiff. It was true; Harriman and Schiff had been buying. How much do you have? asked Hill. "A lot of it, Jim," said Schiff.[14]

Believing that Hill might be willing to make a deal that would satisfy Harriman, Schiff invited him to his home that evening and said that Kuhn, Loeb would stop buying if the Northern Pacific would put Harriman on its board. Hill said he would—but he was not telling the truth. Before coming uptown he had stopped in at 23 Wall to see Morgan's partners. Aghast at learning of the Harriman-Schiff maneuver, the partners decided to cable Morgan for permission to buy 150,000 more Northern Pacific shares. Reached at a hotel in the south of France, Morgan gave his approval the next day.

Meanwhile Harriman had become worried. In theory he and Schiff now owned almost 51 percent of Northern Pacific; he wanted to be sure. So the next morning, a Saturday, he phoned Kuhn, Loeb and asked them to buy 40,000 more shares. (The market was then open on Saturdays.) But Schiff was at his synagogue, where an underling found him among the worshipers and relayed Harriman's request. Schiff quietly said, "Do not buy. I'll take the responsibility."[15] So the order was not executed.

One explanation of Schiff's unexpected response was that he had taken Hill's word and felt the purchase was unnecessary—indeed, in bad faith. Another is that he felt that the game had gone too far and that further purchases would spell trouble. In any event, when Morgan's brokers began buying the 150,000 shares on Monday morning they caused a panic. The reason was simple: there were no longer enough Northern Pacific shares to satisfy the order. It was, in effect, a corner—by accident. The price rose, rose farther, and panic set in as brokers who had sold Northern Pacific short could not deliver. (Harriman, when he learned that his order had not gone through, found he could not buy either.) By Thursday the stock, which had opened on Monday around 110, had hit 1,000. Other stocks had plunged. Then Northern Pacific broke, and the panic was over. That day the two sides made peace, and the market returned more or less to normal.

The crisis, which was dubbed the Battle of the Giants, left Morgan chastened. He felt it should not have been allowed to happen. Schiff, for his part, was unhappy too, and he did not want to make an enemy of the man at 23 Wall Street. A few days later he wrote to Morgan saying that the Union Pacific interests had never meant to be antagonistic to him or his firm, and that "we have at all times wished, as we continue to do, to be permitted to aid in maintaining your personal prestige, so well deserved."[16] The two men continued to get on well.

The financial community had come a long way since the days of Uncle Daniel and his rascally companions. But Wall Street's capacity for causing large-scale tremors had not changed. As all the world knows, it would be felt with ever greater impact in the future.

9

The Gilded Age

Barely two years after the irascible Commodore Vanderbilt, the wealthiest citizen of the United States, died in 1877 at the age of eighty-two, his son and heir William Henry Vanderbilt made an unexpected move. He decided to get a bigger house. Few observers thought he cared about such things. All his life Billy, as the Commodore called him, had been eclipsed in his father's shadow and, while evincing a marked talent for business, had carefully avoided asserting himself lest he incur the wrath of the old man. True, he had shown an interest in racing swift trotters on sportsmen's tracks in upper Manhattan, but so had his father. He had also acquired some paintings. But such minor splurging could be expected of any rich man. Now in his late fifties, the stout, bewhiskered Vanderbilt, who had inherited $90 million as well as control of the New York Central Railroad and other lucrative properties, lived with his wife in a relatively modest house on Fifth Avenue at 40th Street, where they had raised a large family. They cared little about society and the display of their wealth. In this regard William Henry seemed much like the Commodore, who had taken pleasure in ignoring or offending New York's top-ranking social leaders. (In response, society scorned him and his entire family.) But now William Henry thought he could safely enjoy his millions. His move, to a vastly more imposing abode at the northwest corner of Fifth Avenue and 51st Street, was significant in that it set in motion a wave of mansion-building on the upper stretches of Fifth Avenue that was to change the face of the city. Furthermore, the trend would end up affecting the ways of high society and eventually, because the new rich collected great art and sponsored other worthy endeavors, would give a powerful boost to New York's already robust reputation as a cultural center. The city had always had wealthy citizens and had seen the amassing of large fortunes like that of John Jacob Astor, but it was unprepared for the ostentation and conspicuous consumption of the last decades of the nineteenth century and the start of the twentieth. The period, marked by elegance as well as vulgarity, is justly known as the Gilded Age.

William Henry Vanderbilt did not build just one house; he built three at once. His massive pile of brownstones (the builders had recommended red and black marble, but he was not ready for that) comprised not only a mansion for himself that included a large art gallery, but also two splendid adjoining houses for his married daughters, Mrs. Elliott F. Shepard and Mrs. William D. Sloane. The assemblage occupied the entire west blockfront from 51st to 52nd Street and cost more than $3 million—and this was just the opening wedge. His sons and other family members would presently erect even more flamboyant palazzos of marble and other deluxe materials in the blocks to the north, bringing about the Vanderbilts' entry into society and—in a demonstration of New York's way of constantly changing its leadership—their eventual domination of it. The Vanderbilt châteaux would point the way to the succession of mansions all the way up Fifth Avenue to the 90s that became known as Millionaires' Row, mansions that more than one commentator observed were worthy of a Doge of Venice or a Lorenzo de' Medici.

Even as late as the 1870s, when William Henry embarked on his move, most of New York's wealthier citizens lived considerably to the south. Polite society's center was in the vicinity of Madison Square, at 23rd Street, and the solid but restrained brownstones of the rich were to be found on lower Fifth Avenue, in Gramercy Park, and along the side streets up to but not much beyond 42nd Street. The immensely successful German Jewish banker August Belmont, who had gained entry into society by marrying the niece of the naval hero Oliver Hazard Perry (which caused his ancestry to be overlooked), lived in an outwardly staid house at Fifth Avenue and 18th Street; only when the front door was opened, revealing a canvas of a voluptuous nude by the French painter William Bouguereau in the downstairs hall, could passersby get a glimmering of the banker's sophisticated way of life. Caroline Perry Belmont, busy presiding over a lavish entertainment schedule, took her husband's zestful ways in stride. On East 20th Street was the very proper Roosevelt brownstone where young Theodore had grown up. An exception to the staid look of the fashionable homes was that of Leonard Jerome, on

East 26th Street overlooking Madison Square. A millionaire who had made a killing by selling short in the panic of 1857, the tall, mustachioed Jerome pursued a dazzling life-style that included the best horses and carriages (his stables were paneled in walnut and richly carpeted), sumptuous dinners, and a series of unconcealed affairs with beautiful singers and actresses. His six-story brick-and-marble mansion, replete with mansard roof and delicate ironwork, had its own private theatre as well as a commodious white and gold ballroom. Unfortunately for Jerome, his amatory entanglements finally were too much for his wife, who decamped to London with their small daughters thereby beclouding his social life. (One of the daughters, Jennie, grew up to marry Lord Randolph Churchill and became the mother of Winston Churchill.)

Most of the fashionable clubs were around Madison or Union squares. The most aristocratic was the Union Club, which occupied an imposing Italianate building on Fifth Avenue at 21st Street; not far off were the Knickerbocker Club, whose members had hived off from the Union in 1871 on the ground that it was becoming too inclusive; and the Century, which put a premium on sobersided intellectual qualities. Affluent opera patrons took boxes at the Academy of Music on East 14th Street, while those seeking lighter entertainment patronized Tony Pastor's Music Hall nearby. Gaudier shows could be taken in at P. T. Barnum's Hippodrome on Madison Avenue at 26th Street just up from the Jerome mansion, on the site of a former railway depot. In 1875 Barnum sold out to a bandmaster named Patrick Gilmore who renamed the facility Gilmore's Garden, while in 1879 the name was changed again, to Madison Square Garden. It continued to offer rodeos, circuses, and other spectaculars. It was the first of four Madison Square Gardens. (In 1889 it was torn down, to be replaced by a large and delightfully ornate structure designed by the architect Stanford White and surmounted by a replica of the Giralda Tower of Seville, which in turn was topped off with a graceful statue of *Diana in the Nude* by Augustus Saint-Gaudens that many New Yorkers felt was too revealing. In the 1920s the Garden moved to Eighth Avenue and 49th Street and in 1968 to its present location over Penn Station.)

Theaters were still clustered around Union Square, although in the 1870s many were beginning to move uptown, along Broadway from 23rd Street up to 34th and even beyond, the stretch being called the Rialto or, alternately, the Gay White Way. But Broadway below 23rd Street in the late 1860s and 1870s was taking on another kind of image. Lined with elegant department stores, it was becoming a de-luxe shopping street for the well-to-do. The procession, referred to as the Ladies' Mile, began with A. T. Stewart's block-long cast-iron establishment at 9th Street; it was now his principal store, the earlier building at Broadway and Chambers Street having been turned into a wholesale outlet. At 11th Street was McCreery's and at 19th was Arnold Constable, while at 20th Street Lord & Taylor, which had opened its doors downtown in 1826 (under the aegis of an English immigrant, Samuel Lord, and the New York native George Washington Taylor), occupied a fine five-story building with a steam elevator. All day long well-dressed women alighted from their carriages and entered Lord & Taylor to select the latest fashions. (The store would move once again, to its present site on Fifth at 39th Street.)

Although New York's top hostesses depended heavily on such stores, catering to the rich was not enough to earn someone social acceptance. It was not forthcoming, for example, to the department store magnate Alexander T. Stewart, although by the 1870s he was worth at least $40 million and by means of shrewd investments had become one of the biggest landowners in New York (among other things he developed a large tract on Long Island into a suburban community that he named Garden City). Stewart by this time also had a respectable art collection. Desperately seeking social recognition, Stewart in 1864 purchased a perfectly adequate house on the northwest corner of Fifth Avenue and 34th Street (surely a gold-plated address), tore it down, and spent ten years building a huge $2 million white marble mansion that boasted grand staircases, ceilings created by Italian craftsmen, a library filled with rare editions, and an art gallery lined with valuable paintings and sculptures. To the city's aristocrats he was still just a peddler, and his house was a tasteless monstrosity. No one from society's top ranks deigned to cross his threshold, and a few years after moving in, lonely and heartsick, Stewart died.

Ironically, the one person who could have most swiftly granted him entry to the ranks of society lived directly across the street, occupying a stolid though ample brownstone on the southwest corner of the intersection. This was Caroline Schermerhorn Astor, who has come down in social history as *the* Mrs. Astor. But to recognize Stewart would have gone against all her principles. The short, stout, heavy-jawed Caroline Astor was born to one of the city's oldest families—the Schermerhorns had been in New York since 1636—and had worked hard to gain her own social supremacy. She would

210

never jeopardize it by recognizing an upstart like Stewart. Her marriage had not been the best one, for she had married William Backhouse Astor, Jr., who was only the younger son of John Jacob Astor's heir. But she had immediately set out to remedy this discrepancy by getting her husband to drop his unseemly middle name and applying rigid standards to her social life, which her sister-in-law, Mrs. John Jacob Astor III, who had married William's older brother, happened not to care about. The other Astors lived right next door to Caroline, occupying a similar brownstone at 33rd Street and Fifth Avenue, but there was little warmth between the two families. Otherwise correct, Mrs. John Jacob liked to invite painters and writers to her parties, which was improper. Society seemed to agree, for soon Caroline was universally acclaimed as New York's number one hostess. When people referred to Mrs. Astor, there was no question whom they meant. (Her husband was rarely in attendance, finding more pleasure in his yacht.)

In her campaign for primacy, however, Caroline Astor had gained expert help from a social-climbing southerner from Savannah named Ward McAllister. Trained as a lawyer but more interested in giving parties than in arguing cases, McAllister felt that New York society needed codifying. A hostess had to know who was acceptable and who was not; the worthy had to be separated from the boors. Shortly after coming to town he had organized a committee of twenty-five gentlemen known as the Patriarchs, who represented Old Money (four generations of wealth were needed to make a gentleman, McAllister felt, although in a pinch one might make it in three, as he decided the Astors had). The Patriarchs' sole purpose was to give a series of formal balls at Delmonico's. They were a stunning success, as invitations to them were seen as authentic passports to society. (As first-generation money, August Belmont could not qualify, but he did not seem to care.) At this point McAllister was ready for bigger game, and soon he had formed an alliance with Caroline Astor. His self-serving admiration for her grew to such a pitch that before long, evidently without reference to her actual looks, he was calling her the Mystic Rose.

Although her weekly dinners, served on gold plates, were the stuff of grandeur (only aristocrats certified by McAllister were invited), the main vehicle for social enforcement was her annual ball, held each January. It was an exclusive event, and only a limited number of invitations were sent out, as Mrs. Astor's ballroom could conveniently hold only about 400 persons. That suited McAllister just fine.

"Why, there are only about four hundred people in fashionable New York Society," he once remarked to reporters. "If you go outside that number you strike people who are either not at ease in a ballroom or else make other people not at ease."[1] Anyone lucky enough to receive an invitation was assured of belonging; those rejected had to swallow their despair and hope to make it next year. The list did not vary markedly from one year to the next, because society did not change that much, Caroline believed. She was wrong. New York society had always been subject to upheavals and was about to experience the biggest one of all.

No Vanderbilts had ever been invited to the January affair. To Caroline Astor they represented "railroad money," which though admittedly plentiful was somehow tainted. Naturally it was only a matter of time before someone broke that barrier. The person who did so was a plump but resolute young woman from Mobile, Alabama, named Alva Smith, who in 1875 was wed to William H. Vanderbilt's second son, William Kissam Vanderbilt. The socially ambitious daughter of a cotton planter, Alva was determined to thwart Caroline Astor, and her strategy was brilliant.

First, she and Willie K., as her husband was universally called, decided to build the most splendid house in New York. What they got far outshone her father-in-law's set of boxlike mansions. Brownstone was out; fairyland castles were in. Designed by Richard Morris Hunt (who was to build many châteaux for the Vanderbilts) and rising directly to the north of William H.'s trio at 52nd Street and Fifth Avenue, the new residence of Mr. and Mrs. William K. Vanderbilt blended the grandest features of two of France's most felicitous castles, the Château de Blois and the town house of the fifteenth-century merchant prince Jacques Coeur in Bourges. Its limestone facades were graced by Gothic tracery, its crests ornamented with delicate ironwork, its clusters of chimneys patterned charmingly. Hunt had scoured Europe for its furnishings, which included a Rembrandt. If architecture alone could breach the Astor reserve, this was it.

While the house was under construction Ward McAllister's Patriarchs, sensing something was afoot, invited Alva and Willie K. to one of their balls. Yet Caroline Astor did not budge. So Alva played her ace. With the new house completed in early 1883, she announced a commemorative fancy dress ball for the evening of March 26. It was to be the most glittering party New York had ever seen, and its crowning feature would be a quadrille performed by the daughters of the aristocracy. Every young lady in New York instantly wanted to be in on the quadrille. Mrs. Astor's daughter Carrie set her heart on taking part and diligently attended the rehearsals. But with the ball imminent Alva made a sorrowful disclosure: she could not invite Carrie Astor because she had never met her mother.

If Caroline Astor was stuffy she was also a realist, and her capitulation was swift. She got into her carriage and was driven up to 52nd Street, where her footman in the blue livery of the Astors delivered her engraved calling card to a domestic in the maroon livery of the House of Vanderbilt. That, in the arcane custom of society, was enough. Aristocracy—such as it was—had yielded to plutocracy, and the Vanderbilts were in. From now on, old money would never again count as heavily for social recognition in New York City.

Carrie and her mother both attended Alva's ball, as did every other socialite in the New York firmament. The *New York World* estimated the cost, including costume rental by the participants, as at least $250,000, a huge sum in those days. The banker Henry Clews, who was present, said later that he would not estimate the expenditure, but "The ball seemed to have the effect of levelling up among the social ranks of uppertendom, and placing the Vanderbilts at the top of the heap in what is recognized as good society in New York. So far as cost, richness of costume and newspaper celebrity were concerned, that ball had, perhaps, no equal in history. It may not have been quite so expensive as the feast of Alexander the Great at Babylon, some of the entertainments of Cleopatra to Augustus and Mark Antony, or a few of the magnificent banquets of Louis XIV, but when viewed from every essential standpoint, and taking into account our advanced civilization, I have no hesitation in saying that the Vanderbilt ball was superior to any of those grand historic displays of festivity and amusement."[2] There was an important footnote: the following January, Mr. and Mrs. William K. Vanderbilt attended with great pleasure Mrs. Astor's annual ball.

They were indeed, in Clews's words, at the top of the heap, although Caroline Astor was not so much displaced as forced to share the summit. The Vanderbilt family at this point owned 640, 642, 644 (actually 2 West 52d Street), and 660 Fifth Avenue, but there was more to come as other family members added their palazzos up the west side of the avenue, the outlay culminating grossly in the outsize mansion of Cornelius Vanderbilt II (Willie K.'s older brother), which took up the entire blockfront between 57th and 58th streets (the current site of Bergdorf Goodman). No other family had ever made such a splash on the local scene, either socially or architecturally; and they were making their presence known elsewhere too with huge "cottages" in Newport and other watering spots. The most lavish of the country places was the Hunt-designed, baronial Biltmore of George Washington Vanderbilt II, another brother of Willie K.'s, outside Asheville, North Carolina, which had forty master bedrooms under a roof that was the largest in the United States.

The Vanderbilt spending was more than just big; it was different. In marked contrast to the Rockefellers later on, the ramified, multi-generational Vanderbilt family, except for a few bequests to worthy institutions like Columbia University and the founding of one important museum (the Whitney), left little that is tangible on the city scene—for example, all their palatial Fifth Avenue mansions are now gone. Their major legacy was behavioral. They lived like royalty and made no attempt to hide their wealth. They were, in fact, America's first real celebrities and, as such, introduced a breed of socialite that would henceforth be inextricably associated with New York: the partying, nightclubbing, yachting, insouciant rich that for a while were known as café society and that have been eternally beloved of tabloids here and elsewhere.

Alva herself gave the legend a large boost in 1895 when, amidst much newspaper publicity, she divorced Willie K. No marriage breakup had previously occasioned such gossip in the city. (Not quite a year later she married Oliver Hazard Perry Belmont, the son of August and Caroline Belmont.) Then toward the end of 1895 she announced yet another milestone, the engagement of her lovely doe-eyed daughter Consuelo to the ninth duke of Marlborough. The betrothal was not the first between an American heiress and foreign royalty: Jennie Jerome had already married Lord Randolph; and Anna Gould, Jay's daughter, had snagged a French marquis named Marie Ernest Paul Boniface ("Boni") de Castellane. But the duke was the biggest game yet. Consuelo was in love with someone else, but Alva ordered her to comply. Marlborough needed Vanderbilt money, for Blenheim, his vast estate near Oxford, required costly repairs. So at midday on November 6, 1895, Consuelo after much weeping was brought to St. Thomas's Church at 53rd Street and Fifth Avenue and, as thousands waited outside, the wedding took place. Directly thereafter Willie K. signed a contract that conveyed to the duke's benefit 50,000 shares, worth approximately $2.5 million, of the Beech Creek Railway, a short but lucrative coal line in Pennsylvania. The duke and the new duchess each got an annual stipend of $100,000 as well. The marriage, however, was destined to fail. They separated in 1907 and divorced in 1921.

Meanwhile, the building of mansions on upper Fifth Avenue that the Vanderbilts had set in motion was proceeding apace. The intersection of Fifth Avenue and 57th Street had the superrich on all four corners. Cornelius Vanderbilt II's pile on the northwest corner had originally occupied only the southern end of the block, but in 1894 the proprietor and his wife doubled its size to give it a formal entrance on 58th Street including an impressive driveway, porte cochere, and high wrought-iron fence. On the northeast corner stood the mansion of Mrs. Paran Stevens, whose husband had made a fortune in the hotel business; in 1895 the house came into the possession of Herman Oelrichs, a shipping magnate. The southeast corner was occupied by the enormous palazzo of California railroad potentate Collis P. Huntington; while on the southwest rose the steep-gabled, Romanesque abode of William C. Whitney, a suave local political operative who had been Grover Cleveland's secretary of the navy and later gained large profits in New York streetcar transit. In 1896 Whitney's son Harry Payne Whitney married Cornelius II's daughter Gertrude, and he gave them the house—so that she conveniently had only to move across the street. (One of the few Vanderbilts with artistic talent, Gertrude not only became a respectable sculptress but also founded the Whitney Museum of American Art.)

With society firmly entrenched on Fifth Avenue in the 50s, the avenue itself and its sidewalks became elegant on Sundays when the fashionable promenaded after church. The ritual became particularly dazzling on Easter Sunday, giving rise to the famous Easter Parade, which endures in less dressy fashion.

Farther up, the avenue was the location of choice for the emerging as well as the already arrived rich. Until the laying out of Central Park, Fifth Avenue above 59th Street had been little more than a lane, but with the park's completion in the 1870s it had come into its own and was being lined with the most astounding series of mansions ever seen in the United States. They came in all styles—Renaissance châteaux, Florentine villas, Moorish castles, Gothic manor houses, Victorian boxes—and were set down with no regard for architectural consistency all the way up to the East 90s. As Allen Churchill has observed, their owners seemed to be jockeying for position, "the homes of aristocrats standing cheek by jowl with those erected by copper kings, railroad kings, sugar kings, wire kings, silver kings, trolley kings, tobacco kings, and others whose fresh greenbacks appeared limitless."[3] At 68th Street William Whitney, having yielded his 57th Street house to the young folk, built a palazzo that contained tapestries designed by Boucher and the largest ballroom in New York. Nearby, the mansion of Thomas Fortune Ryan, who helped form the American Tobacco Company and later controlled the Equitable Life Assurance Society, had a private chapel designed in opulent Counter-Reformation style. At 75th the elegant house of Edward S. Harkness, whose money came from Standard Oil and railroads, was filled with art objects from around the world, while at 77th Street the mining baron and politician William A. Clark erected a Victorian extravaganza with 130 rooms and 21 marble bathrooms. Frank Woolworth, the dime store pioneer, owned a clutch of houses at 80th Street that evoked William Henry Vanderbilt's phalanx down at 51st. The stately palace of Andrew Carnegie was built on the south side of 91st Street. Later, during World War I, Otto Kahn's felicitous Italian Renaissance house was built on the north side of 91st. Only two major barons of the new age held out against the rush to Fifth Avenue: J. P. Morgan remained in lordly isolation at Madison and 36th Street—the new places on Fifth Avenue, he said, were "architectural monstrosities corrupting our landscape"[4]—while the steel executive Charles Schwab went way west to Riverside Drive and 73rd Street, building a French-style château that occupied an entire block.

To the owners of most of these new mansions an art gallery was obligatory, for collecting was a prerogative as well as a pleasure of the very rich. Hunting up and bidding for works of art also tapped the very competitive zeal that had made these men (or their ancestors) millionaires in the first place. The amassing of masterpieces would end up greatly enriching the city's cultural life, as many collectors found that giving their collections to museums, or converting their mansions into museums open to the public, was almost as satisfying as acquiring the paintings or objects in the first place.

A first-class city, to be sure, had to possess a first-class art museum, and to this end a group of civic leaders had met in 1869 at the Union League Club and resolved to found such an institution and to call it the Metropolitan Museum of Art. The first president was John Taylor Johnston, a wealthy New Yorker who had a sizable collection of his own that he often displayed to the public. One of the vice presidents was the poet and newspaper editor William Cullen Bryant, and among the trustees were the painters John F. Kensett and Eastman

Johnson, the architect Richard Morris Hunt, and Frederick Law Olmsted, the cocreator of Central Park. Johnston and Bryant, who wanted the museum to focus on the works of living American artists, were outvoted by other trustees, principally lawyers and men of affairs, who thought it should offer a comprehensive review of great art from the earliest times to the present.

For some time, despite its august sponsors, the museum lacked sufficient contributors and it languished. Johnston rescued it when he learned from one of his trustees that two important collections of paintings had been offered for sale in Europe; he encouraged the trustee to purchase both and helped pay for them himself. Brought to New York, the paintings were a hit and as a result the Metropolitan, after occupying two interim buildings, was enabled in 1880 to move into its own structure in Central Park on Fifth Avenue above 79th Street. Johnston added significantly to the museum's holdings when he bought for it, completely on his own, a massive hoard of classical antiquities that had turned up on Cyprus. And when the authenticity of some of the objects was disputed by an expert, the resulting controversy, which ended with the museum vindicated, helped popularize the institution immeasurably. A few years later the building was enlarged, and in 1902 a new and much more imposing front along Fifth Avenue designed by McKim, Mead & White was dedicated.

The museum, in fact, has never stopped growing.

For Johnston's successors as large-scale benefactors have enriched it nobly. One of the mightiest was J. Pierpont Morgan, who among his other attributes was the archetypal American millionaire determined to acquire objects representing the finest that civilization has to offer. Buying on a gargantuan scale and paying the highest prices, Morgan had dealers all over Europe competing to serve him. In addition to forming his own remarkable collection of paintings, missals, manuscripts, porcelains, miniatures, tapestries, books, and other rarities, which he preserved in his library next to his own house, Morgan purchased outright a great many works of art that he simply handed over to the Metropolitan, specifying that his name not be attached to them. In 1904 he became the museum's president and markedly upgraded its staff.

Morgan was not only a big buyer and an aggressive one; he had learned to tell good from bad. One art dealer, knowing the banker's love of miniatures, allegedly acquired six that were extremely valuable but then tried to expand the sale by including with them twenty-four others that were not so special. Shown the thirty objects as a group, with none identified, Morgan glanced at them for a moment and then barked, "How much for the lot?" The dealer, thinking he had put one over, quoted a price. Swiftly and unerringly Morgan picked up the six good miniatures and put them in his pocket. Then, dividing the dealer's price by thirty and multiplying by six, he announced his price and stormed out.[5]

Nowhere near so overbearing but equally avid in their collecting were Henry O. Havemeyer and his wife, Louisine Elder Havemeyer, who for their era were unusual in that they functioned as a kind of team. They were to become perhaps the most important early benefactors of the Metropolitan. Henry's grandfather had come to New York from Germany in 1802 and opened a bakery but soon moved into sugar refining. Henry's father expanded the business with great success and earned a fortune, while Henry himself was instrumental in founding the American Sugar Refining Company, one of the celebrated trusts of the 1880s, further increasing the family's wealth. A bulky, imposing man with a trim mustache and a zeal for, among other things, chamber music (he would not go to work in the morning before practicing on one of his Stradivarius or Guarnerius violins), Havemeyer was well used to wielding authority and enjoyed purchasing art as he purchased sugar—in quantity.

His first enthusiasm was for Oriental porcelain and other small objects from China and Japan, but Louisine's wider tastes and far-reaching curiosity broadened his view until their possessions included paintings of great variety and importance. Louisine was from Philadelphia, where she had known the painter Mary Cassatt, and Cassatt after moving to Paris had introduced her friend to the works of impressionist painters like Pissarro, Monet, and Degas. When the Havemeyers began traveling to Europe in search of art, Cassatt was an invaluable companion and guide. Their collection became strong not only in Italian Renaissance canvases but also in the French painters of the nineteenth and early twentieth centuries, one of the first in the United States to include them. On one trip to Spain with Mary Cassatt they discovered the works of both El Greco and Goya, making purchases that today seem almost incredible—El Greco's *View of Toledo* for $14,000 and Goya's celebrated portrait of the duke of Wellington for $3,400. According to the writer Aline Saarinen, "the Havemeyers virtually opened the market for Grecos and Goyas in the United States."[6]

All these gems found their way into the Havemeyers' house on Fifth Avenue and 66th Street. An immense structure, it was plain on the outside but sumptuously decorated inside by the imaginative art nouveau glassmaker and artist Louis Tiffany, who put Chinese embroideries on the walls and Japanese silks of many colors on the library ceiling. Chandeliers of glass flowers dazzled guests attending Havemeyer musicales. The painting collection became so large (there were seven Rembrandts in the library alone) that the owners built a large skylighted extra gallery in the backyard. Havemeyer loved to stop off at a dealer's on the way home from work and surprise Louisine with another painting. Although she owned many valuable jewels, she once remarked to an inquisitive guest, "I prefer to have something made by a man than to have something made by an oyster."[7]

Henry Havemeyer died in 1907. Louisine went on collecting and presided with satisfaction over her opulent house. (She also became active in woman suffrage, as did Alva Belmont.) On her death in 1929 much of the vast collection went immediately to the Metropolitan; the rest was put under the control of her three grown children, who soon decided to give virtually all of it to the Met as well, for a total of close to 2,000 paintings and other objects. The value of the overall bequest is almost beyond reckoning.

Not all of the proto-Medicis gave masterpieces to the Metropolitan, and there were other ways to benefit the city and its rapidly expanding array of cultural riches. Only a few blocks up Fifth Avenue from the Havemeyers, between 70th and 71st streets, was the mansion of Henry Clay Frick, the quiet, implacable former partner of Andrew Carnegie. Getting his start as a producer of coke, the form of coal used in steelmaking, Frick had built a reputation for ruthlessness and was cordially disliked by labor. When the workers in his Pennsylvania mills struck in the winter of 1889–90 he imported men from central Europe to supplant them and there was bloodshed; two years later, after he had joined his company to Carnegie's, he directed the closing of the company's Homestead plant whose workers had demanded better working conditions, and in the ensuing violence several men were killed or wounded. In 1899 Frick and Carnegie parted ways after disagreeing over the value of Frick's interest in their company, and Frick sold out to the older man for $15 million and turned to other pursuits, like railroads. After moving to New York in 1900, he leased the epochal William H. Vanderbilt house at 640 Fifth (the old man had died in 1885 and his heirs were otherwise housed) but soon began construction of a mansion that would properly hold his art collection, which he had been accumulating for years.

The palatial French-Italian-style residence, whose interiors were designed by Elsie de Wolfe, the first woman interior decorator, had a gigantic pipe organ (Frick liked to listen to it while reading a magazine) as well as the mandatory art gallery. The magnate kept buying Renaissance masterpieces and other great works of art while constantly upgrading the collection, and by the time of his death in 1919 he owned a dazzling array that included such masters as Titian, Vermeer, Van Dyck, Piero della Francesca, Rubens, Michelangelo, Whistler, Hogarth, and Gainsborough. Under the terms of his will, in a gesture that his old enemies in labor would have found hard to believe, he left both the mansion and the collection to the City of New York, together with a $15 million endowment for its upkeep. It remains a city treasure as well as one of the handful of palazzos remaining from the era when Millionaires' Row was one of the sights of the town.

All through these years New York's wealthy citizens were also helping to establish the city's reputation as a center for serious music. Opera enthusiasts even witnessed a dispute between old money and new somewhat similar to that between Alva Vanderbilt and Caroline Astor. Up until the 1870s the old Academy of Music on East 14th Street had served well as the city's principal opera house. But it was dominated by the old aristocracy, who year after year held title to its eighteen boxes and would not yield. One of the boxes was of course occupied by Caroline Astor, who under McAllister's tutelage adopted the practice, subsequently considered de rigueur, of arriving well after the start of Act I, receiving visitors during intermissions, and departing before the final curtain. Recently minted millionaires had to be content sitting in the orchestra section, where the box-holders could enjoy looking down on them. The new plutocrats asked that more boxes be added; nothing doing. In 1880 William H. Vanderbilt offered to pay $30,000 for a box and was refused. In high dudgeon he got together with other rejects like Jay Gould, J. P. Morgan, and Henry Clews and formed the Metropolitan Opera-house Company, which made plans to build a much larger and more ambitious hall at Broadway and 39th Street. At the last moment the Academy of Music board panicked, and their chairman, August Belmont, offered to add twenty-six boxes to the old house, but by then it was too late.

The new opera house, with a plain exterior but with opulent appointments within, was designed by the architect Josiah Cleaveland Cady, who boasted that he had never previously built a theatre. That did not bother his wealthy clients, for he served them well by allowing for three tiers of thirty-six boxes each, theoretically enough to satisfy all the moneyed persons within sight. Unaccountably, the third tier did not sell well and was soon converted to ordinary seating, but the Diamond Horseshoe (lower tier) and the Golden Horseshoe (upper), became New York society fixtures. Cady did not serve the less affluent patrons as well, for anyone sitting at the side of the hall above the boxes was rarely able to see more than half the stage.

Right from its opening in the fall of 1883 the Metropolitan Opera was a social smash. One observer estimated that the total wealth of all those present on opening night was $500 million; the Vanderbilts alone occupied five boxes. Even Caroline Astor was there, fresh from her comeuppance at Alva's hand and now, perhaps, making sure she did not stumble again. The Academy of Music could not compete, and in a few years it quietly closed down. Luckily there were enough leftover boxes in the new house to accommodate its diehards.

But the Metropolitan did not cover itself with musical glory in its first years, partly because most of its backers were more interested in eyeing each other than the stage. This changed around the turn of the century with the arrival on the opera's board of directors of Otto Kahn, the suave and cultivated—and formidably energetic—younger partner of Jacob Schiff in the Kuhn, Loeb & Company banking firm. A lover of music and the theatre, Kahn had at first been reluctant to involve himself heavily in the Met, fearing it would be bad for business. But others encouraged him to apply himself to the task of upgrading the company; and before long, by buying up stock from retiring directors, Kahn was in virtual control of it. The improvement he brought about was swift and dramatic. Within a year or so he was instrumental in hiring a young Italian tenor named Enrico Caruso, and the Met's staging suddenly began drawing rave notices. And in 1907, having become chairman of the Met's board, Kahn persuaded the general manager of La Scala in Milan, Giulio Gatti-Casazza, to take over the equivalent post in New York. One of the foremost musical figures in Europe, Gatti-Casazza brought further improvement to the company's productions. He also brought with him a little-known conductor from La Scala named Arturo Toscanini. The great days of the Met were at hand. (Kahn also introduced the Russian ballet to New York by sponsoring a tour, the first of its kind, by the Ballets Russes, whose lead dancer, Vaslav Nijinsky, electrified American audiences.)

Though successful as an opera hall—if only for the holders of better seats—the Metropolitan was not usable for symphony concerts as its large, deep stage swallowed up an orchestra's sounds. The man who provided the remedy for this defect was the steelmaker Andrew Carnegie. Symphonic music of superior rank had been introduced to New York by the German conductor Leopold Damrosch, who came to the city from Breslau in 1871 and founded both the Oratorio Society and the New York Symphony Society. But there was no large hall suitable for performances by either group. Damrosch had yearned for a good concert hall, and after his death in 1885 his son Walter, who took over direction of both societies, decided the time had come to do something about it. He went to Carnegie, who was a member of the Oratorio Society's board. Carnegie, after some hesitation, agreed to bankroll the project.

The resulting auditorium, first called the Music Hall but later renamed for its provider, is one of the finest of its kind in the world. Its architect was William B. Tuthill, a competent amateur musician who studied the accoustics of the great European concert halls in preparation for his task. While the building's exterior is unexceptional, the hall itself is not only lovely but also an acoustic gem, as generations of musicians have noted with gratitude. It opened in May 1891 with a concert conducted by Peter Ilich Tchaikovsky (who got along famously with Carnegie), but its guiding musical presence for many years was Walter Damrosch. When the New York Symphony was combined with another to form the New York Philharmonic, Damrosch stayed on as director, his warmth and imagination endearing him to New Yorkers. Late in life he conducted a series of concerts for children at Carnegie Hall that embellished his legend.

If the Metropolitan Museum, the Metropolitan Opera, and Carnegie Hall were products of New York's Gilded Age, so were some of the city's finest hotels—and the wealthy were among their most prominent customers. Two grand establishments are particularly worth noting. The first came about because of a feud in the Astor family. Caroline Astor, who in the 1890s was still living at the corner of Fifth Avenue and 34th Street, was not getting along well with her in-laws next door. When her brother-in-law John Jacob Astor III died, his property was inherited by his son William Waldorf Astor (Waldorf was the town in Germany where the first John Jacob Astor had grown up), and young William was decidedly not partial to his aunt Caroline. He thought his wife should be considered *the* Mrs. Astor, since his side of the family was senior to hers. But society would not abandon Caroline. In a huff Astor packed up and moved to England (where in due course he would become Viscount Astor and the proprietor of a great and famous estate called Cliveden). But first he directed a final blow at his aunt. He razed his house and erected in its place a thirteen-story hotel, the Waldorf, whose bulk he hoped would bring her misery. In this he succeeded, for after a year or so Caroline Astor moved a mile uptown to a new and much larger mansion that William Morris Hunt (not occupied at the moment by the Vanderbilts) had designed for her at Fifth Avenue and 65th Street. It was one of the grandest and most austere of all the Fifth Avenue châteaux. Her son, John Jacob Astor IV, to whom she left the 34th Street house, considered for a moment fighting his cousin out of spite, then decided to make a profitable deal. He demolished the old house and in its place put up a much larger and more grandiose seventeen-story hostelry, the Astoria (after the first John Jacob's trading outpost in Oregon). He then persuaded his cousin to join the two buildings together to form the Waldorf-Astoria Hotel. Directly upon its opening in 1897 the combined structure was recognized as special.

The Waldorf-Astoria was the world's largest (1,000 bedrooms), most expensive ($10 million), and most magnificent hotel. The impressive main carriage entrance on West 34th Street led to a wide corridor more than 100 yards long that connected the principal restaurants and public rooms; so resplendent were the gowns of the women who swept along it that it became known the world over as Peacock Alley. The Waldorf Men's Bar, which featured a huge four-sided bar, became the city's most popular watering spot, frequented by the likes of Henry Frick, Pierpont Morgan, and "Bet-a-Million" Gates, and in Gates's $20,000 apartment upstairs as much as a million dollars might change hands in an evening of gambling. In the huge Palm Garden, whose tables were usually reserved weeks in advance, men were required to wear white tie and tails, women formal evening dress. Presiding over the Palm Garden was a tall, heavyset, dignified gentleman named Oscar Tschirky, whose good taste, cordiality, and sensitivity to New York's upper-class social nuances caused him to be held in high esteem, and he is known to posterity as Oscar of the Waldorf. (Sadly, the hotel was torn down in 1929, to reappear in new guise on Park Avenue and 50th Street, but the loss was mitigated by its highly popular replacement, the Empire State Building.)

Both halves of the Waldorf-Astoria had been designed by Henry J. Hardenbergh in what was called German Renaissance style, with baroque gables rising above its dark, ornate facade, and its magnificence instantly made him America's number one hotel architect. He was the obvious choice, therefore, to design the new Plaza Hotel that was to replace a low red-brick hotel, also called the Plaza, at the corner of Fifth Avenue and 59th Street, facing Central Park. The new building, completed in 1907, is French rather than German Renaissance but exudes the same feeling of romance and grandeur that the old Waldorf did. Kings, sultans, grand duchesses, and all manner of other international personages have called the Plaza home. In a changing city it remains the most delightful evocation of the Gilded Age.

Such large institutions could have ballrooms far larger than any owned by a private citizen, even a millionaire, and thus became the scene of many a dazzling party. The most lavish was that given on February 10, 1897, in the brand-new Waldorf-Astoria by Mr. and Mrs. Bradley Martin, formerly of Troy, New York, whose riches (of uncertain origin) prompted them to move to New York and hyphenate their name. The party occurred to Mrs. Bradley-Martin, it seems, late in 1896 when she learned from her newspaper something of which she had not been aware: the United States was in the midst of a severe depression. In a burst of myopic naïveté she decided that a party would help business, enhance trade, and alleviate unemployment, and so she sent out 1,200 invitations to a costume ball for which guests were instructed to come in the garb of Louis XV's court at Versailles. The hotel, fearful that the well-publicized affair would attract angry mobs resentful of such profligacy, boarded up all its first-floor windows in advance of the event; and one of the invitees, Police Commissioner Theodore Roosevelt, decided it was more prudent to stay outside directing the forces of law and order than to attend. But while many of the thousands of spectators in the streets may have been seething, there were no incidents, and 700 bizarrely garbed guests entered to find the hall massed with roses and lit by chandeliers dripping with orchids. Mrs. Bradley-Martin, who as a result of faulty research came as Mary Stuart, wore jewels valued at $50,000; one of the Belmont family wore a suit of armor inlaid with gold, while another reveler attired as an Indian chief carried a collection of scalps. Guests were served an enormous meal by waiters in powdered wigs and knee breeches. The cost was estimated at well over $9,000, and the ensuing outcry in the press was loud. The

Bradley-Martins, hurt that their public-spirited effort had been so poorly received, packed up and moved to England.

Unusual entertainments were not limited to hotels, however. New York's two grandest restaurants, Delmonico's and Sherry's, were always happy to oblige. A signal event was the dinner given at Sherry's, at Fifth Avenue and 44th Street, in 1903 by the tycoon C. K. G. Billings to celebrate the opening of his new racing stables. The floor was covered with a kind of imitation grass, waiters were dressed as hunting grooms, and the thirty-six guests were served food and drink while mounted on horses specially rented for the occasion (Billings's own horses would not have been quiet enough) and facing each other in a circle, as in some kind of equestrian drill.

One New Yorker who was not there but would have felt right at home was James Buchanan Brady, widely known as Diamond Jim Brady, an immensely successful salesman of railroad equipment whose lavish spending won him a reputation as a monument to high living. The 250-pound, bejowled Brady may have been one of the earliest practitioners of modern expense-account living, as most of his prodigious entertaining was designed to impress potential wheel and brake purchasers. His gluttony was hard to believe. A dinner party staged at Rector's, a prominent restaurant on Broadway, might find the host wolfing down twelve courses, including four dozen oysters, six or seven giant lobsters, and a large steak, the food washed down with gallons of orange juice and finished off with an entire box of candy. Brady habitually covered himself with jewels—diamonds especially but also emeralds and rubies—and liked to give away diamond-studded pins and watches. He was particularly taken with gold-plated bicycles, which were made to order for him. The prize cycle was a $10,000 gold-plated item that he gave to the actress Lillian Russell, which sported handlebars inlaid with pearl and wheels sparkling with diamonds. On a nice day the two would wheel around Central Park.

In such a moneyed atmosphere, gambling was not limited to the friends of Bet-a-Million Gates at the Waldorf. There were gambling dens through the Tenderloin, the wide-open district in the West 20s where prostitution also flourished; and Wall Street was not without its daytime bookmaking and wagering houses. Brady liked to take his friends to Frank Farrell's place, on 33rd Street just a few doors from the Waldorf, whose interior had been remodeled by Stanford White and which was happy to provide the finest cigars, wines, and liquors gratis to its high rollers. But the most exclusive casino in the city, on 44th Street near Fifth Avenue, was operated by Richard Canfield, who maintained similar establishments at Saratoga Springs and Newport. Leonard Jerome was a favored customer, as were Vanderbilts and Whitneys; their privacy was rigorously protected, patrons being addressed only by the initial of their last names. Canfield's was particularly renowned for the sumptuous supper it served at midnight. The proprietor himself never gambled but did very well in the stock market on the basis of tips from his customers. His library, in his private apartment above the gambling floors, included many a rare edition. His art collection was unusual, consisting mainly of works by contemporary artists, among them James McNeill Whistler, who painted Canfield's portrait.

Whistler never lived in New York though he might well have, as the city during the latter part of the nineteenth century was becoming a center for both artists and writers. Young American painters, many of whom had witnessed the artistic ferment in Paris, were gathering in increasing numbers because of the city's atmosphere of openness and experimentation, even though the major collectors rarely bought their work. A few of them banded together in 1877 to rebel against the conservative National Academy of Design, whose older members disapproved of the insurgents, and they formed the more forward-looking Society of American Artists. The society in turn set up a school, the Art Students' League, which was to become preeminent over the next half century, and its first exhibit included works by such pacesetters as the sculptor Augustus Saint-Gaudens and the painters Albert Pinkham Ryder and William Merritt Chase. Other artists congregated in the downtown Greenwich Village area, a neighborhood that would become America's first full-fledged artists' colony.

Writers came to New York not only for many of the same reasons as did the artists, but also because the largest publishers and most important magazines were here. Although Boston had long reigned as the country's intellectual capital, it was ceding that role to New York. The change was symbolized by the move in the 1880s of the distinguished novelist and editor William Dean Howells, who had edited the *Atlantic Monthly* in Boston, to New York, where he proceded to write for *Harper's Magazine*. In New York, he said, "one gets life in curious slices."[8] Mark Twain lived for a while on lower Fifth Avenue, and knowledgeable observers in the 1880s might have recognized an aging Herman Melville walking in Central Park. Although Melville's early works had won critical praise, they had earned him little money. The writer, disheartened and in debt, was forced to take employment as a customs inspector on the Hudson River piers. A few years later Stephen Crane was living a virtually penniless existence while researching the down-and-out world of the Bowery.

The literary cause in the city was given a substantial boost in the 1890s, when the custodians of three fortunes joined to found the New York Public Library. New York's first major library had been bequeathed by John Jacob Astor upon his death in 1848 and was housed in a handsome brick edifice on Lafayette Street. Another great collection was that of James Lenox, a member of a New York banking family and a prominent book collector, who had built a private library at Fifth Avenue and 70th Street (the site later purchased by Henry Clay Frick for his house and art gallery). Unfortunately, neither of these fine libraries was adequate for the growing city. But a third element entered the picture when the Democratic politician Samuel J. Tilden, who had served as governor of New York in the mid-1870s and died in 1886, left the city $5 million for "the establishment of a free library and reading room."[9] One of the trustees of the Tilden trust, Andrew H. Green, initiated the movement that resulted in combining the Astor and Lenox libraries with the Tilden money to create the city-owned public library. The city donated the land at Fifth Avenue and 42nd Street occupied by the now-obsolete Croton Reservoir; and the new library's main building, designed by the architectural firm of Carrère & Hastings, was dedicated in 1911. As a bonus, Andrew Carnegie contributed $5.2 million toward the construction of branch libraries throughout the city. But the 42nd Street building has become one of the world's largest and most heavily used research libraries, exceeded in size in the United States only by the Library of Congress.

Further contributing to the concentration of cultural institutions, attracting talented young writers, and heightening the air of excitement and enterprise were the city's newspapers, which were more rambunctious than ever. The great early pioneers like Horace Greeley and William Cullen Bryant were gone, but in their wake some equally strong personalities moved in. When twenty-six-year-old James Gordon Bennett, Jr., took over the *Herald* in 1867 from his father, few thought he could maintain the paper's reputation for lurid local reporting as well as highly competent coverage of national and international news; a yachtsman and playboy, he seemed not to care. But the young Bennett knuckled down, and the capably edited *Herald* achieved a special niche in journalistic history with its sponsorship of unlikely enterprises: it was Bennett who sent Henry Stanley to Africa to look for Dr. David Livingstone, and he also backed an unsuccessful expedition to the North Pole.

By all odds the preeminent newspaper owner of his day was Joseph Pulitzer, an immigrant from Hungary who had made a success of the *St. Louis Post-Dispatch* and who in 1883 purchased (from Jay Gould, of all people) the *New York Evening World*. It was Pulitzer who would rescue the Statue of Liberty campaign from likely failure in 1885, and his paper was often cited as the most responsible in the city, as well as the most readable. In the 1890s Pulitzer was locked in a circulation war with the *New York Evening Journal*, which had been founded by the headstrong California publisher William Randolph Hearst, each paper trying to outdo the other in sensationalism and each profiting in the process. Meanwhile the staid, respectable *New York Times*, which had languished since its day of triumph in unmasking Boss Tweed, was bought in 1896 by Adolph Ochs of Chattanooga, who painstakingly converted it into a journal remarkable for its integrity and evenhandedness. Few observers, certainly, would have guessed at the turn of the century that the *Times* under Ochs's heirs would outlast them all.

By the turn of the century New York's theatres had moved up Broadway until they were beginning to encroach on Longacre Square, where it crossed Seventh Avenue. Soon Adolph Ochs's *Times* would move to that intersection, which would be renamed for it. Meantime the Gay White Way lit up the West 30s. Lillian Russell was appearing nightly at Joe Weber and Lew Fields's Music Hall at 29th Street, and there were theatres and restaurants all the way uptown into the 40s; at 42nd Street the new Knickerbocker Hotel, built by the Astors, was famous for its bar containing a mural of Old King Cole by Maxfield Parrish (the mural is now in the St. Regis Hotel). But the center of the stretch was commanded by the Casino Theatre at West 39th Street, near the Metropolitan Opera House. There every evening appeared the Florodora sextette, six of the most entrancing girls imaginable, all beautiful, all the same height, all dressed alike in frilly pink. Demand for orchestra seats was fierce, and the audience went wild as the girls, in response to the singing question from six chorus boys, "Tell me, pretty maiden, are there any more at home like you?" would reply demurely, "There are a few, kind sir." It was reported that all of the original Florodora girls married millionaires. The most famous of the girls, however, was not a member of the sextette. She was Evelyn Nesbit, and before she could be chosen as one of the six she had become the mistress of the architect and man-about-town Stanford White, a noted admirer of female pulchritude—who liked to show her off, naked on a red velvet swing, in his studio on West 24th Street. Evelyn hoped to marry White but that was not his way, and so she married a millionaire playboy from Pittsburgh named Harry Thaw. A strange, sadistic, maniacally jealous man, Thaw conjured up a fierce resentment of Nesbit's past relationship with White, and on the evening of June 25, 1906, he went to the roof garden of Madison Square Garden, where White—the building's architect— was dining alone, and shot him dead. It was the most notorious shooting of the decade, and a fitting denouement to the Gilded Age.

10

The Greater City

One day in 1876 a photographer named John H. Beal climbed to the top of the recently completed Brooklyn tower of the Brooklyn Bridge, lugging his elaborate view camera with him, and took a series of pictures looking toward Manhattan. Fitted together, they constitute the first panorama photograph of New York; the composite picture is seven feet wide. The view from such an exalted elevation —271 feet 6 inches above mean high water, much the highest point in the New York area at the time—must have awed the photographer, for the height gave him an unparalleled glimpse of the metropolitan region, and his camera captured all of lower Manhattan from the Battery to well above Canal Street. Dominating the scene is the bridge's unfinished Manhattan tower; soon the two towers will be linked by the graceful suspension cables that support the roadway. On either side of the Manhattan tower are the sailing ships that symbolize New York's wealth and the ferries that up to now have been the only transport link to Brooklyn. Beyond are the crowded blocks of the rapidly growing city. But anyone looking at the panorama today is bound to be struck by something that in hindsight seems almost like an omission: there are no high buildings. The metropolis that has already become one of the most powerful cities on earth presents a skyline in which the tallest structures are still church steeples.

Thirty years later the view had changed radically. A snapshot taken from Brooklyn in 1906 reveals a Manhattan in which no church steeple is visible. All have been masked by a high building. The development of steel-frame construction and the invention of the electric elevator have by this time permitted Manhattan to build up as well as out, and the skyscraper-studded skyline is on its way.

New York had thus undergone a major physical change in the thirty-year period represented by the two photos. By 1906 it actually looked like a different place. Fully as important, however, were two other changes that could not be seen in a photograph. First, the city's population had been given its greatest infusion of immigrants yet, from southern and eastern Europe—mainly Italians and Russian Jews—who in the first decade of the twentieth century were still arriving in vast numbers and who were already enriching and altering the tone of New York. Second, the city had annexed its neighboring counties—not just Kings but also lower Westchester, Queens, and Richmond—to more than triple its area, more than double its population, and create Greater New York, with a new form of government as well as new capability for growth.

With all due regard for the repercussions of the later arrival of large numbers of blacks and, still later, Hispanics, as well as economic shifts that would bring their own convulsions and the profound effect of new technologies like the automobile, it can be argued that the fundamental nature and look of New York City were both largely in place shortly after the turn of the century and would not appreciably change. As Bayrd Still observed in *Mirror for Gotham*, "The generation from 1870 to 1900 saw the advent of present-day New York . . . contemporary comment depicts a community whose basic features bore a close resemblance to those of the present day."[1] A visitor to the city on the eve of World War I would have seen a place not radically different in nature from today's metropolis. New York would keep tearing itself down and rebuilding and would undergo all manner of shifts and crises, but its basic nature and overall urban look had become more or less fixed.

The symbol of the changes that New York would be going through in the late-nineteenth-century generation, as well as a catalyst of some of those changes, was the Brooklyn Bridge itself. For all its grace and extraordinary durability as well as its practicality, it seems almost quaint in today's landscape, an artifact out of another era. But in the context of the 1870s and 1880s it was monumental and revolutionary, with by far the longest span of any bridge built up to that time and a suspension system that was an engineering marvel. Its huge scale when viewed against the existing city pointed the way to the gigantism that was soon to overtake construction in Manhattan. And as it brought New York and Brooklyn closer and facilitated congress between them, it made the eventual consolidation of the two communities virtually inevitable. The bridge led to a Greater New York.

Ironically, although many Brooklynites would bitterly resist the annexation, the impetus for building the bridge that would destroy their isolation came from their side of the river. Brooklyn by the 1860s was a city to be reckoned with, growing at a furious rate. It was already the third largest American city after New York and Philadelphia and a key manufacturing center, and its seaport was even larger than New York's, with eight miles of piers, dry docks, grain elevators, and warehouses. Brooklynites were jealous of their independence, but they saw a brighter future if access to jobs in Manhattan was improved, especially in the winter, when the East River could be made hazardous if not impassable by ice and wind. They also believed that the bridge would increase their property values. (Conversely, the chief opposition to the bridge came from New York real estate interests who feared that development of upper Manhattan would languish as Brooklyn boomed.)

Designed by the German-born wire-rope maker John A. Roebling (who did not live to see his masterpiece built) and carried to completion under the direction of his son Washington A. Roebling (who was invalided by the effects of the bends, contracted in the pressurized caissons used for building the towers), the bridge took thirteen years to construct. Many buildings on both sides of the river had to be demolished to make way for the long approaches and the anchorages for the cables, and more than twenty workers perished from accidents or the bends. Disputes over the funding of the bridge and allegations of corruption involving work contracts slowed or even stopped work on several occasions, but the bridge's official dedication on May 24, 1883, prompted wild celebration throughout both New York and Brooklyn. Barely a week after its opening a false rumor among a crowd of pedestrians that the span might be unstable caused a stampede in which twelve persons were trampled to death or thrown off the bridge, but since that day Roebling's work has been amazingly free of mishap. When the motorcar came, the bridge handled it with ease.

Hardly as masterful as the bridge but of similar import to the city at large was the construction in 1869 of New York's first apartment house, the Stuyvesant, on East 18th Street near Third Avenue. London and Paris had seen such compound residences, but middle- and upper-class New Yorkers felt that it was somehow indecent for more than one family to live under the same roof. Luckily the builder, Rutherford Stuyvesant, was a descendant of the Dutch governor, which seemed to make his experiment proper, and in any event the five-story house was an immediate success, all of its "French flats" renting readily. Soon apartment buildings would be found everywhere.

A feature of the Brooklyn Bridge that is no longer extant but was of great importance during its early years was its rail line, which could speed commuters across the river far faster than any ferry. The line was thus an extension of the city's rapid transit system, which was then being developed on a broad basis. As New York expanded up Manhattan Island, the problem of moving large numbers of people from its outlying sections down to the business district was becoming acute. Other cities could expand in several directions, but New York, constrained by Manhattan's insularity and not yet encompassing Brooklyn, could go only uptown. The north-south avenues were served by horsecars that ran on rails, but they were slow and overcrowded.

In the 1860s an inventive soul named Alfred Ely Beach, who was the editor and publisher of *Scientific American*, decided that the city needed swift underground transportation, and he proposed to build a subway under Broadway. The prospects for such a line seemed dim, however, as Boss Tweed, who was then at the height of his power and would have to approve the project, was firmly committed to elevated transport (he also held investments in surface transit). So Beach resolved to build his line on the sly. Acquiring a permit to construct a pneumatic tube for moving mail, he caused a block-long subway under Broadway to be built secretly, his crews working only at night, just a stone's throw from City Hall. Cars were to be blown along it by a large reversible fan mounted at one end of the tunnel. In February 1870 he proudly unveiled his creation, which included an elaborate entranceway with a fountain and a grand piano. Tweed, furious, ordered Governor Hoffman (who was under his thumb) to reject Beach's charter, and the scheme went no further. New York would have to wait another three decades for its first subway.

Thanks partly to Boss Tweed, however, elevated transit did receive the necessary backing. Here the pioneer was a corpulent, bearded inventor named Charles T. Harvey, who thought cars could be hauled along an elevated line in a city like New York by a cable running to a stationary steam engine. After building a half-mile demonstration track above Greenwich Street, he donned a frock coat and top hat, climbed up to the track, seated himself on the small car, and sped along the rails at five miles an hour as onlookers cheered. After some months he decided that cables would not do—they kept breaking—and so he introduced small steam engines on each car, which proved dependable. The age of the elevated was at hand. By the mid-1870s elevated lines were being built along Second, Third, Sixth, and Ninth avenues; and while inhabitants of houses along the routes and pedestrians beneath complained of the smoke and cinders (electrification did not come until this century), the lines were well patronized.

The els, as they were called, opened up for intensive development large tracts in upper Manhattan that had hitherto seemed too far away. The most notable of these was the Upper West Side, above 59th Street, which the Ninth Avenue el made accessible after its extension to West 110th Street in 1879. The West Side's main thoroughfare was the old meandering route out of town that had originally been called the Bloomingdale Road, as it led to the Bloomingdale district today known as Morningside Heights; this was the route taken by the colonial troops when they fled the pursuing British in 1776. In 1868 the city had widened the street and renamed it the Western Boulevard, or simply the Boulevard; in 1899 the avenue would be renamed Broadway. But until the 1880s the West Side area was still open land, dotted with shantytowns, country houses, and small farms, with a tavern here and there.

A few large structures had been built, like the American Museum of Natural History, whose first building (on 77th Street near Central Park West) was dedicated in 1877. But such interlopers seemed woefully isolated. When Edward S. Clark, the president of the Singer Sewing Machine Company, conceived the idea of a luxury apartment building at Central Park West and 72nd Street in 1880 and hired the eminent architect Henry J. Hardenbergh to design it, most New Yorkers thought he had lost his mind. The building was so far out of town, they said, that it might as well be out West somewhere, and they began to call it the Dakota, a name the imposing structure has since carried with pride.

Once building got under way in the West 70s and 80s it went forward with a rush. As the *New York Times* reported in 1886, "The west side of the city presents just now a scene of building activity such as was never before witnessed in that section . . . Streets are being graded, and thousands of carpenters and masons are engaged in rearing substantial buildings where a year ago nothing was to be seen but market gardens or barren rocky fields."[2] But development

235

did not occur as real estate investors had predicted. They had envisioned Central Park West and the Boulevard as elegant residential streets, with Eleventh Avenue—renamed West End Avenue north of 59th Street in 1880—serving as a business center lined with shops. Instead the Boulevard (Broadway) became the commercial street, and West End Avenue got the mansions as did Riverside Drive, west of it. Central Park West, with the Dakota as a model, was taken over by elegant apartment buildings and hotels. Meanwhile, speculative builders filled the side streets with handsome row houses exhibiting the latest architectural styles, many of them highly felicitous. Brownstone, the material of choice when the West 40s, 50s, and 60s were being developed, was now considered too staid, and the West Side houses on their quiet treelined streets were often faced in limestone or brick with results that were in many cases superb.

Meanwhile the Upper East Side, which one day would supplant the West Side as the city's most posh residential district, had little to recommend it. True, the mansions of the ultrarich were beginning to decorate Fifth Avenue above 59th Street, and Madison Avenue was enjoying a subdued version of the same splurge. But any kind of proper development farther east seemed unlikely because of the rail traffic that besmirched Park Avenue. The trains leading out of the city had originated at Fourth Avenue and 26th Street, spewing ashes on their way uptown along Fourth Avenue, but in 1871 Commodore Vanderbilt, responding to a city ordinance forbidding steam locomotives below 42nd Street, built Grand Central Terminal in honor of his new rail combination, the New York Central. The stretch of Fourth Avenue between 34th and 38th streets on which the steam trains had run had meanwhile been roofed over, with gardens planted along the middle of the avenue, and it was renamed Park Avenue. The avenue leading uptown from the new terminal was also called Park, but as far north as 51st Street it was an open train yard, noisy and sooty, and even though the tracks were roofed over from 56th up to 96th Street the roof barely contained the smoke. With steam-driven elevated lines running up both Second and Third avenues, and with First Avenue almost too far east for proper habitation, the whole East Side above 42nd Street was literally under a cloud and increasingly filled with tenements and the modest homes of the lower middle class. Not until the railroad line was electrified and buried in a tunnel under Park Avenue after the turn of the century, and after the els were converted to electricity, did the area begin to acquire its present style and grandeur.

But the city was bursting beyond the confines of both the Upper West and the Upper East Sides. Above 110th Street near the Hudson River the land now known as Morningside Heights was being made into a major institutional center. Columbia College, which had moved from its original location near City Hall to 49th Street and Madison in 1857 and had later reconstituted itself as a university, found the midtown area too crowded in the last decades of the century and in 1897 moved all the way up to the Heights, where it would soon incorporate a great number of other institutions like Barnard and Teachers College. Near it the Episcopal Diocese of New York was building the mammoth Cathedral of St. John the Divine (a structure that still defies completion), and St. Luke's Hospital was also under way. To the east of the Heights lay Harlem, a very proper middle-class community whose residents, a large proportion of them Jewish, valued their conservative, traditional way of life. Harlem's main thoroughfare was 125th Street, which boasted fine shops, restaurants, and theatres; there was no need to go downtown for anything. The Harlem Opera House built by Oscar Hammerstein occasionally showed somewhat daring plays from Paris, but most residents wanted nothing to do with such unconventional entertainments.

New York City had even extended its corporate area in 1873 to take in some land in the Bronx, on the other side of the Harlem River. The new holdings were known as the Annexed District and encompassed Kings Bridge, West Farms, and Morrisania. The following year the city added twenty square miles that filled out the southern portion of the Bronx. Although the rest of the Bronx—still a part of Westchester County—was rural, the annexed areas were being rapidly built up and by 1890 had nearly 90,000 residents. In 1895 New York University, finding its Washington Square campus increasingly congested, opened a branch at University Heights overlooking the Harlem River, which it would maintain until after World War II. It was there that it built its well-known Hall of Fame, a display of bronze busts of great Americans.

Brooklyn, too, was expanding, partly because of its readier access by means of the new bridge. Down at its southern end Coney Island was being developed into an elaborate resort, the eastern end (Manhattan Beach) occupied by luxury hotels, the other given over to an amusement park. New Yorkers could get to the resort either by railroad from Brooklyn's center or via steamboat from the Battery.

Each workday, furthermore, thousands of people were coming into the city from the newly settled suburbs. Commuters from the Westchester County communities of Yonkers, Mount Vernon, New Rochelle, and White Plains came in on the New York Central or New Haven Railroad, down Park Avenue to Grand Central. Long Islanders traveled via the Long Island Rail Road to its terminal at Hunter's Point, in Queens, and thence by ferry to Manhattan (Penn Station would not be built until 1910); New Jerseyites from Jersey City, Newark, Montclair, or the Oranges took one of several rail lines to the Hudson's west shore and similarly transferred to ferries. And the Staten Island Ferry was adding to the flow. At the end of the day the great tide would be reversed as the hordes scrambled to get home.

Staten Island Ferry riders were especially lucky in the 1880s—they could watch the erecting of the Statue of Liberty, a gift from the French people in commemoration of the centennial of American independence. Designed by Frédéric Auguste Bartholdi and constructed in sections in his Paris studio, the statue was given a preview in the United States when its torch-bearing arm was shown at the 1876 Philadelphia Centennial Exhibition. Just as the rest of the statue was to be delivered in 1885, the American campaign to raise funds for the statue's pedestal, which was to stand on Bedloe's Island in the Upper Bay, bogged down, and the whole project was thrown into doubt. The publisher Joseph Pulitzer undertook to raise the required sum by carrying on a vigorous campaign in the *New York World*, and within months the goal was reached. The 151-foot statue looking out over the harbor was formally dedicated on October 28, 1886, and has ever since symbolized America's—and New York's—role as a haven for needy and oppressed people the world over.

Throughout the 1880s and 1890s, and into this century, there were enormous numbers of the needy and oppressed coming up the harbor to land at New York. These decades represented the height of what has been described as the greatest population transfer in history, and although New York had seen great numbers of immigrants earlier in the century—principally Germans and Irish—it was scarcely prepared for this onslaught. It is estimated that between 1880 and 1919 more than 23 million Europeans came to America, of whom more than 17 million landed at New York. During the 1880s alone more than twice as many aliens came through New York as had come in any two consecutive decades. A surprising proportion of them went no further. They were city dwellers by background or by choice, and as this was the biggest city in the country, why go anywhere else? They helped cause Manhattan's population to double in the last three decades of the century; at the same time the population of the neighboring counties almost tripled.

The new influx was so huge that it swamped Castle Garden, the reception depot at the Battery that the city had inaugurated in 1855. There also were complaints that immigration officials at the garden were corrupt and allowed unsuspecting aliens to be exploited by outsiders or by other officials. In 1890 the federal government took over the processing, and in 1892 the whole operation was transferred to Ellis Island, near the Statue of Liberty, where a series of buildings was constructed especially for handling aliens. Although complaints of unfair and harsh treatment persisted, the new center worked surprisingly well considering the tremendous numbers it was called upon to handle.

Those numbers were of a different sort from the earlier immigrants, who had been principally from northern and western Europe: English, Irish, French, Dutch, Germans, and Scandinavians. This later influx was from southern and eastern Europe, at first mostly Italians, then more and more Russians, Poles, Austrians, Hungarians, and people from the Balkans, whose outlook was not the same as that of their predecessors. To a greater extent than those who had come before, they were fleeing poverty or oppression. Of the Russians and to a lesser extent the Poles, a large percentage were Jewish. The overall result of the mammoth new influx was to alter New York City's population mix and thus its general tone—perhaps, in the long run, for the better.

Until the 1860s the city had a very small Italian population, mostly from northern Italy and including a few musicians and opera singers (Mozart's librettist Lorenzo da Ponte had opened an Italian opera house here in 1832). But the later group was made up largely of peasants and landless laborers from the poorer southern half of the country, whose already meager livelihoods back home had—ironically—been further depressed by the success of fruit growers in Florida and California, as well as by French tariffs that hurt vineyards in Apulia, Sicily, and Calabria. Increasingly after 1870, entire villages and rural towns in southern Italy decamped to the New World, and in the two decades ending in 1880 almost 70,000 people left for the United States. Still greater numbers were to follow. By 1900 there were 145,000 Italians in the city; by 1920 there were 391,000. The total number who traveled to the United States during this period was actually much larger than these figures indicate. Many young

Italian men came on a temporary basis, to earn a modest sum that they could take back to their families in the old country. Many returned later, however, bringing their families for good.

It was not by chance that most of the new immigrants stayed in New York and other cities. Most of them, though they had come from the soil, had no desire to go back to it. As one observer wrote, the former peasant felt that farming was "a punishment, not only for his ill-nourished stomach but for his soul as well . . . It humiliated his sense of being."[3] Some were masons and could readily find semi-skilled jobs, but the great mass were not only uneducated but illiterate (Italy's rulers had ruthlessly denied them schooling) and scarcely prepared for skilled work of any kind. So most newly arrived Italians became day laborers, often replacing Irish workers who had moved on to other occupations.

Most of the southern Italians moved first into the wretched Five Points area below Canal Street previously dominated by the Irish, but they also took over a neighborhood north of Canal along Mulberry Street in such force that it remains known as Little Italy. Within it, certain streets became the domain of specific groups, the Neapolitans focusing on Mulberry Street, the Sicilians on Prince, the Calabresi on Mott. Many northern Italians in the neighborhood took a dislike to their newly arrived compatriots and moved out, establishing a smaller Little Italy to the northwest in Greenwich Village, which also persists today, centering on Bleecker Street. Of all the immigrant groups, the Italians were the most cohesive, exhibiting a distrust of strangers or outsiders that stemmed from living in isolated rural communities. But as their numbers continued to increase they formed other distinctly Italian neighborhoods, for example in East Harlem, in the Red Hook section of Brooklyn, and eventually in the Bronx south of Fordham Road.

Not having been exposed to the advantages of education in the old country, the southern Italians for the most part did not subscribe to the notion that the next generation should achieve an improved station in life. Higher education was deemed a waste of time and an unnecessary prolonging of childhood. But in time the Italians moved into white-collar jobs and developed a strong professional class, and their contribution to the city's government has been strong—no mayor has been as beloved as Fiorello La Guardia in the 1930s. Beyond that, they have bestowed on the city an atmosphere of warmth, of gusto and cultural enrichment, and of melody and the good life that is more enduring than the heritage of almost any other ethnic group.

The eastern European Jews came from an entirely different environment. They were basically urban, and a large proportion were at least semiskilled. They also put a high value on schooling, which made them more eager to better their lot—to be more upwardly mobile—than most other immigrant groups. Finally, as they had fled from an oppressive political system, their commitment to remaining in the United States was strong.

The event that precipitated the flight of so many Jews from eastern Europe was the assassination of Czar Alexander II in 1881. The lot of the Jews in Russia had never been good, but Alexander, a man of moderate views who had freed Russia's serfs, had caused the relaxation of many statutes that discriminated against the Jewish minority. His killing was followed by vicious pogroms and severe restrictions that plunged the Jews into despair. Some 150,000 of them fled Russia in the decade after 1881, mostly for the United States, but as the pogroms intensified after 1890 the flight gathered momentum. In 1907, the peak year, 259,000 eastern European Jews came to America, and by 1910 there were 1,100,000 Jews in New York City, the great preponderance of them from Russia or Poland (at that time part of the Russian Empire). Their influx made the earlier arrival of German Jews seem almost inconsequential. Jews now made up a quarter of the city's population, a percentage that has generally persisted down to this day.

They came not from the farmlands of Russia (or Rumania or Austria-Hungary) but from towns and cities, and fully two-thirds of those who were employable—that is, men or single women rather than wives and children—were skilled or semiskilled, an unusually high proportion. Among the arrivals, for example, 145,000 gave their occupation as tailor, 23,000 as shoemaker, and 17,000 as clerk or accountant. And because they had seen what education could do, they were eager to advance themselves in their new homeland. As Thomas Kessner put it in *The Golden Door*, they were "fired by a hunger for material success and its accompanying security."[4]

Their sheer numbers, however, made success seem remote at first. Their German predecessors had settled in the German neighborhood on the Lower East Side, and it was to this area that the new group came, often moving into buildings owned by German Jews. The result was fearful overcrowding: the density of the area climbed to 524

241

inhabitants per acre, the highest in the city, and one block containing 39 tenement buildings had 2,781 inhabitants—but only 264 toilets and no bathtub.

The clothing industry was virtually the only activity in the city at this time in which Jews were employers of appreciable numbers of workers, and many of the new immigrants, skilled in the needlework trades, found jobs there, not in factories but in sweatshops, rooms in the homes of subcontracting "sweaters" who worked them long hours and paid them a pittance. Wrote the Danish-born journalist Jacob Riis, whose descriptions of substandard working conditions in such precincts are classics, "Take the Second Avenue Elevated and ride up half a mile through the sweaters' district. Every open window of the big tenements, that stand like a continuous brick wall on both sides of the way, gives you a glimpse of one of these shops . . . Men and women bending over their machines or ironing their clothes at the window, half-naked . . . Morning, noon, or night, it makes no difference."[5] New kinds of machinery and the development of ready-made clothing had brought boom times to the garment industry since the Civil War, and so there were many jobs, albeit poor-paying ones. Children were frequently employed as well and were shamelessly exploited. Although many Jews eventually found their way out of the industry, an appreciable number rose through it and came to dominate it. In New York today the major garment concerns, still a vital force in the city's economy, are overwhelmingly Jewish.

Those who could find no job resorted to peddling, which became a major undertaking on the Lower East Side, streets like Hester, Ludlow, and Orchard swarming with kerchiefed women and bearded men noisily hawking bread, dry goods, candles, matches—anything at all. It was grueling, but the resourceful could make it the first rung on the entrepreneurial ladder. The immigrant, said one observer, "goes on from day to day, changes the basket for the bundle, the bundle for the horse and wagon peddling, and finally . . . emerges a sleek, thrifty merchant."[6] For many this was the route to proprietorship of a small business. Others managed to put aside small sums which they later used as security for renting property, and which they then subleased at a modest profit; this led to their owning property outright, first one parcel, then many. Real estate became a favorite vehicle out of the slums, and many a New York fortune started this way.

But because many of the Jewish immigrants dressed in long black coats, spoke with a thick, strange accent, and possessed unfamiliar habits, and because there were suddenly so many of them, many Americans—even those who had not been here very long themselves—began to feel somewhat threatened. The first signs of anti-Semitism appeared. The United States, and New York in particular, had been remarkably free of this scourge. The German Jews in their desire to conform and to be assimilated had, with a few exceptions, escaped such condemnation; they had not been seen as a disturbing, alien force. The eastern European Jews found a different reception. As Irving Howe reports in *World of Our Fathers*, stereotypes arose of "the Jew as an Oriental figure hoarding secrets of recondite wisdom and trained in the arts of commercial deception" and of "the Jew as a figure of surreptitious accumulation, gothic or medieval in style, performing mysterious rites in the dives of the modern city."[7] Moreover, the Jews' persecution at the hands of the Russian authorities had turned many into political radicals, and this greatly magnified the threat. One result was that Jews of every kind, even those of German descent who had earlier been accepted, began to face discrimination, such as exclusion from societies, clubs, and neighborhoods to which they might formerly have enjoyed access. Another was that proposals to limit immigration, perhaps by establishing quotas for different groups, gained new credence.

Such feelings were becoming rife throughout the United States. If they were particularly virulent in New York it was because the city was absorbing much the largest number of new immigrants, and even if the community at large was made up of prosperous and diligent workers (like so many of the Jews), the social problems arising from the massive influx would be felt here first. New York had seen more than its share of racial animosity, mostly involving blacks as in the infamous 1741 "conspiracy" trials and the bloody Civil War draft riots. Its citizens were no more accepting of aliens than were residents of other cities. But it is possible that because New Yorkers encountered such challenges before others did, they were quicker over the long run to acknowledge the necessity for people of different races and beliefs to coexist—if not in harmony, then at least in wary accommodation and a measure of mutual respect.

For many of the newcomers, respect was a long time coming, and in the meantime the Jews more than other groups seized on education as a way of advancing in the world. With many institutions of higher education barred to them, their young people gravitated in tremendous numbers to the publicly supported City College, centered after 1907 at Convent Avenue and 137th Street. Its rules required it to accept all students who could pass its entrance examinations, even if they could not afford any tuition. By 1900 Jews made up 85 percent of City College's enrollment, a figure that would remain constant for many decades until other colleges and universities opened their doors to these students. Among City College's most eminent graduates are the financier and adviser to presidents Bernard Baruch, Supreme Court Justice Felix Frankfurter, Senator Robert F. Wagner (whose son would become mayor in the 1950s), and the great liberal rabbi, Stephen Wise.

Those who were able to move out of the Lower East Side did so, for example to Brownsville and Williamsburg, in Brooklyn, where a number of clothing concerns had built factories. The more prosperous Jews moved to Harlem or the Bronx, and in the summer many of them began going to the Catskills, where lodging was inexpensive and open to all.

The surest road out of the ghetto, however, was through sheer achievement. One area in which the Jews shone was entertainment and the arts. Isidore Baline, the son of a Russian cantor, who came with his family in 1893, demonstrated a marked musical talent and changed his name to Irving Berlin. Morris and Rose Gershovitz, from St. Petersburg, Russia, decided to change their name to Gershvin; their sons won distinction as Ira and George Gershwin. Two onetime synagogue choirboys, Reuben Ticker and Jacob Perelmuth—who later were brothers-in-law—became professional singers, changed their names to Richard Tucker and Jan Peerce, and became stalwarts of the Metropolitan Opera. But by far the most memorable entertainers who came out of the Lower East Side and other New York Jewish communities were the comedians—an astonishing list that includes Eddie Cantor, Fanny Brice, George Jessel, Groucho Marx, Jack Benny, George Burns, and Milton Berle. Rising out of a world that was well acquainted with unhappiness, they had a genius for making America laugh.

The eastern European Jews brought a special spark, a zest to New York City that it did not previously have and that has become a key part of its personality. The city had always been known for its feeling of energy and drive; this now was heightened and given an edge. One special contribution of the Jews—of both the earlier German group and the later eastern European wave—has also been that of patronizing and supporting cultural activities. Artists, musicians, and all sorts of other creative persons have much to thank them for.

In the meantime, in the early decades of the great Italian and Jewish immigration booms there seemed to be few chances to escape the slums, which got worse with each passing year. The more fortunate New Yorkers could afford to move uptown; but below 14th Street, except for Greenwich Village, almost every neighborhood not taken up with business and commerce had become a slum. This polyglot world was a far cry from the uptown world of the wealthy. On the Lower East Side the noisy streets were thronged with people speaking Yiddish; around Mulberry Street the language was Italian; north of the Bowery and east of Third Avenue, German was heard, while near St. Mark's Place, east of Greenwich Village, Hungarian was spoken; just a bit further uptown one would hear Czech. In the Chatham Square area below Canal Street, which had been Irish, there were now Chinese—the beginnings of New York's famed Chinatown—while the district around the Brooklyn Bridge approaches was Greek, and across town near the Battery there were Turks, Syrians, and Arabs.

Crowding was endemic and the housing was abominable. The angled lower end of Mulberry Street, known as Mulberry Bend, had the highest crime rate in the city. Slum buildings were filthy and decrepit, and landlords had no reason to improve them. If a family became disgusted and moved out, another immediately moved in to replace them. In 1879 a new, supposedly improved tenement design was mandated. Called the dumbbell plan, it featured a narrow air shaft in its interior to provide light and air. In practice, the shaft served as a dumping ground and soon filled up with garbage.

There were a number of notorious slum areas north of 14th Street, too. The East 20s and 30s, known as the Gashouse District for its round gas-storage tanks, was ridden by gangs; while on the West Side in midtown, beyond the Tenderloin between 23rd and 42nd Streets (a neighborhood containing a great many blacks), conditions were so bad that the area was known as Hell's Kitchen.

Forced to live in such surroundings, the newcomers were all too likely to feel disillusion or even despair. One Italian immigrant summed it up: "All the time I hear about the grand city of New York. They say it is something to surprise everyone. I learn New York is twice, three, four, ten times bigger than Italian city. Maybe it is better than Milano. Maybe it is better than Naples . . . I think I am going to great city, to grand country, to better world . . . I arrive in New York. You think I find here my idea?"[8]

Jacob Riis, in *How the Other Half Lives*, revealed in words and photographs the sordid nature of slum life. But officialdom, aside from creating a few new small parks, was not disposed to do much about the problem. The city government in the 1890s and at the turn of the century was still dominated by Tammany Hall under Richard Croker, who saw no reason to disturb the status quo as long as it was profitable to his machine. Whatever help was available to slum dwellers was likely to be offered by individuals or private voluntary groups. One of the most zealous benefactors was Lillian D. Wald, a young woman from a middle-class German Jewish background who had taken nurse's training. Learning of the dreadful living conditions and dire health problems on the Lower East Side, she decided to move there and minister to the sick.

With Mary Brewster, Wald founded a nursing service that grew into the Henry Street Settlement, a pioneering social welfare organization many of whose programs were subsequently taken over by the city (among other things she persuaded the Board of Education to put nurses in all the public schools). People worshiped her. Jacob Riis wrote, "The poor trust her absolutely, trust her head, her judgement, and her friendship. She arbitrates in a strike, and the men listen . . . When pushcart peddlers are blackmailed by the police, she will tell the mayor the truth, for she knows."[9] Settlement houses like hers would be founded throughout the United States.

If not enough was being done to clean up the slums, a great deal was happening in other ways to change New York. A handful of inventions in the latter part of the nineteenth century had a profound effect on the city. One was the telephone, first demonstrated in New York by Alexander Graham Bell in 1877. Two years later the first telephone exchange was opened, downtown on Nassau Street. The new service even provided a "directory," a card containing 252 names. By the early 1890s there were 9,000 subscribers, most of them businesses (to make personal calls people went to a nearby hotel or store), and the telephone was well on its way to helping New York bolster its role as the nation's communications center. In 1882 Thomas Edison began generating electricity at a plant on Pearl Street, which sent electric current to a number of businesses and eighty-five private homes that the inventor had previously wired. The financier J. P. Morgan had already installed his own generating apparatus in the backyard of his mansion on Madison Avenue at 36th Street, but few individuals could afford such a luxury and it was many years before electricity supplanted gas in private homes. For businesses the advantages were immense—better and more dependable lighting and the innumerable uses to which electric motors could be put.

Edison had elected to put his wires and cables underground, but the city's streets were rapidly becoming a snarl of overhead wires installed for both telegraph and telephone transmission. Many utility poles carried fifteen or more arms and some bore as many as fifty, which not only was unsightly but also posed considerable danger when the wires broke during storms. In 1884 the city ruled that all wires must be buried. Compliance was spotty due to the complexity of installing so many conduits, but on March 12, 1888, the great freakish snowfall struck that has been enshrined as the Blizzard of '88. Phone and power lines went down everywhere (including two-thirds of all the poles in Manhattan), creating chaos and convincing the public of the danger of exposed wires. Within a few years the poles and wires were gone.

Fully as significant as the telephone and the harnessing of electricity were two innovations that went hand in hand: the electric elevator and steel-frame construction. Elevators powered by steam were nothing new—the Fifth Avenue Hotel, at 23rd Street, proudly possessed one when it opened in 1859—but they could not work above a height of five or six stories. Few buildings higher than that were therefore built, as nobody wanted to climb stairs much farther. Similarly, buildings constructed of masonry were limited in height by the thickness of the walls necessary to support a tall structure: the thick walls robbed valuable space from the lower floors. In the last two decades of the nineteenth century improvements in elevators and steel construction combined to erase these limitations. Soon the solid bedrock of Manhattan Island would give rise to buildings of ever increasing height.

The honor of putting up the world's first skyscraper is rightly claimed by Chicago, where the architect William Le Baron Jenney in 1884 built the ten-story Home Insurance Building, the first structure based on a steel skeleton. New York followed three years later with the thirteen-story Tower Building at 50 Broadway, whose architect, Bradford Lee Gilbert, decided the best way to erect such a high building on the narrow plot (it was barely twenty-one feet wide) was to take a steel bridge design and stand it on end. He announced that such a building was perfectly safe and would be able to withstand hundred-mile-an-hour gales. The notion seemed foolhardy, and every day as the building went up crowds gathered along Broadway expecting it to topple. One day a storm blew up bearing winds of eighty miles an hour, and Gilbert hurried downtown to check on his project. Climbing up through the construction to the top, he reeled out a plumb line that stretched all the way down to the sidewalk and found that there was no vibration or swaying of any kind. The watching crowd cheered. When the building was completed, to demonstrate his own confidence in it, Gilbert installed his own architectural offices on the top floors, remaining there until the building was demolished in 1913 for a taller structure.

The success of the Tower Building was soon followed by much higher efforts, as well as many buildings approximating it. In 1890 Joseph Pulitzer unveiled his new sixteen-story *World* building on Park Row opposite City Hall; soon after its opening a visitor is reputed to have gotten off the elevator on the top floor and asked, "Is God in?"[10] Down the street from it, eight years later the Park Row Building boasted twenty-nine stories and topped off at 386 feet, a new record. Not as tall but much more memorable was the wedge-shaped Fuller Building, better known as the Flatiron Building, which was completed in 1902 at the point where Broadway and Fifth Avenue come together at 23rd Street; to an entire generation it symbolized the drama of New York's skyline. Then just a few years later, in 1908, came the forty-seven-story Singer Building at Broadway and Liberty Street, at 612 feet the tallest building in the world. It held that record for only one year, when it was topped by the fifty-story Metropolitan Life Tower, facing Madison Square just east of the Flatiron Building.

All this was prelude, however, to the Woolworth Building, a 792-foot wonder erected by the five-and-ten-cent-store magnate Frank W. Woolworth and completed in 1913 on Broadway opposite City Hall Park. A soaring Gothic tower designed by Cass Gilbert, it bore flying buttresses, spires, gargoyles, and elaborate terra-cotta decoration. An admiring New York clergyman called it the Cathedral of Commerce, and the name stuck. The lobby contained not only sumptuous mosaics but also humorous wood carvings honoring the project's creators—Gilbert is shown holding a model of it, while Woolworth carefully counts out coins. The building cost $13.5 million, which Woolworth paid in cash, and it reigned for almost twenty years as the tallest in the world. The company that Woolworth founded still makes its headquarters there.

The increasing financial power that such high buildings represented, combined with the surge in Manhattan's population brought about by the massive immigration from southern and eastern Europe, placed increasing pressure on the city in the closing decades of the nineteenth century to expand by annexing its neighboring communities, in particular Brooklyn. The first real call for consolidation, however, arose not from any desire to annex territory but from a plan to upgrade the feature that had made New York great in the first place: its harbor and port. The plea was made as early as 1868 by Andrew H. Green, an esteemed lawyer and public servant who occupies a place in nineteenth-century New York somewhat comparable to that of Robert Moses in the twentieth. Always close to the pinnacle of power but never becoming mayor, Green was involved in the planning or building of many public works such as Central Park, the bridges over the Harlem River, the American Museum of Natural History, and the New York Public Library. And he spearheaded the early drive for consolidation. His proposal called for uniting the various municipalities (excluding those in New Jersey) that fronted on the harbor, thereby encouraging its efficiency and promoting the development of docks, bridges, terminals, and markets for the good of all. The harbor municipalities concerned were New York (Manhattan), Brooklyn, Queens, the Bronx, and Staten Island—the very units that eventually formed the Greater City.

The proposal was submerged in the Tweed scandals and in the business downturn of the 1870s, but Green did not give up. He secured the backing of the Chamber of Commerce and other civic groups and in 1890 asked the state legislature to appoint a study commission to explore the idea. New York was in competition with London, Paris, Chicago, and even Brooklyn, he told the legislators, and all of those had grown by increasing their boundaries; consolidation would enable the city to hold its own. The legislature agreed, and Green headed the resulting study group, which came out solidly for his scheme. All five counties voted on the proposal in 1894, and all backed it, although Brooklyn, many of whose residents were vehemently against it, did so by only a narrow margin. At this point the opponents, largely Brooklynites but also including some politicians who felt change would hurt them, staged a counterattack and persuaded the state legislature to shelve the program. Downcast after his long effort, Green withdrew from the fight.

The cause was saved by an unlikely figure, Boss Thomas C. Platt of New York's Republican Party. A quiet, spare, almost professorial upstate politician, Platt liked to conduct party business from his office in the Fifth Avenue Hotel—or from a sofa in a corridor off the lobby that came to be known as the Amen Corner from the obsequiousness of lowly pols petitioning him for favors. This resourceful man saw a way to build the prestige of the Republicans by stealing a march on Tammany Hall and the Democrats: triumphant Republicans might then capture City Hall. He probably wanted also to be known as the Father of Greater New York, and if so he succeeded, for it was Platt's maneuverings that won the day. Threatening, scheming, cajoling, and otherwise neutralizing the opponents of consolidation, he got the legislature to reverse itself. A new charter was written, and on January 1, 1898, the City of Greater New York came into being accompanied by fireworks, parades, the firing of guns, and the incessant blowing of boat whistles. (Ironically, Platt's great ulterior dream came to naught. Although he had elected a Republican mayor, William L. Strong, in 1894, Tammany Boss Richard Croker foxed him in 1897 by winning with his pliable candidate Robert van Wyck, and the Republican resurgence never took place.)

The new amalgam consisted of five boroughs, which were synonymous with the former counties; the counties remained as subdivisions of the state, while the boroughs were units of the city (thus Brooklyn, a borough of the city, was and is synonymous with Kings County, and the Borough of Manhattan corresponds to New York County). New York was to be governed by a much more powerful mayor and by a municipal assembly of two chambers. A third body, the Board of Estimate and Apportionment, had come into being in 1864 to supervise a regional police force, but at this point it was given some say over the annual budget. It consisted of the mayor and two commissioners. In 1901, in response to clamoring that the mayor's power should be curbed, the chief executives of each borough (called borough presidents) were added to the board, and it is this body, its name shortened to Board of Estimate, that has ever since wielded the true power in New York—until the 1980s, when the Supreme Court ruled that it was unconstitutional as it defied the one-man—one-vote principle.

The consolidation produced a city that covered 320 square miles and in 1900 counted 3,437,202 inhabitants—twice the population of Chicago and more than all but six American States. In the entire world only London was more populous. Well over a third of that population was foreign-born, and of these, Germans were still the largest bloc with the Irish next, but Italians and eastern European Jews were coming on strong and would eventually surpass them. The city had 578 miles of waterfront and an annual budget of $90 million.

But the boroughs were very different from each other. Brooklyn, with just over a million people, was more built up than any of the others (except for Manhattan) and contained the bucolic Prospect Park, designed (as Central Park had been) by Olmsted and Vaux; the extensive and parklike Green-Wood Cemetery; and a first-class newspaper, the Brooklyn *Eagle*, founded in 1841. Queens was heavily built up along its western edge, on the East River, with Long Island City and Astoria given over largely to factories, warehouses, and office buildings; to the east the borough was mostly a collection of overgrown towns like Flushing and Jamaica. In the consolidation Queens had lost three of its easternmost settlements, Hempstead, North Hempstead, and Oyster Bay, which voted to stay out and to become part of a new county, Nassau. The Bronx was vastly increased in area, the original Annexed District being augmented by Riverdale, at the western end on the Hudson, and a large chunk of Westchester County that became the East Bronx and included parts of Pelham and Eastchester. Much of the Bronx was still rural, a condition that the city took advantage of by creating Van Cortlandt Park, Bronx Park (which would be given over to the Bronx Zoo and the New York Botanical Garden), and Pelham Bay Park (in the northeast corner of the borough); the Bronx also included St. John's College, a Jesuit institution, which in 1907 became Fordham University. Even more rural was Staten Island, also known as the Borough of Richmond, which had only 67,000 residents and remains to this day the city's least populous borough.

Given such an immense area, the need for fast, efficient rapid transit became acute, and this finally led to the building of New York's first subway line. The elevated railroads had proved only a limited success; they were noisy, dirty (before being converted to electricity), and not fast enough—trains moving at more than about 20 miles per hour shook the supporting structure ominously. Brooklyn and parts of the Bronx were served by electric streetcars that took their power from overhead wires (Brooklynites took such pride in dodging the cars that they later named their baseball team the Dodgers), but the aerial wires were ruled out for Manhattan. Cable cars made a brief appearance in Manhattan but were involved in so many accidents that the experiment was abandoned. A key consideration that delayed the city's first subway was technological: because Manhattan was so long and narrow, experts said that a train must be capable of speeds up to forty miles an hour or more, and until the 1890s there was simply no electric motor capable of delivering such speed.

When a powerful enough motor became available, the project snagged over financing. Private interests could not come up with the money, and so the city eventually footed the $50 million bill itself —though it decided to turn over the operating of the subway to private concerns. On March 24, 1900, ground was broken, and 12,000 laborers set to work, a great many of them recent Italian immigrants. More than four years later, on October 27, 1904, the first train was dispatched. The mayor, George B. McClellan, Jr. (the son of the Civil War general), took the controls wearing a top hat and a chesterfield coat and with some trepidation guided the train on its journey from one end of the nine-mile system to the other. His route led from City Hall up Lafayette Street and Fourth Avenue to 42nd Street, west (today's Shuttle route) to Times Square, and then under Broadway all the way up to 145th Street. Attaining a top speed of forty-five miles an hour at times, McClellan and his trainload of dignitaries made the run in twenty-six minutes, a clocking that would be perfectly acceptable today. That day some 110,000 New Yorkers used the system, and within a week the daily ridership was 350,000. The fare was five cents, and it was to remain at that level for more than forty years, rising only after World War II.

Work was already under way on a tunnel to Brooklyn that would extend the subway all the way to Borough Hall, and soon tunnels were being dug to the Bronx and Queens and a new and separate system gave additional access to Brooklyn. During World War I the original route taken by McClellan was extended by adding a line up the East Side above 42nd Street and another south of Times Square on the West Side, the link between them being made into the Shuttle. In the 1930s a third system, the Independent, but also known as the Eighth Avenue line and immortalized by Duke Ellington and Billy Strayhorn's "Take the 'A' Train," was added. Eventually New York's system, with all its mammoth problems and annoyances, would be the most heavily traveled railroad in the world.

More than the subways were linking Manhattan to its outer boroughs and the rest of the United States. A second span over the East River to Brooklyn, the Williamsburg Bridge, was completed in 1903, and six years later the Queensboro Bridge, to Queens, and the Manhattan Bridge, just above the Brooklyn Bridge, were added. New Jersey got a rapid transit connection to the city in 1908 with the opening of the subwaylike Hudson & Manhattan Railroad under the Hudson, better known as the Tubes.

Up to 1910, any railroad passenger coming to New York from the south or west was deposited on the west shore of the Hudson and had to take a ferry to the city, an irksome arrangement. The inconvenience was eliminated, at least for Pennsylvania Railroad customers, with the opening in 1910 of the stately Pennsylvania Station on Seventh Avenue at 33rd Street, designed by McKim, Mead & White, which trains could reach via a brand-new tunnel under the Hudson. The station was also connected with Long Island by means of a tunnel under the East River, and in due course a line was added that brought trains from the Long Island City yards through Queens and over to the Bronx, and thence north and east to New England. From this time on, through service was possible from Washington all the way to Boston by way of New York.

The Pennsylvania Station building was unfortunately lost to New York when it was demolished in the early 1960s, but still operating today is its counterpart, the Grand Central Terminal that opened in 1913 at Park Avenue and 42nd Street, the last of three terminals on that site. The structure itself, designed by Warren & Wetmore, is a spacious and handsome Beaux Arts design. But even more remarkable is the engineering scheme, drawn up by the New York Central's chief engineer, William J. Wilgus, which allows for an astonishing twenty-seven miles of track on two levels in a space not quite half a mile long and three blocks wide, all underground. Because the terminal's approaches and yards occupy the underground space all the way up to East 50th Street, all of the buildings built above the previously open yards are without basements. Their steel-beam supports go down through the rail yards.

By the time World War I broke out in Europe, just a year after Grand Central's opening, New York was in many ways unrecognizable from the city it had been in the 1870s. As recently as 1898, South Street had still been the center of the American shipping world, and sailing ships were still seen everywhere in the harbor, but by 1914 steam had entirely supplanted sail, and the docks along the Hudson River were handling the greater part of the maritime traffic. New York no longer held such a commanding lead over other port cities, for New Orleans and even Baltimore could more conveniently be reached from many western inland areas. But as the nation's economy was still growing swiftly, the port of New York continued to expand in absolute terms, and during the war it passed both Liverpool and London to become the world's busiest port. The city's role as a headquarters town continued to expand, as did its manufacturing activities, and thanks to the addition of Brooklyn the city remained the nation's chief industrial center. But the manufacturing scene was changing, as industries with large production orders found it cheaper to do business outside of Manhattan; more and more manufacturers were setting up in Brooklyn, Queens, or the Bronx. In Manhattan, small-time producers were becoming more prevalent, for example in the garment industry where the ability to shift, adapt, and bring out new products overnight was vital.

Manhattan was by now entirely built up from river to river and almost all the way up the island except for parts of Harlem and Washington Heights. Midtown Manhattan, centered on 34th and 42nd Streets, was becoming a prime office location, and both here and downtown buildings of twenty and thirty stories were almost commonplace, so that the skyscrapers stood out, as Henry James wrote, like "extravagant pins in a cushion already overplanted."[11] The advent of electricity had turned Times Square into a nighttime marvel (masking its daytime tawdriness), with illuminated signs and billboards lighting up the sky. In the outer boroughs, elevated lines were built extending the run of trains that ran underground in Manhattan's subways. New York's 1910 population was 4.8 million and climbing. The increased number of people necessitated new sources of water; and the city, which up to now had been adequately served by water from Croton in Westchester County, was forced to reach out to the Catskill Mountains to meet the demand.

Consolidation had made New York even harder to govern; and although Boss Croker finally retired as Tammany leader, his successor, Charles Francis Murphy, continued to wield considerable power. Two mayors, William Gaynor and John Purroy Mitchel, stood out in their efforts to contain Tammany and improve the city. Gaynor, a trim, gray-bearded former judge, had been nominated by Tammany but immediately upon taking office in 1910 turned against it, ruthlessly cut the city payroll, made sure municipal employees put in a full eight-hour day, and otherwise showed himself to be his own man. Unfortunately, after little more than seven months in office he was wounded by a would-be assassin as he prepared to embark on the SS *Kaiser Wilhelm* for a European vacation. The bullet lodged in his throat and could not be removed, and Gaynor spent the rest of his term in pain and subject to bouts of irascibility that cut short his promising career. He was succeeded as elected mayor by Mitchel, who had been president of the Board of Aldermen (roughly comparable to today's City Council) and proved himself a thoroughgoing reformer; his most notable accomplishment was to put the city on a pay-as-you-go basis. But he was an elitist and a poor politician and, sadly, did not win reelection. In the 1917 election Tammany Hall, under Murphy, won back its former power.

A new factor had intruded onto the political scene: organized labor. Unions had enjoyed little success in the nineteenth century as state laws tended to weaken them, but worsening conditions in the garment industry led in 1900 to the founding of the International Ladies' Garment Workers Union, followed by others. One notorious anti-union shop was the Triangle Shirtwaist Company, which was known for exploiting its workers—its female employees were billed for the needles they used and taxed for their lockers. When some of the employees tried to join the ILGWU they were fired; the union attempted to call a strike against the firm but its pickets were beaten up. Then on March 25, 1911, fire broke out at the company's factory on Washington Place near Washington Square. Spreading quickly, it soon engulfed the building, which was equipped with neither fire escapes nor sprinklers. A total of 146 workers died, 125 of them women. New Yorkers were shocked and outraged, and as a result the state rewrote its labor code and the labor movement gained new status and urgency. In due course New York would become the nation's preeminent "union town," and union leaders would play a major role in local politics.

Another key shift under way at this time was the movement of blacks to Harlem. Although New York had been regarded by many blacks as hostile territory due to the implications of the Civil War draft riots, there was a considerable influx of blacks from the rural South during the latter part of the nineteenth century, and in 1900 their number stood at 60,000. Most of them lived in Manhattan between the West 20s and 50s, although a few had established outposts in Brooklyn. As the West Side was becoming more and more congested there was pressure on the blacks to move, and it happened that after the turn of the century an overextended building boom in Harlem had left many landlords with empty space on their hands. Blacks were encouraged to occupy these buildings, though they were charged higher rents than whites would have paid. By the start of World War I the sudden invasion was virtually complete, and Harlem had become transformed into a black city within a city.

So New York City, though it had achieved a kind of maturity and was in most respects the city of today, continued to change. Two developments in the decade before World War I, though they might not have seemed earthshaking at the time, were to have lasting repercussions. One was the Armory Show, an international exhibit of highly controversial modern art held at the 69th Regiment Armory on Lexington Avenue in 1913. Most New Yorkers were dumb-founded or offended, or both, by what they saw, which included works by such innovators as Pablo Picasso and Marcel Duchamp. But a seed had been planted, out of which grew the city's growing acceptance of, and involvement with, avant-garde painting and sculp-ture. Decades hence, with hefty infusions of New York money, this would lead to the city's establishment as the art capital of the world.

The other development was the arrival of the automobile. Cars had first been seen on the city's streets shortly before the turn of the century. Most were custom-made and expensive, and many were electric. The nation's first automobile show was held at Madison Square Garden (on East 26th Street) in 1900, and the following year New York State required motorists to buy license plates at a dollar apiece. By 1910 the streets were full of cars, most of them now gasoline-powered—honking, roaring contraptions that poured out smoke and fumes. In no time at all these convenient, space-consuming carriers would be remaking the face of New York.

11

Boom, Bust, and Triumph

New York in the 1920s was riding high. It was at the peak of its glory, its power seemingly limitless. It was now the nation's indisputable cultural and economic capital, the place that everyone envied and wanted to see. In the words of the writer W. L. George, it was "all the cities ... the only American city where people work and play; in the others they work ... the oil and cotton of the South, the wheat of the Middle West, come to fuse themselves in the crucible of pleasure that lies on the Hudson."[1] The air of excitement, almost of fantasy, seemed to be summed up in the skyline, now bristling with towers and never failing to inspire awe. As F. Scott Fitzgerald wrote in *The Great Gatsby*, "Over the great bridge, with the sunlight through the girders making a constant flicker upon the moving cars, with the city rising up across the river in white heaps and sugar lumps all built with a wish out of nonolfactory money. The city seen from the Queensboro Bridge is always the city seen for the first time, in its first wild promise of all the mystery and the beauty in the world."[2]

Hymned in the works of its artists and writers and given a special tinge of unreality by the peculiar national experiment known as Prohibition, the city's ebullience was to become legendary—while it lasted. But the glory and the good times proved to be transitory when the October 1929 stock market collapse signaled the end of one world and the beginning of another. The Great Depression changed the United States, and it surely changed New York. Ironically, despite the terrible hardships of those years, the New York of the 1930s proved to be an even better and certainly more humane city than it had been in the 1920s. For just as the feckless Mayor Jimmy Walker had symbolized the carefree, irresponsible 1920s, his successor Fiorello La Guardia—by far the best mayor in the city's history—would lead New York in triumph out of scandal and despair in the 1930s. He would bring an air of decency and compassion to New York and preside over a virtual remaking of its outward look more than anyone had thought possible, making the city once again the envy of the nation.

But there was one significant difference between the New York of these decades, with all its ups and downs, and the city that had existed previously. The colossal tide of immigration had ebbed, due to legislation enacted in the isolationist wake of World War I. The nation was no longer accepting virtually anyone who showed up at its door. The emergency quota act of 1921 not only reduced the total number of immigrants allowed to enter but also set quotas for each nation based on the number of nationals of a given country who had lived here in 1910. Three years later, in response to a misguided popular sentiment that this system gave undue recognition to the recent, prewar influx from southern and eastern Europe, the Johnson-Reed Immigration Act of 1924 pushed the quota-basing year back to 1890, when northern Europeans had still formed the dominant group in the country. The effect on New York City was substantial and long-lasting. Except for a continued (indeed increasing) influx of blacks from the southern states, the city's racial mixing was brought to a standstill. The Lower East Side was no longer packed with new arrivals, and ethnic neighborhoods stopped elbowing each other for breathing room. Ellis Island operated at half speed; immigration from the Orient was reduced to a trickle. For New Yorkers it was an odd, unexpectedly quiet interim. The calm came to an end only in the mid-1930s when the city began welcoming Jewish refugees from Hitlerite Germany, and the partial reopening of the Golden Door brought back some of the old sense of energy.

In this atypical interlude, for half a dozen years at least, the city flourished. National prosperity caused investment money to flow to Wall Street in ever greater amounts and the stock market surged upward. New York had by the end of World War I displaced London as the financial center of the globe. Thanks to thriving factories and industrial plants mainly in the outlying boroughs, the city also retained its lead as the nation's number one manufacturer—an industrial as well as a commercial and financial nexus.

And with money so plentiful, New Yorkers were not hesitant to enjoy themselves. The war was over, and if there was still trouble in Europe, who cared? Reminders that the world was an ugly place were dismissed. Just before noon on September 16, 1920, a horse-drawn wagon came up Wall Street from the east and stopped in front of J. P. Morgan & Company. The driver strolled away, and precisely at noon, as Trinity Church was sounding the midday, the wagon exploded in a deafening yellow-white ball of fire, killing 38 people and wounding 130. The crime was never solved but was universally assumed to have been staged by anarchists. No matter—Wall Street was cleaned up (although the bank chose to proclaim its defiance by leaving its scarred wall unrepaired; the pockmarks are still there), and the city went back to work—and to play.

The era has been called the Roaring Twenties and the Jazz Age. Its most distinctive symbol was the flapper, a carefree young woman in short skirt and shingled hair, and its most memorable icon was the speakeasy, wherein otherwise law-abiding New Yorkers cheerfully defied Prohibition. An illicit bar, the speakeasy—so called presumably for the quiet tone in which one muttered the password that gained entry—was usually disguised behind a store or in a basement (one of them was entered through a fake telephone booth) and served exorbitantly priced drinks in a coffee cup or other camouflage device. There were said to be anywhere from 20,000 to 100,000 of them in New York, and they came and went. One of the few that survived past the repeal of Prohibition in 1933 was a very posh establishment called Jack and Charlie's, at 21 West 52nd Street, which as "21" has been a gustatory fixture at that address ever since.

The most illustrious of them, however, were a succession of clubs presided over by a hearty middle-aged blonde from Texas named Mary Louise Cecilia Guinan, known to everyone as Texas Guinan. She liked to greet patrons by enthusiastically singing out "Hello, sucker!" and the key to her success was the mix of clientele that she managed to attract. In any of her establishments one would typically find a smattering of socialites, some Broadway (or Hollywood) stars, plenty of show girls or flappers, a sprinkling of writers or artists, and, significantly, a few racketeers or gangsters. The heady combination was a great drawing card, and it gave rise to café society, the nightclubbing set of the 1930s and 1940s whose descendants include the tabloid-fueled celebrity world of today.

To find a speakeasy, one had only to ask a policeman for directions, as these illegal establishments were for the most part winked at because of their great popularity. One unfortunate side effect of the whole charade, to be sure, was the rise of big-time rumrunners, racketeers who specialized in smuggling liquor into the United States in defiance of the law, and whose cunning and savagery (and that of their successors in other fields) would bedevil the authorities from then on. Many operatives who had been small-time hoodlums or gang leaders in the city rose to positions of great power and wealth in the underworld this way and, after repeal or even before, branched out into other rackets. The longshoreman Big Bill Dwyer made millions and was adept at paying off the police as well as the Coast Guard. Arthur Flegenheimer, better known as Dutch Schultz, profited handsomely by his control of beer distribution in Harlem and the Bronx and then entered the numbers racket. Francesco Castiglia, who called himself Frank Costello, earned a fortune importing liquor before moving into slot machines; he operated out of a proper-looking office on Lexington Avenue near Grand Central. So powerful did these men become, flagrantly bribing judges and Tammany Hall politicians, that they were able virtually to subvert the government of New York City.

And very little could be done to thwart them. With only 178 agents in the entire metropolitan region, the Treasury Department, the governmental body charged with enforcing Prohibition, concentrated on making speakeasy arrests. Although such crackdowns were cordially disliked by the citizenry, two federal agents became popular heroes because of their imaginative tactics. The former postal clerk Izzy Einstein, five feet five inches tall and weighing 225 pounds, was a natural clown, as was his even more rotund friend Moe Smith, and together they cut a wide swath through New York's gin mills. Specializing in disguises, they staged raids dressed as football players, grave diggers, waiters, icemen, musicians, fishermen, and poultry salesmen (to name just a few) with stunning results. Over a five-year period they seized an estimated 5 million bottles of liquor and made 4,392 arrests until their embarrassed superiors, worried that the pair were making fools out of other agents, dismissed them "for the good of the service."[3] Izzy switched to amateur theatricals and later wrote his memoirs.

The delight with which New Yorkers viewed the exploits of Izzy and Moe was echoed in their enthusiastic patronage of Broadway plays and musicals. Among the most successful musical productions of the 1920s were *Show Boat* and *A Connecticut Yankee*, while the *Ziegfeld Follies* established another kind of tradition. Meanwhile, motion pictures were being offered in ever-grander and gaudier movie "palaces," of which by far the most splendid was the Roxy Theatre, opened at the northeast corner of Seventh Avenue and 50th Street in 1926 by the showman Samuel "Roxy" Rothafel. Costing $12 million and seating 6,200 moviegoers, this monument to kitsch boasted a lobby large enough to hold 2,500 patrons, an ornate auditorium decorated in multiple shades of gold leaf, three pipe organs, and an orchestra pit capable of seating 110 musicians. An elaborate stage show alternated with the featured movie. The Roxy and another of Rothafel's creations, the Capitol Theatre at Broadway and 51st Street, formed the northern boundary of the Times Square district, which now was dominated by movie houses on Broadway and Seventh Avenue; the legitimate theaters had almost all retired to the side streets. The city's entertainment center had been moving uptown (all the way from the City Hall district) for a century and a half; having reached Times Square, it would move no more. But other entertainments were to be found elsewhere. The concert world centered on West 57th Street, where Carnegie Hall was located. The old Madison Square Garden on 26th Street was torn down and reopened in 1925 on Eighth Avenue and 50th Street, almost part of Times Square. Up in the Bronx the success of the New York Yankees—and of the club's sterling home run hitter, Babe Ruth—led the club's owner, beer baron Jacob Ruppert, to construct Yankee Stadium on 161st Street. The "house that Ruth built" was an instant success.

Hand in hand with New York's ever-increasing influence as an entertainment bazaar went its central role in literature and the arts. Greenwich Village was no longer a hotbed of radicalism, as it had been before and during World War I. Although it was still the kind of place where Willa Cather, Edna St. Vincent Millay, and Eugene O'Neill preferred to live, the literary scene was inching uptown. Book publishers were mostly ensconced along Fourth Avenue around or above 23rd Street, although many of them would soon pull up stakes and move farther up, to the midtown area. A key event was the founding, in 1925, of the *New Yorker* magazine, whose editor, Harold Ross, orchestrated an ingenious mix of humor and serious writing. Soon the magazine's wits and other literary luminaries, like Robert Benchley, Alexander Woollcott, and Dorothy Parker, began meeting for lunch at the Algonquin Hotel a block away from the magazine's offices, to be joined by such other banterers as the columnist Franklin P. Adams, the playwright George S. Kaufman, and the newspaperman Heywood Broun. The rapierlike conversations at the Algonquin Round Table, as their meeting spot became known, were the stuff of legend and may have been almost as scintillating as reported. A different kind of tradition got under way in New York with the initial publication, in 1923, of *Time* magazine, which under the idiosyncratic leadership of its founder, Henry R. Luce, introduced an entirely new kind of sharp, opinionated weekly news reporting and gave rise to a host of other Luce publications (like *Life* and *Fortune*) whose influence would be vast.

If the literary lights had moved away from Greenwich Village, the artists had not. Painters and sculptors who had been involved in the epochal Armory Show in 1913 were centered there, many of them befriended or otherwise encouraged by Gertrude Vanderbilt Whitney, a great-granddaughter of the Commodore and a talented sculptor in her own right, who although she maintained her residence on upper Fifth Avenue had opened an art gallery on West 8th Street. There she exhibited the work of such realist painters as John Sloan, William J. Glackens, and Robert Henri, whose depictions of the workaday world of the city earned them the name of the Ashcan school. Her gallery in 1931 became the Whitney Museum of American Art, which would remain in the Village until well after World War II. A kindred soul was the photographer Alfred Stieglitz, who presided over a small gallery at 291 Fifth Avenue that became famous for showing the work of modern or avant-garde painters like John Marin as well as that of gifted photographers. Stieglitz's own photographs of the city were imbued with the same spirit of realism that motivated the Ashcan school.

Another cultural center, however, existed far uptown in Harlem. There had long been plenty of gifted black writers, artists, and musicians, of course, but white New Yorkers and other Americans had never heard of most of them—except for the jazz players. But in the 1920s, as Harlem came to recognize itself as a strong black community (counting a population of more than 200,000, many of whom had come north during World War I in response to wartime job openings), and as black writers from other parts of the United States began gravitating to it, white intellectuals downtown discovered it. This was due partly to outright recognition of hitherto unnoticed talent, but it was also due to a romantic feeling for what blacks seemed to represent in a rebellious age: they were outcasts whose complaints about the nature of society struck a chord among many whites. They were also seen as endlessly fascinating and somehow exotic. The result was the Harlem Renaissance, in which the works of such writers as James Weldon Johnson, Countee Cullen, Claude McKay, Zora Neale Hurston, and Langston Hughes, such composers as William Grant Still, and painters like Aaron Douglas became known. The white writer Carl Van Vechten, a fixture of the New York literary world who had a wide acquaintance in Harlem, helped spread the word through his 1926 novel *Nigger Heaven*. Meanwhile the black singers Roland Hayes and Paul Robeson were achieving great prominence.

Harlem was becoming popular among downtown whites for another reason too: it was seen as a citadel of jazz and laughter whose night clubs symbolized gaiety and adventure. Limousines would collect after midnight in front of spots like the Cotton Club, Connie's Inn, and Small's Paradise. In any of the clubs might be heard bands led by the likes of Duke Ellington or Cab Calloway, and Harlem had already sent the tantalizing personality Josephine Baker to Paris.

The romance and notoriety masked the true Harlem—crowded, poverty-stricken, and disease-ridden. Blacks generally paid much higher rents than whites did for equivalent space, yet they tended to take home smaller paychecks than whites doing the same work. Strapped for cash, they subdivided their apartments and sublet the space, or held rent parties whose proceeds went to an extortionate landlord. Crime was rampant and so was every form of gambling; drugs were rife. But Harlemites had few leaders who could effectively fight such conditions. One who seemed to offer hope was Marcus Garvey, a Jamaican who had come to Harlem in 1917 and soon began publishing a weekly paper called the *Negro World*, which advocated black unity and the return of blacks to Africa. Membership in his Universal Negro Improvement Association was in the hundreds of thousands, and no black stirred the popular imagination more than he did. In 1922, however, he was indicted by the federal government for mail fraud in connection with a steamship company, the Black Star Line, which he had founded to transport blacks to Africa, and was convicted and sent to prison. Things got no better in Harlem, and the rest of New York (and the country) was having too good a time and making too much money to care.

Personifying the happy, unconcerned spirit of the times was New York's mayor, James J. Walker, a genial, wisecracking, dapper man who was every inch the product of Tammany Hall. Born on Leroy Street in Greenwich Village in 1881, he was the son of a Tammany ward leader and state assemblyman. At first he did not want to follow his father into politics; his ambition was to be a songwriter. After completing high school he hung around New York's Tin Pan Alley —on 28th Street between Sixth Avenue and Broadway, where music publishers had their offices—and in 1905 wrote "Will You Love Me in December as You Do in May?" which became a hit. But that was his only success, and in 1910 his father persuaded him to enter politics and arranged for his election to the state assembly. Walker attracted notice there, and in 1914 Tammany boss Charles Murphy, successor to Boss Richard Croker, upped him to the state senate. Again Walker did well, becoming Democratic floor leader and sponsoring bills to legalize boxing in New York State and to allow Sunday baseball games. He had an engaging personality and was known for his florid speaking style. By 1924 he was being touted for mayor.

The incumbent, Mayor John F. Hylan, was a bumbler. Scrupulously honest but ponderous and slow-witted, he was a product of the Brooklyn Democratic machine and had been swept into office in 1917 in the city's overreaction to the rigidly reformist John Purroy Mitchel. Called Red Mike for his red hair and mustache, he was bereft of the fire that such a name would imply; but he had won reelection in 1921 and, as the 1925 election drew closer, let it be known that he would be happy to accept a third term. By now, however, Tammany was fed up and decided the time had come for a new face. With the halfhearted blessing of Governor Alfred E. Smith, who though himself a Tammany sachem and a personal friend of Walker had little respect for him, the bosses picked Walker to run. He sailed into office.

Jimmy Walker had no administrative experience, but it did not seem to matter. The city was healthy and its government seemed to run itself. Walker became a part-time mayor, which suited most New Yorkers just fine. Rarely showing up at City Hall before noon, he might preside over a Board of Estimate meeting by making a few wisecracks, then depart for some party or civic ceremony, his thin figure nattily set off by a sleek broad-shouldered suit, custom-made tie, spats, and walking stick. Deep down, it is now known, Jimmy was neurotic and insecure—he feared crowds and cars and was terrified if he was driven around town at a speed greater than twenty miles an hour—but few people were aware of any of this. His nightclubbing (he personally helped redesign the Central Park Casino, an exclusive restaurant and eatery overlooking the Mall, and patronized it assiduously) and his mistress Betty Compton made good copy. His forgiving wife observed many years later, "He made everyone happy wherever he went. I don't know just how he did it, and neither did he."[4] But happiness was almost official city policy, as Walker's official greeter Grover Whalen organized all-out ticker-tape parades up Broadway for the benefit of any sudden celebrity like Charles Lind-bergh, English Channel swimmer Gertrude Ederle, or Queen Marie of Rumania. New York was a party and Walker was the host. In 1929 the mayor easily won reelection over Fiorello H. La Guardia, a Republican congressman from the Upper East Side, despite the challenger's angry and unrelenting charges that city officials were being paid off by prominent underworld figures. La Guardia also attacked Walker for having accepted an increase in salary from $25,000 to $40,000, a high figure in those days. Retorted the mayor, "That's cheap! Think what it would cost if I worked full time."[5]

Prosperous, the city continued to grow. Despite the cutback in immigration, New York's population climbed from 4.8 million in 1910 to almost 7 million in 1930, most of this registered in the outer boroughs rather than in Manhattan—which for the first time experienced a slight decline. Buildings climbed higher and higher, although there were now limitations on the space they were allowed to occupy. As early as 1907 complaints had been voiced that gargantuan new structures were cutting off light and air and hurting their neighborhoods. But nothing came of the agitation until the Equitable Life Assurance Society put up a mammoth structure at 120 Broadway in 1912–1915. The building occupied a full block and rose forty stories straight from the sidewalk, with no setbacks. The bulky structure dominated everything around it. New Yorkers were incensed and in 1916 forced the passage of a building zoning resolution that set limits on heights of street facades and mandated setbacks for all tall buildings. It was the nation's first zoning ordinance, and among other things gave the downtown skyline a distinctly spiky look that would last for several decades, until air conditioning and other developments changed things again.

Midtown was getting high buildings too, most of them along East 42nd Street near Grand Central: the Lincoln Building was fifty-three stories high and the Chanin Building fifty-six, while in 1930 the 77-story Chrysler Building, at 42nd and Lexington, was completed and became (for a year) the world's tallest structure. (The steel spike that crowns the Chrysler Building's glittering modernist sleekness was an afterthought. While the building was under construction its architect, William Van Alen, feared that the Bank of the Manhattan Company's new skyscraper on Wall Street might turn out to be higher, for its architect had added floors when he heard of Van Alen's plans. So Van Alen designed a 185-foot spire and had it assembled on the sly, within the Chrysler Building's fire shaft. When he was certain that the Manhattan Company's tower had topped off just slightly higher

265

than what was visible in his own design, he had the spire brought up and triumphantly installed to give him the record.) Van Alen's (and Chrysler's) glee was short-lived, for less than a year later the height record was taken over by the 102-story Empire State Building, at Fifth Avenue and 34th Street, on the site of the old Waldorf-Astoria Hotel. (The Waldorf had been re-created at Park Avenue and 50th Street.)

Fifth Avenue was undergoing grave changes. The great palaces of the millionaires were disappearing: below 59th Street the avenue was becoming commercial, invaded by department stores and smart shops, while to the north the mansions were giving way to large and luxurious apartment buildings. Both of the spectacular Vanderbilt mansions, Willie K.'s pseudo-château at 52nd Street and Cornelius II's immense pile at 58th, were demolished in the 1920s. Park Avenue, a choice address now that the railroad tracks were covered over, became lined with hotels and big apartment houses all the way to 96th Street; it could claim to be the wealthiest residential highway in the world. Building boomed all over the Upper East Side, as did construction in the outlying boroughs, which were rapidly becoming urbanized. Brooklyn had few tall buildings but mile after square mile of pleasant small houses on tree-shaded streets, plus a share of slums in Williamsburg, Brownsville, and Red Hook. Queens, burgeoning on the basis of its subway link to Manhattan, was a borough of drab two-story homes and an occasional affluent development like Forest Hills or Kew Gardens, both planned communities. The Bronx, except for the proper residential districts of Riverdale and Marble Hill, was becoming filled with cheap apartment buildings but boasted one thoroughfare that aspired to respectability, the Grand Concourse. (Unfortunately the Concourse enjoyed little more than a generation of grandeur and began to decline soon after World War II.) Only Staten Island, connected to the rest of the city just by ferry, remained generally rural.

The city's harbor facilities, which had been severely strained to keep up with demands made on them during World War I and badly in need of upgrading, received a welcome boost with the creation in 1921 of the Port of New York Authority. A bistate nonpolitical agency administered jointly by New York and New Jersey, the authority concentrated port management in one central office, which was empowered to float bond issues and use the revenue to keep harbor facilities in top condition. It was thanks to the authority's efficiency that the port retained its world leadership through the interwar years.

The authority was also empowered to build tunnels and bridges (and collect tolls therein) as needed, and in due time, with the increasing importance of interstate motor traffic, this activity would become virtually as big a part of its franchise as running the harbor. When the authority came into being, planning was already under way for constructing the Holland Tunnel, to connect Jersey City with lower Manhattan, but the authority took over its operation soon after it was finished in 1927. The first long tunnel in the world designed for automobile traffic, it necessitated a complex and ingenious ventilating system that was the brainchild of the project's chief engineer Clifford M. Holland. Meanwhile the authority itself initiated work on a great bridge to cross the Hudson from upper Manhattan. Designed by the Swiss-born and -trained engineer Othmar Ammann and named for George Washington (who had fought battles in the Revolution nearby), the structure was dedicated in 1931 and was the longest suspension bridge ever built up to that time. It is noteworthy especially for its openwork steel towers. Originally they were to be clad in granite, but as the work progressed the public grew fond of the look of the steel and raised an outcry for abandoning the stone. (With the onset of the depression, the authority was also grateful for an excuse to save money.) The unclad steel has captivated onlookers ever since. A critical link, the bridge has been largely responsible for the swift growth of New Jersey's Bergen County as a bedroom community for New York.

During the booming 1920s New York City also reinforced its position as a headquarters town by becoming the nation's undisputed communications center. Because of its financial role, the city had long been the focus of economic news; with the development of commercial radio in the 1920s it also became the broadcasting center. The first person to sense radio's potential was the Russian-born David Sarnoff of the Marconi Wireless Telegraph Company, in New York, which dominated transatlantic wireless communication before World War I. In 1919 the Marconi Company was combined with other concerns to form the Radio Corporation of America, with Sarnoff as general manager, and presently the RCA radio stations became the nucleus of the National Broadcasting Company, with offices in midtown. At about the same time the Columbia Broadcasting System came into being, to be controlled after 1928 by William S. Paley.

The two big networks would be joined much later by the American Broadcasting Company, and their influence would escalate with the coming of television after World War II. NBC, CBS, and ABC would all remain headquartered within a few blocks of each other.

In this pleasant, confident era it seemed as if nothing could go wrong, but of course the good times did not last. For Mayor Walker there was an intimation even before his first term had ended that trouble might lie ahead. One Sunday evening in 1928 he and Betty Compton were having dinner in a suburban restaurant frequented by underworld figures. A man came up and whispered something to Walker, who appeared distressed by the news and announced he had to leave. On the way out he confided to a friend that he had been told that the gangster Arnold Rothstein had been shot. A notorious hoodlum, Rothstein had earned the title of Banker to the Underworld, and while having heavily invested in all manner of illegal activities he was also suspected of having loaned or given money to many persons in public office. The mayor, in spite of his storied hands-off attitude toward his job, must have sensed that members of his administration would be implicated. He was right. When Rothstein died a few days later his office files were impounded, and the revelations they yielded were to bring down Walker and critically wound Tammany Hall as well.

Little of this was known to the public, however, and when La Guardia charged during his unsuccessful mayoralty campaign in 1929 that among the recipients of Rothstein loans was a city magistrate named Albert H. Vitale, who had gotten $19,940 from him, few people paid any attention.

In late October 1929, however, the crash of the stock market changed everything. During the ensuing months, with Wall Street in disarray and business reeling, and with the city's finances suddenly looking less than rosy as a result of the downturn, the public was ready to look at rumors of payoffs. The upshot was a series of three state-ordered investigations conducted by a former judge and high-minded lawyer named Samuel Seabury, who found that Vitale was only one of a number of persons paid off or otherwise corrupted, many of them in the ruling circle of Tammany Hall and some embarrassingly close to the mayor himself. Judges were being bribed, Tammany politicians were profiting from rigged contracts and hiding the ill-gotten cash in "little tin boxes," and many of the city's departments were bureaucratic nightmares.

As the revelations unfolded, the city descended further into the depths of the depression. Businesses failed, public construction was almost at a standstill, unemployment skyrocketed until nearly one out of every four employable New Yorkers was jobless, and breadlines became a common sight. Well-dressed, respectable men took to selling apples on the street. The homeless were everywhere, many of them eking out an existence in shacks in Central Park. Harlem was particularly hard hit, as blacks as usual were the first to be laid off in bad times. The city itself was approaching bankruptcy.

The Seabury probe was getting closer to the mayor. There was the matter of the Equitable Coach Company, run by a friend of Walker's; the mayor had worked hard to push a franchise for it through the Board of Estimate and shortly thereafter left for a vacation in Europe armed with a $10,000 letter of credit from Equitable's New York representative. Well-placed friends had given the mayor securities, enabling him to profit heavily in the stock market without investing a dollar. Walker's personal financial agent, Russell T. Sherwood, somehow had deposited almost $1 million in various banks although his salary was only $10,000 a year.

Finally, on May 25 and 26, 1932, Seabury succeeded in putting Walker himself on the stand. The mayor was debonair and cheerful as ever—and thoroughly evasive. Although Seabury bored in relentlessly, he could produce little from him. But on June 8 he wrote a letter to Governor Franklin D. Roosevelt (who had succeeded Al Smith in Albany in 1928) summing up the case against Walker and accusing him of such malfeasance and nonfeasance "as to render him unfit to continue in the office of Mayor."[6] The governor held public hearings on the case and examined Walker personally. Roosevelt had a dilemma. He had just become a candidate for president and was reluctant to offend Tammany, whose help might be vital to him in carrying New York State in November; but failure to remove Walker would be seen as a sign of weakness or opportunism. As it happened, the governor was spared the agony, for Walker on September 1, 1932, resigned his office. He sailed for Europe ten days later.

Some vigorous politicking ensued. Becoming acting mayor by right of temporary succession was the president of the Board of Aldermen, Joseph V. McKee, a cultivated and experienced protégé of the Bronx Democratic boss, Edward J. Flynn. McKee immediately put through a number of cost-cutting reforms that eased the city's crisis. Would he be the next mayor? Tammany Hall's leaders, operating from their Manhattan power base, had other ideas; they were not about to allow Flynn such unexpected influence. For the special election to be held in November 1932, to choose a mayor for the final year of Walker's term, Tammany chose a political hack named John P. O'Brien. In the interests of party unity Flynn abandoned McKee and backed O'Brien. But in the election McKee received a big write-in vote, almost beating O'Brien. Flynn thereupon switched back and formed a Recovery party to back McKee for the regular election a year hence, against O'Brien.

With the Democratic vote thus split, Republicans and independents (including Seabury) saw an opportunity. Forming a Fusion party under which anti-Tammany groups could unite, they looked around for a candidate. They immediately ruled out La Guardia: he had, after all, lost to Walker in 1929 and was believed to be impulsive, difficult to get along with, and unpredictable. No one else of stature, however, would agree to run, and La Guardia made no secret of his desire for the job. He had just lost his congressional seat in Roosevelt's 1932 Democratic landslide and was fighting for his political life. He hinted that if he were not nominated he would enter the Republican primary and knock out the official candidate—whoever that was. Finally, Seabury decided La Guardia should be chosen, as he was both capable and incorruptible, and he argued for him strongly. With some reluctance the other Fusion leaders came around and gave La Guardia the nomination. He did not disappoint them. Campaigning with tremendous vigor, he defeated both O'Brien and McKee in the November 1933 election.

In view of La Guardia's stunning record as mayor over the next twelve years it is hard to understand why he was not chosen more readily. He was certainly unusual. About five feet tall, stout, sloppily dressed, and with a high squeaky voice, he was easy to laugh at. He was both autocratic and stubborn, and unable to take criticism. His rages could be devastating. His scorn for capitalists and industrialists was exceeded only by his hatred of anything to do with Tammany. Yet he was also kind, generous, and possessed of a telling sense of humor. He was a talented mimic and could play the cornet passably well. He was a tireless worker and his honesty was beyond reproach. Known as the Hat because of the broadbrim black Stetson he habitually wore, and as the Little Flower because of his first name, he was a one-man balanced ticket: his father was Italian, his mother was Jewish, and he himself was an Episcopalian.

Although born in lower Manhattan in 1882, La Guardia was raised mostly in Arizona, where his father, an army bandmaster, was stationed. When La Guardia was in his teens his father became ill, and

ictorian clutter permeates the art gallery in the home of the leader of society, Mrs. William B.
stor, on Fifth Avenue at 34th Street in 1887. The gallery also served as a ballroom for her annual
ll; it could conveniently hold—so her social adviser proclaimed—no more than 400 persons.
urtesy of The New-York Historical Society

succession of Vanderbilt mansions
es the west side of Fifth Avenue in
1885 in a view looking north from
50th Street, with St. Patrick's
Cathedral on the right. The first
large pile, at 51st Street, is that of
illiam H. Vanderbilt, while next to
it is a virtually identical building
that is actually two houses, for his
two married daughters. On the far
side of 52nd Street is the much
lighter château of his son, William
K. Vanderbilt, scene of Alva
anderbilt's triumphant fancy dress
ball in 1883. Courtesy of
The New-York Historical Society

The most lavish party ever given in New York up to that time was the Bradley-Martin ball at the Waldorf-Astoria Hotel in 1897, which was condemned in the press for costing more than $9,000.
Museum of the City of New York

The pleasure of socialites in showing off their finery while strolling on Fifth Avenue led to the annual Easter Parade, very elegant at the time of this photograph (1898) but today much debased. At the left is the reservoir at 42nd Street, which would shortly be demolished for construction of the New York Public Library. Museum of the City of New York

Opposite: Guests at a famed dinner given by millionaire industrialist C. K. G. Billings at Sherry's 1903 consumed a hearty repast while seated on horses rented for the occasion. Waiters were dressed as hunting grooms, bucolic scenes adorned the walls, and the floor was covered with grassy material to protect the horses' hooves. Museum of the City of New York

Steerage passengers on their way to the United States from Europe crowd the decks of the SS Patricia around the turn of the century. Museum of the City of New York

What was perceived as the menacing atmosphere of some immigrant neighborhoods is evoked in Jacob Riis's photograph of the denizens of Bandit's Roost, an alley off Mulberry Street. Museum of the City of New York

opposite: Hester Street on the Lower East Side, a center for recently arrived Jewish immigrants, is jammed with shoppers buying food and clothing from pushcarts. Museum of the City of New York

Skaters in 1890 enjoy the ice in Central Park not far from the Dakota, the imposing apartment house so named after being derided as ridiculously far from the center of town. Courtesy of The New-York Historical Society

Opposite: *Hansom cabs await passengers along the edge of Madison Square at 24th Stre* *and Fifth Avenue in 1901.* Museum of the City of New Yo

The Florodora sextette, all of whom reputedly married millionaires, were the toast of New York in 1900. Museum of the City of New York

The increasing complexity of the city is evoked in an aerial photograph of the Manhattan approaches to the Lincoln Tunnel in the 1950s. Margaret Bourke-White, *Life* Magazine © Time Inc.

Opposite: *Crowds accustomed to commuting by subway to the Bronx wait in the dark outsi* *Grand Central to take special railroad trains home during the bitter transit strike of 196* Arthur Schatz, *Life* Magazine © Time I

The relocated port, which began to be developed in the 1950s and is now centered in Port Newark on Newark Bay, is seven miles from Manhattan (visible in the distance). Here containers can be efficiently stored and transferred to trucks or railroad cars. Courtesy of The Port Authority of New York and New Jersey

Showing his concern for the problems and frustrations of slum residents during the tense hot summer months of 1968, Mayor John Lindsay walks the streets of Bedford-Stuyvesant.
N.Y. Daily News Photo

Beleaguered and beset during the fiscal crisis of 1975, Mayor Abraham Beame, in City Hall, listens noncommittally as real estate mogul Robert Tisch tries to make a point. Janie Eisenberg

Below: *In a festive mood, New Yorkers jam a West Side pier to view the tall ships during Operation Sail in 1976.* N.Y. Daily News Photo

In the first concerted action to gain protection for the city's valued buildings, architects belonging to the Action Group for Better Architecture in New York (AGBANY) picket Pennsylvania Station in 1962 to protest its announced demolition. Although they were unable to save the station, their effort and the belated anger of other New Yorkers at the loss of the magnificent building resulted in a strong landmarks law three years later. New York Times Pictures

Opposite: In the 1980s, oriental signs crowd out English ones on Union Street in Flushing, Queens, one of New York's newest ethnic neighborhoods. Dorothy Alexander

Celebrating the end of a tight primary race in 1989, Manhattan Borough President David Dinkins at left, makes peace with Mayor Edward Koch, whom he has just defeated for the Democratic mayoralty nomination. Dinkins went on to become New York City's first black mayor. N.Y. Daily News Photo the family moved to Trieste to live with his maternal grandparents; at eighteen he took a job as a clerk in the American consulate in Budapest. Later he became consular agent in Fiume, but in 1906 he returned to the United States and went to work as an interpreter on Ellis Island; he already was fluent in Italian, German, and Croatian and now added Yiddish, French, and Spanish, resources of great benefit when he became mayor. (Once when an opposing candidate accused him of anti-Semitism, Fiorello challenged him to a debate, to be held in Yiddish. The man failed to show up.) Evenings he attended the New York University Law School, and upon graduating in 1910 he set up a law practice and represented men's clothing workers during strikes in 1913 and 1914. He had joined the Republican party out of dislike for Tammany, and when the party sought a candidate in 1914 to run for Congress in a lower Manhattan district—one that historically was solidly Democratic—he volunteered, was nominated, and amazed everyone by almost winning. Two years later he did win.

Soon after entering Congress, with the United States now at war, La Guardia enlisted, learned how to fly, and served with distinction as a captain (later major) on the Italian front in the Army Air Service. On returning home he was reelected to Congress, then in 1919 became president of the Board of Aldermen and spent two years mostly working with "Red Mike" Hylan in matters before the Board of Estimate. He confidently expected to be the Republican nominee for mayor in 1921, but his party, evidently fearing he was something of a wild man, preferred another and La Guardia lost the primary. Disillusioned, he returned to his law practice. Three years later he ran for Congress again, this time in a district on Manhattan's Upper East Side mainly covering East Harlem, and triumphed. By 1932 he had served seven terms as a congressman and achieved a national reputation for his effective work on behalf of liberal causes.

He had told New Yorkers he wanted to prove that "nonpartisan, nonpolitical local government" was achievable, and in office he showed he meant it. His first act was to order the arrest of Lucky Luciano, the narcotics and prostitution overlord, and he followed up with a campaign against gambling of every kind, at one time delighting the public by personally wielding a sledgehammer to smash impounded slot machines. Faced with an impending $30 million deficit in the city budget and the severe terms of agreements that McKee and O'Brien had been forced to accept from bankers loaning money to the city, La Guardia instituted a 2 percent sales tax and other levies and forced city employees to accept pay cuts (thereby reluctantly breaking a campaign promise not to do so). By means of such measures and by rigidly controlling expenditures, within a year he was able to balance the city's budget and raise its credit rating. Perhaps most remarkable were his appointments to top posts in his administration: virtually all were free from political ties and were of top caliber. The sole criterion was merit. New Yorkers could hardly believe it.

His Honor's behavior could, however, be bizarre. He would tear out of City Hall to follow fire engines to a blaze. Distrusting the newspapers, which he was convinced were out to get him, he once seized a notebook from a reporter's hands, flung it to the ground, and jumped up and down on it. He was unfailingly on the side of the poor and the less fortunate. His onetime aide Ernest Cuneo tells of a group of laundry owners who went to City Hall to protest the assigning of police around their establishments, allegedly to maintain law and order during a strike of their female employees. They said it hurt their business and also showed the city was on the side of the strikers. The owners' spokesman said they merely asked that the city remain neutral in the dispute. La Guardia asked if they could put that request in writing. They did so, hastily, and the mayor after glancing at the paper announced that their application was granted; the city would be absolutely neutral. In their presence he then picked up a telephone, called the water commissioner and ordered him to turn off all the water in the laundries, as the city was neutral. The owners withdrew their request and departed in disarray.[7]

Like Jimmy Walker before him, La Guardia was likely to turn any public session into a piece of theatre enlivened by jokes and humorous asides. But where Walker's quips often showed how little he cared for the city's people and their problems, La Guardia's were the opposite. Soon after taking office, Cuneo recalls, the mayor held hearings on an all-important relief budget designed to alleviate some of the distress caused by the depression. An alderman interrupted the presentation to state that relief money was already being misdirected: some of it, he said with disgust, was going to prostitutes. This would have to stop. The mayor listened in disbelief and then remarked, "I thought that question was settled two thousand years ago, but I see I was wrong." He raised his voice and exclaimed, "Mr. Sergeant-at-Arms, clear the room! Clear the room—so this big bum can throw the first stone!"[8]

Admittedly, many of the La Guardia administrations's greatest achievements were offshoots of Roosevelt's New Deal—projects funded largely or entirely by the federal government. But the mayor might not have received anywhere near so much federal money if he had not put the city's house in proper fiscal order. Furthermore, the money was, for the most part, spent efficiently and honestly. The existence of so much largess can make for widespread corruption, and there were certainly cases of petty graft here and there, but La Guardia established a record of honest government to a degree that few thought was possible in a city of such size and complexity.

And the results, in new housing, parks, and other public facilities, were impressive: the city was in some ways physically reborn. Public housing today may have acquired a bad reputation, but in the 1930s it was badly needed and generally welcomed. The so-called First Houses, completed in 1935 on the Lower East Side, was the first public housing project in the United States. Others followed in Harlem, Williamsburg, and other areas; altogether the New York City Housing Authority, which LaGuardia had brought into being, built thirteen such projects and had fourteen more planned by the time he left office in 1945, a truly pioneering effort.

Equally tangible were the new or rehabilitated parks and other recreational facilities. Here La Guardia had the good fortune to be able to appoint as parks commissioner the indomitable but immensely creative Robert Moses. Previous administrations had allowed New York's parks to deteriorate; zoos were rundown and uninviting; playgrounds were woefully inadequate. Moses was a whirlwind who got things done. As head of the state park system he had already achieved renown for constructing the magnificent Jones Beach State Park, a huge and handsomely designed seafront project on the south shore of Long Island. When La Guardia approached him about the city post, he said he would take it—provided he could also continue as state parks chief and provided the city's borough-run parks operations could be combined into a single office. The mayor, who never hesitated to take on a capable person no matter how headstrong, acquiesced and made the necessary arrangements. Thereupon Moses fired hundreds of incompetent workers, brought in energetic new staff, and began showing dramatic results. Central Park was cleaned up and its zoo rebuilt. By the end of 1934 sixty new parks had been constructed, and more were to come. During the La Guardia years Moses also built seventeen outdoor swimming pools in congested neighborhoods, added two hundred tennis courts to the city's plant, and almost doubled the number of public golf courses. Two waterfront facilities, Orchard Beach in the Bronx and Jacob Riis Park in Queens, were vastly enlarged and upgraded, and Randall's Island in the East River was made over for recreational use. For the first time in quite a while New York could be proud of its parks.

Even more dramatic and of greater consequence were the highways and bridges that Moses built, partly in his capacity as parks commissioner and partly through other posts that he assumed over the years. By the 1930s the automobile had largely taken over the city (which had not been laid out to handle it efficiently), and traffic jams were worsening. Moses literally ringed the city with big new highways designed to speed traffic flow and relieve congestion, and although critics have claimed that the net effect of the new roads was to bring more vehicles into town, eventually compounding rather than relieving the automobile glut, the initial effect was unquestionably beneficial. Furthermore, many of the roads were set in parklike surroundings that everyone praised. The first true limited-access parkway had come into being just outside New York, in Westchester County, with the building in 1912–25 of the Bronx River Parkway, a scenic road designed to allow motorists a pleasant Sunday afternoon drive. Moses took the idea and raised it to a new and more efficient level.

The first of the new highways, and in some ways the most notable, was the Henry Hudson Parkway along the Hudson River on Manhattan's Upper West Side. Although the riverfront above West 72nd Street contained Riverside Park, designed by Frederick Law Olmsted in the 1870s, the area seemed permanently blighted by the existence of New York Central rail tracks along the river. And Riverside Drive could not handle the traffic now pouring onto it. In one vast reclamation project Moses roofed over the tracks, extended the park with landfill, added a brace of recreational facilities, and planted his new well-landscaped roadway at the river's edge. The architecture critic Lewis Mumford disputed some of the project's features but praised the overall result, calling it "the finest single piece of large-scale planning . . . since the original development of Central Park."[9] The new parkway when completed ran all the way up to the tip of the island, crossed over to the Bronx, and connected with other parkways at the city line.

Following soon after the Henry Hudson were the Grand Central, Interborough, and Laurelton parkways in Queens and Brooklyn, and the Belt Parkway, which ran along the Brooklyn shoreline and up toward the Brooklyn Bridge. Moses was also instrumental in pushing the construction of the East River Drive, along Manhattan's eastern shore, although he did not supervise it directly. By 1941 it was possible for a motorist to drive most of the way around New York City without stopping for a traffic light, a feat previously not dreamed of.

Connecting many of the new roads were new bridges and tunnels masterminded by Moses. The Triborough Bridge—actually four bridges connected by an elaborate set of causeways—linked Manhattan, the Bronx, and Queens; the Henry Hudson Bridge carried its parkway over the Harlem River; the Bronx-Whitestone linked the Bronx with Queens. In addition Moses built more than one hundred smaller bridges. He caused the Queens-Midtown Tunnel to be burrowed under the East River. Meanwhile, in 1937, the Port Authority added a second tunnel under the Hudson, the Lincoln Tunnel from the midtown area to Weehawken, New Jersey.

All these vehicular improvements were admittedly of little advantage to the city's poor, few of whom owned automobiles. The vast construction program, however, did generate jobs and income for the depression-ridden city, and the highways when added to the new parks made for a far more handsome and more livable city for everyone.

While he was giving scope to Robert Moses to promote so much building, La Guardia was also carrying on a full-scale war against crime, in the persons of gangsters like Dutch Schultz and Frank Costello. The mayor's arrest of Lucky Luciano had been prophetic: more was to come. The crux of the problem was that gangsters had moved from rum-running not only into other illegal activities like gambling and prostitution but also into legitimate trades like restaurants, theatres, and the garment industry, until their hand was felt all over the city. They dominated certain unions, threatened employers, and demanded protection money from manufacturers eager to avoid trouble; and to safeguard their operations they paid off politicians like those in Tammany Hall. The Seabury probes had hardly put a dent in such practices.

The mayor's first move was to clean up the police department. He chose as chief inspector of the department (later commissioner) an outstanding career policeman, Lewis J. Valentine, and announced that corruption would not be tolerated and that crooks and racketeers would be ruthlessly pursued and prosecuted. Soon the department's ties to the underworld were largely cut. La Guardia moved against slot machines (smashing many of them personally) and pinball machines. He wiped out the rackets in the city's wholesale food markets. Although none of this got at the top malefactors, it did create a climate for further enforcement and led in the summer of 1935 to the naming, by Governor Herbert Lehman (Roosevelt's successor in Albany), of a special state prosecutor to investigate all forms of organized crime in New York County. The young lawyer chosen, Thomas E. Dewey, was to become a major political figure in his own right.

Born in Michigan but a graduate of Columbia Law School, the prim, mustachioed Dewey had attracted notice as an assistant U.S. attorney. Known for building his cases with meticulous care and presenting them with a marked dramatic flair, he proceeded to go after Lucky Luciano (who had evaded earlier charges against him), brought him to trial for operating a prostitution racket, and convicted him. Investigation of the bakery-trucking and garment-trucking rackets led to the indicting of Louis (Lepke) Buchalter and Jacob (Gurrah Jake) Shapiro, who were eventually convicted. Dewey did not have to prosecute Dutch Schultz—he had been killed by other gang leaders who disapproved of his plan to assassinate the special prosecutor, a tactic they considered risky. But Dewey's biggest quarry was James J. Hines, a Tammany Hall leader who had long been known as gangdom's principal political protector in the city. A large, heavyset, and soft-spoken man, Hines at first seemed to evoke confidence and respect, but witness after witness told of his accepting payment in return for keeping the forces of law away from racketeers. After the first Hines trial ended in a mistrial, he was convicted and sent to Sing Sing.

Hines's conviction was a severe blow to a Tammany Hall already hard hit from several directions. Its power base had been eroded first of all by the decline in immigration; no longer were there great numbers of people just off the boat needing help and guidance as they adjusted to a new world. Second, comprehensive welfare programs enacted by both the federal government and the city had sapped the appeal of the old system of clubhouse relief; the poor were no longer dependent on politicians. Third, better schooling had made New Yorkers more politically independent and so less prone to accept the machine's blandishments. Finally, Tammany no longer had rich political plums to hand out to the faithful, for La Guardia had put many city jobs under the aegis of the civil service and, in any event, tended to freeze Tammany out of those that remained.

The days of the ancient Society of St. Tammany were numbered, and it would not long survive the years immediately after World War II.

With bossism on the decline, and with so many physical improvements like parks and highways to point to, La Guardia became more and more popular. He was further aided by two new minor parties, the American Labor party and the Liberal party, both of which, organized by labor leaders, attracted independent voters and anti-machine Democrats. The mayor was also given credit for some popular changes in the city charter that were put through at this time: the Board of Aldermen was abolished and a City Council set up, and the mayor's powers were enhanced. Ironically, the only political group that was truly uneasy about La Guardia at the end of his first term was the Republican party, to which he nominally belonged. They were unable to settle on a substitute, however, and the mayor was elected in 1937 to a second term with a plurality of 450,000 votes—the first Fusion candidate in the city's history to win re-election.

Never one to pass up an opportunity to promote the city, the mayor had long claimed that New York should have its own first-class airport. At one time he made a great show of refusing indignantly to get off a plane at Newark Airport—for many years the only field serving the city—because his ticket said New York as its destination, not someplace in New Jersey. He got his wish with the so-called North Beach Airport, next to Flushing Bay in Queens. It was dedicated in 1939 and soon thereafter was renamed for La Guardia himself. In the years since then it has never stopped expanding.

Local transportation was being upgraded as well. The elevated railroads that had preceded the subways in the nineteenth century were by now considered detrimental to the central sections of the city, and during the 1930s most of them in Manhattan were torn down, first the Sixth Avenue el, then the Ninth and the Second Avenue els. Only the Third Avenue el, beloved by sentimentalists, lasted into the 1950s, although elevated extensions of the city's subways continue to rumble through the outer boroughs. The benefits of removing the elevated lines were startling, with long stretches of avenues suddenly becoming ripe for development; the long-term changes along Third and Sixth avenues have been especially dramatic. In the meantime La Guardia acted to take over control of all the city's subways. It had never made sense for the three lines (the IRT, the BMT, and the IND or Independent) to compete with each other, especially since the city owned the IND. And both of the privately held lines were bankrupt, unable to make a profit charging the five-cent fare that by this time had become politically sacrosanct. In 1938 the mayor asked Albany for legislation enabling the city to purchase the two bankrupt lines, and in 1940 the unified system came into being. The five-cent fare remained for eight more years, however, before doubling, and fare hikes remain a major source of political dispute.

Even though the lingering depression continued to cast a pall over New York's overall economic health during the 1930s, one development right in midtown Manhattan was to prove a gigantic boon. It came about in a roundabout way, from the desire of the Metropolitan Opera Company in the 1920s to acquire a new house. The old opera house, on Broadway at 39th Street, had never been satisfactory, even though boxholders loved the Diamond Horseshoe that displayed them so prominently; sight lines were inadequate for most of the less expensive seats, backstage facilities were cramped, and there was virtually no space for storing scenery. Such problems were long tolerated, but now the wealthier opera patrons were complaining that the Met's neighborhood was no longer fashionable and was also inconvenient. The company's major patron, Otto Kahn (chairman of Kuhn, Loeb & Company), purchased property on West 57th Street, between Eighth and Ninth avenues, with the intention of building a great new hall there, and even had plans drawn. But the boxholders torpedoed the scheme; they did not like that location either. Presently it became known that property between Fifth and Sixth avenues north of 48th Street owned by Columbia College (which had once been situated nearby) might be available for lease. Kahn and his fellow benefactors were delighted and had a whole new set of architect's drawings made.

A benefactor would be needed, for the Met could not itself afford the project. John D. Rockefeller, Jr., was approached and showed keen interest: his residence was not far away, on West 54th Street, and so he was desirous of protecting the neighborhood. Moreover, the area could be developed commercially as well as culturally and thus was a good investment. He agreed to develop the site, which was to be known as Metropolitan Square.

Then the deal went sour. When Kahn and his associates saw what the Rockefeller interests were envisioning they were profoundly uneasy: the Square was to be very much a commercial proposition in which the opera would play a relatively minor role. There were other troubles, too. Costs were escalating, and it did not help that in the midst of the negotiations the stock market collapsed. In December 1929 the Met withdrew. (Its move from 39th Street would not occur until 1966, when it transferred to Lincoln Center.)

Rockefeller was plunged into gloom. He had signed long-term leases with Columbia and was committed; but he no longer had the Met as a centerpiece, and the financial situation was worsening daily—a prospect to worry even a multimillionaire. In a full-scale depression, who would be able to pay the inevitably high rents needed in such a central area? He decided to go ahead anyway.

The result, as everyone now knows, was a triumph. A city within a city, and taking form progressively throughout the 1930s (and later), the development consisted of a single thin slab of a skyscraper—a brilliant design by the architect Raymond Hood—surrounded by lesser buildings, all handsomely relating to each other and interspersed with gardens and other amenities, and all connected via underground passageways lined with shops. In the middle of it all lay a sunken plaza that was flooded for ice-skating in winter. Rockefeller's agents persuaded the Radio Corporation of America to establish its headquarters in the skyscraper, which accordingly was named the RCA Building; certain parts of the building not leased by RCA were declared a duty-free zone to attract international trading firms, which responded in droves. In deference to RCA's formidable presence the development became known at first as Radio City, and the larger of the two theatres located at the Sixth Avenue end of the project was called the Radio City Music Hall. (Both the Music Hall and its companion, the Center Theatre, were managed by Roxy Rothafel, who was lured away from his own Roxy Theatre just a block away.) But "Radio City" never quite caught on, and the public soon began referring to the complex as Rockefeller Center.

It has produced more than its share of institutions popular among New Yorkers and visitors alike. The Music Hall was so immense, seating an audience of 5,960, that it seemed to dwarf performers on its huge stage, and critics felt a new kind of show would have to be devised—and so it was, the Rockettes, thirty-six seemingly identical pretty girls high-kicking in flawless precision into the hearts of on-lookers. Atop the RCA Building were two nightclubs, one of which, the Rainbow Room with its rotating dance floor and stunning views, was (and is) arguably the grandest nitery ever built. Lower down in the RCA Building is NBC's Studio 8H, which the NBC Symphony Orchestra under Arturo Toscanini put on the map and which was later the venue of television's *Saturday Night Live*. The Center's skating rink at the height of the season is such a drawing card that tourists line up three- and four-deep to view it. And every December the lighting of the Center's mammoth Christmas tree next to the skating rink—a custom that dates back to the setting up of a small tree by the Center's construction workers in the depths of the depression—produces gridlock and wall-to-wall people for blocks around. In the 1960s the area was allegedly the number one American tourist attraction, outranking Niagara Falls and the Grand Canyon.

In view of its extraordinary reputation, the Center, amazingly, was originally seen by some critics as a dreadful mistake—just a real estate promotion, they said, with little thought given to scale or efficient traffic flow. Over the years it has proved them wrong and is now universally regarded as a model of good urban planning.

None of this astonishing transformation of a large area of midtown, admittedly, was the work of La Guardia. Indeed, it was a celebration of capitalism, and the mayor had an instinctive contempt for capitalists as a group. Yet Rockefeller Center's splendid design could not be denied, and La Guardia's belief in such orderly, sensible development was well known because of his espousal of Robert Moses' vast projects. So its glory to some extent rubbed off on him. In addition, the Center's popularity and success were made possible in part because the scrappy mayor had somehow helped New Yorkers regain their confidence—not to mention their pride—after the disillusion and despair of the worst depression years. The city was on an even keel, and it was okay to play once again.

New York's overall health was far from rosy when examined closely, of course. Unemployment was still too high in the late 1930s, and the slums were as bad as ever. The worst now was Harlem, packed ever more densely by the continued migration of blacks from the rural South. Yet their very arrival showed that the city was still a place of hope, even of opportunity, to people everywhere, even if it could not live up to some of those hopes. Toward the end of the decade New York once again became, in a small but significant way, a city of European immigrants. Many thousands of Jewish intellectuals were fleeing persecution in Germany, and a large proportion of them ended up in New York. An educational institution in Greenwich Village, the New School for Social Research, hired so many of them as teachers that it came to be called the University in Exile.

Perhaps the culmination of La Guardia's administration was the staging of the New York World's Fair of 1939–40. The idea of making New York the site of a fair marking the 150th anniversary of Washington's inauguration had been promoted by a group of businessmen including Grover Whalen, who was La Guardia's official greeter as he had been for Jimmy Walker. But the realization of it was another masterstroke by Robert Moses, who had insisted that it be held at the former Corona ash dump in Queens and who thereupon converted the dump into a 1,216-acre park for the event and for the future benefit of Queens residents. Well designed, its central buildings dominated by the Trylon and Perisphere—a huge spike and accompanying sphere that were its symbols—the fair presented a vision of a confident "World of Tomorrow." Depression-weary New Yorkers and other Americans, who were also concerned about the imminence of war in Europe, found the whole affair captivating and reassuring, in particular the Futurama, an elaborate model of a utopian United States that fairgoers viewed from seats on a moving belt. Although the fair was not a financial success, it was visited by some 44.9 million people, some of whom at least heeded the mayor's remark at its opening that the greatest display of all was New York City itself, with its 7,454,995 inhabitants.

More popular than ever, La Guardia had little trouble winning a third term in 1941, although his margin of victory was cut because of some ill-tempered remarks directed to Governor Herbert Lehman during the campaign. A month after his election the nation was at war, and New York with its unexampled harbor became a key staging area. The mayor's third term was less successful than his first two; the city was necessarily preoccupied with the war effort, and La Guardia himself was increasingly disconsolate because he was refused a top-level commission in the armed forces for which he longed. But it was during the wartime years that La Guardia did something for which he will always be remembered. A newspaper deliverymen's strike in 1945 had left New Yorkers without their papers, and the mayor instinctively knew who would be the worst hit by the deprivation. Taking to the airwaves on the city's station, WNYC, he read the comic strips to the children of New York.

In the spring of 1945 he had announced to a surprised city that he would not run for a fourth term. He certainly could have been reelected, but he was weary, and there were signs that his health was not good. The signs were correct. Little more than two years later, in September 1947, he was dead of cancer at the age of sixty-four. He left behind a more humane, more livable, and infinitely more prosperous city.

12

At the Summit

Nearly half a million jubilant New Yorkers jammed Times Square on the evening of August 14, 1945, to rejoice over the news that Japan had surrendered and that World War II was over. The mood of the mammoth crowd was one of happiness tempered with relief, for although New York itself had not been physically harmed by the war, almost 900,000 of its citizens had served in the armed forces, and more than 16,000 had been killed or reported missing in action. But the celebrating extended throughout the city, and flags and bunting broke out everywhere, accompanied by honking horns and wailing sirens. Strangers hugged and kissed each other, and bars were hard put to keep up with the demand. As a French visitor noted, "Statistics will never say exactly how much alcoholic beverage passed from production to consumption that night, but the figure would certainly be expressed in tons rather than liters."[1]

Many of those celebrating so lustily were quick to recognize the more sobering side of the news. Victory had been hastened by the dropping of the atomic bomb, which signaled a new era in world affairs. In another all-out war, no one would be safe; next time the city might not be spared—indeed, might be destroyed. There was another reason, too, for those who rejoiced to reflect soberly: New York now stood alone at the summit. No other city approached it in sheer power. London and Paris had been severely weakened by the conflict, as well as by other forces largely beyond their control, and would probably never again enjoy their former influence. Berlin, Tokyo, and other great centers were decimated. But partly because of its isolation, lucky New York, the biggest and by far the most potent city of the strongest nation, was unimpaired—indeed, strengthened. Its harbor had operated full blast throughout the war and was much the busiest in the world. The city was unrivaled in the United States as a manufacturing center, and it had for some time been the world's financial leader.

Because of all this, no one could have been surprised when the newly constituted United Nations organization decided, late in 1945, to establish its permanent headquarters in New York. After occupying several temporary sites, the world body eventually moved into its own complex on the eastern edge of midtown Manhattan. The city's economic muscle and its strong cosmopolitan character also propelled it during these years into global primacy as a cultural center. There was good reason now to call New York the capital of the world. As the English writer J. B. Priestley put it in 1947, "The New York that O. Henry described 40 years ago was an American city, but today's glittering cosmopolis belongs to the world, if the world does not belong to it."[2]

The thought was heady and not without its perils, for life at the top can be uneasy: all roads from the summit lead down. Over the next quarter of a century the city would learn that power does not cause problems to dissolve, and that bigness and complexity constantly generate new difficulties. The 1950s and early 1960s saw extraordinary prosperity in New York. But seemingly uncontrolled expansion and new construction would bring ever worsening congestion. Boom in one area would be accompanied by decay in another. New technologies and relentless cost factors would cause the city's economic base to shift perceptibly. New immigration would foment new ethnic discord and give rise to new social dilemmas. At the end of the era the city, to many of its residents, did not seem such a wonderful place after all, and much of the optimism that had characterized New Yorkers for so many generations had worn away.

If disillusion was to make its appearance, an early harbinger was the strange case of Mayor William O'Dwyer, who was elected in 1945 to succeed the great Fiorello La Guardia. In many respects O'Dwyer seemed ideal to lead the city. Born in Ireland, he had come to New York in 1910 with $25 in his pocket, had become a policeman, earned a law degree, served as a city magistrate, and eventually, in 1940, was elected district attorney of Brooklyn. There he compiled what seemed to be an impressive record as prosecutor of a notorious crime ring that an imaginative newspaper reporter had dubbed Murder, Incorporated. Tammany Hall looked with favor on him. Charming, warmhearted, and unbigoted, with blue eyes and wavy hair, he personified Tammany's great hope to regain its lost status, and during his first term he was highly popular throughout the city. He extended the rent controls imposed during the war (still largely in existence today, they are now widely deplored), reorganized the city's welfare department, and successfully mediated a number of potentially damaging labor disputes. He appeared to be a shoo-in for reelection in 1949. Yet he inexplicably delayed announcing his candidacy, and rumors began circulating that his record as Brooklyn D. A. had not been as advertised—that he had gone after minor hoodlums while protecting the bosses, notably the waterfront racketeer Albert Anastasia. He was also reported to be embarassingly close to the underworld leader Frank Costello.

Finally O'Dwyer announced his bid and was handily reelected. Hardly a month later, however, the *Brooklyn Eagle* began publishing a series of articles describing widespread payoffs to policemen to protect gambling operations, and the corruption appeared to reach high in the department. Twelve days after being sworn in for his second term, O'Dwyer retreated to Florida with what was described as nervous exhaustion, and seven months later Bronx Democratic boss Edward Flynn—not a Tammany man but influential in national Democratic party affairs—persuaded President Truman to protect the local branch of the party by naming the mayor ambassador to Mexico.

Later revelations, including the confession of a big-time bookmaker named Harry Gross, showed that gambling had become rife during O'Dwyer's regime. The mayor himself seemed to have benefited directly from this and other arrangements; when a congressional investigating committee chaired by Tennessee Senator Estes Kefauver held hearings on the matter, one of the witnesses, John Crane of the Greater New York Uniformed Firemen's Association, testified that he had personally met O'Dwyer on the porch of Gracie Mansion and handed him an envelope containing $10,000 in cash as a campaign contribution. Crane had also given $55,000 over the years to O'Dwyer's friend James J. Moran, who had also received substantial sums from Harry Gross and had presided over a lucrative extortion racket involving fire department inspectors. It was not clear how much of this may have gone to the mayor, and O'Dwyer himself was not prosecuted, but Moran went to prison. It began to look as if the bad old days of Jimmy Walker were back.

Luckily, O'Dwyer's successor, former City Council President Vincent Impellitteri, was untainted by scandal. A decent, likable Sicilian-born municipal functionary, he declared himself independent of Tammany and every other city machine, and grateful city voters in a special election in 1950 chose him to fill out O'Dwyer's unexpired second term. "Impy" was popular but had no clear-cut program and no organized following, and his record was lackluster. By 1953 the city was ready for something better, and they got it in the person of Robert F. Wagner, Jr., the son of a former Democratic senator from New York known for his pioneering federal labor legislation.

Highly educated, courtly, and the beneficiary of an upbringing in which he was constantly surrounded by politicians and immersed in political lore, Wagner presented a deceptively mild appearance. Not only did he seem not very bright, he made a virtue out of procrastination. His father had advised him, "When in doubt, don't," and Wagner never seemed to accomplish much. The reputation was misleading. He was a consummate political operator, a gifted compromiser with strong connections not only to the business community but also to social welfare reformers and many ethnic groups; and when he had to act, he did so promptly and judiciously. He was honest—there was no major scandal connected with his administration. Until his last year, all his budgets were balanced. Admittedly the country as a whole was prospering during those years. But when many of Wagner's critics looked back years later they realized that the city during his three terms of office had never been so prosperous or free of strife. It was the last era of good feeling New York would enjoy for some time.

The 1950s were a time of major construction, and the look of the city once again changed. Glass was the new magic building material, and architects were espousing the international style derived from Europe in the 1930s and based on steel frames and glass curtain walls. Air conditioning and improved lighting techniques now also made possible much thicker buildings, whose tops were squared off (partly to hold air conditioning equipment) instead of pointed. The first office building in this style was Lever House, a handsome glass box on spindly columns completed in 1952 at Park Avenue and 53rd Street; it was to signal the rapid ensuing conversion of that section of Park Avenue into a glass-walled office canyon. Less than ten years later the first big office building west of Sixth Avenue, the Time and Life Building at Sixth Avenue and 50th Street, opened up the entire west side of midtown Manhattan to gigantic steel-and-glass structures, first along Sixth Avenue and later along avenues farther west.

Meanwhile a new zoning law in 1961 permitted builders to add extra floors and to omit the previously mandated setbacks if they promised to set aside a certain amount of street-level space for a public plaza. This resulted in still more gargantuan buildings all over the midtown area—with the new "plaza" spaces often clumsy and sterile and of scant benefit to the public. Nor was change confined to midtown. Although many banks in the 1950s were moving their headquarters to midtown from the Wall Street area, David Rockefeller (a grandson of John D.) as chairman of the Chase Manhattan Bank opted to stay downtown, and the resulting Chase Manhattan Building—another boxy, straight-walled glass-and-steel structure— showed the way to a transformation of the lower end of Manhattan. Once admired for its spires and slim towers, downtown became dominated by another mass of huge flat-topped boxes. The ultimate steel boxes were the twin towers of the World Trade Center, completed in the early 1970s just to the west of the Wall Street district along the Hudson River. At 110 stories, they surpassed the Empire State Building and were the world's tallest buildings until Chicago's Sears Tower captured the title. By the late 1960s any sense of scale tended to be lost in the rush to build. As historian Bayrd Still noted, the pervasiveness of towering structures throughout the central city created "a vertical mass unmatched in magnitude and density by any other city in the world."[3]

New housing further changed the look of New York. Shortly after World War II the federal government made immense sums of money available for mass housing, which was badly needed, and in New York the grants were effectively under the control of Robert Moses, the parks and highway builder who now was given extraordinary supervision over all city construction. Headstrong, opinionated, brooking no criticism or second-guessing, Moses was a constant thorn in the side of the city's mayors and was tolerated only because he relentlessly accomplished his aims—and outmaneuvered his opponents. Warren Moscow, a former newspaper reporter who served as an aide to Wagner, tells about the vain attempt by Wagner, on his inauguration as mayor in 1954, to limit Moses' power. His own swearing-in completed, Wagner began administering oaths of office to those who would be his key aides. Moses had held three jobs under Impellitteri, parks commissioner, city construction coordinator, and member of the planning commission. The new mayor intended to keep Moses only in the first two; his advisers had urged him not to retain him in the third, and he thought he could simply not include it in the ceremony. He swore Moses into the first two and turned to the next man. Moses asked him where the third oath was. Taken aback, Wagner mumbled that his clerks must have overlooked the form. Moses strode out of the room and into the clerk's office, demanded a blank form, sat down and filled it out himself, then brought it back to Wagner and held it in front of him. Wagner capitulated and swore him in.[4]

Under Moses' guidance, slum areas throughout the city were leveled and replaced by high-rise apartment buildings, some of them for low-income residents and others middle-income projects. The campaign was called urban renewal, and if its aims were laudable, the results were often disastrous. Maintenance in the low-income projects tended to be inadequate, and the buildings themselves became vertical slums. Where the new tenants were middle-income, they supplanted the poor who had lived in the area. In a process that came to be referred to as urban removal, the uprooted were forced to move into other slum districts, compounding the squalor and congestion there. In the case of both low- and middle-income projects the special character of a neighborhood tended to be lost. Furthermore, many of the projects became breeding grounds for crime.

While overseeing the public housing campaign, Moses also continued to remake the city by building more—and bigger—highways. In the 1930s his major road projects had been intended mainly for pleasure driving and for the relief of midtown congestion. By the 1950s the task was far more complex and the stakes were higher. First of all, trucks were supplanting rail transport in moving goods of all kinds in, out of, and around the city, so that heavy commercial traffic was crowding the roads. Second, suburbanites were increasingly commuting by car into the city every day. And, finally, the sheer number of cars traveling within and around the city had skyrocketed. Fearsome traffic snarls were a daily phenomenon and were getting worse.

Many experts believed, and would continue to believe with increasing conviction, that the new roads were simply bringing more traffic into the city rather than alleviating the existing mess and that at least part of the answer was better mass transit. Moses was not interested in public transportation, and he proceeded to bulldoze wide swaths through the city for bigger expressways, many of which have now become so accepted that it is hard to imagine their not existing. The Brooklyn-Queens Expressway joined those two boroughs; the Major Deegan Expressway ran along the Harlem River, while the Van Wyck led to Idlewild (later John F. Kennedy) Airport;

the Bruckner Expressway cut through the East Bronx; the Long Island Expressway carried traffic from the Queens-Midtown Tunnel out of town to the east. (Moses also masterminded the Brooklyn-Battery Tunnel, connecting the lower tip of Manhattan with Brooklyn, and the Verrazano Narrows Bridge, linking Brooklyn with Staten Island.) Most of the massive highway projects went through with only token controversy, but the Cross-Bronx Expressway was another matter. Designed to link the George Washington Bridge with the Whitestone and the Throgs Neck bridges to Long Island (both also built by Moses), it became highly controversial when Moses' route was seen as threatening several hitherto stable mid-Bronx neighborhoods. All attempts to persuade Moses to adjust his plans to save these areas were rebuffed. The blight that was to afflict the lower Bronx in the 1960s and 1970s was at least partly due to the highway's destructive effect.

One major Moses project, toward the end of his career, was stopped. It was the Lower Manhattan Expressway, which would have barreled through the Canal Street area to connect the Holland Tunnel with the Manhattan Bridge to Brooklyn; tributary roads would have devastated Little Italy and other neighborhoods. The public outcry against the scheme was vehement and unrelenting, and at length the scheme was abandoned. (Moses continued in power until the late 1960s, when he was edged out not by the mayor but by Nelson Rockefeller, who was then governor.)

Meanwhile traffic tie-ups got worse. During the 1950s most of Manhattan's north-south avenues were made one-way; the last street-cars had been replaced by buses; zones in which parking was banned during business hours multiplied; parking garages were built—and then often torn down to be replaced by apartments or offices, which compounded the problem. But the cars and trucks kept coming. By the early 1970s it was estimated that some 650,000 automobiles entered the Manhattan area south of 60th Street daily. New Yorkers wondered how the city could survive such an onslaught, whereas the cars in fact represented the heightened, intensified superactivity and drive of the city itself.

Crowded, glutted, replete with difficult problems but endlessly exhilarating, New York was also attracting more and more intellectuals, artists, musicians, dancers, and all those who surround, support, and promote them. Even before World War II the city had been able to offer artists, writers, and others greater stimulation and also greater commercial and critical exposure than any other American city. The advance of Hitlerite Germany and the fall of Paris accelerated the move toward Manhattan. To New York from Europe came such painters as Piet Mondrian, Fernand Léger, and Jacques Lipchitz; the pioneering dancer and choreographer George Balanchine was already here; architects like Le Corbusier and Mies van der Rohe were frequent visitors. But American artists were also coming to the city in greater numbers, and by this time, impatient with the condescension that had frequently been their lot, they were demanding to be accorded the same respect as the Europeans. It happened sooner than many of them had expected. The turning point came in 1942 when a young Russian painter named John Graham organized a show in which the paintings of his still-unknown friends Jackson Pollock, Lee Krasner, and Willem de Kooning (who had emigrated from Holland in 1926) were hung amidst the canvases of Henri Matisse, Pierre Bonnard, Georges Braque, and Amedeo Modigliani. A later show juxtaposed the works of such young Americans as Robert Motherwell and Joseph Cornell with those of Pablo Picasso and Jean Arp. Both shows were a success, and the critics were happy to acknowledge the newly proclaimed equality.

Art galleries in the 57th Street area were increasingly showing the works of American painters, and the campaign was also being helped along by larger institutions. Principal among these was the Museum of Modern Art, founded back in 1929 by a trio of well-to-do art patrons led by Abby Aldrich (Mrs. John D., Jr.) Rockefeller. Under its first director, Alfred H. Barr, Jr., the Modern soon established itself as a flagship of the avant-garde, and the building it erected on 53rd Street just west of Fifth Avenue in 1939 has constantly outgrown its space and necessitated rebuilding and expansion. Virtually as influential in promoting American artists was the Whitney Museum of American Art, which moved uptown from Greenwich Village in the 1950s and then in 1966 moved into its distinctive cubelike building designed by the architect Marcel Breuer on Madison Avenue at 75th Street. The Guggenheim Museum was founded in the 1930s by a European noblewoman named Hilla Rebay with the backing of copper-mining millionaire Solomon R. Guggenheim; in 1959 it moved into its startling circular building at Fifth Avenue and 88th Street designed by Frank Lloyd Wright, where it continues to show many of the more radical contemporary artists.

Abetted by all this attention, homegrown artists were becoming familiar to a large segment of the public as "the New York school," which ranks as one of the most important American painting movements. The common thread linking the artists was abstract expressionism, which the historian Leonard Wallock in *New York: Culture Capital of the World, 1940–1965* describes as "abstract in form and international in esthetic."[5] New York's cosmopolitan background kept the new style from becoming provincial; it had a universal quality. The overall tendency was the abandonment of all tradition. The painters of this school—artists like Pollock, de Kooning, Motherwell, Franz Kline, Arshile Gorky, and Barnett Newman—believed that art was an expression of the individual psyche, and some of them seemed to want deliberately to shock viewers. It took a while for the public to get used to Pollock's almost chaotic canvases composed of random paint drippings, for example, or Mark Rothko's almost intrusive stark masses of bold color. But the New York school's work caught on and was recognized as the mainstream of American art.

The painters, and sculptors like David Smith, were enthralled by the city. As the sculptor Louise Nevelson remarked to an interviewer, New York was "teeming with energy and everything else . . . When you walk anywhere and you see the skyline around New York and you see the buildings, and you see the millions of people, and each mind in itself is a creation, it's overwhelming."[6] Not only was the city exciting; it was also receptive to them, providing a ready audience that included a large number of patrons and collectors. Wartime and postwar prosperity helped generate the kind of wealth needed to support the arts successfully, and so New York now found itself the unquestioned center of the world art market.

That center, hitherto located on 57th Street between Park and Sixth avenues, now expanded geographically. Bursting up Madison Avenue into the East 70s and 80s (where the Whitney was providentially located) it also established outposts in other districts, the most important being Soho, the area so named as it lies south of Houston Street. A onetime warehousing district filled with handsome cast-iron-front loft buildings, Soho had been discovered in the 1950s and 1960s by artists who valued its ample interior spaces and low rents. In the 1970s many of the major art galleries began opening branches there, to be followed by restaurants and boutiques, until the area ironically became too expensive for the artists who had put it on the map. Many of them moved on to the area south of Soho known as Tribeca, to other low-cost districts like Long Island City, or even out of the city completely to Hoboken, across the Hudson in New Jersey. Few artists remained in Greenwich Village, which likewise had become too expensive for all but the most successful, and the same was true of writers and intellectuals, who were now increasingly gathering on the Upper West Side—their world generally centering on Columbia University, where many of them taught. For all, however, the city was the lodestone.

As with the art world, so did America's performing arts find that their center was inevitably New York. The city had been the jazz center since the late 1920s, when such pioneers as Louis Armstrong, Jelly Roll Morton, King Oliver, and Red Allen moved here; and after the repeal of Prohibition, West 52nd Street with its nightclubs became a jazz mecca. In the 1930s most of the famous swing bands like those of Benny Goodman, Tommy Dorsey, and Duke Ellington made their base here, and New York had long been the center of music publishing as well as recording. Jazz continued to flourish in the city after World War II, although the top clubs were increasingly located in Greenwich Village. Rock music when it began appearing in the 1950s was centered here. In classical music New York has been not so much a leader as a powerful gathering place of fine performers, many of whom augment their concert income by teaching. A New York debut has continued to be a make-or-break event in the career of any American musician and even for those from abroad.

Just as New York crowds pack the city's museums and art galleries, so do they throng its concert halls. Testimony to the size and enthusiasm of New York's potential concert audience came in the late 1950s when construction began on Lincoln Center, the area along Broadway in the West 60s that was projected as a performing arts center. The Metropolitan Opera was to move there, as would the New York City Ballet, George Balanchine's company, which had previously performed at the City Center on West 55th Street. Finally, the New York Philharmonic decided to make the transfer as well, leaving Carnegie Hall without a principal tenant. Convinced that the city could not support two major concert halls, Carnegie's owners made plans to demolish it and replace it with an apartment building. Nonsense, said a group of musicians and patrons led by the violinist Isaac Stern; the hall's superlative acoustics, they argued, must not be thrown away. So they mounted a fund-raising campaign and saved the hall, which has been welcoming full houses ever since—as has the Philharmonic's new home, Avery Fisher Hall at Lincoln Center.

The theatrical scene is different, for although Broadway continues to reign at the top of American theatre in general, it is not the Broadway of old. The major problem has been costs: staging even a nonmusical play in any of the major theatres in the Times Square area has become almost prohibitively expensive. Although the 1950s were boom times on Broadway, with musicals like *South Pacific* and *West Side Story* enjoying extended runs, plays were increasingly being offered elsewhere in the city where costs were lower and where more innovative or daring works could be more hopeful of at least breaking even. These out-of-the-way theatres became known as Off Broadway, and their number grew rapidly. In due course even they found costs escalating, and a third group of houses, referred to as Off-Off Broadway, began operating from lofts, storefronts, churches, and many other unexpected locations.

Two other reasons exist for the decline of Broadway. One of them, of course, is television, for many dramas are now written directly for TV and thus siphon off part of the potential audience for serious drama (as well as preoccupying some of the dramatists). The other reason stems from the increasing sophistication of American cultural life. The past half century has seen a surge in regional cultural activity throughout the United States, with local drama groups, symphony orchestras, and opera companies competing for both talent and financial support and thus supplying a counterweight to New York City's leadership.

The kind of shifting that was taking place in the theatre was also taking place, and with more significant repercussions, in the city's overall economy. New York was losing its factories. Because Wall Street's long-term success had called attention to Manhattan's dominance of finance, many city dwellers had failed to realize that New York's prosperity had in the past been due at least as much to its role as a manufacturing center. But starting in the 1950s its manufacturers began drifting away. In previous decades industrial concerns had been moving from Manhattan to the outer boroughs; now they were leaving the city entirely, some moving to the suburbs, others decamping to another part of the United States.

There were several reasons for this exodus. One major cause was the high cost of labor in the city, which in turn was due to the cost of housing, transportation, and many other elements. Not only was labor generally more costly, but with the increased use of automation the percentage of skilled workers was going up in many industries, resulting in higher salaries. Another cause was the higher cost of space, driven up by high land values and the expense of construction. City taxes were a significant factor, and with the city providing so many services there seemed little reason to expect these could ever recede very much. And on top of everything else, the city's storied congestion was driving businesses away: moving goods from here to there was both time-consuming and expensive, and so was delivery to the customer within the city or elsewhere.

To an increasing extent, the only manufacturing industries that could afford to stay in New York—at least in Manhattan—were those that might enjoy an advantage in being close to the customer, like printing, or that were organized to adapt swiftly to changes in the market, like garment making. But the decline in the number of factories and smaller manufacturing enterprises was steady and sizable. In one two-year period, from 1953 to 1955, the city lost some 80,000 manufacturing jobs. Meanwhile the proportion of people employed in the so-called service industries—banking and brokerage, communications, radio and television, advertising and marketing— was going up. But service-oriented jobs generally demanded a higher level of skill than manufacturing jobs, and so produced a problem that New York had not faced in the past: finding entry-level jobs for unskilled workers, who tended to make up the majority of recent immigrants. The dilemma was not easily solved.

Not as critical now for the city's economic health but of great importance and historical interest was the fact that the port of New York—the extraordinary money-maker responsible for the city's original surge to prominence almost two centuries ago—was undergoing vast changes. The main reason was technological and could be summed up in one word: containers. Traditionally, cargo had been handled in New York and at other ports by means of break-bulk packing: items to be shipped by sea were individually packaged or crated and loaded onto the ships by cranes that hoisted them in slings and deposited them in the hold; then each item was individually stowed. Unloading was similarly complex. The process involved many steps and many workers—principally longshoremen, who did the heavy manhandling. Containers—big standardized metal boxes in which items to be shipped were prepacked, and which could be easily transferred from truck (or rail car) to ship and carried as is— changed all that. Whereas unloading and reloading a ship formerly had taken ten or twelve days, containers reduced the turnaround time to twenty-four hours or less. This alone meant a critical saving for the shipper. But the process also required far fewer workers, and as a result thousands of longshoremen (whose work had also given rise over the years to all manner of waterfront rackets) suddenly found themselves obsolete.

Equally to the point, the docks that ringed the entire lower half of Manhattan and a large part of the Brooklyn waterfront were rendered useless. Containers required mammoth hoisting devices that could not fit on most of the old piers, plus acres of open space where containers could be stored and then swiftly dispatched via rail lines or major highways. Except for one stretch in Brooklyn, no spot within New York City lent itself to the new arrangement. Within the jurisdiction of the Port Authority of New York and New Jersey, but on the Jersey side of the harbor, there was ample space, at the newly made Port Newark and Port Elizabeth. So as the years passed, shipping abandoned Manhattan and Brooklyn and moved over, and the old docks and piers that had made New York great were deserted and one by one were removed. Gone from the upper harbor around Manhattan were the thousands of large and small vessels whose whistles (especially on a foggy day) had always been a reminder to New Yorkers of their maritime past. Today the big container ships, which astonishingly enough account for virtually as much tonnage as was formerly handled by all the smaller craft that docked at the Manhattan and Brooklyn piers, come up through the Narrows and turn west to the new port facilities, unseen by all but a small number of city dwellers. The one saving note in the whole transformation is that the city's waterfront, which was formerly monopolized by commerce, can now be used for recreation and other beneficial activities never considered practicable for the city's shoreline.

A contributing cause of the port's change in the 1950s and 1960s was air travel. Particularly with the development of jet aircraft, transatlantic and most other ocean liner traffic was doomed. Travelers to Europe now congregated at Idlewild (later renamed Kennedy) Airport, not along West Street. So if cargo dispatching by sea was altered in the city, oceanic passenger traffic was virtually wiped out, and this too helped remove shipping from the harbor. One by one the gigantic liners that had so stirred the imaginations of New Yorkers—the *Queen Mary, Ile de France, Nieuw Amsterdam,* and *United States* —slunk silently out of the great harbor and were laid up or sold for scrap. Cruise ships continued to call at the remaining West Side docks, particularly in the summer months, but even this traffic was depleted as customers were increasingly content to fly to Miami and sail from there instead of debarking from New York.

Shifting, changing, the city continued to grow. By the 1950s few places within the city limits, except for parks, had not been given over to residential or commercial development. Manhattan had long since been totally built up, the Bronx had only a few isolated sections still given over to farming, Brooklyn continued to absorb new residents, and Queens presented mile after square mile of two- and three-story homes—although they in turn were rapidly being supplanted by large, characterless apartment houses. Only Staten Island remained rural, but the opening of the Verrazano Narrows Bridge promised to eventually destroy the borough's isolation. Each of the outlying boroughs pointed with pride to its own educational institutions: in the Bronx it was Fordham University and Lehman College; in Brooklyn, Long Island University, Brooklyn College, and Pratt Institute; in Queens, Queens College; and on Staten Island, Wagner College. By the 1960s the city's population was in excess of 7.7 million; that of the entire metropolitan area was more than double that.

One institution that enjoyed a brief comeback during the prosperous 1950s was Tammany Hall, under the guidance of Carmine DeSapio, its first Italian-American chief. Courtly but humorless, and somewhat sinister-looking because an eye ailment required him to wear tinted glasses, DeSapio had reputedly been selected for his leadership post on the advice of the gangster Frank Costello, who felt that Italians needed a better image and that DeSapio might provide it. Along with Edward Flynn of the Bronx, DeSapio had backed Wagner in the 1953 election, and Wagner's victory was good for both Tammany and its leader—who now proceeded to fill great numbers of city posts with party men loyal to him. Luckily, the great preponderance of these appointees were extremely capable, and although Wagner barely tolerated him, DeSapio seemed to thrive. He was a "good" boss. Then he overestimated his power and made a bad mistake: using his influence at a state nominating convention in 1958, he directed the choice of his own handpicked candidate for senator—New York District Attorney Frank Hogan—against the will of most of the delegates, and in the November election Hogan was swamped, as was the Democratic governor, Averell Harriman. DeSapio's image was badly tarnished, and he never recovered. Wagner turned on him and resolved to end Tammany's influence once and for all. The final break came in 1961 when Wagner decided to run for a third term. DeSapio entered an opposing candidate in the race, but Wagner trounced him in the primary and went on to victory in the general election. During the rest of his mayoralty Wagner controlled all patronage from City Hall and ended for all time the power of Tammany. So the great political machine fostered by Aaron

Burr, fattened notoriously by William Tweed, and brought to its zenith by Richard Croker and Charles Murphy finally vanished as a significant political force. (DeSapio himself, after losing his own political base in Greenwich Village—one of those who unseated him was the future mayor, Edward Koch—was later convicted of bribery and went to prison.)

More than Tammany took a beating in the 1960s; the city's good times began to seem only skin-deep. Many divisive issues coming to the force were national ones: the decade was, after all, a time of increasing concern over women's rights, consumerism, black power, student activism, and especially the Vietnam War; and New York was strongly affected by them along with a host of other issues lurking just beneath the surface. Of central concern was the city's unbalanced budget; more and more, income was proving inadequate to cover expenses. The mayor who would succeed Wagner would have to deal energetically and decisively with these issues. New Yorkers thought for a while that they had found such a person in the candidate elected on a combined Republican-Liberal ticket in 1965, John Vliet Lindsay. A popular congressman from Manhattan's East Side, the tall, handsome, dashing Lindsay seemed to have everything.

A possible omen of what lay in store, however, came just a week after Lindsay's election when, on November 9, 1965, the city experienced a power blackout—as did almost all of the Northeast. Occurring just after sundown, the episode lasted all night and brought the city to a virtual stop. Although the breakdown was not due to any error in New York, and although New Yorkers suffered through it with unexpected cheerfulness (or perhaps more than good cheer —nine months later the city's birth rate briefly zoomed), the calamity seemed symbolic of urban America's inability either to solve its own problems or to cope with crises thrust on it.

A more damaging breakdown, to Lindsay especially, began on January 1, 1966, the very morning the new mayor was sworn in: the city's subway and bus workers went on strike. In the past, the Transport Workers Union, led by a colorful Irishman named Mike Quill, had always threatened a strike when their contract came up for renegotiation but had always been willing to settle—after much dickering—for a compromise package offered by mayors like O'Dwyer and Wagner, who believed a transit strike was unthinkable for a city the size of New York. Lindsay, trying to look tough, instead called Quill's bluff. Quill pulled his men out and upped the ante. No trains or buses ran and roads were clogged, and Lindsay was caught.

297

The walkout lasted twelve disastrous days and wreaked great harm on the city's economy (not to mention the shoe leather of pedestrians). Midway in the strike the mayor had Quill jailed for calling what was technically an illegal work stoppage; Quill laughed at Lindsay from behind bars, and the newspapers laughed too—at the mayor's expense. In the end, a desperate Lindsay had to settle for a great deal more than Quill had originally demanded. His reputation for decisiveness was gone.

From that point on he seemed to drift downward. Many of his appointments to office were mediocre, and even his good commissioners tended to quit after a year or two in office. He also found himself unable to cure the city's chronic budgetary distress. Manhattan's well-to-do residents had initially adored him. He was one of them, a certified white Anglo-Saxon Protestant who believed in good government, and he had delighted them by talking about New York as Fun City, a pleasant if meaningless notion. But his inability to grapple with the city's ills eventually disenchanted them. Meanwhile, residents of the other boroughs became convinced early on that he looked down on them, for they saw him spending money on Manhattan projects while ignoring their problems. To Queens residents the last straw came after a crippling blizzard hit New York in February 1969. Snowdrifts five and six feet high paralyzed entire neighborhoods; but while streets in Manhattan were generally cleared within a day or two, some areas in Queens were unplowed for a week or longer. After that, Lindsay could hardly make an appearance in Queens without being roundly booed.

Despite all these negative signs, Lindsay astonished everyone in 1969 by getting reelected. He had been the beneficiary of a fluke: although the Republican party turned him down, the Democrats put up a political hack named Mario Procaccino, and Lindsay was able to secure the Liberal party's nomination. In the general election he just managed to squeak through. Given this demonstration of residual political appeal, he might have been expected to accomplish great things in his second term. Instead, at this point he was smitten by the presidential bug and spent much of the next couple of years campaigning (in vain) all across the United States and hardly minding the city, and the opportunity passed.

There was one area, however, in which John Lindsay could claim to have made a difference and benefited the city, and that was in his handling of race relations. Demonstrating a rapport with blacks and Puerto Ricans (a rapport that ironically hurt him badly in his dealings with other ethnic groups), he was able to defuse many of the potentially explosive racial issues that so racked the rest of the nation in the 1960s and early 1970s. And when there were threats of rioting, as after the assassination of Martin Luther King, Jr., in 1968, Lindsay walked the streets of the ghettos to show that he cared—very possibly averting major troubles.

The difficulty of dealing with the problems presented by the increasing percentage of blacks and Puerto Ricans (as well as other Hispanics) in New York had been growing ever since World War II. Large numbers of blacks came to the city from the South during the war itself, partly in search of employment, and their arrival helped boost New York's black population from 458,000 in 1940 to 748,000 a decade later. But many more were to come, and by 1970 there were 1.6 million blacks in New York. By this time they were a major factor in the city's makeup. In 1900 blacks had made up only 2 percent of the city's population; by 1960 their proportion had climbed to 10 percent; in 1970 it was greater than 21 percent. And except for a small minority who were highly skilled or well educated, most blacks lived in segregated ghettos, had trouble finding employment, and were likely candidates for welfare support. New York had always been a city of immigrants, but it was unprepared for this influx. And the fact that the newcomers were black made their plight different and more perplexing than that faced by earlier arrivals. Many of them were angered, furthermore, by the slum conditions they found themselves in, surrounded by disintegrating housing, insufficient police protection, and a rising crime rate.

Complicating the situation was the sudden and huge increase in Hispanics, principally Puerto Ricans, after World War II. Puerto Rico, acquired by the United States at the turn of the century, had always been a poverty-stricken island whose inhabitants would be prime candidates for emigration, but until the 1940s few of them could afford to leave. What happened after World War II was the introduction of inexpensive air service between San Juan and New York—some airlines charged less than $50 for the nine-hour flight. During these years there was an additional reason why Puerto Ricans might want to leave: their island was undergoing economic change, and tremendous numbers of people were suddenly out of work. So they flocked to New York—by the thousands. And as they were already American citizens, the city could not stop them from coming even if it had wanted to (the same was, of course, true of the blacks). New York had counted only 45,000 persons of Puerto Rican ancestry in 1930 and 70,000 in 1940, but by 1950 their number had soared to 246,000, and seven years later the figure had more than doubled, to 570,000.

The majority of them jammed into East Harlem, which became known as El Barrio (the neighborhood), but there were sizable enclaves also in Washington Heights, the south Bronx, and downtown Brooklyn. Although many Puerto Ricans stayed only briefly, returning to their island whenever conditions improved, their total in the city continued to grow. By the 1970s they were counted at more than a million, and Spanish had become New York City's official second language. Meanwhile they had been joined by others from the West Indies, particularly Jamaicans, Haitians, Dominicans, and Cubans. A large proportion of the West Indians, furthermore, were of African ancestry and therefore difficult for many native New Yorkers to distinguish from American blacks.

By and large, the Puerto Ricans and other West Indians, despite their woeful lack of education and (except for the Jamaicans) severe language problems, did not represent as great a challenge as the southern black influx, for most of them had come purely to get work and were more patently eager to advance themselves (admittedly against daunting odds). But their sheer numbers, combined with those of the blacks, frightened many New Yorkers, who saw a hostile tide advancing toward them and threatening their way of life. As a result there commenced during the 1950s a large-scale exodus of middle-class whites, mainly to the suburbs, transforming the city's overall population and thus, perhaps in the long run, its character. In the 1950s, as the number of blacks and Puerto Ricans was multiplying, an estimated 800,000 whites left New York. During the 1960s the city's white population was reduced by a full million, while the number of nonwhites increased by 62 percent. One consequence was a lowering of the city's potential tax revenue, as the newcomers could not be expected to spend money at the same rate as those who had departed or to pay as much in taxes. At the same time the new population tended to require more city services like unemployment compensation and health care. While paying less into the city budget, in other words, they would be taking more out of it. And many New Yorkers were distressed at the prospect of the city divided as never before, made up of a small white upper class surrounded by an ever-larger and often hostile-seeming dark-skinned underclass.

Not only was there a big exodus of middle-class whites; other ethnic groups moved elsewhere within the city before the onset of the new arrivals. The Italians of East Harlem, confronted by the advent of the Puerto Ricans, decamped mainly to the Bronx. The Jewish residents of the south Bronx fled when their neighborhoods began to turn black, many of them moving eastward in the borough, in particular to a massive new development called Co-op City in the northeastern corner of the city that was constructed in the 1960s. The Brownsville section of Brooklyn had been second only to Manhattan's Lower East Side as a Jewish district, but when better housing in other parts of the city led some Jews to move out after World War II and blacks began moving into the vacant buildings, there was a mass exodus of Jews, and by the late 1970s Brownsville was almost entirely black.

As with their predecessor immigrant counterparts, the blacks in due course began organizing politically to work for better living and working conditions and for other matters of importance to them. One of their earliest effective leaders was the Reverend Adam Clayton Powell, Jr., a congressman from Harlem, whose flamboyant personality masked a considerable record of achievement on behalf of his constituents. New York's militant blacks led many a local demonstration during the nationwide civil rights movement of the early 1960s; at one point it was estimated that the city was paying as much as $15,000 a day for extra police protection to make sure that such activities did not get out of control. To dramatize their cause, the militants tried to disrupt the formal opening of the 1964–65 New York World's Fair on April 22, 1964, by stalling cars on the approach roads and tying up the subway system. Although the tactic did not appreciably mar the opening, the urgency and depth of the blacks' complaints made many whites fear that the ghetto might explode at any time. So it was that Mayor Lindsay's subsequent gestures of reaching out toward the pockets of discontent were appreciated by so many New Yorkers.

One area that blacks and Puerto Ricans focused on with special intent was education. They knew that previous immigrant groups had found that acquiring a sound education was one of the surest ways out of the ghetto, and they looked to New York's public schools to provide it. This was a tall order for the city's school system; its record of educating impoverished newcomers had never been as successful as legend claimed. The system's weakness—as demonstrated by the poor reading scores of the city's schoolchildren—indeed was one of the major reasons why so many middle-class whites were leaving New York. Yet the blacks and their allies persisted, and their struggle was to provide some intriguing insights into the role of minorities in the city's social fabric. In particular it was to set them on a collision course involving the great immigrant group of yesteryear, the Jews.

The Supreme Court's pivotal decision in 1954 outlawing school segregation had led many black leaders to believe that integration was the answer to their educational needs. Because it had been shown that segregation, brought about by racism, was demeaning and harmful to children, and because it resulted in schools that were made up largely of blacks, these leaders were convinced that schools predominantly black were to be avoided. But how could meaningful integration be achieved in a city like New York? Attempts to redraw school district boundaries solved little—most ghetto schools remained solidly black. Busing was politically unworkable and ran head on into the sacrosanct concept of the neighborhood school, which most citizens (including blacks) were loath to give up. Finally, such ghetto schools as had been partly integrated showed little or no improvement in student test scores. For this reason, sentiment not only among militants and parents but also among many educators in the late 1950s and early 1960s began to turn away from integration to the notion of community control as the solution. It was the Board of Education's rigidly centralized control of the schools that was at fault, they said; it resulted in teachers who were unresponsive to the needs of black youngsters. Give parents and local leaders authority to run their schools, and improvement was sure to come—black children would learn better in a black-controlled school. Integration was out; the new byword was decentralization.

Achieving decentralization was not easy, however, and Lindsay in 1966 turned for advice to McGeorge Bundy, president of the Ford Foundation and an experienced educator. Bundy recommended that three demonstration school districts be set up and given considerable independent authority. One of these was to be established in a Brooklyn area known as Ocean Hill–Brownsville. The Ford Foundation also provided some funds to pay for the experiment. So far so good, but there were two difficulties—and they would prove fatal. One was that the city's Board of Education, although it backed the idea of decentralization, was unwilling to cede full power to the locally elected governing board, asserting that its role was only advisory; but the local board insisted that its control was complete. The other was the presence of the United Federation of Teachers, the union that in 1961 had won the right to represent all the city's public school teachers; most of its members were from Jewish families that had emigrated from eastern Europe a half century or more earlier, and they held strong trade-union convictions concerning both job security and academic freedom. The UFT members in Ocean Hill–Brownsville were deeply suspicious of the district's local board, which was dominated by blacks convinced that the UFT was not only obstructionist but also replete with mediocre teachers. The Jewish teachers, many blacks claimed, practiced "intellectual genocide."

In April 1968 the district administrator hired by the local board, a quiet but determined black educator named Rhody A. McCoy, brought matters to a head by dismissing thirteen teachers and six other UFT members from the district on the ground that they were incompetent and uncooperative. The UFT refused to obey the order, as the teachers had not been given a hearing—which the local board would not allow. The teachers called a strike. McCoy hired substitutes prepared to teach the way the board wanted. Both sides girded for what was to become the most significant confrontation between blacks and Jews in New York in decades. It was black power and the perceived needs of an aggrieved minority against an entrenched group who believed they were defending academic freedom and due process. It was also today's immigrants against yesterday's, as well as black versus white. Emotions ran high, angry crowds threatened the picketers, and the Board of Education was for the moment unable to resolve the dispute.

In late May, McCoy knuckled under and filed charges against the fired teachers. The judge assigned to weigh them, a retired black jurist, decided they were insufficient to warrant dismissal of the UFT members. McCoy still would not take the teachers back and proceeded to hire more substitutes. The first strike ended with the conclusion of the school year, but in September the UFT called a two-day citywide teacher's strike. Finally, in November 1968 after months of bitter invective on both sides, an agreement was hammered out under state auspices. The district took back the teachers who had struck and was put under the temporary stewardship of a state trustee until the local board was prepared to comply with the Board of Education's directives. The demonstration district was quietly disbanded, and McCoy departed for new ventures. For its part, the United Federation of Teachers was fined $250,000 for violating a law that forbade strikes by public employees. It could claim to have won the fight, though at some cost to its image as a progressive union. Blacks were infuriated by what had been done to their hopes, but they knew they had learned much about the city's political realities. And the struggle had not been without its benefits, for presently the entire city school system was restructured to provide for locally elected boards and for much more local control. Under the new arrangement there was reason to hope that the performance of children in ghetto schools would improve.

So the tempest subsided and the wounded participants went about their business. Once again New York's many discordant ethnic groups found they could get along together. Bigger troubles, however, lay ahead for the city. As the 1970s got under way a crisis arose that would prove to be much the most serious in New York's history. It had to do not with race, or education, or political control. It had to do with money.

13

Crisis

The tone of voice of the mayor's press secretary on the phone was somber. "I think we're going down," he said. He was calling from Gracie Mansion just before midnight on October 16, 1975, advising *New York Times* reporter Fred Ferretti to come to the mansion as soon as possible.

"Down?" asked Ferretti.

"Default. It looks bad."[1]

When Ferretti arrived at the elegant house that serves as the mayor's official residence, he found a motley collection of the city's top officials already assembled. Mayor Abraham Beame was wearing white tie and tails, having been hastily called from the annual Alfred E. Smith dinner at the Waldorf-Astoria. Some of the members of the Board of Estimate, summoned from their homes, were in sweat shirts. Gloom pervaded the house. The unthinkable seemed likely to occur within hours: America's richest and most powerful city, the money capital of the world, would be forced after years of unbalanced budgets and runaway borrowing to default on its financial obligations, the next thing to declaring bankruptcy. When investors in the city's short-term notes showed up at the Municipal Building the next day to redeem them, they would have to be told that the city could not pay up: it had run out of cash and could not raise any more.

As the group sweated through the night awaiting the outcome, Mayor Beame pondered a list of the city's emergency priorities in case of default: first was police protection, then fire protection, and so forth. But municipal employees would have to be paid in scrip, for New York City's bank accounts would be empty.

The sudden escalation on October 16 of the city's fiscal crisis, which had been mounting since the beginning of the year, was brought about by the unlikely and unexpected last-minute reluctance of the trustees of the city's teachers' retirement system to permit their pension funds to be used to bail out the city. Seemingly fearful that their assent might be construed as violating their fiduciary responsibilities, they refused to go along with the plan. (Their obduracy was actually a political move directed by the head of the union, Albert Shanker, but that did not mitigate the gravity of the emergency.) And New York had long since run out of other sources of funds. The banks had ceased loaning the city money, having found that investors were not buying the bonds issued to back up the advances. The state had already provided the city with many millions; its legislators would give no more. The federal government had turned thumbs down on the city's pleas, at least until now; New York should mend its ways and make some more sacrifices, said President Gerald Ford, before it could expect any help from Washington. The teachers' fund was apparently the last resource.

Perhaps the strangest aspect of this harrowing turn in the city's dilemma, however, was that nothing could be done about it by those city leaders called to Gracie Mansion. They could only wait—and make plans in the event that the end actually came the next day. Months earlier, Mayor Beame might have been able to stave off the disaster, but in October 1975 it was too late. He no longer had the power; all control over the city's finances had been taken away from him. Indeed, the pension fund trustees were not even at Gracie Mansion that evening. They were across town at the New York office of Governor Hugh Carey, who earlier that year had moved in to rescue the city from its distress and, other means not succeeding, had finally arranged for the appointment of an Emergency Financial Control Board chaired by him and given total power over New York's finances for a three-year period.

All that evening Carey and his panel of banker advisers had tried unsuccessfully to persuade the pension fund trustees to relent. The following morning, as news of the deliberations spread, prices on the New York Stock Exchange suffered a sharp decline, the bond market was paralyzed, and currency trading in Europe virtually shut down —a clear harbinger of the widespread havoc that could ensue if default were to take place. Shortly after midday on October 17, Carey and the others finally succeeded in convincing Shanker that his reputation would not be enhanced by his becoming known as the man who triggered the city's final ignominy; Shanker reluctantly told the trustees to vote yes, and the cataclysm was averted.

But New York's fiscal crisis was not over, for the infusion of pension money gave only a few days' relief. It would be another six weeks before President Ford reversed himself and backed the federal loan guarantees that would save the city. Even so, several years would pass before the city was restored to full fiscal health. It would emerge from its travail bruised and perhaps a bit more hardheaded about the ways in which it collected and spent its money; the crisis was a watershed in the way the city ordered its affairs. New York had been living beyond its means for many years; unable to curb its spending, it had kept borrowing and borrowing, even borrowing to pay interest on its borrowing until, as Ken Auletta put it in his thoughtful book, *The Streets Were Paved with Gold*, it had become a "short-term note junkie."[2] Such a baleful, wrenching state of affairs must not be allowed to recur.

The seemingly uncontrolled excess of spending was, however, an outgrowth of New York's long history as a city that provided more benefits and services than any other, without perhaps knowing how to limit them. One way to look at the fiscal crisis of the 1970s is to see it as a collision between the two main forces that have shaped New York: its financial prowess on the one hand and its role as a cosmopolitan haven on the other. Being a haven can be costly, and it was New York's bankers and brokers who blew the whistle in 1975 and told the city it must set limits to its generosity or face ruin. When the city's leaders balked, the bankers moved in, took over, and compelled New York to mend its ways.

New York had always prided itself on its municipal services. No other city, for example, offered a free college education to all its citizens, and in 1961 its educational system was enlarged with the establishment of a City University offering advanced degrees. New York's nineteen municipal hospitals are elaborate and expensive; Chicago, in contrast, has only one public hospital, and it is funded by Cook County rather than the city. Cultural and recreational amenities are widespread. So are welfare benefits. At the same time, like all the older cities of the country, New York suffers from a decaying infrastructure, its roads, bridges, and other undergirdings constantly requiring repair or replacement. And because of the city's role not only as a business center but also as a tourist attraction, it must provide services to a great many people who are not residents or taxpayers.

Meanwhile in the 1950s New York found its welfare costs escalating because of the large-scale influx of poverty-level blacks and Hispanics. There was no question about the necessity of caring for them. True to its liberal traditions, says Auletta, "New York often thought with its heart. Suffused with a commitment to help people, when the federal or state government wouldn't, the city reached to do the job alone."[3] Because of the city's apparent abundance of resources, there always seemed to be enough money to go around. Mayor Robert F. Wagner, who presided over the city from 1954 to 1966, bespoke what he saw as the priorities: "I do not propose to permit our fiscal problems to set the limits of our commitments to meet the essential needs of the people of the city."[4]

Another element was injected into the picture when Wagner in 1958 signed an executive order permitting the city's own employees—around 100,000 at the time but soon to increase greatly—to join unions and bargain collectively. Not only would this bring about significantly higher labor costs for New York, but the city would also find itself funding its workers' health and welfare benefits, including their pension plans.

Last, it must be noted that in the 1960s the entire nation was overtaken by a wave of concern about society's needs and an optimism toward meeting them. Though the enthusiasm was nowhere greater than in New York, it was accompanied by a sense of urgency grounded in fear: if slum conditions were not addressed, many people felt, the poor might rise up and bring about racial polarization and even civil war. Occasional near-riots lent cogency to the idea.

So as the years progressed more and more money was needed. Where to get it? The first "innovative solution" that, combined with other artful devices, would lead many years later to New York's fiscal crisis was made in 1963 by that well-meaning and concerned citizen Mayor Wagner. Finding a projected budget out of balance, he turned for advice to his comptroller, Abraham Beame, who suggested that the mayor simply increase his estimate of anticipated revenues. Whereupon Wagner, announcing that a "brighter economic outlook" justified a more sanguine forecast, reached into thin air and upped his budget by $26.3 million.[5] A breach had been made in the wall of fiscal integrity.

The following year Wagner came up with another device that would help him make ends meet, but this time the idea was handed to him by his friend Governor Nelson Rockefeller, who thereby merits consideration as one of the more imaginative creators of New York

City's fiscal shambles. Wrestling with yet another budget that threatened to go out of whack, Wagner asked the governor for suggestions. Rockefeller, who rejoiced in such challenges and also liked to help his friends, recommended that the mayor charge to his capital budget the cost of a special census that the city was undertaking, as the census project would take longer than a year to complete.

Up until this time, there had been an inviolable barrier between the city's expense budget, which covers city salaries and wages and other day-to-day needs and is paid for by tax revenues, and its capital budget, which pays for such things as new schools and bridge repairs and is funded by the sale of bonds on which interest must be paid. And there was good reason to keep them separate: paying for today's needs by floating securities that will have to be supported tomorrow is merely postponing the reckoning and can thus be viewed as hoodwinking the citizenry. Wagner may have felt the tactic was a bit suspect—a census hardly seems comparable to something as solid as a school building—but he nevertheless went along with it, and the governor obliged him on April 3, 1964, by signing an amendment to the state's Local Finance Law that made the dodge legal, permitting city officials to sneak expenses into the capital budget. What Wagner did was admittedly minor, but the door had been opened, and the technique was to be used increasingly by subsequent mayors until it grew to magnificent dimensions. By 1975, when everything came apart, Beame's capital budget included an unbelievable $835 million for what were essentially day-to-day expenses. The sum constituted more than half of Beame's entire capital budget. What made the practice doubly unfortunate was that it resulted in fewer dollars being available for true capital needs that were demonstrably apparent at the time.

One final contribution made by Robert Wagner in his earnest desire to bring in more cash was the use of so-called revenue anticipation notes, or RANs, to borrow money against estimated future expenses. Up to now the city had been able to borrow money against anticipated revenues (like federal grants or uncollected taxes) that were genuinely forthcoming in the current fiscal year. Such notes were in effect bridge loans on a short-term basis, to be paid off when Washington actually came across or when taxes were truly collected. They could be no larger than the revenue from that source had been the previous year. Wagner wanted to issue RANs that were to be paid off with revenues that were larger than those of the past year and that he merely thought—or hoped, or dreamed—would be coming in—but that might never come in at all. As Fred Ferretti points out in *The Year the Big Apple Went Bust*, this was quite simply borrowing without collateral. Once again Nelson Rockefeller approved, furnishing the necessary legislation to make it all seem proper.

The lid was off. All the ingredients were in place to create New York City's time of disgrace in the 1970s. Budgets could be based on estimates that might or might not be real; the city could borrow money on the basis of such estimates—and around this time it also began to "roll over" its debt, borrowing further when it found itself unable to redeem previously issued notes; and it could also hide expenses in its capital budget. As New York's Senator Daniel Patrick Moynihan has remarked, "From Wagner's third term to Beame's second year, the city was, in effect, printing money."[6]

In capable hands such subterfuges might not have gone out of control. Unfortunately, Wagner's successors, John Lindsay and Abraham Beame, were not equal to the task. And all the time these dodges were being used with increasing frequency, the stakes were being raised. Welfare costs were going up, as were the costs of running the city's government; not only were municipal employees earning more, their ranks had to be increased to handle the city's expanding needs. Debt service, the cost of paying interest on all that borrowing, was an increasing expense, and city pension funds were siphoning off larger sums. But at the same time the city's revenue base was declining, as manufacturing enterprises departed and large numbers of middle-class residents moved to the suburbs. New York was facing bigger and bigger bills with fewer and fewer resources on which to base payment.

Admittedly, the sheer size of New York's budget was and is intimidating. Observers like to point out two mind-boggling facts: New York City's population is larger than that of Sweden, and the city's budget is virtually equal to that of India. Balancing it is not easy under the best of circumstances.

In his 1965 campaign for the mayoralty, John Lindsay railed against what he termed Wagner's fiscal irresponsibility. The suspect practices, he said, would end once he took office. They did not; in fact they were resorted to with ever greater abandon. To his credit, Lindsay, whose abilities were formidable, was acutely concerned about the problems both fiscal and social that confronted the city. And he did introduce budgeting procedures that seemed to limit the number of ways in which income and expenses could be juggled. But he was unable to stanch the budgetary hemorrhage that was already under way. During his first two years on the job he held the line fairly well on borrowing, but then the city's short-term debt began climbing steeply. In 1967 it stood at $2.4 billion. Two years later it had risen to $4.4 billion, and in 1970 it was at $6.5 billion and heading higher. The city's budget was growing at a rate of more than 15 percent annually, but significantly the major increase was not in basic services like police and fire protection but in welfare costs, medical services, and higher education. A tremendous leap in costs came in 1970 with the adoption of open admission to the City University: henceforth any graduate of a city high school could enter one of the city's two- or four-year colleges without further examination. Between 1969 and 1971 admission to the city's colleges zoomed from 19,000 to 39,000. The aim was laudable, but could the city afford it? In Lindsay's view it was mandatory. The city would find the money somewhere.

Finding the money became a kind of game, with the most imaginative players praised for their creativity. One year the projected budget was several million dollars in the red, and there appeared to be no further sources of revenue. Whereupon Abraham Beame, who after an absence was once again comptroller, produced a neat answer: he declared the fiscal year to be only 364 days long, so that a big payment due to be made on the 365th day could be ascribed to the following year. Everyone applauded. Often it seemed as if the participants had dealt in mammoth sums for so long that they had lost any real sense of what they were talking about. As one Lindsay aide put it, paraphrasing a remark allegedly made by former Senator Everett Dirksen of Illinois, "You get a million dollars here and a million dollars there and, before you know it, you've got some real money."[7]

Even politicians who were not members of the Lindsay administration played the game. Ken Auletta recalls that in 1972, when he was serving as executive director of the New York City Off-Track Betting Corporation, the profits of which were classed as city revenues, he and others appeared before the City Council's Finance Committee to explain their estimate of $43 million as profits for the corporation for fiscal 1973. The previous year OTB had earned only $14 million, but they felt they might get up above $40 million this time around—certainly not much more than that. Finance chairman Mario Merola, with nothing to go on, said, "I can't see why we can't go to $70 million next year." He smiled at them and added, "I've got that much confidence in your operation." The OTB staffers objected that such a figure was illusory, but the $70 million figure went into the budget. That year the corporation earned $34.3 million.[8]

One of Lindsay's favorite tactics during budget-making time was to announce that if his very high proposed budget was not approved in toto he would have to fire umpteen thousand police officers, cut way back on sanitation pickups, close hospitals, and the like. Much politicking would ensue, out of which a lower budget would emerge. But then, marvel of marvels, it would turn out that no one would have to be laid off after all, nor would any services have to be curtailed, for the mayor had found the money. He had indeed—at the public's eventual expense.

One party to most of these tactics was Beame. As comptroller, if he was doing his job, he had to know where all the money was coming from and where it went. From time to time he expressed public disapproval, even dismay, at what was happening before his eyes, particularly as the enormity of the city's budgetary problems was by 1973 beginning to be taken seriously by the press. This was seen as routine political maneuvering—for the comptroller was pondering higher office. With John Lindsay's stock running low at the end of his second term, Beame was the odds-on favorite to become the next mayor. He proceeded to campaign as "the man who knows the buck," the one person who could put an end to all the shenanigans and return the city to fiscal rectitude. Even New Yorkers with a short memory might have recalled with misgivings that this line was suspiciously similar to what Lindsay had trumpeted eight years earlier, but enough of them believed him to put him over the top. On January 1, 1974, Abraham Beame became the first Jewish mayor of New York City.

His qualifications were good. A Democratic party regular, he had worked hard and risen steadily through the civil service to positions of great responsibility, and he had the reputation of being thorough and painstaking. He was short (five foot two), polite, and dapper, and he thought carefully and moved with caution. Unfortunately, he proved unable to grasp the seriousness of the situation into which the city was drifting, and when the crisis hit he was unable to cope with it. When the times called for decisive action he seemed paralyzed.

In the spring of 1974, not long after Beame's taking office, the first murmurs of uneasiness were voiced by New York's major banks. At the rate things were going, said an official of Chase Manhattan, the market in the near future might not be able to absorb more city bond issues; indeed, brokers were having trouble selling issues that had already been floated. Beame hardly took notice. While complaining that he had inherited a $1.5 billion deficit from Lindsay (ignoring the fact that he had helped push it that high), he projected a 1974–75 budget that put New York still further in debt. The document was filled with fictional figures. Although the national economy was depressed, the Beame budget predicted a decrease in welfare costs, and it pegged interest costs at $145 million while city accountants were saying the true figure would be closer to $200 million. True, the habit of stretching the numbers was so widespread and so deeply ingrained in the city government that it was hard to know what was real. Said a Beame adviser at one point, "It's not Abe's fault. The commissioners and the budget bureau are sending him rubber numbers."[9]

The sluggishness of the market in city notes was now having a destructive side effect: because the bonds had to be priced lower, the city would end up paying ever-higher interest rates on them, further widening the budget deficit. In July 1974 Beame's comptroller, Harrison J. Goldin, was forced to pay interest charges of 8.586 percent on a new issue; the following December the rate would go up to a devastating 9.479 percent. That November, Goldin issued a report stating that unless the city's borrowing could be contained, the city might soon find no purchasers for its short-term bonds. While this gloomy prognostication was being digested, Mayor Beame was admitting that his current budget, which had been in effect for only a few months, was already showing a deficit of $430 million. To make up for it, he promised to lay off thousands of city employees over the next several months, though he truly had no idea who they would be.

All of these warnings, however, were prologue. The first real shock came in the early weeks of 1975 when a state-funded housing construction agency called the Urban Development Corporation appeared near collapse. The UDC's financing was based on "moral obligation" bonds, securities backed not by anticipated revenues but by the state itself and its reserve fund. Another brainchild of Nelson Rockefeller's, the bonds did not require voter approval and had always been considered slightly suspect, and now the suspicions were being proved correct. New York's newly elected governor, Hugh Carey, hastily put together a coalition to rescue the corporation temporarily—the first of a series of judicious moves that he was to make over the ensuing months—but in late February the UDC actually defaulted on one of its obligations, and the damage was done.

Investors began to shun New York State bond offerings; asked one Wall Street bond trader, "Why should I buy the moral obligations of immoral politicians?"[10] And Wall Street became even more suspicious of what the city would be trying to sell. Within days, lawyers from a syndicate of banking underwriters asked Goldin for permission to look at the city's tax receipts, a request he grudgingly granted.

What they found did not please them. The city's books were a mess. When the underwriters' discoveries became known, New York's credit plummeted. Early in March, when the city attempted to sell $587 million in bond anticipation notes, there were no takers. In the next few weeks the city did succeed in squeezing some money out of a syndicate of the city's banks at exorbitant rates, but basically Wall Street had slammed the door. The market would take no more New York bond issues.

Thus began an eight-month nightmare marked by desperate attempts by Goldin and others to scrape up cash to keep the city going, by increasing exasperation on the part of the bankers at the city administration's inability to change its ways, by stronger attempts by the banking community to force the city to put its finances in order, by critically needed help arranged by Governor Carey in the face of almost total lack of concern by Washington, and by the all-but-ineffectual performance of Mayor Beame.

Responding to the pleas of Hugh Carey, the state legislature in April authorized an emergency loan of $400 million to the city to head off a collapse. Incredibly, Mayor Beame responded by declaring his faith in New York City and by canceling the layoffs he had threatened a few months back. Observers could hardly believe it.

With the public spurning New York's securities and the state legislature showing increased reluctance to advance any more aid, Beame and Carey journeyed to Washington in May to ask President Ford for help. After they had made their plea, Ford merely delivered a few pronouncements about how families should live within their means, and a few days later he wrote the mayor that until the city came up with a plan to mend its ways there could be no special aid from the federal government. Later that month the City University was forced to close temporarily, and its faculty and other city workers for a while went unpaid. Default, or even bankruptcy, seemed to be staring New York in the face.

Something drastic had to be done, and Carey was prepared to do it. In early June he got the state legislature to authorize the appointment of a nine-member board of bankers, lawyers, and business leaders to be known as the Municipal Assistance Corporation, their mission being to refinance the city's debt and, with the state's backing, to make New York bonds once again marketable. More to the point, Big MAC (as it was called) was given the power to guide the city's borrowing policies for the near future. A sizable chunk of Beame's power was thereby stripped from him, although he was slow to acknowledge the loss. Ultimate power in the city was being transferred to a group of unelected citizens, surely a risky arrangement but one that under the circumstances may have been unavoidable. By far the strongest member of the board, and later its chairman, was Felix Rohatyn, a partner in the prestigious global investment banking firm of Lazard Frères. Tough-talking and at ease in the world of high finance, he became known for his quotable observations on the city's plight. Default, he once remarked, would be "like someone stepping into a tepid bath and slashing his wrists—you might not feel yourself dying, but that's what would happen."[11] Over the next several months it was Felix Rohatyn and Hugh Carey more than any others who led the fight to bring New York back from the brink.

The newly appointed board immediately began trying to sell its own bonds, which superseded those of the city. Sales were slow, for the investment community remained highly doubtful of the city's reliability. Beame promised again to trim the city's payroll but neglected to follow through. On July 10 he invited reporters to his office in City Hall and announced that New York's fiscal distress was "reasonably behind us now." There really hadn't been a crisis at all, he said, just a cash flow problem.[12] A week later the Big MAC board, furious, called him in and in effect ordered him to get going. The mayor agreed to institute a wage freeze for all city employees, but a day or two later when he told the municipal employees' unions about it, they objected with such vehemence that he backed down. Very gradually during August he gave way, trimming here and there (and raising the subway fare), but it was not enough. Toward the end of the month a panel of accountants who had been studying the city's books reported that the 1975–76 budget deficit was not $641 million, as Beame had been stating, but an astonishing $3.3 billion.

The MAC board informed Governor Carey that the situation had become grave and that "emergency action of a new and decisive kind" was called for.[13] Again Carey was ready, and in early September he called a special legislative session that approved a complex plan that he and his aides together with Rohatyn and other MAC members had drawn up. It provided for a $2.3 billion aid package and, to make sure the money was put to good use, the appointment of an Emergency Financial Control Board, chaired by Carey, which was to have total control of city finances for a three-year period, including the power to reject any labor union contracts that it considered inappropriate. All city revenues would be funneled through the board, and it would make all disbursements. Although Beame would be a member of the Board, what lingering power he had possessed was now swept from him. He had become a figurehead.

But this Draconian arrangement did not turn things around. The financial community was relieved, but the MAC bonds still were not moving. On October 2 Moody's Investor Service, whose ratings are taken seriously throughout the nation, downgraded both New York State and New York City securities, casting a pall on the entire MAC effort. Another plea to the White House again yielded a cold response. Looking around for untapped sources, Rohatyn decided to approach the city pension funds (the state comptroller had ruled out using the state equivalents for the purpose), and it was this effort that produced the sudden and unexpected crisis on the night of October 16–17. To pay off the notes due on the seventeenth and to meet other expenses that day, the city would need $477 million; but it had only $34 million in its bank accounts. And if the teachers' fund did not come through, its counterparts were hardly likely to decide differently. The city would go under. As Rohatyn said, "The dikes are crumbling and we are running out of fingers."[14]

Albert Shanker's last-minute assent, freeing the use of the teachers' fund, saved the day—but just barely, for New York was assured of funds only until December 1. Carey sent a telegram to President Ford urging federal aid simply because default would have a devastating effect on the rest of the country, a view echoed by many economists on the national scene. "We need not a handout," Carey wrote, "but the recognition by the federal government that we are part of this country." Ford answered through his press secretary: "This is not a natural disaster or an act of God. It is a self-inflicted act by the people who have been running New York City."[15]

Members of Congress, for their part, were at long last moving to help the city, but on October 29 Ford in a speech to the National Press Club went even further than he had up to that time. "I can tell you—and tell you now," he exclaimed, "that I am prepared to veto any bill that has as its purpose a federal bailout of New York City to prevent default."[16] That evening the managing editor of the New York *Daily News*, William Brink, tried to think of a headline that would do justice to the thunderbolt that the president had just flung. His first attempt was FORD REFUSES AID TO CITY, but that did not seem strong enough. He tried another but did not like it either. His third try, which he decided to run, now ranks as a classic: FORD TO CITY: DROP DEAD.[17]

There were political reasons for Ford's attitude. Mindful of the resentment that much of the United States feels toward New York for its swaggering and egocentricity, he was tightening the screws for all the gain that might result. New York State must do more, he said, and the city must put through additional cutbacks to ensure that its books balance.

Although Ford had reason to feel that his intransigence would play well, he was mistaken. Polls taken immediately after his speech showed that a majority of Americans disagreed with him and felt New York should be helped. Gradually the White House softened its stand, and by the end of November a complex package was approved by Ford and enacted by Congress whereby the federal government granted $2.3 billion in loan guarantees to the city in return for some major concessions engineered by Carey. The most important concessions were a major increase in income taxes paid by New York City residents and the further use of city workers' pension funds. As part of the deal, the state also permitted the city to postpone redeeming its short-term notes for a three-year period: investors could either keep their notes or exchange them for higher-paying MAC bonds. Ironically, this constituted default—though no one wanted to admit it at the time.

The cost to the city was widespread and deep. City workers had their wages frozen for several years, and thousands of jobs were eliminated. The subway and bus fares went up. Free education at the City University became a thing of the past. Many social programs in such areas as nutritional guidance and consumer education were eliminated or cut back. Twenty-eight day-care centers closed, and a number of medical services were shut down. Cultural institutions like public libraries reduced their hours, and some were forced to close. And all manner of new capital projects like the renovation of obsolete housing were put on indefinite hold.

At long last, then, the city was suffering in concrete ways. The cutbacks touched virtually everybody in one way or another, and during the winter and spring of 1975–76 the atmosphere of pessimism was thick citywide. It would be several years before recovery from the crisis was achieved financially. Oddly enough, the aura of gloom was mitigated in the summer of 1976 by an event that was only marginally local. Although the bicentennial of the United States was observed nationally, the sight of magnificent tall sailing vessels moving majestically up the New York harbor past the extraordinary skyline—the proceedings were televised nationwide—had the effect of reminding people elsewhere of New York's historical greatness and of providing New Yorkers themselves with a much-needed resurgence of civic pride. The fiscal crisis had scarred them, but they felt this old city would endure and prosper again, even if it turned out to be not quite the same place they had known before.

The fiscal crisis, then, marked a significant shift in the way New Yorkers felt about their city, about its needs and responsibilities. Unrelated to the crisis but of equally great importance as a sign of how New Yorkers might change their thinking was a pair of developments in the 1960s and 1970s that related to land use. Throughout its history, the city had always expanded, built, and rebuilt, tearing down the old with scant regard for its value in order to put up something new. A prime example was the magnificent abode of Mrs. William Astor on the corner of Fifth Avenue and 34th Street, built in the 1850s, which was torn down in the 1890s for the erection of the Waldorf-Astoria Hotel, which in turn was removed in 1929 to make way for the Empire State Building. New Yorkers habitually took the destruction in stride because it was a seemingly inevitable side effect of prosperity and success. Even the massive bulldozing by Robert Moses for the construction of new highways and bridges was generally accepted, for the city seemed to need new roads and something obviously had to give to make them possible. At least New Yorkers in general tolerated this sort of thing with some amusement and with only minor objection—until the 1960s. Then their attitude changed.

What triggered the shift was the demolition, in the early 1960s, of Pennsylvania Station, the glorious monumental structure at Seventh Avenue and 33rd Street designed after the turn of the century by Charles McKim of the prestigious architectural firm of McKim, Mead & White. When the station was completed in 1910, the Pennsylvania Railroad was a thriving carrier. But by the 1950s the line had fallen on hard times, and its managers said the station was a drain on its resources and should give way to a more profitable structure. The wreckers would soon begin taking it apart. Suddenly taking notice, a group of New York architects banded together in 1962 and tried to stop the destruction, and they and their friends picketed the station, but to no avail. It was only after the demolition had been completed that popular indignation was aroused. More and more the conviction gained ground that the city could not afford to lose such magnificent and valuable buildings and that the best of the physical past in New York must be preserved, lest the city lose all sense of what made it distinctive and special.

Out of the clamor, in 1965, came the establishment of the Landmarks Preservation Commission, an official city body empowered to designate for protection not only individual buildings but also entire neighborhoods, or historic districts. Such buildings or districts could be modified only with the permission of the commission. Since that time more than 900 buildings all over the city have been awarded landmark status, as well as more than fifty historic districts, among the most notable of which are Brooklyn Heights, Greenwich Village, and Soho. In the mid-1970s a serious challenge was mounted against the commission's powers by the owners of Penn Station's counterpart, Grand Central Terminal at Park Avenue and 42nd Street, who wanted to build a high-rise office tower above the already-designated structure, again because they felt the station was a financial lemon. When the commission turned them down they sued and carried their fight all the way to the Supreme Court, which by a narrow margin rejected their arguments and affirmed the commission's powers. New York's preservationists rejoiced, and the commission continued designating.

If the campaign to preserve New York's architectural gems can be seen partly as a latter-day reaction to the relentless drive for new construction epitomized by Robert Moses, the other land-use reversal in recent decades was an even more direct manifestation of it. This one concerned an ambitious and costly plan for the development of the West Side waterfront of Manhattan. Ever since Manhattan's harbor traffic had begun to decline in the 1950s, the area had cried out for attention: piers were rotting, commercial buildings nearby were vacant and run-down, and even the elevated highway that ran over Twelfth Avenue was deteriorating. In 1972 the city unveiled a massive plan, known as Westway, whereby the shoreline all the way from Chambers Street downtown near City Hall to 42nd Street in midtown would be extended into the river by a full three blocks of landfill. Part of the new land would be given over to parks and the rest to residential development, and beneath the parkland would run a new superhighway that proponents said was a much-needed link in the interstate highway system as well as yet another means of relieving

319

the city's fearful traffic congestion. Opponents of the plan claimed that the money needed to build it, first estimated at $2 billion but later closer to $4 billion (most of which would come from the federal government as part of its highway program), would be much better spent improving the city's mass transit. They also said that the new road would simply shift the congestion rather than allay it and would increase air pollution, and that the entire project was nothing more than a plum for the real estate interests.

Although all these objections were valid, it was another—and highly unlikely—one that would prove Westway's undoing. Environmental tests showed that the Hudson shoreline, with its rotting piers, was a key spawning ground for striped bass; the landfill, it was said, would have a devastating effect on these fish. Most New Yorkers were ready to shrug off that revelation with a chuckle until they learned that the striped bass fishery is a multimillion-dollar industry along the Atlantic Coast. At any rate, Westway's opponents, led by a spirited, hardworking, and zealous woman named Marcy Benstock, fastened on the striped bass issue and used it to block the entire project. Their court challenges, which among other things revealed that the Army Corps of Engineers had deliberately misled the public concerning the impact of the project on the striped bass, consumed eleven years and finally ended in September 1985, when Congress voted to deny the federal government's funds for the landfill. The great West Side expansion plan was dead.

For a city that throughout its history had added to its shoreline with nary an objection from anyone, and that once gloried in its ever-improving highway network, it was a startling turn. Coming on top of the traumatic fiscal crisis, which mandated a leaner and more circumspect New York, it was the sort of thing only a city well used to dramatic change would be able to take in stride.

14

New Departures

Few people would have guessed during the fiscal crisis of 1975 that barely half a dozen years later New York City would be well on its way to renewed prosperity and confidence. But just as the city had in the past confounded its observers by rebounding dramatically from severe difficulties, so it did in the 1980s. Barely a year after bankruptcy had seemed imminent, the Municipal Assistance Corporation's bonds were selling at a good pace, and New York's credit rating was on its way back to acceptability. By 1981, one year earlier than expected, the city budget was in balance, and in the mid-1980s the unbelievable was occurring: New York's books were showing a surplus.

Part of the remarkable turnaround was admittedly caused by factors outside New York. The United States was increasingly prosperous, and because the city's economy was tied to the country's, the benefits were bound to rub off. There were also what might be called self-correcting changes within the city itself: bad times had depressed both wages and rents, reducing at least temporarily the cost of doing business here. This in turn dissuaded many enterprises from departing and allowed others to become established—thus improving the business climate. But above all, the recovery was brought about because of the city's belt-tightening. Fiscal sanity had returned. The promised layoffs were indeed made, expenses were curtailed, and the regrettable practice of constantly borrowing huge sums to meet huge deficits was banished. The renewed budgetary honesty fostered increased confidence in the city's future, and by the end of the 1970s there was a distinct feeling of optimism.

If any one figure personified that optimism it was New York's new mayor, Edward I. Koch, who was elected in 1977 to succeed the discredited Abraham Beame. Brash, abrasive, and wisecracking, Koch had come to prominence as a Reform Democrat in Greenwich Village and had established a liberal record as a congressman, but in the mayoralty he became known for his tough-minded approach to civic issues and his conservative views. The city's rapid comeback from its misfortunes was due in no small part to his leadership. He craved attention and applause, but at least in the first years of his mayoralty this was forgiven. When he yelled "How'm I doing?" at crowds, they invariably yelled back their approval, somehow taking "I" to mean "we" and acknowledging that the mayor in his strident way was personifying the city itself. In his inaugural address he had proclaimed, "New York is unique in the history of human kindness . . . New York is not a problem. New York is a stroke of genius."[1] And there was never any doubt that he had a profound affection for the city. But he was tough enough to force the municipal bureaucracy to conform to rigid accounting principles, which was a strong plus. Although poor blacks and Hispanics distrusted him for what they saw as his insensitivity to their needs, his overall popularity was high, especially among lower-middle-class whites. So overwhelming was his sway that when he ran for reelection in 1981 he captured the nomination not only of the Democratic party but also of the Republicans, an unprecedented feat in New York City. If his three terms were not without discord and failure, the 1980s nevertheless were the Age of Koch.

It was an age marked above all by astonishing developments in the two areas that from the very beginning set New York's tone: its ability to attract those who would foster its mercantile and financial power, and its role as a safe harbor for peoples from everywhere on earth.

The business boom was mind-boggling. Throughout most of the 1970s the world's economy had been in the doldrums, hobbled by the OPEC oil embargo among other things. But starting in the late 1970s and continuing into the 1980s, world trade picked up and the international economy took off. So did the nation's. As the world's financial capital, New York was ready for the upsurge, and Wall Street underwent a furious expansion, its brokers straining to keep up with the stock market's rise, its major money manipulators putting together ever more gigantic deals, and its back-office minions laboring into the night to feed the computers processing the millions and millions of transactions. Manufacturing in the city continued to de-

cline, but businesses in the so-called service sector—banking, bro-
kering, insurance, importing and exporting, and other financial
activities—more than made up for the loss, so that New York was
gaining jobs rather than losing them. And while the city continued
to lose the headquarters offices of major corporations (J. C. Penney
and Mobil Oil both departed during the decade, and Exxon announced in 1989 that it would soon leave for Texas), other businesses
found new reasons to move to the city. With the heightened activity
in international finance, for example, major foreign banks all found
it advisable to set up offices here, as did every law firm with an
international clientele.

For although computers, advanced telephone systems, and other
electronic marvels were making it increasingly possible for businesses
to operate at a distance from each other, and thus to function effectively far from expensive urban centers like New York, tremendous
numbers of concerns kept finding powerful reasons to remain in
town. As one observer noted, "Nothing can replace the efficiency of
face-to-face contact, whether at formal meetings or power break-
fasts."[2] While it is true, says Louis Winnick of the Ford Foundation,
that sophisticated electronics systems can process prodigious
amounts of data, of equal importance are what he calls "the primitive
communications systems." "Body language," he notes, "the lift of
an eyebrow, a wave of a hand, the wink, the nudge, the whispered
confidence constitute a subtext for elaborate transactions and nu-
anced deals. Such elemental modes of information transfer [render]
much of New York's economy resistant to the powerful dispersive
pulls of modern communications technology."[3] Proximity could be
an overwhelming advantage—one could almost say that the expense
account lunch was the savior of New York. In 1989 when Time Inc.
and Warner Communications decided to merge, the negotiations
were greatly facilitated by the fact that the head offices of the two
organizations were located in Rockefeller Center barely a block from
each other.

There were those who said that the gain in service industries at
the expense of manufacturing was risky, as these operations were
more vulnerable to swings in the economy and other sudden changes.
Indeed, the stock market collapse of October 1987 resulted in severe
employee cutbacks in a number of large brokerage firms, losses that
were only partially recouped when the market recovered. But the
new emphasis could also be seen as a strong asset, for the city's
conversion to a postindustrial economy based on financial manage-

ment and information processing would in the long run extend and enhance its dominance as the money capital of the world.

With the business expansion came a boom in residential and office construction. Massive new high rises were shoehorned into the unlikeliest spots, especially in midtown and the Wall Street area, and neighborhoods heretofore largely bereft of recent construction, like Brooklyn Heights and Manhattan's Upper West Side, blossomed forth with sleek tall new structures, often to the indignation of old-time residents who disapproved of the changed skyline. Queens got its first skyscraper, an office building erected in Long Island City by Citicorp, and in downtown Manhattan along the Hudson River the monumental urban development known as Battery Park City and consisting of both apartment complexes and big office buildings came into being atop landfill deposited by excavations for the World Trade Center. Not every mammoth new project came to fruition. An ambitious scheme announced by the builder Donald Trump for a large patch of vacant land in the West 60s (and including what he said would be the world's tallest building) was sidetracked because of vociferous community opposition, and plans for a huge new office building at Columbus Circle had to be scaled down due to similar outcry. But the spurt of building helped raise the assessed valuation of New York's taxable real estate to a new high of $64 billion by 1988 (the actual market value of the city's land would, of course, be infinitely greater).

Furthermore, the extraordinary and increasing value of real estate in New York, particularly in Manhattan, was not ignored in other parts of the world. When Ferdinand Marcos of the Philippines wanted a good place to park his ill-gotten millions, he invested in a number of choice Manhattan buildings. And in late 1989 New Yorkers were startled to learn that their great showcase, Rockefeller Center, had been sold by the Rockefeller family to a major Japanese corporation, Mitsubishi, whose directors were pleased as punch to be able to afford it. Not for them were all the claims that New York had no future.

Symbolic of the city's constant change and adaptation were new neighborhoods reclaimed from old ones. One of the most remarkable was the downtown Manhattan area known as Tribeca, an acronym for Triangle Below Canal Street. Made up almost completely of warehouse and market buildings as late as the 1960s, it was becoming a predominantly residential neighborhood, as artists and young professionals moved into its sturdy old structures that had been made over into studios and apartments. And the south Bronx, ravaged by the seemingly endless burning of abandoned buildings in the 1960s, was making a strong comeback, its streets thronged with residents, mostly Hispanic, eager to bring new stability to it.

Many of those Hispanics were recent arrivals. For immigration into New York from foreign countries was going full blast all during the 1980s—so much so that the city's population, which had gone down by almost a million during the 1970s, was during the following decade well on its way to making up most of that loss. The spurt in growth, which was the second of the major developments coloring the decade, was all the more remarkable because it was dominated by large-scale influxes from countries whose peoples had previously been only modestly represented in the city.

The new influx came as an odd result of legislation passed in 1965 that abolished the favoritism heretofore granted to immigrants from Europe and gave every country in the world a quota of 20,000 persons annually. The sponsors of the act assumed that Europeans would continue to dominate the scene—but that is not the way it worked out. Western Europeans in particular, enjoying prosperous conditions at home, no longer had such a desire to depart, and many eastern Europeans were prevented by repressive regimes from emigrating. Instead, great numbers of Asians and Latin Americans (especially West Indians and Central Americans) poured in.

Their numbers were inflated by two special features of the law: it gave special preference to persons with skills deemed in short supply in the United States (Korean doctors and Jamaican nurses, for example, were not subject to the quota); and it allowed a naturalized immigrant to bring in other members of his or her family (so that a Chinese engineer, once permanently lodged in this country, could bring in many of his relatives). So the Asians and Latin Americans tended to build up their numbers far in excess of expectations. The newcomers were arriving not only in New York but also in California, Florida, and Texas, of course, but New York as in the past was receiving a disproportionate share. Of the 14 million foreign-born counted in the 1980 census, no fewer than 1.7 million were in New York City, many more than had come to any other American city, and by the end of the 1980s they were arriving at the rate of almost 90,000 a year. As a result a total of 121 languages were being spoken on the streets of New York.

The onrush was changing the face of the city. The population of Chinatown was quadrupling, from a meager 25,000 to 100,000, and Chinese were taking over not only much of the former Italian enclave of Little Italy near Canal Street but also a large part of what used to be the Jewish Lower East Side. Immigrants from the Dominican Republic had come to New York in tremendous numbers in the preceding quarter century; by 1980 there were at least 120,000 in the city and they had become New York's second-largest foreign-born group (after the Italians); most of them were clustered in the Washington Heights and Inwood sections of northern Manhattan. Korean-born New Yorkers have seen a similar explosion in numbers; for although in 1960 there were only 562 of them, in 1980 there were 20,380, and with immigrants from India they now make up a sizable portion of the population of Flushing, in Queens. So many Asians, in fact, have settled in Flushing that the subway line serving the area has come to be known as the Orient Express. A Methodist church in Jackson Heights conducts four separate services each Sunday—in English, Spanish, Korean, and Chinese. Meanwhile, Haitians have congregated in Brooklyn's Crown Heights, Greeks are to be found in Astoria (Queens) and Bay Ridge (Brooklyn), and Soviet Jews—an exception to the paucity of recent European immigrants —have come in great numbers to Kew Gardens (Queens) and Brighton Beach (Brooklyn).

Furthermore, these recent city dwellers have not only pumped new vigor into old neighborhoods but also displayed a capacity for hard work that rivals (if indeed it does not exceed) the legendary industriousness of the immigrants who came before World War I. They display, says one observer, "a work ethic beside which the vaunted Protestant ethic shrinks to limp indolence."[4] The Korean takeover of the greengrocery trade has been nothing short of astonishing; the operator of one Korean vegetable stand was shown in a magazine article to be regularly working a twenty-two-hour day. Koreans are also heavily engaged in the dry-cleaning business. The Chinese, in addition to operating restaurants, are represented in banking and real estate, and Chinese women (along with Hispanics) are a major force among garment workers. New Yorkers in recent years have gradually awakened to the fact that many of their newsstands are operated by Indians, and that three-fourths of the self-employed drivers of the city's 11,700 officially medallioned taxis are foreign-born (often leading to bizarre communication gaffes). For some reason many sidewalk vendors who hawk dubious luxury items on midtown streets are Senegalese, energetic immigrants from West Africa.

And just as the recent newcomers have poured themselves into certain occupations, so have yesterday's arrivals moved on to other things. The Irish, for example, who once dominated city politics, have now in large measure abandoned it for occupations they consider more worthy of their talents, or they have been shouldered aside by other groups. Their role has been taken over to a large extent by blacks and especially by Jews, leading to the quip that today it was becoming "easier for an Irish-American to achieve sainthood than a seat on the Board of Estimate."[5]

Virtually lost in New York's political picture today, in fact, are the White Anglo-Saxon Protestants, or WASPs, who until the great rise of Tammany Hall—and even thereafter—controlled the city. To be sure, they still dominate the world of Wall Street—it was mostly members of the WASP minority who stepped in and set the city straight during the fiscal crisis—but their influence otherwise is small. And although blacks and Hispanics now make up almost half the city's total population, they rarely act cohesively as a group. Because no other body has moved into the forefront, New York has become a city without a genuine majority. For a number of reasons that are mainly national rather than local, the political parties exercise nowhere near the sway they once did. As a result, the city's affairs tend to be shaped by constantly shifting alliances among one or more special-interest groups like ethnic minorities, labor unions, and neighborhood organizations, with no one in the ascendancy. Among other things, this has rendered the city even more difficult to govern than its huge size and complexity would otherwise indicate.

Moreover, despite all the favorable economic news and the constant influx of new peoples who contribute so much, New York City in its maturity confronts formidable problems, each of which has been cause for serious concern.

One is municipal corruption, a continuing danger in any city but of special import in a place like New York where so much money changes hands in the governing process. Although recent mayors have been men of scrupulous personal honesty, and none more so than Edward Koch, the same has not always been true of those occupying lesser official positions. This was borne out by the strange case of Donald Manes, the borough president of Queens and a powerful figure in the city's Democratic party, who one night in January 1986 was found in his car along a highway suffering from severe knife wounds. Although Manes said he had been attacked, the wounds appeared to be self-inflicted, and this turned out to be true. As he was recovering in the hospital and the city was trying to unravel the mystery, he was found to be heavily implicated in fraud centering in

327

the city's Parking Violations Bureau, the unit that collects parking fines, and he also had close ties to a number of other fraudulent schemes citywide, some of which were just coming to light. Within a few weeks, back home, and as evidence against him continued to accumulate, he again attempted suicide—this time successfully. In the aftermath a number of his accomplices, in particular the Bronx County Democratic leader Stanley Friedman, went to jail, and other instances of corruption were unearthed. It was a severe blow to the Koch administration and one from which the mayor had difficulty recovering.

Another concern is the city's crumbling infrastructure, a matter that would challenge any large municipality but afflicts New York with special urgency because the city is so old. The situation is aggravated by the deferral during the fiscal crisis of the 1970s of much badly needed maintenance. In 1988 the Williamsburg Bridge to Brooklyn was found to be severely corroded and had to be closed to all traffic for repairs for two months, and the following year a series of steam pipe explosions in or near midtown caused many blocks in the surrounding areas to be closed off because of the threat caused by toxic asbestos, which had been used to line the pipes. Luckily the subways were being upgraded after decades of poor care, but many New Yorkers believed that so much of the city's underpinning was so old and so poorly kept up that anything might give at any time.

Narcotics are a blight throughout the United States but nowhere on a more damaging scale than in the nation's largest city, which is sorely put to contain the resulting wreckage. On top of the threat posed for so many years by the abuse of heroin, cocaine, and other harmful drugs, the smokable cocaine derivative known as crack made its appearance in the mid-1980s and immediately aggravated a severe problem, so addictive and strong was the new substance. As experts and city authorities searched for ways to halt its spread, crack became a scourge bedeviling the work of police, public health officials, and many others and virtually overwhelming the criminal justice system.

Crack was almost certainly responsible, at least in part, for the upsurge in crime that has undeniably had an adverse effect on millions of New Yorkers. To be sure, the city has always had its criminal element and has never been without its perils to person and property. In past eras, however, crime tended to be localized: there were dangerous areas—like the Five Points neighborhood a century and a half ago or Hell's Kitchen in the early 1900s—but other parts of town during those years tended to be safe. Today no area can be considered without menace, and this has generated a climate of fear that genuinely disturbs even the city's most vociferous partisans.

The most serious and perplexing of all New York's problems, however, is racial discord. For if the city has always been a refuge for peoples of every stripe, it has undeniably seen some of the most disgraceful incidents of racial persecution as well, notably the orgy of killings of blacks that occurred in the summer of 1741 and the infamous Draft Act riots of 1863. The very fact of the city's continued growth and change makes for racial unrest as peoples move and neighborhoods shift, inevitably producing new suspicions and resentments. No community, furthermore, is free of at least some racial prejudice, and the resulting enmity is all too frequently directed against blacks. Because a high proportion of young black males are poorly served by the city's schools and unwilling to conform to the customs of a white-dominated society and are thus all too likely to be attracted to activities on the edges of crime, a great many New Yorkers feel threatened by blacks as a whole, whom they automatically link to narcotics abuse, crime, and other threats to their safety. The upshot has been a series of tragic incidents that have shaken the city. On many occasions the police have acted with what has seemed to be undue rigor against purported black offenders; in one celebrated case a black youth named Michael Stewart was picked up by police in the subway for what was considered suspicious behavior and, when he objected, was beaten to death. Two incidents in which bands of white youths set upon individual blacks whom they did not want entering their neighborhood caused widespread outcry. In one, a young black named Michael Griffith, attacked by a group of whites in the Queens district of Howard Beach in 1986, was pursued onto a highway where he was killed by a car. Three years later another black youth, Yusuf Hawkins, who had come to Bensonhurst in Brooklyn on an innocuous errand with some friends, was also attacked by a band of whites and shot to death.

That such ugly events could take place in New York, the bastion of cosmopolitan acceptance, was attributed by many thoughtful observers not just to the inevitable enmities present in any large metropolis but also to what was seen as Mayor Koch's disdain for blacks and their manifold problems, which were viewed as exacerbating tensions in the city to the breaking point. For all his successes in guiding the city out of its travails and presiding over its good times in the 1980s, Koch was surely vulnerable to the charge, and this blind spot, when combined with the harm done him by the Manes-

Friedman scandals, ended up causing his defeat when he ran for a fourth term in 1989. Instead, the city by a narrow margin acted to address the racial turmoil directly by electing its first black mayor, David Dinkins.

It was a historic departure for the city. And in the same election New York took another decisive step by voting to adopt a new brand of government. The Supreme Court had ruled the city's Board of Estimate unconstitutional because it violated the principle of one man, one vote, and a charter-revision committee had proposed a new alignment in which the board would be abolished and its power taken over principally by an enlarged and more muscular City Council. The voters said yes.

So New York City, triumphant after more than three and a half centuries, headed for new ventures, new headaches, and new exploits. Crowded, perplexing, annoying, brimming over with difficult and baffling problems, always generating excitement, always changing, the great city was ready—as it had always been—for the novel, the creative, and the unexpected.

Notes

Prologue: The Incomparable Setting

1. Milton M. Klein, "Shaping the American Tradition," p. 174
2. Bayrd Still, "The Personality of New York City," p. 85
3. Ibid., p. 85
4. E. B. White, *Here Is New York*, p. 43
5. John Strong Newberry, *The Geological History of New York Island and Harbor*, p. 13
6. Carl Condit, *The Port of New York*, p. 11
7. Edward R. Ellis, *The Epic of New York City*, p. 12
8. I. N. Phelps Stokes, *New York Past and Present*, p. xi
9. Michael G. Kammen, *Colonial New York*, p. 5

1:    The Businesslike Dutch

1. Henry H. Kessler & Eugene Rachlis, *Peter Stuyvesant and His New York*, pp. 179–80
2. Ibid., p. 180
3. John E. Bakeless, *The Eyes of Discovery*, p. 238
4. John Franklin Jameson, ed., *Narratives of New Netherland*, p. 18
5. Ibid., p. 22
6. Kammen, op. cit., p. 26
7. Thomas J. Condon, *New York Beginnings*, p. 139
8. Jameson, op. cit., p. 188
9. Edmund B. O'Callaghan, *History of New Netherland*, p. 171
10. Kessler & Rachlis, op. cit., pp. 56–57
11. Ellis, op. cit., p. 41
12. Kessler & Rachlis, op. cit., p. 66
13. Ibid., p. 93
14. Ibid., p. 187

15. Ellis, op. cit., p. 63
16. Kessler & Rachlis, op. cit., p. 192
17. Ibid., p. 195
18. Ibid., p. 196
19. Ellis, op. cit., p. 66
20. Kammen, op. cit., p. 71

2: The British Overlords

1. Ellis, op. cit., p. 74
2. Kammen, op. cit., p. 88
3. Ellis, op. cit., p. 99
4. Robert C. Ritchie, *The Duke's Province*, p. 238
5. Carl Bridenbaugh, *Cities in the Wilderness*, p. 176
6. Bayrd Still, *Mirror for Gotham*, p. 18
7. Bridenbaugh, op. cit., p. 176
8. Kammen, op. cit., p. 155
9. Ellis, op. cit., p. 102
10. Kammen, op. cit., p. 155
11. Ellis, op. cit., p. 111
12. Ibid., p. 122
13. Ibid., p. 123
14. Ibid., p. 127
15. Ibid., p. 132
16. David Kobrin, *The Black Minority in Early New York*, p. 28
17. Kammen, op. cit., p. 281
18. Arthur E. Peterson & George W. Edwards, *New York as an 18th Century Municipality*, p. 171
19. George J. Lankevich & Howard B. Furer, *A Brief History of New York City*, p. 44
20. Still, *Mirror for Gotham*, p. 27
21. Lankevich & Furer, op. cit., p. 44
22. Still, *Mirror for Gotham*, p. 20
23. Carl Bridenbaugh, *Cities in Revolt*, p. 52
24. Virginia D. Harrington, *The New York Merchant on the Eve of the Revolution*, pp. 256–57
25. Ibid., p. 62
26. Milton M. Klein, *The Politics of Diversity*, p. 39

3: The Cataclysm of Revolution

1. Klein, *The Politics of Diversity*, p. 209
2. Ellis, op. cit., p. 146
3. Wilbur C. Abbott, *New York in the American Revolution*, pp. 56–57
4. Kammen, op. cit., p. 344
5. Thomas J. Wertenbaker, *Father Knickerbocker Rebels*, pp. 27–28

6. Abbott, op. cit., p. 127
7. Bruce Bliven, Jr., *Under the Guns*, p. 53
8. Kammen, op. cit., p. 370
9. Wertenbaker, op. cit., p. 71
10. Ibid., p. 81
11. Bliven, op. cit., p. 319
12. Ibid., p. 343
13. Bruce Bliven, Jr., *Battle for Manhattan*, p. 103
14. Wertenbaker, op. cit., p. 100
15. Lankevich & Furer, op. cit., p. 54
16. Oscar T. Barck, *New York City During the War for Independence*, p. 114
17. Wertenbaker, op. cit., p. 165
18. Ibid., p. 236
19. Ibid., p. 257

4: The City Reborn

1. WPA Writers Program, *A Maritime History of New York*, p. 82
2. Arthur D. Howden Smith, *John Jacob Astor*, p. 47
3. Robert A. Hendrickson, *The Rise and Fall of Alexander Hamilton*, p. 192
4. Ibid., p. 279
5. Lankevich & Furer, op. cit., p. 65
6. Still, *Mirror for Gotham*, p. 55–56
7. Hendrickson, op. cit., p. 352
8. Sidney I. Pomerantz, *New York: An American City*, p. 189
9. Susan E. Lyman, *The Story of New York*, p. 111
10. Ellis, op. cit., p. 203
11. Ibid., p. 204
12. Ibid., p. 225
13. Lyman, op. cit., p. 113
14. Smith, op. cit., p. 110
15. Ellis, op. cit., p. 210
16. Dorothy Bobbé, *De Witt Clinton*, p. 160
17. Lankevich & Furer, op. cit., p. 83
18. Ibid., p. 83

5: The Heyday of the Merchants

1. Robert G. Albion, *Square-Riggers on Schedule*, pp. 2–3
2. WPA Writers Program, op. cit., p. 141
3. Joseph A. Scoville, *The Old Merchants of New York City*, Vol. 2, p. 89
4. Ibid., p. 191
5. Robert G. Albion, *The Rise of New York Port*, p. 263
6. Scoville, op. cit., pp. 73–74
7. Joseph A. Scoville, *The Old Merchants of New York City*, Vol. 1, pp. 396–97
8. Albion, *The Rise of New York Port*, p. 241

9. Richard C. McKay, *South Street*, p. 94
10. Scoville, op. cit., Vol. 1, p. 195
11. Albion, *The Rise of New York Port*, p. 251
12. WPA Writers Program, op. cit., p. 160
13. Philip Hone, *The Diary of Philip Hone*, p. 250
14. Charles Lockwood, *Manhattan Moves Uptown*, p. 89
15. Albion, *The Rise of New York Port*, p. 317
16. Wayne Andrews, *The Vanderbilt Legend*, p. 8
17. Ibid., p. 12
18. Ibid., p. 50
19. Ibid., p. 75

6: Expanding and Changing

1. Hone, op. cit., 209
2. Robert Ernst, *Immigrant Life in New York City*, p. 27
3. Ibid., p. 39
4. Herbert Asbury, *The Gangs of New York*, pp. 10–11
5. Still, *Mirror for Gotham*, p. 136
6. Edward K. Spann, *The New Metropolis*, p. 26
7. Lockwood, op. cit., p. 121
8. Spann, op. cit., p. 71
9. Lockwood, op. cit., pp. 9–10
10. Still, *Mirror for Gotham*, p. 81
11. Hone, op. cit., p. 395
12. Lockwood, op. cit., p. 154
13. Ibid., p. 126
14. Ibid., pp. 127–28
15. Ibid., p. 136
16. Ibid., p. 129
17. Ibid., p. 144
18. Hone, op. cit., pp. 186–87
19. Ellis, op. cit., p. 252
20. Lyman, op. cit., p. 154
21. Spann, op. cit., p. 402
22. Still, *Mirror for Gotham*, p. 129
23. Lockwood, op. cit., p. 172
24. Henry Hope Reed & Sophia Duckworth, *Central Park*, p. 3
25. Ibid., p. 14
26. Ellis, op. cit., p. 305
27. Quoted in Ellis, op. cit., p. 316

7: The Bosses

1. William L. Riordon, *Plunkitt of Tammany Hall*, p. 153
2. Morris R. Werner, *Tammany Hall*, p. xvii

3. Riordon, op. cit., p. 154
4. Alexander B. Callow, Jr., *The Tweed Ring*, p. 74
5. Lankevich & Furer, op. cit., p. 170
6. Callow, op. cit., p. 210
7. Lothrop Stoddard, *Master of Manhattan*, p. 37
8. Leonard Chalmers, "Fernando Wood and Tammany Hall," p. 380
9. Ibid., p. 380
10. Alfred Connable & Edward Silberfarb, *Tigers of Tammany*, p. 131
11. Callow, op. cit., p. 40
12. Ibid., p. 40
13. Ibid., pp. 45–46
14. Connable & Silberfarb, op. cit., p. 150
15. Callow, op. cit., p. 35
16. Ibid., p. 38
17. Connable & Silberfarb, op. cit., p. 148
18. Callow, op. cit., p. 248
19. Ibid., p. 254
20. Connable & Silberfarb, op. cit., p. 166
21. Ibid., p. 167
22. Werner, op. cit., p. 303
23. Ibid., p. 277
24. Connable & Silberfarb, op. cit., p. 209
25. Ibid., p. 180
26. Ibid., p. 180
27. Ibid., p. 198
28. Lyman, op. cit., p. 190
29. Werner, op. cit., p. 444
30. Ibid., p. 462
31. Stoddard, op. cit., p. 125
32. Ibid., p. 78

8: Wall Street Takes Command

1. John Steele Gordon, *The Scarlet Woman of Wall Street*, p. 27
2. Ibid., p. 110
3. Ibid., p. 151
4. Maury Klein, *The Life and Legend of Jay Gould*, p. 73
5. Gordon, op. cit., pp. 167–68
6. Ibid., p. 256
7. Ibid., p. 268
8. Frederick Lewis Allen, *The Great Pierpont Morgan*, p. 35
9. Sidney M. Robbins & Nestor E. Terleckyj, *Money Metropolis*, p. 33
10. Frederick Lewis Allen, *The Lords of Creation*, p. 18
11. Allen, *The Great Pierpont Morgan*, p. 175
12. Ibid., p. 177
13. Ibid., p. 179
14. Stephen Birmingham, *"Our Crowd,"* p. 231

15. Ibid., p. 233
16. Ibid., p. 236

9:   The Gilded Age

1. Lloyd Morris, *Incredible New York*, p. 156
2. Andrews, op. cit., p. 260
3. Allen Churchill, *The Upper Crust*, p. 141
4. Ibid., p. 146
5. Aline B. Saarinen, *The Proud Possessors*, p. 72
6. Ibid., p. 164
7. Ibid., p. 161
8. Quoted in *American Heritage*, April 1989, p. 64
9. Maxwell F. Marcuse, *This Was New York!*, p. 379

10:   The Greater City

1. Still, *Mirror for Gotham*, p. 205
2. Lockwood, op. cit., p. 317
3. Thomas Kessner, *The Golden Door*, p. 39
4. Ibid., p. 59
5. Irving Howe, *World of Our Fathers*, p. 81
6. Kessner, op. cit., p. 19
7. Howe, op. cit., p. 395
8. Kessner, op. cit., p. 13
9. Howe, op. cit., p. 94
10. Lockwood, op. cit., p. 279
11. Still, *Mirror for Gotham*, p. 257

11:   Boom, Bust, and Triumph

1. Robert A. M. Stern et al., *New York, 1930*, p. 15
2. Ibid., p. 18
3. Lankevich & Furer, op. cit., p. 214
4. Gene Fowler, *Beau James*, p. 59
5. Ellis, op. cit., p. 526
6. Charles Garrett, *The La Guardia Years*, p. 77
7. Ernest Cuneo, *Life with Fiorello*, p. 193–94
8. Ibid., p. 192
9. Stern, op. cit., p. 700

12: At the Summit

1. Still, *Mirror for Gotham*, p. 305
2. Ibid., p. 315
3. Milton M. Klein, ed., *New York: The Centennial Years*, p. 124
4. Warren Moscow, *What Have You Done for Me Lately?*, p. 196
5. Leonard Wallock, ed., *New York: Culture Capital of the World*, p. 11
6. Ibid., p. 141

13: Crisis

1. Fred Ferretti, *The Year the Big Apple Went Bust*, p. 327
2. Ken Auletta, *The Streets Were Paved with Gold*, p. 78
3. Ibid., p. 255
4. Ibid., p. 255
5. Ibid., p. 55
6. Ibid., p. 97
7. Ferretti, op. cit., p. 28
8. Auletta, op. cit., p. 100
9. Jack Newfield & Paul Du Brul, *The Abuse of Power*, p. 173
10. Auletta, op. cit., p. 88
11. Ferretti, op. cit., p. 196
12. Newfield & Du Brul, op. cit., p. 174
13. Ferretti, op. cit., p. 299
14. Lankevich & Furer, op. cit., p. 299
15. Ferretti, op. cit., p. 341
16. Ibid., p. 349
17. Ibid., p. 358

14: New Departures

1. Lankevich & Furer, op. cit., p. 303
2. Peter D. Salins, ed., *New York Unbound*, p. 42
3. Ibid., p. 9
4. Ibid., p. 8
5. Ibid., p. 12

Bibliography

Abbott, Wilbur C. *New York in the American Revolution.* New York: Charles Scribner's Sons, 1929.

Albion, Robert G. *The Rise of New York Port, 1815–1860.* New York: Charles Scribner's Sons, 1939.

———. *Square-Riggers on Schedule.* Princeton, N.J.: Princeton University Press, 1938.

Allen, Frederick Lewis. *The Great Pierpont Morgan.* New York: Harper & Brothers, 1949.

———. *The Lords of Creation.* New York: Harper & Brothers, 1935.

Andrews, Wayne. *The Vanderbilt Legend.* New York: Harcourt, Brace & Co., 1941.

Archdeacon, Thomas. *New York City, 1664–1710: Conquest and Change.* Ithaca, N.Y.: Cornell University Press, 1976.

Asbury, Herbert. *The Gangs of New York.* New York: Alfred A. Knopf, 1928.

Auletta, Ken. *The Streets Were Paved with Gold.* New York: Random House, 1979.

Bakeless, John E. *The Eyes of Discovery.* Philadelphia: Lippincott, 1950.

Barck, Oscar T. *New York City During the War for Independence.* New York: Columbia University Press, 1931.

Berger, Meyer. *The Eight Million.* New York: Simon and Schuster, 1942.

Birmingham, Stephen. *"Our Crowd," The Great Jewish Families of New York.* New York: Harper & Row, 1967.

Bliven, Bruce, Jr. *Battle for Manhattan.* New York: Henry Holt, 1956.

———. *Under the Guns: New York, 1775–1776.* New York: Harper & Row, 1972.

Bobbé, Dorothy. *De Witt Clinton.* New York: Minton, Balch & Co., 1933.

Bogen, Elizabeth. *Immigration in New York.* New York: Praeger, 1987.

Bonomi, Patricia U. *A Factious People: Politics and Society in Colonial New York.* New York: Columbia University Press, 1971.

Bridenbaugh, Carl. *Cities in Revolt: Urban Life in America, 1743–1776.* New York: Alfred A. Knopf, 1955.

———. *Cities in the Wilderness: The First Century of Urban Life in America, 1625–1742.* New York: Ronald Press, 1938.

Bibliography

Brown, Wallace. *The Good Americans: The Loyalists in the American Revolution.* New York: Morrow, 1969.

Buttenwieser, Ann L. *Manhattan Water-Bound.* New York: New York University Press, 1987.

Callow, Alexander B., Jr. *The Tweed Ring.* New York: Oxford University Press, 1966.

Caro, Robert A. *The Power Broker.* New York: Alfred A. Knopf, 1974.

Carosso, Vincent P. *Investment Banking in America.* Cambridge, Mass.: Harvard University Press, 1970.

Chalmers, Leonard. "Fernando Wood and Tammany Hall, The First Phase." *The New-York Historical Society Quarterly* 52 (1968): 379–402.

Chandler, Alfred D., Jr. *The Visible Hand: The Managerial Revolution in American Business.* Cambridge, Mass.: Harvard University Press, 1977.

Churchill, Allen. *The Improper Bohemians.* New York: Dutton, 1959.

———. *The Upper Crust.* Englewood Cliffs, N.J.: Prentice-Hall, 1970.

Clews, Henry. *Fifty Years in Wall Street.* New York: Irving Publishing Co., 1908.

Condit, Carl. *The Port of New York.* 2 vols. Chicago: University of Chicago Press, 1980–1981.

Condon, Thomas J. *New York Beginnings: The Commercial Origins of New Netherland.* New York: New York University Press, 1968.

Connable, Alfred, & Edward Silberfarb. *Tigers of Tammany.* New York: Holt, Rinehart & Winston, 1967.

Cuneo, Ernest. *Life with Fiorello.* New York: Macmillan, 1955.

Depew, Chauncey M., ed. *1795–1895: One Hundred Years of American Commerce.* New York: D. O. Haynes, 1895.

De Voe, Thomas F. *The Market Book.* New York: A. M. Kelley, 1970.

Dodge, Phyllis B. *Tales of the Phelps-Dodge Family.* New York: New-York Historical Society, 1987.

Duffy, Francis J., & William H. Miller. *The New York Harbor Book.* Falmouth, Me.: TBW Books, 1986.

Ellis, David M. *New York, State and City.* Ithaca, N.Y.: Cornell University Press, 1979.

Ellis, Edward R. *The Epic of New York City.* New York: Coward-McCann, 1966.

Emerson, Frederick V. "A Geographic Interpretation of New York City." Doctoral thesis, University of Chicago, 1909.

Ernst, Robert. *Immigrant Life in New York City, 1825–1863.* New York: King's Crown Press, 1949.

Ferretti, Fred. *The Year the Big Apple Went Bust.* New York: G. P. Putnam's Sons, 1976.

Flick, Alexander C. *Loyalism in New York During the American Revolution.* New York: Columbia University Press, 1901.

Foner, Nancy. *New Immigrants in New York.* New York: Columbia University Press, 1987.

Fowler, Gene. *Beau James: The Life and Times of Jimmy Walker.* New York: Viking Press, 1949.

Garrett, Charles. *The La Guardia Years: Machine and Reform Politics in New York City.* New Brunswick, N.J.: Rutgers University Press, 1961.

340

Gilchrist, David T., ed. *The Growth of the Seaport Cities, 1790–1825.* Charlottesville, Va.: University Press of Virginia, 1967.

Glazer, Nathan, & Daniel Patrick Moynihan. *Beyond the Melting Pot.* Cambridge, Mass.: M.I.T. Press and Harvard University Press, 1963.

Gordon, John Steele. *The Scarlet Woman of Wall Street.* New York: Weidenfeld & Nicolson, 1988.

Green, Martin B. *New York 1913: The Armory Show and the Paterson Strike Pageant.* New York: Charles Scribner's Sons, 1988.

Hammack, David C. *Power and Society: Greater New York at the Turn of the Century.* New York: Russell Sage Foundation, 1982.

Hansen, Marcus L. *The Atlantic Migration, 1607–1860.* Cambridge, Mass.: Harvard University Press, 1940.

Harrington, Virginia D. *The New York Merchant on the Eve of the Revolution.* New York: Columbia University Press, 1935.

Hawkins, Stuart. *New York, New York.* New York: W. Funk, 1957.

Headley, Joel T. *The Great Riots of New York, 1712 to 1873.* New York: E. B. Treat, 1873.

Hendrickson, Robert A. *The Rise and Fall of Alexander Hamilton.* New York: Van Nostrand Reinhold Co., 1981.

Hershkowitz, Leo. *Tweed's New York: Another Look.* Garden City, N.Y.: Doubleday & Co., 1977.

Holbrook, Stewart H. *The Age of the Moguls.* Garden City, N.Y.: Doubleday & Co., 1953.

Hone, Philip. *The Diary of Philip Hone, 1828–1851.* Edited by Allan Nevins. New York: Dodd, Mead & Co., 1936.

Howe, Irving. *World of Our Fathers.* New York: Harcourt Brace Jovanovich, 1976.

Innes, John H. *New Amsterdam and Its People.* New York: Charles Scribner's Sons, 1902.

Jameson, John Franklin, ed. *Narratives of New Netherland.* New York: Charles Scribner's Sons, 1909.

Jones, Pamela. *Under the City Streets.* New York: Holt, Rinehart, and Winston, 1978.

Kammen, Michael G. *Colonial New York: A History.* New York: Charles Scribner's Sons, 1975.

Kenney, Alice P. *Stubborn for Liberty: The Dutch in New York.* Syracuse, N.Y.: Syracuse University Press, 1975.

Kessler, Henry H., & Eugene Rachlis. *Peter Stuyvesant and His New York.* New York: Random House, 1959.

Kessner, Thomas. *The Golden Door: Italian and Jewish Immigrant Mobility in New York City, 1880–1915.* New York: Oxford University Press, 1977.

Ketchum, Richard M. *The Winter Soldiers.* Garden City, N.Y.: Doubleday & Co., 1973.

Klein, Alexander. *The Empire City: A Treasury of New York.* New York: Rinehart, 1955.

Klein, Maury. *The Life and Legend of Jay Gould.* Baltimore: The Johns Hopkins University Press, 1986.

Bibliography

Klein, Milton M., ed. *New York: The Centennial Years, 1676–1976*. Port Washington, N.Y.: Kennikat Press, 1976.

————. *The Politics of Diversity: Essays in the History of Colonial New York*. Port Washington, N.Y.: Kennikat Press, 1974.

————. "Shaping the American Tradition: The Microcosm of Colonial New York." *New York History* 59 (1978): 173–97.

Kobrin, David. *The Black Minority in Early New York*. Albany, N.Y.: N.Y. State Education Department, 1971.

Kouwenhoven, John A. *The Columbia Historical Portrait of New York*. Garden City, N.Y.: Doubleday & Co., 1953.

————. *Partners in Banking. . . . Brown Brothers Harriman & Co., 1818–1968*. Garden City, N.Y.: Doubleday & Co., 1968.

Lankevich, George J., & Howard B. Furer. *A Brief History of New York City*. Port Washington, N.Y.: Associated Faculty Press, 1984.

Leder, Lawrence H. *Robert Livingston, 1654–1728, and the Politics of Colonial New York*. Chapel Hill, N.C.: University of North Carolina Press, 1961.

Lee, Basil. *Discontent in New York City, 1861–1865*. Washington, D.C.: Catholic University of America Press, 1943.

Lichtenberg, Robert M. *One-Tenth of a Nation*. Cambridge, Mass.: Harvard University Press, 1960.

Lockwood, Charles. *Manhattan Moves Uptown*. Boston: Houghton Mifflin Co., 1976.

Lossing, Benson J. *History of New York City*. New York: G. E. Perine, 1884.

Lovejoy, David S. *The Glorious Revolution in America*. New York: Harper & Row, 1972.

Lyman, Susan E. *The Story of New York*. New York: Crown, 1964.

Lynch, Denis Tilden. *"Boss" Tweed: The Story of a Grim Generation*. New York: Boni and Liveright, 1927.

Lynes, Russell. *Good Old Modern: An Intimate Portrait of the Museum of Modern Art*. New York: Atheneum, 1973.

Mack, Edward C. *Peter Cooper: Citizen of New York*. New York: Duell, Sloan & Pearce, 1949.

Mahoney, Tom, & Leonard Sloane. *The Great Merchants*. New York: Harper and Row, 1966.

Mandelbaum, Seymour J. *Boss Tweed's New York*. New York: J. Wiley, 1965.

Marcuse, Maxwell F. *This Was New York! A Nostalgic Picture of Gotham in the Gaslight Era*. New York: Carlton Press, 1965.

Mason, Bernard. *The Road to Independence: The Revolutionary Movement in New York, 1773–1777*. Lexington, Ky.: University of Kentucky Press, 1966.

Mayer, Martin. *Wall Street: Men and Money*. New York: Harper & Brothers, 1955.

McCoy, Samuel D. "Lost Island of Sailing Ships—The Port of New York, 1783–1789." *New York History* 17 (1936): 379–90.

McCullough, David. *The Great Bridge*. New York: Simon and Schuster, 1972.

McKay, Richard C. *South Street: A Maritime History of New York*. New York: G. P. Putnam's Sons, 1934.

Ment, David. *The Shaping of a City: A Brief History of Brooklyn*. New York: Brooklyn Educational & Cultural Alliance, 1979.

342

Mohl, Raymond A. *Poverty in New York, 1783–1825.* New York: Oxford University Press, 1971.

Monaghan, Frank, & Marvin Lowenthal. *This Was New York: The Nation's Capital in 1789.* Garden City, N.Y.: Doubleday, Doran, 1943.

Moorhouse, Geoffrey. *Imperial City: New York.* New York: Henry Holt & Co., 1988.

Morris, Lloyd. *Incredible New York.* New York: Random House, 1951.

Moscow, Warren. *What Have You Done for Me Lately?* Englewood Cliffs, N.J.: Prentice-Hall, 1967.

Myers, Andrew B., ed. *The Knickerbocker Tradition: Washington Irving's New York.* Tarrytown, N.Y.: Sleepy Hollow Restorations, 1974.

Myers, Margaret G. *The New York Money Market: Origins and Development.* New York: Columbia University Press, 1931.

Neill, Humphrey B. *The Inside Story of the Stock Exchange.* New York: Forbes, 1950.

Nettels, Curtis. "The Economic Relations of Boston, Philadelphia, and New York." *Journal of Economic and Business History* 3 (1930–31): 185–215.

Nevins, Allan. "The Golden Thread in the History of New York." *The New-York Historical Society Quarterly* 39 (1955): 5–22.

Nevins, Allan, & John A. Krout, eds. *The Greater City: New York, 1898–1948.* New York: Columbia University Press, 1948.

Newberry, John Strong. *The Geological History of New York Island and Harbor.* New York: D. Appleton & Co., 1878.

Newfield, Jack, & Paul Du Brul. *The Abuse of Power.* New York: Viking Press, 1977.

O'Callaghan, Edmund B. *History of New Netherland.* 2nd ed. 2 vols. New York: D. Appleton & Co., 1855.

Osofsky, Gilbert. *Harlem: The Making of a Ghetto.* New York: Harper & Row, 1966.

Peterson, Arthur E., & George W. Edwards. *New York as an 18th-Century Municipality.* Port Washington, N.Y.: I.J. Friedman, 1967.

Pomerantz, Sidney I. *New York: An American City, 1783–1803.* New York: Columbia University Press, 1938.

Pound, Arthur. *The Golden Earth: The Story of Manhattan's Landed Wealth.* New York: Macmillan, 1935.

Raesly, Ellis L. *Portrait of New Netherland.* New York: Columbia University Press, 1945.

Ravitch, Diane. *The Great School Wars: New York City, 1805–1973.* New York: Basic Books, 1974.

Reed, Henry Hope, & Sophia Duckworth. *Central Park: A History and a Guide.* 2nd ed. New York: Clarkson N. Potter, 1972.

Riordon, William L. *Plunkitt of Tammany Hall.* New York: McClure, Phillips & Co., 1905.

Ritchie, Robert C. *The Duke's Province: A Study of New York Politics and Society, 1664–1691.* Chapel Hill, N.C.: University of North Carolina Press, 1977.

Robbins, Sidney M., & Nestor E. Terleckyj. *Money Metropolis: A Locational Study of Financial Activities in the New York Region.* Cambridge, Mass.: Harvard University Press, 1960.

Saarinen, Aline B. *The Proud Possessors.* New York: Random House, 1958.

Salins, Peter D., ed. *New York Unbound: The City and the Politics of the Future.* New York: Basil Blackwell, 1988.

Schlesinger, Arthur M. *The Colonial Merchants and the American Revolution, 1763–1776.* New York: Columbia University Press, 1918.

Schuberth, Christopher J. *The Geology of New York City and Environs.* Garden City, N.Y.: Natural History Press, 1968.

Scoville, Joseph A. *The Old Merchants of New York City.* 3 vols. New York: Carleton, 1864–1870.

Simon, Kate. *Fifth Avenue: A Very Social History.* New York: Harcourt Brace Jovanovich, 1978.

Singleton, Esther. *Social New York Under the Georges, 1714–1776.* New York: D. Appleton & Co., 1902.

Smith, Arthur D. Howden. *John Jacob Astor: Landlord of New York.* Philadelphia: J. B. Lippincott Co., 1929.

Spann, Edward K. *The New Metropolis: New York City, 1840–1857.* New York: Columbia University Press, 1981.

Stansell, Christine. *City of Women: Sex and Class in New York, 1789–1860.* New York: Dodd, Mead & Co., 1973.

Starr, Roger. *The Rise and Fall of New York City.* New York: Basic Books, 1985.

Stern, Robert A.M., Gregory Gilmartin, & Thomas Mellins. *New York, 1930: Architecture and Urbanism Between the Two World Wars.* New York: Rizzoli, 1987.

Stevens, John A. "The Physical Evolution of New York City." *American Historical Magazine* 2 (1906–7): 24–43, 92–128, 173–86, 242–60.

Still, Bayrd. *Mirror for Gotham.* New York: New York University Press, 1956.

———. "The Personality of New York City." *New York Folklore Quarterly* 14 (1958): 83–92.

Stoddard, Lothrop. *Master of Manhattan: The Life of Richard Croker.* New York–Toronto: Longmans, Green and Co., 1931.

Stokes, I. N. Phelps. *The Iconography of Manhattan Island.* 6 vols. New York: R. H. Dodd, 1915–1928.

———. *New York Past and Present.* New York: Plantin Press, 1939.

Taylor, George R. *The Transportation Revolution, 1815–1860.* New York: Rinehart & Co., 1951.

Vail, Philip [pseud.]. *The Great American Rascal: The Turbulent Life of Aaron Burr.* New York: Hawthorn Books, 1973.

Wallock, Leonard, ed. *New York: Culture Capital of the World, 1940–1965.* New York: Rizzoli, 1988.

Walton, Frank L. *Tomahawks to Textiles: The Fabulous Story of Worth Street.* New York: Appleton-Century-Crofts, 1953.

Warshow, Robert I. *The Story of Wall Street.* New York: Greenberg, 1929.

Werner, Morris R. *Tammany Hall.* Garden City, N.Y.: Doubleday, Doran, 1928.

Wertenbaker, Thomas J. *Father Knickerbocker Rebels: New York City During the Revolution.* New York: Charles Scribner's Sons, 1948.

White, E. B. *Here Is New York.* New York: Harper and Bros., 1949.

White, Norval. *New York: A Physical History.* New York: Atheneum, 1987.

Wilson, James G. *The Memorial History of the City of New York.* 4 vols. New York: New-York History Co., 1892.

WPA Writers Program. *A Maritime History of New York.* Garden City, N.Y.: Doubleday, Doran, 1941.

Index

Index

Index

Index

Index

Index

Index

Index

Index